Future of Business and Finance

The Future of Business and Finance book series features professional works aimed at defining, analyzing, and charting the future trends in these fields. The focus is mainly on strategic directions, technological advances, challenges and solutions which may affect the way we do business tomorrow, including the future of sustainability and governance practices. Mainly written by practitioners, consultants and academic thinkers, the books are intended to spark and inform further discussions and developments.

Claus Sneppen

The Future (R)Evolution of the Office Workspace

How to Succeed in a Digital Reality

Springer

Claus Sneppen
Copenhagen Institute for Futures Studies
Associated Partner and Futurist
Copenhagen, Denmark

ISSN 2662-2467 ISSN 2662-2475 (electronic)
Future of Business and Finance
ISBN 978-3-031-85228-2 ISBN 978-3-031-85229-9 (eBook)
https://doi.org/10.1007/978-3-031-85229-9

This Springer imprint is published by the registered company Springer Nature Switzerland AG
The registered company address is: Gewerbestrasse 11, 6330 Cham, Switzerland

Picture generated by use of AI depicting an imaginary office workplace. Image credits: Katrine Blaeum/Midjourney

Maersk HQ. *Image credits:* Tomas Bertelsen PLH Architects

Preface

Are you excited about the future of the office and working life? Undertaking the task of writing a book on such a timely and pertinent topic is inherently an exhilarating personal endeavour. The aspiration of *The (R)Evolution of the Hybrid Office* is, however, to inspire a renewed focus on the office as an institution and work-life concept, as it is expected to undergo even more profound changes. These changes are anticipated to have far-reaching implications for the existing office workplace model and the working lives of all office employees.

You are about to invest your most valuable resource—your time—in immersing yourself into *The (R)Evolution of the Hybrid Office*. I am not striving to revolutionise the office to improve the planet or elevate humanity, nor am I embarking on an idealistic crusade to liberate employees to work from anywhere. My aim is far more practical and grounded: to equip organisations with the capability to conceptualise offices as competitive and resilient assets within an increasingly fast-paced and ever-changing environment. I consider my ambitions fulfilled if you make slight adjustments to your approach and henceforth address the development of the office workplace for knowledge workers in a more thoughtful manner. For a "more thoughtful" approach can make a world of difference for the workplace, employees, management, and, most importantly, the organisation for many years to come. However, it is evident that leaders in the office workplace are not tasked with overseeing minor adjustments but rather substantial changes, if the competitive strength of the office—and, by extension, the organisation—is to be secured in an increasingly dynamic environment for knowledge workers. In essence, this book can be encapsulated by the theme of time—how to derive greater value from the knowledge worker's time, and perhaps even more importantly, how to avoid wasting it. Wasting time, whether for the individual employee, the team, the manager, or the organisation as a whole, is a critical issue that demands our attention.

The saying "work is something you do, not somewhere you go" has become increasingly prevalent and meaningful. The renowned futurist Alvin Toffler suggested that "work is not necessarily going to take place in offices or factories. It is going to take place everywhere, anytime" (A. Toffler, *The Third Wave*, 1980). This foresight highlighted the shift towards flexibility and mobility in work long before the advent of digital technology made such arrangements feasible, anticipating a future where work transcends traditional physical spaces. When we in the proximate future look back at the current period, it will become evident that organisations that were able to embrace and take advantage of the opportunities presented by the widespread implementation of the hybrid workplace thrived. Simultaneously, it will be natural to see that others failed to do so and consequently lost competitiveness. The future is already here; it's just not evenly distributed, as we like to say at the Copenhagen Institute for Futures Studies. The significant question for all participants in the office workplace is, who will emerge as the winners and losers in the race towards a hybrid office workplace that is prepared for and successful in the future? Organisations must now reevaluate and refine their office workplace model to sustain or enhance value creation for individual employees, the organisation as a whole, and ultimately the market and its customers. For instance, it is essential to identify scenarios within the hybrid workplace where physical, synchronous presence in the office provides significantly greater value than remote, non-linear, and predominantly asynchronous digital work.

"All truth passes through three stages. First, it is ridiculed. Second, it is violently opposed. Third, it is accepted as being self-evident" (Arthur Schopenhauer, Philosopher 1788–1860). The three stages of truth prompt the readers of *The (R) Evolution of the Hybrid Office* to contemplate essential questions regarding anticipatory forecasts of the future hybrid office workplace: which ideas and anticipations should indeed be ridiculed, which ones will face strong opposition, and which ones will eventually be accepted as self-evident? Only time and the future can provide the answers. However, one thing is certain: the future of the office workplace for knowledge workers is bound to undergo significant changes and look markedly different within the next decade. As we explore and embrace these changes, it is essential to keep an open mind, challenge assumptions, and be prepared to adapt to the evolving landscape of knowledge work and the workplace.

Nivaa, Denmark Claus Sneppen

Competing Interests

The book has been produced in my capacity as Associate Partner and Futurist at the Copenhagen Institute for Futures Studies. It has been written independently, on my own initiative and funding, without any external editorial influence on the content. However, as the Institute is committed to highlighting the impacts of trends and changes over time, and our livelihood depends on doing so, we may tend to overestimate actual trends, developments, and implications to become valued, capture attention, and make the audience more receptive to the content. In other words, we are inclined to exhibit a bias towards *change optimism* rather than a *status quo bias*.

Acknowledgements

I extend my gratitude to all contributors for their dedication to sharing knowledge, insights, and actively shaping the content of *The (R)Evolution of the Hybrid Office*. First and foremost, I would like to extend my heartfelt gratitude to my colleagues at the Copenhagen Institute for Futures Studies for their unwavering support and invaluable foresight contributions.

Special acknowledgement for providing current data, hindsight, insights, and knowledge to the evolution of the hybrid office workplace:

- Christine Ipsen, Professor, Management Division DTU
- Danish FM
- Danish HR
- Danish IT
- Gensler
- McKinsey & Company
- Microsoft Denmark
- Nickolas Bloom, Professor of Economics, Stanford University
- Rob Sadow, CEO and co-founder of Scoop and Flex Index

Further acknowledgement to the predominately Danish organisations and companies listed below, which through participation in in-depth workshop sessions, interviews, and workspace cases have contributed to uncovering significant insights into the potential implications of development for the future hybrid office workplace: Alleroed Municipality, Arla Foods, Bankdata, BEC, Copenhagen Properties (The Finance Administration, City of Copenhagen), Danish Building and Property Agency, Danish National Bank, Danske Bank, Erik Architects, Frederikssund Municipality, Genmab, Grundfos, Maersk, Mast-Jaegermeister, Novartis Pharmaceuticals, Novozymes (Novonesis), Nykredit, Radiometer, Roerbaek & Moeller Architects, Scania, The LEGO Group, and Woods Office (Nrep).

About the Book

After a brief introduction to the scope and foresight methodology of the book, *The (R)Evolution of the Hybrid Office* is broadly structured into four main parts (I–IV).

I. The first part delves into the current dominant state of the hybrid office workplace, drawing on pre-pandemic status quo and the accelerated changes and trends of recent years.
II. The second part focuses on office workplace trends, future developments, and anticipated consequences.
III. The third part aims to unfold the implications for the central components of the hybrid office, namely the analogue and digital workplace infrastructure, management, and the employees.
IV. The final section presents recommendations to prepare and equip stakeholders and organisations, ensuring they are aware and proactive in safeguarding the potential benefits of a continuously modern hybrid office environment.

Contents

About the Author

Claus Sneppen

brings a wealth of knowledge and insight at the intersection of people, culture, and business. He holds a master's degree in business and culture from the University of Southern Denmark. His expertise contributes a sociological understanding of business to the future hybrid office workplace, drawing from his extensive management consultant experience in various fields, including experience economy, experience-based communication, workplace design, meeting design, and retail store design. As an advisor and consultant, he is passionate about translating new knowledge, analyses, and foresight into concrete, actionable initiatives within organisations. Notably, he has co-authored the book *Experience-Based Communication* (Oernbo, Würtz, and Sneppen, Springer 2008). Additionally, he established the think tank

"Meetings of Tomorrow" with a specific focus on exploring the impact of digitalisation on collaborations, meetings, and meeting places (2017–2019). These accomplishments underscore his significant contributions to understanding and shaping the dynamics of the future hybrid office workplace.

The Copenhagen Institute for Futures Studies is an independent, non-profit think tank established in 1969 on the initiative by former Danish Minister and OECD Secretary-General Professor Thorkil Kristensen. Our purpose is to help people and organisations imagine, work with, and shape their future. Our core advisory offerings include megatrend analysis, scenario planning, risk assessment, innovation processes, and strategic foresight. Besides our advisory services, we publish reports and magazines, host various events, organise talks, classes, and courses, and create and launch various joint venture initiatives. All the Institute's profits are allocated to further futures studies and to realising our purpose (www.cifs.dk).

Claus Sneppen. Image credits: Emil Monty Freddie

Introduction 1

Abstract

The transformation of the office workplace, primarily driven by digitalisation, changing employee behaviour, and new management practices, has led to a profound structural and systemic shift in how office work is conducted and organised.

The COVID-19 pandemic accelerated this transformation, making remote work a permanent feature for many knowledge workers. This shift challenges the traditional office-centric model, necessitating a re-evaluation of workplace design to align with contemporary needs. As organisations navigate the transition to a hybrid workplace, they must address critical questions about flexibility, productivity, and employee well-being. The hybrid model, which blends digital and physical elements, offers opportunities to enhance collaboration and efficiency but also presents challenges, particularly in managing remote and in-person interactions and communication.

Despite the initial expectation that remote work would decline post-pandemic, it has remained a key component of the modern office work landscape. This has raised concerns among managers, who struggle to balance the demands of upper management with the expectations of their teams. As economic hardships and unpredictability loom, organisations face further complexity in adopting a hybrid workplace model, with some reverting to traditional practices while others embrace flexibility.

The end of the office as the predominate epicentre of work-life for knowledge workers marks a significant departure from the post-industrial office factory. The hybrid workplace, driven by digitisation and automation, offers a new model for work that transcends time and location constraints. However, this shift raises important questions about how to design and manage an office workplace that supports both individual and organisational goals in a rapidly changing environment. Addressing these challenges requires effective management, a focus on employee well-being, and a willingness to embrace new technologies and work

C. Sneppen, *The Future (R)Evolution of the Office Workspace*, Future of Business and Finance, https://doi.org/10.1007/978-3-031-85229-9_1

practices. The ongoing development of the hybrid workplace will have far-reaching implications for productivity, efficiency, and the future of office work, requiring organisations to adapt to remain sustainable and competitive.

1.1 *The (R)Evolution of the Hybrid Office*

Welcome to the era of office employee consumerism—a transformative phase in the world of knowledge work, where the dynamics of the digital realm are reshaping how employees engage with their office workplaces and organisations. Today, office employees dedicate their work time to creating value in an omnichannel reality. Much like understanding what motivates your customers, organisations must *now ask: Do you truly understand what motivates your employees? And do you truly understand the why, how, and what of employee behaviour in both the analogue and digital realms?*

The (R)Evolution of the Hybrid Office is partly a discussion paper but primarily a vision for the anticipated future development of the office workplace from the Copenhagen Institute for Futures Studies. Its main goal is twofold. Firstly, it aims to provide primary office workplace actors and stakeholders with a more nuanced understanding of the most significant changes in the market that have already been realised, are nearing realisation, or are anticipated to drive the transformation of the office workplace towards a hybrid model. Secondly, the paper also seeks to equip primary workplace actors with foresights to anticipate and prepare for the future office workplace model. It achieves this by offering recommendations and strategic tools to facilitate internal processes, enabling organisations to transition towards a more sustainable and future-ready office workplace model. While it does not, nor aspire to, serve as an A-Z manual on developing and implementing a future-proof hybrid workplace model, the publication strives to encompass all major trends and components that will shape the evolution of the hybrid office workplace. As such, it seeks to provide a framework and vocabulary that enable workplace stakeholders to contemplate and develop the optimal office workplace model for their organisation.

The book adopts a comprehensive yet specific approach to envisioning the future office workplace. The hybrid office workplace is a multifaceted concept, intricately connected to various components, challenges, and opportunities that together shape the productive power and potential of a knowledge organisation. The analogy to a yarn cone suggests that whichever thread one pulls on is ultimately intertwined with the whole, forming a complete structure. Each of these elements fully warrants deeper exploration, but such depth lies well beyond the scope of this book. In this book, I have deliberately chosen to focus on the hybrid office workplace model and its anticipated development, while also addressing related components and their inherent challenges and opportunities throughout.

The publication sheds light on the office workplace in the post-pandemic era, amidst an evolving and potentially severe economic crisis characterised by high inflation, rising interest rates, and international geopolitical conflicts (2023–2024). These crises have unexpectedly accelerated trends and put working life and the workplace under significant stress, particularly for knowledge and office workers (Fig. 1.1). The pandemic has been a profound teacher, demonstrating that knowledge work can effectively and productively be carried out in locations beyond the traditional office setting. Hundreds of millions of office employees experienced remote work during the pandemic, underscoring that distance work is here to stay for knowledge workers. Hybrid working may indeed represent the "best of both worlds" for such employees (Choudhury et al. 2022).

To understand and navigate the hybrid office, it is essential to grasp the interplay and relationships that shape the workplace. Consequently, this book focuses on both the tangible and intangible aspects of the office environment, covering not only the physical and digital infrastructure but also the human dynamics between employees and management. This comprehensive approach aims to provide a holistic view of the modern office, addressing both structural and relational elements critical to a successful hybrid model. The term "analogue and digital workplace" distinguishes between work conducted on screens or through in-person interactions with physical presence. Knowledge workers predominantly carry out their tasks digitally, regardless of time, location, or space, but they collaborate either through digital means, analogue methods, or a combination of both. The redefined meaning of the workplace for knowledge workers, currently taking place, impacts all workplace actors to different extents. The publication primarily concentrates on the workplace itself and the potential ramifications for key stakeholders, including employees, management, and those responsible for the digital and analogue infrastructure. While many secondary actors and potential consequences will be mentioned, they are all intended to understand the possible implications for the primary actors and components of the workplace. However, the publication remains relevant for all internal and external actors in office workplaces and the working lives of knowledge workers.

The transformation holds structural and systemic significance for the office workplace. Due to the pandemic, the physical workplace was closed, and in response to the looming economic crisis, it has, figuratively speaking, been partially switched off to reduce costs and align with environmental, social, and governance (ESG) principles. This shift raises important questions about employee behaviour, preferences, management practices, and sustainability in both the short and in the long term. Will the physical shared office continue to exist in its current form in the future, albeit in a reduced and altered form? In truth, the ecosystem of the office

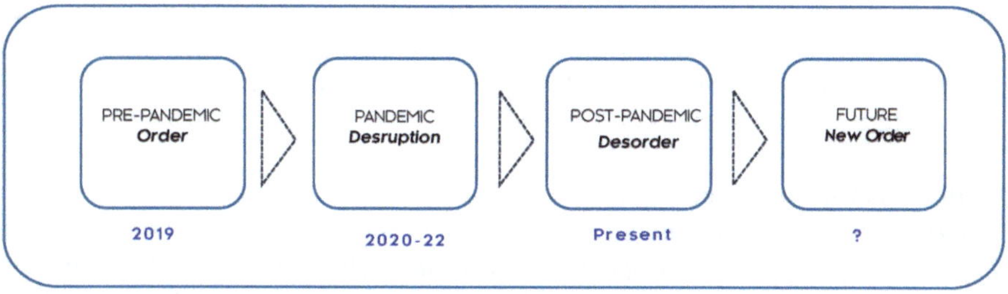

Fig. 1.1 A workplace model in motion: from order, to disruption, to disorder, to new order

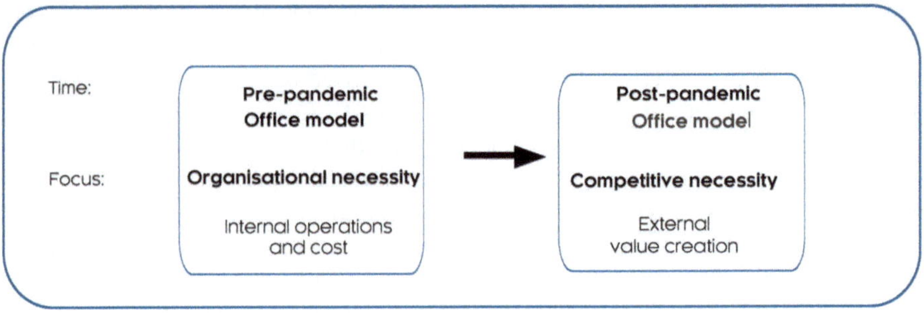

Fig. 1.2 Changing strategic objectives for the design of the workplace model

workplace has been significantly and fundamentally disrupted and deeply influenced by the growing presence of digital technology. Finally, it seems that after decades of resistance to change, there is a growing temptation to acknowledge this reality in the work-life of knowledge workers. As we adapt to a post-pandemic world, it is becoming evident that the office workplace and working life of the future will differ significantly from what we have been accustomed to, with the office serving as the primary, and in many cases only, epicentre of work for knowledge workers.

For knowledge workers, the hybrid and flexible working life is here to stay. This is simply because it is predominantly a mutually beneficial situation for both employers, employees, and society (e.g. Erdsiek 2021). We have only witnessed the beginning of the transformation of the workplace and work-life, particularly for knowledge workers. With ever-expanding and improved digital opportunities to create value, the development will continue to evolve. Basically, because in the future, it is reasonable to anticipate that ground-breaking new technologies and further digitalisation will increase productivity and significantly reduce the dependence on specific places and spaces for work. This development is briefly illustrated in Fig. 1.2, as this shift reflects a change in focus from the physical office as a necessity for the organisation to a renewed emphasis on the holistic office workplace model as a competitive necessity and a new framework for understanding how knowledge work is best organised.

This transformation cannot be resolved with a relatively simple management decision, such as allowing remote work for 2 days a week or make the office more accommodating and attractive. However, at the same time, we are increasingly realising that physical presence in the office remains essential for activities such as relationship building, onboarding of new employees, conflict management, innovation, culture, and co-creation.

Office Workspace Case: Maersk

Maersk employs approximately 130,000 people globally, with around 3000 based at the headquarters in central Copenhagen. The main office spans 32,049 sqm, including 25,386 sqm of office floors and 6663 sqm of common areas. There are 1670 desks, which can host 2385 employees with a 70 percent desk-sharing ratio.

In 2019, we began renovating the older part of the HQ, built in 1978. Previously, each employee had an assigned desk. We implemented an 80 percent desk-sharing ratio, which was later, after Covid, reduced to 70 percent in 2023. The renovation included adding various space types to support diverse work styles.

Our vision is to continue creating a flexible, digitalised, and sustainable office environment. We aim to optimise spaces with occupancy sensors and provide effective workplace tools. We are also expanding our HQ with a new building planned for 2026–2027, featuring a modern and sustainable workplace.

Maersk HQ. *Image credits*: Tomas Bertelsen PLH Architects

We expect that the future development of the office workplace will focus on creating more flexible and digitalised environments to support diverse work styles, enhance productivity, and meet constantly changing needs.

We strive to create an Iconic Cool Campus that embraces a different culture and flexible ways of working, which is key to servicing our customers on the digital transformation journey.

One of our biggest challenges is integrating the right technologies to create a smart and sustainable environment, including but not limited to occupancy sensors and digital workplace assistants. It is also crucial to stay on top of changes in work culture, as employee expectations are constantly evolving.

Recommendations:

Employee expectations are under constant change, especially with the new generations coming in, hence it is recommended to follow this development closely and proactively to ensure our workplace can meet these expectations. An office building should not be constructed in a static way that makes it difficult and expensive to adjust to the constantly changing needs.

Maersk HQ. *Image credits:* Tomas Bertelsen PLH Architects

Currently, nobody knows the exact formula or framework for a successful hybrid working life, which means that, to an unforeseen extent, we are unable to anticipate what the future hybrid office workplace or working life will look like for office workers. We are in uncharted territory (e.g. Kniffin et al. 2021). In this rapidly changing environment, successful collaborative approaches and models for the workplace must be developed despite the challenges that individuals and organisations face. These challenges put the development and implementation process under pressure, and we can expect increasing friction between workplace actors until organisations find a new balance between in-office and remote work in an increasingly digitalised realm. However, this balance is anticipated to be constantly challenged at an unprecedented pace as trends and dynamics change with progress. This implies, quite intuitively, that office workplaces must continuously adapt their current interpretation of the office model to remain relevant. In essence, the unfolding of hybrid work life and workplaces presents numerous ongoing and emerging dilemmas and paradoxes that workplace actors will be compelled to address, whether proactively or reactively.

Post-pandemic, I have observed that numerous organisations have redirected their attention from the hybrid workplace to address other urgent challenges or attempting to retrace to a pre-pandemic office-first model. I assume that this is partly because the hybrid workplace and the concept of a more flexible work-life with a workforce have not yet reached a definitive form, leading to considerable uncertainty especially when it comes to leadership (e.g. Wong and Berntzen 2019). Moreover, many management teams do not view the ongoing changes in the office workplace model as crucial for the organisation's competitiveness. In my opinion, it is important to recognise that while many organisations have taken steps in preparation for a hybrid workplace model, only a few have managed to find a sustainable solution. This is understandable because the development of the hybrid workplace is still in its early stages, and workplace actors are currently facing significant challenges in understanding the implications for the office workplace and the overall work-life value chain. The evolving nature of this model requires ongoing exploration and adaptation as we strive to establish a successful and long-lasting hybrid working environment.

During the process of writing *The (R)Evolution of the Hybrid Office*, I have identified significant elements and potential implications for the future hybrid office workplace model. The prioritisation of these elements has been determined somewhat arbitrarily, drawing on Copenhagen Institute for Futures Studies foresight method approach, experiences, available knowledge, and interactions with workplace actors, including accredited collaborators and contributors. I fully acknowledge that the list of elements and potential implications provided may not be exhaustive or thoroughly detailed.

The book has been in progress for several years, and, like many other aspects of the hybrid workplace, it was initially conceptualised due to the pandemic (2020–2022) and the foundational work for the book was conducted in 2023. Countless days, weeks, and months have been dedicated to contemplation, development, and finally, it has been documented in writing. Contemplating an idea is one thing, but articulating it in writing is quite another. The process, as is often the case with substantial publications, has been challenging yet rewarding, offering deeper insights and, ultimately, a clearer understanding of the potential and anticipated significant implications for the future office workplace.

The publication has been primarily developed within a Danish and Western context, with local national collaborative input from Danish HR, Danish Facilities Management, Danish IT, and Microsoft Denmark—each network and organisation representing significant stakeholders and co-creators of the future hybrid office workplace. Concrete workspace cases have been incorporated to illustrate the current developments, changes in organisational approaches, and how they interpret and implement office workspace interventions to remain competitive. The cases have been submitted by the organisations and should therefore be regarded as citations. At the same time, throughout the book, I have included challenge sub-chapters as a way to inspire reflection and provoke thought on the projected future development of the office workplace.

Data sources and contemporary knowledge on the hybrid workplace and working, along with its implications, remain relatively scarce, as our understanding of this concept is still in its early stages (hybrid working previously often referred to as teleworking, working from home or remote working). Consequently, the available data is often limited to specific areas and sub-topics, but it has been included in the book as indicators of trend development. The data and sources are, unsurprisingly, often conflicting, yet they reflect the underlying tensions that are shaping the future of the office workplace. A further note: much of the available data comes from office workplace stakeholders and should be regarded as potentially biased, as it often aligns with their specific agendas. This data serves as foundational context for the insights and perspectives in this book, incorporating a broad range of sources. However, for reasons of copyright and economics, the data itself is not directly presented. Additionally, much of the data is historical rather than current, partly become this book has been in development for several years. While this may make the foundation of the book's conclusions appear somewhat less robust to the critical eye, it is essential to recognise the dynamic and evolving nature of these trends. As is always the case with future-oriented work, this project has required a delicate balance between the pursuit of certainty and the understanding that we are navigating uncertainties and potential scenarios for future developments.

We cannot predict the future, but we can certainly anticipate and ready ourselves for the office workplace of tomorrow. Nevertheless, I will make an exception and make one prediction. A decade from now, in 2035—looking back at the office workplace of 2025—we will likely be astonished by how we operated and structured it, recognising the vast untapped potential that lay within reach, just waiting to be realised (the book manuscript was concluded in the fourth quarter of 2024). The prediction indicates that most office environments, along with current initiative, projects, and changes, will not meet the future ideal standards. Consequently, they will become outdated and be seen merely as preliminary steps towards a more optimal and competitive office workplace model. The prediction is, in fact, not so far-fetched, for who would have believed 5 years ago (in 2019) that most knowledge workers around the world would, to varying degrees, spend significant portions of their working hours remotely rather than in the office? The continued digitisation of knowledge work and its prominence will inevitably lead to the office transitioning wholly, or almost wholly, to the cloud. This shift will place the current analogue office in a precarious position, requiring it to be redefined radically. While the work infrastructure is already cloud-based, our behaviours have yet to adapt. It is merely a matter of time, and more intriguingly, a question of how this transformation will unfold.

My proposals and arguments concerning scenarios, possible futures, consequences, and recommendations reflect a probable and likely development—one that, for many, may not be particularly likable—as is often the case when engaging in foresight, rather than an absolute truth. I acknowledge that no one is truly deserving of the title of a present, let alone future, "hybrid workplace oracle". The evolution and future of the hybrid office workplace are being forged at the intersections and amidst the tensions between various stakeholders, technologies, and emerging trends. It is within this dynamic environment that the path towards the future hybrid office workplace will unfold, and uncertainties will be navigated.

1.2 The Transformation of the Office Workplace

The physical workplace and the office have historically served as the cornerstone for shaping the working life of knowledge workers in industrial and modern societies. However, the office workplace and working life are currently experiencing a rapid and profound structural and systemic transformation (e.g. Kane et al. 2021). With digitalisation, shifting employee behaviour, and new management principles, the office workplace and working life are undergoing an accelerated structural and systemic transformation. This profound change justifies describing the era we are living in as a pivotal turning point for the concept of the office. Structural, because the design of the workplace components changes significantly, and systemic, because the shared experience and interactions of workplace actor's change. The concept of a changing office workplace within a digital realm is far from new, as illustrated in *The New Office* by Francis Duffy and Kenneth Powell, which examines the evolution of office spaces in response to technological, social, and economic changes (Duffy and Powell 1997). Published in 1997 (almost three decades ago), this book offers insights into how modern office design can align with shifting work practices, employee needs, and organisational objectives. On the one hand, this development offers the opportunity to increase competitiveness through rethinking the office workplace model and the organisation of the workforce. But on the other hand, actors feel that the development threatens the existing and well-known model. As the office workplace is considered vital for organisations, this (r)evolution could be regarded as a wicked problem—a complex, multifaceted issue that is difficult, or at times impossible, to resolve through traditional, linear problem-solving methods (Churchman 1967). A wicked problem is characterised by ambiguity, a lack of clear solutions, interconnectedness, and a resistance to straightforward answers due to multiple, often competing perspectives. However, it will become evident that the challenge of the hybrid office workplace is more constructively understood as a series of critical dilemmas that management must address, rather than as a single problem with a straightforward solution. As the environment evolves, the organisation's response to these dilemmas must adapt accordingly.

The pandemic has played a significant role in permanently accelerating remote working, equivalent to almost four decades of pre-pandemic growth (Barrero et al. 2021). I once again use the word "accelerated" rather than "changed", as the pandemic has not altered the development but merely accelerated it. This rapid evolution clearly suggests that the traditional office workplace model was, to some extent, out of sync with the contemporary potentials and opportunities introduced by these changes. The traditional, purely analogue office space has largely ceased to exist, and digital work has become the cornerstone of working life for an increasing number of individuals. Data from Statistics Denmark (governmental institution) in 2024 now indicates that the level of remote work in Denmark is as high as it was at its peak during the early stages of the COVID-19 pandemic in 2021 (Statistics Denmark 2024). Statistics Denmark divides the group into individuals who frequently work from home—defined as more than half of their working days—and those who work from home occasionally. Currently, the latter group is the largest, whereas during the pandemic, when many were mandated to work from their home offices, the frequent remote workers formed the majority. In essence, for knowledge and office workers, the computer has surpassed the desk in importance. As a result, a thorough re-evaluation of the office workplace model is imperative to ensure that it aligns with the evolving needs and realities of the modern workforce and organisation.

Woods co-working space. Image credits: Woods Office

The accelerated pace of change institutively necessitates a proactive approach to adapt and harness the opportunities presented by the evolving office work landscape. A study published in 2021 revealed that nine out of ten organisations acknowledged the importance of flexibility and it was no longer a question of whether to be flexible, but rather how to achieve flexibility (Mckinsey and Company 2021). This sentiment resonates with the current transformation taking place in the office workplace, where digitalisation has revolutionised the way we work and collaborate. The office space has evolved to embrace a hybrid approach, combining digital and physical elements to support the changing needs and preferences of the modern organisation.

The organisation of employees' working lives plays a critical role in enhancing productivity and efficiency. As we consider the changed workplace, it is essential to approach it with a strategic mindset. How should the changed workplace be thought of? How can complexity and uncertainty around future hybrid working life and the workplace be reduced? How can the individual's and the organisation's productivity, efficiency, and well-being be continuously maintained and increased? How do you ensure that all work time is time best spend for both the individual and the organisation at the workplace as an entity? How do you create a way of working that attracts, retains, and develops talents and employees?

The immediate and pressing question that all organisations and stakeholders have addressed is: What proportion of employees will, and must, regularly attend the workplace in person? Nevertheless, this question only scratches the surface of the broader concept of the hybrid workplace. It extends well beyond guidelines for remote work and physical attendance; it is not solely about flexibility. Once an organisation embraces increased flexibility, the transformation towards a hybrid workplace has already commenced and cannot be easily reversed (as numerous workplaces are currently experiencing as they attempt to revert, or hold on, to an office-first model). A movement known as Return-to-Office (RTO) has gained momentum. By autumn 2024, a substantial number of large organisations have underscored this trend by announcing a shift back to a pre-COVID office model, requiring employees to work in the office 4 or 5 days a week rather than three. However, when analysing data across the Western Hemisphere, it becomes clear that this RTO trend is not widespread, as will be discussed in later chapters of the book. For example, in the USA, full-time in-office mandates have been steadily declining over recent years (Fig. 1.3).

Looking at the anticipated future development of the hybrid office workplace, rather than focusing on anecdotal, cherry-picked examples, a more indicative projection can be found in a study by WFH Research (Barrero et al. 2021). In fact, the current trend in balancing office and remote work remains relatively stable (Fig. 1.4). These findings underscore a growing acceptance of flexible work models among corporate leaders.

Furthermore, remote and hybrid job opportunities are still on the rise. The speed of development from pre-pandemic times is evident looking at data from before the pandemic. This trend highlights employees' preference for flexibility, offering employers a valuable opportunity to broaden their talent pool (Cui and Salomon 2024).

The hybrid office workplace presents a framework and opportunities for both digital and analogue work at both individual and organisational levels. This brings forth diverse challenges, one of which, e.g., is how to approach meetings, collaboration, and interactions (e.g. Yang et al. 2021). How should meetings be conducted when some employees are physically present while others join digitally? Which meetings are better suited for digital platforms, and which require physical presence? Determining when employees should gather in person and when interactions can take place asynchronously becomes critical. Navigating these challenges

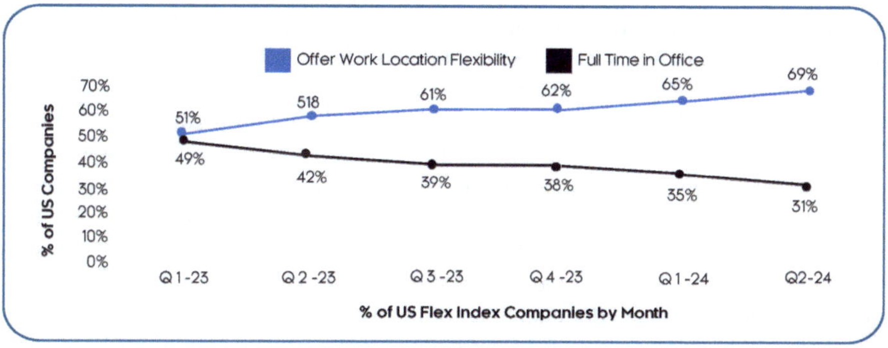

Fig. 1.3 US flex index companies offering work location flexibility over time. Source www.flex-index.com

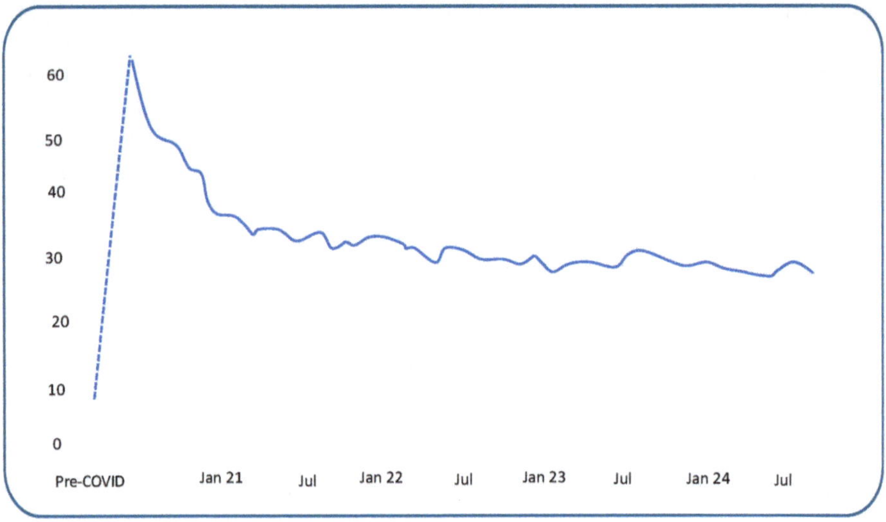

Fig. 1.4 Percentage of full paid days worked from home. Source: https://wfhresearch.com

requires careful consideration, effective communication, and embracing a hybrid approach that seamlessly blends digital and analogue elements.

1.3 The Pandemic Forced a Rethink of the Office Workplace Concept

In the past, forced behavioural changes under exceptional circumstances have often had limited or no lasting effect on subsequent behaviour. E.g. in previous publications from CIFS (Copenhagen Institute for Futures Studies), we addressed the potential impact of the pandemic on the balance between online and on-site retail. Initially, we expected it to have a lasting effect, leading to a permanent acceleration and influence towards more online commerce. Contrary to our expectations, this has not been the case, as online commerce has returned to its expected upward trend in most markets. This return to the trend may have been influenced by the economic development with expanding uncertainty and challenges.

The disruption in the office workplace is a completely different story. There has been a definitive and permanent shift in the balance towards more remote work and flexibility for knowledge workers. Unlike the retail sector, the office workplace has experienced a fundamental transformation, and remote work has emerged as a prominent and lasting feature of the new working landscape (see Fig. 1.5). This shift is likely to continue shaping the future of the office workplace, with remote work becoming an integral and dominant part of the working model for knowledge workers. This will be a long-tail shift because both employers and employees have come to realise that remote working is a valuable and viable digital alternative for in-office work performance. The last several years highlight the potential of remote

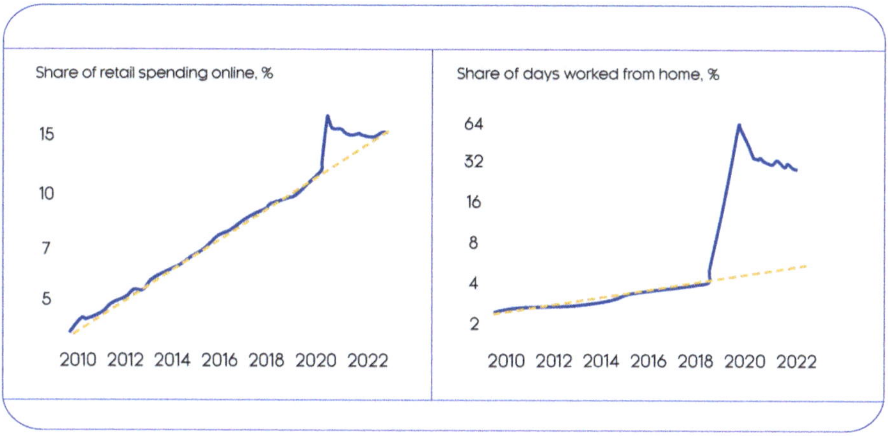

Fig. 1.5 Rise in WFH is permanent—Online shopping is back to pre-pandemic trend. Source: www.wfhresearch.com and data cover the USA

work, demonstrating that it can be a value-creating option for organisations and individuals alike. This realisation has led to a significant shift in attitudes towards remote work and has opened new possibilities for the future of the office workplace.

The pandemic lasted for approximately 3 years and during this time, both organisations and individuals became aware of viable alternatives to traditional office working habits. Research suggests that habits can be formed anywhere between 18 and 254 days, depending on the individual and the behaviour in question (P. Lally 2009). With approximately 5 years of new and increasingly digital work routines (2024), the workplace and working life have long passed the threshold of learning new behaviour and establishing new habits. However, contrary to initial expectations, the post-pandemic workplace did not adopt "social distancing" measures as anticipated. Phrases like "workplace distancing" or "office distancing" did not become the new norm in office work environments. Instead, the workplace has evolved to embrace a more flexible and hybrid approach, allowing employees to work in a manner that suits their individual needs and preferences, whether it be in the office or remotely. This shows that even in the face of significant changes and challenges, the workplace has adapted and found innovative solutions to create a more adaptable and inclusive working environment. As is often the case, the development of the office workplace has landed in the middle ground between the extremes of fully remote and fully in office. The revolution has matured into a gradual transformation and evolution, aptly reflected in the book's title. Yet, the question remains whether we will experience another revolution as digitalisation continues to advance.

The pandemic has once again highlighted the importance of managers and leadership in hybrid workplaces and a search for rising strategies in relation with others—both human and non-human—that enable and constrain the possibilities for actions (Nansen et al. 2010). Nevertheless, many middle managers find themselves in a challenging position, torn between the expectations of upper management and the needs of their team members. Many managers frequently feel they lack the authority and resources needed to effect meaningful change within their teams. A substantial number believe that organisations leadership is out of touch with employee expectations, and an even larger proportion sense they do not have sufficient influence or resources to bring about positive developments for their teams. This disconnect underscores the challenges managers face in aligning with both leadership goals and the needs of their teams (Microsoft 2022). The source of this tension is clear as business leaders push to restore pre-pandemic work structures. Around half indicate that their company has either mandated or intends to mandate full-time, in-person work in the coming year, with even greater support for this approach in sectors like manufacturing, retail, and consumer goods. This outlook, however, stands in stark contrast to employee preferences, as a considerable number of employees express intentions to pursue hybrid or remote work arrangements in the near future. This disparity highlights the ongoing struggle between leadership priorities and employee desires for flexibility.

There is no doubt that technology played a significant role in maintaining productivity during the pandemic. However, concerns about losing progress may be contributing to the push for in-person and office-first work. Although the vast majority of employees report being as productive, if not more so, since moving to remote or hybrid work, over half of leaders remain concerned that this shift has negatively impacted productivity (Microsoft 2022). During the pandemic, leaders faced immense pressure as they guided their employees and organisations through uncertainty and unprecedented economic challenges. It is understandable why they might view a return to the office as the solution. However, now leaders face a new and urgent challenge in an uncertain economy and labour market: establishing a standard for flexible work that balances business outcomes with the new expectations of employees. In the end, it is all about staying competitive.

The change in behaviour has challenged the previous functional fixedness bias associated with the use of the office. This bias previously limited the ways the workplace was used and understood within a modern and ever more digitised context. Employees and organisations that have worked remotely have now developed new habits and experiences that shape their preferences for the future workplace. This brings up several important and immediate questions for both employees and organisations, e.g.: "Which workplace model provides the most value?" "What have been the advantages and disadvantages of remote work?" "When does working in the office add value?" "How do we design and structure the physical office for this new reality?

1.4 The End of the Office as the Universal Hub for Knowledge Work

The office factory in the post-industrial society is increasingly being replaced by the hybrid workplace in the digitalised knowledge and network society. New information and communication technologies enable the spatial reconfiguration of work, allowing it to take place across multiple locations (Halford 2005). This spatial hybridity transforms the nature of work, organisation, and management, bridging domestic, organisational, and virtual spaces. For defenders of the traditional office-first model, the digital advancement of collaborative tools arrived as a Trojan horse, embedding itself unnoticed at the heart of the office stronghold—seemingly benign yet largely ignored by many. It was not until the pandemic that its true impact was unleashed, dismantling the very walls of the office. While most have partly adapted to this new reality, some are attempting to rebuild the walls and reinforce their office defences. Yet, the question of what the competitive office should be in the future remains wide open.

The ongoing development predominantly impacts knowledge workers, but it also extends to other areas of work that previously required physical presence. The advent of digitisation and automation is liberating work and productivity from the constraints of time and location (e.g. Egan 2020). While many of these trends are not novel, their significance lies in how they interact and collectively shape the landscape of productivity, efficiency, and employee well-being in a transformed labour market, enriched by the availability of new technologies. The key lies in fully understanding how these trends interact and collectively shape work practices across sectors. While the office is far from obsolete, it is set to evolve into a more modern, adaptable version (Moran 2020). This transformation reflects the shift towards hybrid work models, where physical offices serve as collaborative hubs rather than the default workspace, accommodating a more flexible and responsive approach to where and how work is conducted.

Embracing the hybrid workplace serves various reasons and objectives, but it is crucial to remember that the hybrid workplace model is merely a means to achieve the unique goals set by each organisation. From a broader perspective, organisations that hesitate to adopt an up-to-date and flexible office workplace are likely to face challenges in terms of digitisation, productivity, efficiency, and sustainability (the dominant workplace competitive advantages and objectives will be addressed in the later chapter). Moreover, they may struggle to attract and retain valuable employees compared to those that wholeheartedly embrace the flexible workplace model. Looking to the future, we can, in a black-and-white perspective, anticipate two types of organisations with corresponding office work models: those that embrace flexibility to varying degrees and those that, consequently, will face intense competition and potentially be outpaced by their more forward-thinking counterparts. The key to success lies in recognising the potential benefits of a flexible and adaptable workplace and aligning it with the specific needs and objectives of the organisation. By doing so, organisations can position themselves to thrive in an evolving and dynamic work environment. The ongoing development will profoundly impact the structure and functioning of the workplace, leading to significant and direct consequences for various stakeholders. This includes employees, top management, middle management, facility management, real estate, IT, People and Organisation, and all other stakeholders involved in shaping and managing the physical and digital workplace.

The changes in the workplace model will necessitate a comprehensive reassessment of how work is conducted, how teams collaborate, and how technology is leveraged to support remote and digital work. It will require organisations to adapt their policies, processes, and infrastructure to accommodate the evolving needs of a hybrid workforce. This transformation will undoubtedly shape the future of work and require active engagement and collaboration from all workplace actors to ensure a successful and future-ready workplace environment. However, the shift towards new workflow raises several important questions:

- How should the office be dimensioned and designed to accommodate the future hybrid work-life?
- How can the changed workplace effectively support a digitised reality, contrasting the predominant past mindset where the digital supported the analogue?
- How can complexity and uncertainty about future working life and the workplace be minimised while simultaneously ensuring continuous improvement in individual and organisational productivity, efficiency, and well-being?
- How do you create a workplace that not only attracts but also retains and develops employees, fostering a positive and engaging work environment?
- How can a workplace model be established that promotes shared structure and work behaviour in a digitalised reality, where working life and private life increasingly merge?

Addressing these questions and embracing the possibilities offered by the hybrid workplace is essential for organisations to remain competitive, adaptive, and future-ready in an ever-evolving working environment.

1.5 Hybrid Office Workplace Amid Economic Hardship and Uncertainty

The present economic hardship has added further complexity and unpredictability to the evolution of the hybrid workplace. During an economic recession, organisations are more likely to focus on cost-cutting measures and may revert to past practices that are known and proven. One way to achieve cost-cutting is by reducing or eliminating remote work options. Some organisations may view remote work as a luxury they can no longer afford when resources are scarce. Moreover, a recession can result in heightened competition for jobs, with more individuals being willing to work in a traditional office environment. This may make remote work less desirable and harder for employees who prefer it to find suitable job opportunities.

However, by end -2024, the job market remains largely driven by employee preferences, operating as an employee's market, or more commonly known as a job seeker's market, with workers in most sectors and industries holding greater influence than employers over their working conditions. This is captured in the following statement made during an interview for this book by a senior HR Director: "In the current challenging geopolitical and economic situation, it takes extremely courageous leaders to say, 'We need to work on our culture and how we define the future workplace', unless there is a burning platform. The question is whether there will be stability again in the previous understanding. If there is a burning platform, the situation is entirely different. For example, if we cannot attract employees, then we also need to build flexibility. They might be allowed to live in another country. What do we do about well-being? Should we focus on inclusion? Perhaps we should explore AR technology to attract stronger digital talents? It is the burning platform that has propelled some organisations further in developing the hybrid workplace model, and I expect that population to grow as more organisations come under pressure due to ongoing developments".

On the other hand, a potential recession can also accelerate the adoption of remote work. Organisations, to cut costs or searching for crucial competitiveness, may recognise the advantages of remote work, including reduced office expenses. Additionally, during a recession, technology becomes increasingly important. Organisations may need to invest more in remote work-enabling technologies, such as video conferencing and project management tools, to maintain smooth operations. This heightened reliance on technology may lead to a higher demand for remote work and create new opportunities for workers skilled in remote work technologies. With the looming economic hardships, interpretations of the future workplace model have become even more varied and divergent. Some believe in reverting to the old model and perceive the market to have shifted in favour of employer dominance, leading to widespread attempts by management to return to a "traditional" office-first model with limited remote work opportunities. On the other hand, many organisations have wholeheartedly embraced the hybrid workplace and are actively working to develop and implement this model.

1.6 Burning Hybrid Office Controversies

In a historical context, the workplace model has evolved gradually and slowly over the past century, with most office workplace models and spaces showing only minor differences. Therefore, the sudden shift to forced remote working during the pandemic was unexpected, requiring an abrupt and immediate change. As offices reopened, we encountered a new workplace paradigm, where Pandora's box of challenges has been irreversibly opened. The tale of Pandora's Box speaks to the challenge of attempting to put things back under the lid, only to seal in hope. What are organisations missing by clinging to a predominantly office-first workplace model? Firstly, as I will repeatedly emphasise throughout the book, employees aspire to a more balanced life. Consequently, a renewed approach to the office environment and work-life balance is essential. On a less positive note, this shift could also be likened to lifting the lid on a can of worms, revealing complexities that cannot easily be contained. Since the current workplace model has been developed based on existing knowledge and data, adopting a more experimental approach to the workplace will eventually lead to a paradigm shift at the management level (Economist 2021).

The workplace has traditionally served as the space for conducting work, socialising with colleagues, and pursuing professional ambitions. However, as the physical workplace, specifically the office, transforms from a daily routine and central point to an option and a means to achieve specific objectives, several contentious issues arise concerning the workplace model. Is your workplace prepared to face these challenges and address the fundamental office workplace controversies?

WHERE WE WORK: Hybrid, Remote, or In-person

The ongoing debate about remote versus in-person work shows no signs of abating. Organisations will continue to grapple with the challenge of developing fair and sustainable policies regarding remote and on-site work. The future hybrid workplace is a work environment where employees have the flexibility to work both remotely and on-site. In a hybrid workplace, employees are not tied to a physical office and can work from any location, such as their home or a co-working space, if they have the necessary tools and technologies to perform their job. The hybrid workplace model is gaining popularity as it offers several benefits for both employees and employers. For employees, it provides greater flexibility in achieving work-life balance and the ability to work in a comfortable environment. For employers, it can enhance productivity, reduce costs related to maintaining a physical office, and offer access to a broader talent pool (Coskun et al. 2024).

HOW WE WORK: Input or Output Focus

Traditionally, work has been measured in terms of hours worked. However, this approach may not be suitable for evaluating the performance of creative roles. Researchers at Stanford University have shown that while quantifying simple tasks, such as certain manufacturing steps, can improve productivity, attempting to quantify complex and creative work can actually hinder productivity. In a hybrid workplace, the focus is shifting towards output, rather than the number of hours worked or the physical location of the employee. This means that employees are evaluated based on the quality of their work, regardless of whether they are working from home or the office. To support an output-focused approach in a hybrid workplace, employers must provide their employees with the necessary tools, framework, and resources to work efficiently. This includes access to technology, communication tools for collaboration, and project management software. More importantly, employers need to establish clear performance metrics and expectations and communicate them effectively to their employees to ensure that everyone is aligned and aware of what is expected, especially as employees become more independent in performing their daily chores.

WHY WE WORK: Pay or Purpose

Even though the Great Resignation and Quiet Quitting are no longer dominating headlines, employees are still resigning in significant numbers. E.g. in Denmark, more than one in three employees changed employers in 2022 (Berlingske 2022). This means that in 2024, even amid ongoing layoffs in some sectors, organisations will need to adopt creative strategies to retain their valuable employees. With the hybrid and flexible workplace model, there is a shift in employees' priorities and the balance between pay and purpose (Burbano 2016). On one side, employees, as they spend more time at home, demand a more purposeful reason for being emotionally attached to the workplace and organisation. Additionally, employees have rediscovered the cost of being partially detached from their private lives by spending most of their daily time commuting and working away from home and family. They now prioritise achieving a better work-life balance. Moreover, the megatrend of doing good is rising, and working for a greater cause holds more appeal than a marginal increase in pay for an increasing number of employees. Tight budgets, growing social responsibility awareness, and a new focus on efficiency and flexibility are set to collide with challenges over hybrid work, productivity, and compensation.

1.7 Office Workplace Knowledge, Myths, and Bias

With the forced transformation of the workplace and work-life, all organisations, including management, are confronted with making decisions based on limited knowledge and data about the hybrid office workplace. Historically, the work model has been developed based on existing knowledge and data. Over the past 50 years, the office workplace model has evolved slowly, resulting in virtually all office workplaces looking quite similar with minor variations. The advent of the hybrid workplace is creating a radical and significant shift towards a more experimental approach until workplaces find a future-proof balance in this new hybrid reality.

In a classic VUCA approach, (Bennis and Nanus 1985), Volatility, Uncertainty, Complexity, Ambiguity, the situation moves towards ambiguity, characterised by unknown connections and causality, leading workplace actors to face "unknown unknowns". This necessitates a growing need for workplace actors to experiment, voluntary or involuntarily, to understand the connections and effects of different initiatives. They must be willing to continuously adapt, and discard approaches based on the experiences generated. The experimental approach to the workplace presents considerable challenges and signifies a major shift from current workplace management paradigms, particularly when it encompasses the office as a central workplace.

Workplace actors are expected to respond differently to this changed reality, with approaches ranging from "go back to the past", "maintain and wait" to "transform and revolutionise". Regardless of the approach, workplace actors must proactively address the changes, as employees and other stakeholders expect to be actively involved in shaping the workplace. Failing to address these changes is also a choice with consequences in the competition to attract and retain valuable employees and to ensure overall competitiveness. To determine what is best for the organisation's future regarding remote work, management must consider it within the broader context of goals and objectives. In other words, management needs to have a clear vision of what it aspires to achieve. Then, management must visualise the "workforce system" that will enable the accomplishment of those objectives (Johnson and Suskewicz 2020).

Organisations should exercise caution when shaping the future hybrid workplace, ensuring it is not built upon assumptions grounded in habitual biases and past experiences. This is particularly evident, for instance, when we examine varying preferences across age groups regarding flexibility and hybrid work environments (Fig. 1.6).

In essence, the development of the hybrid workplace must be approached with more knowledge, less myth, and less biases.

- Do you possess the answers to the crucial workplace questions based on data and insights?
- Do you know when, where, and how the employees and teams create most value?
- Do you know when, where, and how collaboration creates most value?
- Do you know and understand the value hierarchy of the different components of the workplace model?
- Do you understand the optimal flexibility structure for your organisation?
- Do you understand the preferences and behaviour of the employees for the sustainable workplace value creation?
- Do you comprehend the future implications of the development on the capabilities of management?

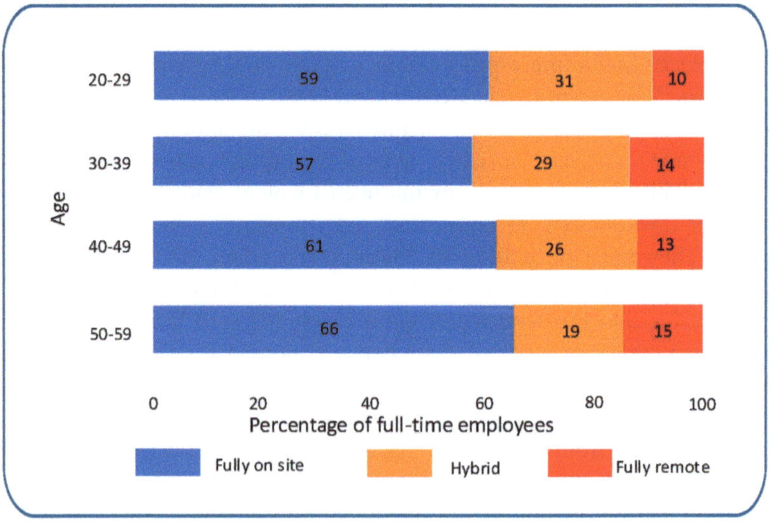

Fig. 1.6 Workers in their 50s and 60s are more fully on-site and fully remote more often than younger workers. Source WFH Research Barrero, Bloom, Buckman, and Davis 202

More Knowledge With the sudden transformation of work life, all organisations, including management, are confronted with making decisions based on limited knowledge, experience, and data about the hybrid workplace. This new workplace entails an expanding portion of work being carried out digitally and remotely. The speed of workplace changes shifts the perceived reality from being static, with a high degree of knowledge and predictability, towards a more complex, uncertain, and ambiguous workplace. They need to be ready to continuously adapt and discard initiatives based on experiences. Workplace actors are expected to approach this changed reality in various ways, from an office retention-focused approach to a transformation-focused approach. However, workplace actors should also be cautious not to unnecessarily destabilise an already changing workplace, which could further amplify uncertainty and complexity. There is a widespread need for stability and predictability regarding work life and the workplace model. Maintaining a sense of calmness creates more space to focus on work tasks. Regardless of the approach, workplace actors must proactively address the changes, as employees and other stakeholders expect to be actively involved in shaping the office workplace of tomorrow.

Less Myth Creating the hybrid workplace of the future requires dispelling myths about the workplace and taking a stand against them (e.g. Fig. 1.7. The data debunking these myths will be presented later in the book). The ongoing transformation of the workplace model puts pressure on organisations to improve access to data, hasten development processes, and make more informed decisions. The hybrid workplace approach reflects this progress and addresses the need to digitalise individuals and organisations in terms of scale and speed. Simultaneously, this hybrid approach challenges traditional notions of when, where, and how employees and organisations are most productive and effective.

Developing the hybrid office workplace model demands purposeful efforts to create a scalable, hybrid workplace model that aligns with the organisation's business goals while reducing costs, allowing resources to be optimally allocated towards core objectives. It is becoming increasingly important to consider the future workplace strategy and model. Although the current market in certain regions and segments may appear to favour employers, this perception is illusory, particularly concerning talent attraction and retention.

Less Biases All too often, we confuse the *likeable* with the *likely*, thereby accommodating our ever-present biases. There are numerous diverse opinions on how the transformed workplace should be designed. However, more often than not, a single focus is chosen as the starting point. This approach can increase the likelihood of less objective and holistic solutions, which may distort competition and hinder the creation of a sustainable model for the transformed office workplace. The starting points for workplace transformation introduce biases that influence the process of creating a successful future workplace. These biases can take the form of status quo

MYTH	DEBUNKED
• Hybrid work reduces productivity.	> Research indicates that hybrid models can maintain or even enhance productivity.
• Collaboration suffers in hybrid settings.	> Modern tools and practices ensure collaboration is effective across settings.
• Hybrid work is only for tech-savvy organisations.	> Hybrid work can be tailored to fit a variety of sectors with the right planning.
• Hybrid work leads to unequal opportunities.	> Proper policies can ensure inclusivity and equal access to opportunities.
• Hybrid work makes culture building impossible.	> Culture thrives through intentional efforts, regardless of location.
• Hybrid work is a temporary trendnitiatives.	> The hybrid model is becoming a permanent feature of modern work life.
• A hybrid workplace model is a reflection of our analogue infrastructure.	> The resilient organisation continuously adapts and develops IT strategies and infrastructures towards the "Everywhere Enterprise"

Fig. 1.7 Myths about the hybrid office workplace

bias, confirmation bias, or optimism bias, leading to a subjective approach in developing the future and transformed workplace. The complexities increase as biases intertwine and, in many cases, are at play when decisions related to the workplace are made, as it is a subject that often provokes strong opinions. Here are typical forms of bias that actors should be aware of when developing the office workplace:

- Status Quo Bias: The workplace functions as it is, and it just needs incremental changes over time. E.g. If employees are allowed to work remotely 1 day a week, we have implemented the hybrid workplace.
- Confirmation Bias: The future workplace should be developed based on historical data and experiences.
- Optimism Bias: The workplace should be radically changed, and all development is seen as positive. It is also named the Overconfidence Bias. The tendency for decision-makers to overestimate their understanding and abilities, leading them to make bold assumptions about future workplace success without adequate testing or feedback mechanisms.
- Expert Bias: The expert believes they know everything, but few actually know anything about the successful model for the future hybrid office workplace. And even fewer, if any, know a lot or everything about it (I for one most certainly do not).

- Group Thinking Fallacy: We, as a group, know how the future hybrid workplace should be developed and implemented. Typically, when a limited group of management representatives share the same beliefs and are empowered to make significant decisions without being challenged.
- Survivor Bias: We observe that successful organisations often commit to a specific workplace model, which can create the impression that this approach is inherently the most effective. For example, some well-resourced organisations prioritise exceptional in-person office environments, while others, catering to distinct employee groups unlike your own, may pursue alternative strategies. Likewise, highly digital organisations with advanced assessment frameworks may operate entirely remotely. Survivor bias lies in failing to consider the broader context and relying solely on partial data from successful organisations and their workplace models.
- Functional Fixedness Bias: The tendency to see the office workplace only in terms of the traditional use or function, e.g. using the in-person office-first as the core of the development of the hybrid workplace model. An example of functional bias is to primarily focus on interior design and services as a means of embracing and defining the hybrid workplace model.
- Anchoring Bias: The tendency to rely heavily on the first piece of information encountered when making decisions. For example, if an initial hybrid workplace model emphasises limited remote work, future strategies may become anchored to this structure, stifling more innovative or flexible developments.
- Recency Bias: Giving disproportionate weight to the most recent events or experiences. For instance, if a recent remote-work pilot failed due to temporary issues (e.g. technological hiccups or unexpected staff shortages), decision-makers might avoid pursuing further remote options, overlooking their potential benefits.
- Sunk Cost Fallacy: The tendency to persist with a project or policy due to the significant resources already invested, rather than assessing its current and future merits. Organisations may continue to adhere to an office-first model if they have heavily invested and committed to an analogue office setup.
- Authority Bias: The tendency to believe or rely on the opinions of authoritative figures or perceived experts without adequate scrutiny. If a senior executive strongly advocates for a particular workplace model, others might follow suit without offering counterarguments or objections.
- Cultural Bias: Assuming that the way the workplace functions within one cultural or organisational context is the best or only way. For example, imposing a hybrid model designed for one region's norms and practices onto global branches with different work cultures and needs.

1.8 The Office Workplace Model Is Inherently Change Adverse

The office workplace model is resistant to change primarily because it continues to function relatively effectively, and people have grown accustomed to it (Gratton 2023). Why has it been challenging to alter the workplace model? The reason is that there is a lot at stake. The emergence of the hybrid work model goes beyond deciding whether employees should return to the office full-time, work 2 or 3 days a week at the office, or have the option to work from home. As these questions are debated and navigated, organisations are confronted with the need to challenge long-standing assumptions about the nature of work and collaboration and how it should be conducted.

The evolution of the workplace model is largely influenced by market economic forces. In an offensive perspective, the most sustainably productive workplace model prevails. On the defensive side, organisations maintain their workplace model as long as it remains competitive compared to the broader market and often specific competitors within the same sector or industry. This includes competing for market share, customers, employees, etc. If everyone else adopts essentially the same workplace model, there is a reluctance to experiment unnecessarily, but it also means that everyone ends up with an equally good or bad model. The defensive strategy for workplace development could partly be rooted in Hotelling's Law from 1929 (Ridley 2016), which overall suggests that rational organisations are inclined to make their workplaces as similar as possible, thus favouring homogeneity over differentiation (formulated in an oligopolistic market setting, and reflecting that the office workplace landscape is characterised near-identical environments.) Additionally, in the context of behavioural game theory, this approach aligns with the concept of Nash Equilibrium of 1950 (Holt and Roth 2004), where workplaces strategically position themselves at the centre of the market.

Another perspective for understanding the underlying processes behind organisational workplace similarity can be found through the lens of neo-institutionalism (Wasserman 2011). What is essentially a rather simple concept is referred to by the sophisticated term "isomorphism". In essence, isomorphism merely refers to the processes that lead organisations within the same organisational field to resemble one another—in other words, to become isomorphic. This concept is crucial not only for understanding why organisations tend to resemble each other, but also because isomorphism plays a significant role in an organisation's legitimacy. So, why do organisations and workplaces end up looking alike? The answer lies in three main drivers of isomorphism: coercive, mimetic, and normative isomorphism. Coercive isomorphism refers to the formal and informal pressures on an organisation, exerted by other organisations or institutions on which they are dependent, such as customers, trade unions, legislation, and so on. Mimetic isomorphism occurs when, due to uncertainty and ambiguous conditions, an organisation responds by modelling itself on another organisation's workplace model. Finally, normative isomorphism arises from the professionalisation of employees, which leads to shared understandings of work life and the workplace. As a result, professions, work processes, and practices begin to resemble one another across organisations.

Consequently, there is an inherent resistance and aversion to taking risks by changing the existing workplace model to a different one from competitors and the broader market. The development of the workplace is thus partly hindered by resistance to change, and the focus may not be on establishing the optimal model. As a result, various degrees of development and, in some cases, stagnation are observed in the adoption of the hybrid workplace, despite the potential for significantly increased competitiveness. In this context, it is important to recognise that some of the key differences in the interpretation of the office workplace can be observed between various countries or states, as legislation and regulation have a significant impact on the model, rather than a lack of aspiration to attain or maintain competitiveness.

However, we have already reached the tipping point regarding the balance between working in-person and working remote. According to Malcolm Gladwell (2001), a tipping point is the moment when an idea, behaviour, or trend crosses a threshold, tips, and spreads rapidly and extensively throughout a society or system. And the tipping point is not the qualitative equilibrium, but when key actors change their behaviour or stance. In the case of transitioning to a hybrid workplace, this tipping point can occur when a critical mass of employees and managers adopt this new work model, making it the new norm for contemporary organisations. Once this tipping point is reached, the benefits of a hybrid workplace can become self-reinforcing. For instance, remote work can, if implemented wisely, lead to a better work-life balance for employees. This, in turn, can lead to higher job satisfaction, attracting and retaining more talented employees who value flexibility and autonomy. This virtuous cycle can continue to reinforce the hybrid work model as the dominant norm, as indeed appears to be the case.

Most office workplaces now have updated policies for distributed and flexible work. However, we are yet to fully experience the implications of this shift on the workplace ecosystem as the development and internal and external pressure continue to build on the "old" prevalent analogue office-first model. The upcoming tipping points in the adoption of the hybrid workplace are anticipated to involve radical changes in the size and design of offices, a shift from an input-focused to an output-focused work-life, an increased focus on employee well-being as a crucial competitive advantage, reduced carbon footprint, decentralised and distance management, and other related factors.

The challenged office workplace will continue to evolve and not stabilise in the traditional sense. It is anticipated to be subject to ongoing change as new technology and further digitisation are adopted and integrated into organisations. The real long-term challenge for the workplace model is to remain up-to-date and relevant, as the physical office involves both short-term and long-term structures and commitments. Long-term investments pertain to the fundamental digital and analogue infrastructure and may have timeframes of 10 to 30 years through binding agreements and significant costs in case of change. Short-term investments involve user interfaces such as furniture, work screens, IT hardware, and service subcontractors. The most substantial workplace investment and commitment revolve around the organisation of "soft" resources, namely management and employees. As always, the culture and behaviour of the organisation are the most challenging aspects to embrace in a change process.

Precisely because the workplace model holds crucial importance for organisations and due to the significant external changes, there is a corresponding resistance to making significant decisions. Additionally, the hybrid workplace has not yet reached its final form, which further contributes to the reluctance in engaging in "experiments" around such a central aspect as the workplace institution. From a broader perspective, various actors are to different extents held back in the change process and the ongoing liberation of work through the adoption and development of the hybrid workplace. However, eventually, most workplaces will adopt a hybrid model and will be compelled to experiment and adapt to the changing landscape.

1.9 Management Bias

Ultimately, the successful development of the hybrid workplace in any organisation depends on the management's willingness to prioritise and drive the necessary changes. However, it is crucial for management not to rely predominately on their own preferences and habits when approaching the development of the workplace. Instead, they need to be open to new ideas, consider the evolving digital reality, and be receptive to the changing needs and preferences of employees. In this context, it is important that top management don't reflect their own work-life reality onto the organisation. For example, studies have shown that the effectiveness of remote working arrangements between CEOs and their companies is often challenged (Duchin and Sosyura 2024). CEOs working remotely tend to underperform in terms of operating performance, firm valuation, insider reviews, and market reactions to their departures. These negative effects are more pronounced when the CEO lives farther away and crosses multiple time zones. As a result, top management, all else being equal, are generally less inclined towards hybrid working arrangements from this narrow perspective.

The pressure for change is particularly significant on management, as they are responsible for setting the direction and vision for the organisation (Kohntopp and McCann 2020). Their approach to creating an optimal workplace will directly impact the success of the transition to a hybrid model. It is essential for management to thoroughly understand the consequences of the digital reality on the workplace model and be proactive in addressing the challenges and opportunities it presents.

The traditional 9-to-5 office model which originated in the early 1900s and was popularised by industrialists like Henry Ford, offered a structured and predictable environment that suited both management and employees. It provided a clear routine and rhythm, making it easy for both parties to navigate. This model was a significant step in reducing the working week from 6 days to five and limiting daily work hours to eight, whether employees worked in offices or on assembly lines. The decision to implement these changes was also influenced by the understanding that workers, who were also consumers, needed time for leisure and consumption activities. Ultimately, however, it was a means for Ford to attract and retain the best talent and employees for his organisation and production lines.

Executives are likely to experience higher levels of work satisfaction than their employees, a disparity that can be attributed to several factors. Executives often enjoy superior living conditions, more comfortable office environments, and significantly higher pay. Even when working from home, they typically have access to better resources, such as larger living spaces and the financial means to arrange childcare during school closures. In the workplace, executives benefit from private offices with doors, affording them privacy, while other employees may contend with open-plan hot desks. Furthermore, their positions grant them greater autonomy and flexibility in their work. This advantage, however, may lead to a form of confirmation bias, where executives mistakenly assume that other employees share the same level of satisfaction with the current work setup.

The pre-pandemic, office-first workplace naturally facilitated, to varying degrees, the development of a shared organisational culture, collaboration, psychological safety, and trust-building by offering a common, face-to-face meeting point: the office. Management was relatively straightforward through linear, synchronised, and symmetric in-person attendance, and the office had predominately a post-industrial design and distribution of the workforce that contributed to facilitating in-person specialised collaboration and management. The dark side of the old workplace model and office was the actual mismatch between the model and how employees worked and desired to work, as well as the opportunities provided by digitisation for work. The network and knowledge society operate independently of specific formats and channels. The "old" office-first did not align with what organisations truly desire, which is agility and flexibility in a dynamic reality characterised by constant change. There is a constant pressure to deliver fast responses to evolving challenges regardless of time, location, or physical space.

In the current development of the hybrid workplace model, management often uses the so-called unquestionable truths about how the work life of knowledge workers is best organised (Fig. 1.8). These are often unchallenged so-called truths and statements that are frequently used to defend the present office-first model and are predominantly not based on knowledge or data but on personal anecdotes, preferences, and habitual behaviour (All of the arguments and responses will be explored and examined in greater depth later in the book). Top-management "trump" arguments often involve selective use of evidence, effectively amounting to automated cherry-picking. These trump arguments suppress counter-evidence or rely on the fallacy of incomplete evidence by highlighting specific cases or data that appear to support the notion of the shared physical office as the central hub for organisations and knowledge workers that suppress evidence, or the fallacy of incomplete evidence, in the act of pointing to individual cases or data that seem to confirm a particular position for defending the shared physical office as the centre of gravity of organisations and knowledge workers. In some instances, this goes beyond selective use of data to what could be termed "data mirages"—fabricated or misleading data presented as valid. The intent is to reinforce an already fixed position on how the

Fig. 1.8 Six management office trump cards: played by management to limit flexibility in the office workplace model

office workplace model should be optimally designed. The fundamental challenge to the use of management office first trumps is that it often reflects the paradigm that the office is the epicentre of the work life of knowledge workers. Post-pandemic, it is in fact predominately hybrid, combining remote and in-person work performance, and consequently organisations are to find the balance and competitive advantages in navigating a more distributed workforce.

In my view, the objections and counterarguments put forth by top-management frequently outweigh the reasons often cited to hinder the progression of the hybrid office workplace. Many of the prevailing arguments made by management during the current turbulence surrounding hybrid work will, both when examined in the present and over time, be recognised for what they truly were: responses rooted in a period of evolutionary transition, as the post-industrial office workplace shifts towards a more digitally dominated future.

References

(Barrero, Bloom, and Davis, 2021). "Why working from home will stick," National Bureau of Economic Research Working Paper 28731. www.wfhresearch.Com

(Bennis and Nanus 1985) Harper and Row, Leaders: The Strategies for Taking Charge https://www.amazon.com/Leaders-Strategies-Taking-Warren-Bennis/dp/006015246X

(Berlingske 2022) Jobmarkedet koger: En million danskere har fået nyt job det seneste år – »det er nu, man har chancen https://www.berlingske.dk/oekonomi/jobmarkedet-koger-en-million-danskere-har-faaet-nyt-job-det-seneste-aar

(Burbano, 2016) Social responsibility messages and worker wage requirements: Field experimental evidence from online labor marketplaces. https://psycnet.apa.org/record/2016-45906-003

(Choudhury et al., 2022) Choudhury, P., Khanna, T., Makridis, C. & Schirmann, K. Is hybrid work the best of both worlds? evidence from a field experiment. *Rev. Econ. Stat. Forthcom.* *9*, 1–24 (2024). https://www.hbs.edu/ris/Publication%20Files/22-063_639195cc-e7b5-47d3-9281-62d192c5b916.pdf

(Churchman, 1967) C. Churchman, "Wicked Problems" Management Science 14, no. 4 (December 1967 B-141–B-146. https://www.jstor.org/stable/i344811

(Coskun, Wolfgang, Gartner, Stops and Enzo 2024) Working from Home Increases Work-Home Distances https://papers.ssrn.com/sol3/papers.cfm?abstract_id=4761332

(Cui and Salomon 2024) The Global Market for Remote White-Collar Jobs https://papers.ssrn.com/sol3/papers.cfm?abstract_id=4942498

(Duchin and Sosyura 2024) Remotely Productive: The Efficacy of Remote Work for Executives https://papers.ssrn.com/sol3/papers.cfm?abstract_id=3761972

(Duffy and Powell, 1997) Duffy, Francis and Kenneth Powell. The New Office. London: Conran Octopus 1997 https://www.amazon.com/New-Office-Francis-Duffy/dp/1850298912

(Economist 2021) The rise of working from home. (Special Report). The Economist. https://www.economist.com/special-report/2021/04/08/the-rise-of-working-from-home

(Egan 2020) The office, as you know it, is dead. https://edition.cnn.com/2020/08/25/business/office-space-remote-work-pandemic/index.html. (CNN Business)

(Erdsiek 2021) Erdsiek, Daniel, Working From Home During COVID-19 and Beyond: Survey Evidence From Employers (2021). ZEW - Centre for European Economic Research Discussion Paper No. 21–051, Available at SSRN: https://ssrn.com/abstract=3875337

(Gladwell 2001) Malcolm Gladwell Little Brown and Company, The Tipping Point: How Little Things Can Make a Big Difference https://www.amazon.com/Tipping-Point-Melcolm-Gladwell/dp/0316679070

(Gratton 2023) HBR Redesigning How We Work https://hbr.org/2023/03/redesigning-how-we-work

(Halford, 2005) Hybrid workspace: Re-spatialisations of work, organisation and management. New Technology, Work and Employment, 20(1), 19–33. https://onlinelibrary.wiley.com/doi/10.1111/j.1468-005X.2005.00141.x

(Holt and Roth 2004) The Nash equilibrium: A perspective https://www.pnas.org/doi/full/10.1073/pnas.0308738101

(Johnson and Suskewicz 2020) HBR Does Your Company Have a Long-Term Plan for https://hbr.org/2020/07/does-your-company-have-a-long-term-plan-for-remote-work

(Kane, Nanda, Phillips and Copulsky 2021) Redesigning the post-pandemic workplace. MIT Sloan Management Review, 62(3), 12–14. https://sloanreview.mit.edu/article/redesigning-the-post-pandemic-workplace/

(Kniffin et al.; 2021). Kniffin KM, Narayanan J, Anseel F, Antonakis J, Ashford SP, Bakker AB, Bamberger P, Bapuji H, Bhave DP, Choi VK, Creary SJ, Demerouti E, Flynn FJ, Gelfand MJ, Greer LL, Johns G, Kesebir S, Klein PG, Lee SY, Ozcelik H, Petriglieri JL, Rothbard NP, Rudolph CW, Shaw JD, Sirola N, Wanberg CR, Whillans A, Wilmot MP, Vugt MV. COVID-19 and the workplace: Implications, issues, and insights for future research and action. Am Psychol. 2021 Jan;76(1):63–77. doi: 10.1037/amp0000716. Epub 2020 Aug 10. PMID: 32772537.COVID-19 and the workplace: Implications, issues, and insights for future research and action https://pubmed.ncbi.nlm.nih.gov/32772537/

(Kohntopp and McCann 2020) Leadership in virtual organizations: influence on workplace engagement. In: Dhiman S (eds) The Palgrave handbook of workplace well-being. Palgrave Macmillan https://doi.org/10.1007/978-3-030-02470-3_12-1

(P. Lally 2009) https://onlinelibrary.wiley.com/doi/abs/10.1002/ejsp.674

(Mckinsey & Company 2021) "What Executives Are saying About the Future of Hybrid Work" https://www.mckinsey.com/capabilities/people-and-organizational-performance/our-insights/what-executives-are-saying-about-the-future-of-hybrid-work

(Microsoft 2022) Work Trend Index: Annual Report 2022) https://www.microsoft.com/en-us/worklab/work-trend-index/great-expectations-making-hybrid-work-work

(Moran, 2020) Despite Covid-19, the end of the office is far from nigh. https://www.irishtimes.com/business/commercial-property/despite-covid-19-the-end-of-the-office-is-far-from-nigh-1.4354658. (The Irish Times)

(Nansen, Arnold, Gibbs and Davis, 2010) Nansen B, Arnold M, Gibbs M, Davis, H. (2010) Time, space and technology in the working-home: an unsettled nexus. N Technol Work Employ 25(2):136–153. https://doi.org/10.1111/j.1468-005X.2010.00244.x

(Ridley 2016) Hotellingers Law https://www.researchgate.net/publication/311907851_Hotelling's_Law

(Statistics Denmark 2024) https://www.dst.dk/da/Statistik/nyheder-analyser-publ/nyt/NytHtml?cid=49082

(Wasserman 2011) To be (alike) or not to be (at all): aesthetic isomorphism in organisational spaces

(Wong and Berntzen 2019) Transformational leadership and leader–member exchange in distributed teams: the roles of electronic dependence and team task interdependence. Comput Hum Behav 92:381–392 https://www.researchgate.net/publication/329015643_Transformational_leadership_and_leader-member_exchange_in_distributed_teams_The_roles_of_electronic_dependence_and_team_task_interdependence

(Yang et al., 2021) Yang, L., Holtz, D., Jaffe, S. *et al.* The effects of remote work on collaboration among information workers. *Nat Hum Behav* **6**, 43–54 (2022). https://doi.org/10.1038/s41562-021-01196-4

Foresight and Anticipatory Leadership in an Era of Uncertainty and Complexity 2

Abstract

Strategic foresight is a critical tool in navigating the uncertainties of the future. It involves structured methods to anticipate and prepare for potential changes, guiding decision-makers towards sustainable, long-term solutions. While many rely on extrapolating existing trends to predict the near future, this approach limits our understanding of the complex, volatile forces shaping the long term. Studies show that companies adopting strategic foresight are more likely to outperform competitors, demonstrating the value of foresight in a rapidly changing environment.

Megatrends, fundamental uncertainties, unexpected events, and human biases are central components of future analysis. Each plays a vital role in shaping the trajectory of organisations. As futurists stress, the future cannot be predicted with certainty, but strategic foresight allows businesses to adapt and respond more effectively. Acknowledging human biases, such as confirmation and optimism biases, helps leaders make more informed decisions. Ultimately, understanding future customer needs and potential disruptions is crucial for maintaining competitiveness in an evolving landscape.

2.1 Why Work with the Future and Foresight

As we stand on the brink of the future (r)evolution of the office workplace, it is timely to explore and share insights into the nature and value of futures studies, and how they can enhance our understanding of the hybrid office workplace model.

Nobody knows the future, and there is obviously no data available. When working with the future, it is rare to know when real value is created. The best possible value exploring the future comes from making observations and drawing attention to potential scenarios that influence stakeholders to make more intentional,

C. Sneppen, *The Future (R)Evolution of the Office Workspace*, Future of Business and Finance, https://doi.org/10.1007/978-3-031-85229-9_2

forward-thinking, and sustainable decisions. In many cases, the true value lies in developing a mutual vocabulary and understanding within an organisation regarding the potential future situational landscape, thereby enabling the evaluation of and response to changes as they arise. In futures studies, the term "strategic foresight" is used to describe the discipline of working in a structured manner to understand and act upon possible futures.

Who hasn't been caught off guard by an unforeseen event, or found themselves needing to rethink their plans because of something unanticipated? Perhaps even discovered that a usual problem-solving approach is no longer effective? In times of rapid change and growing uncertainty, these challenges are increasingly faced by governments, companies, and organisations alike. As a colleague recently remarked, *"Organisations should not engage in foresight to seek certainty. Quite the opposite. Organisations should engage in foresight to challenge the misguided assumptions that underpin a false sense of certainty".*

2.2 Development: A Non-linear Journey

Development is not always linear or predictable based on past progress and data. When combined with the tensions present in today's office environments, it is more important than ever to look ahead to stay ahead of ongoing developments. For example, a survey of over 200 organisations revealed that more than 90 per cent of executives expect COVID-19 to drive fundamental changes in business practices within the next 5 years, with nearly as many believing the crisis will have a lasting effect on customer needs (Bar Am et al. 2020).

One of the most comprehensive studies on the value of strategic foresight tracked several companies over a seven-year period (Rohrbeck and Kum 2018). The study concluded that companies employing a structured approach to understanding and positioning themselves in relation to long-term developments had a 44 per cent likelihood of outperforming their industry peers (Fig. 2.1). In contrast, those that did not take a structured approach to the future had only a 15 per cent chance of being top performers. Much like navigating an ice cap, the likelihood of survival is significantly higher when working with a structured, strategic foresight approach.

In 2020, the Copenhagen Institute for Futures Studies conducted a survey in which over 1000 top Danish decision-makers were asked about their approach to strategic foresight. While 26 per cent indicated that they had identified it as a priority, only 11 per cent were found to be systematically scanning for potential long-term developments (over 5 years). Paradoxically, nearly half of these decision-makers expected their core business to undergo fundamental changes within the next 3–5 years. Despite studies highlighting the value of taking a structured approach to understanding and responding to long-term change, a significant competitive advantage remains for those willing to commit resources to this work. From extensive experience in the field, the core issue lies in the ongoing challenge of distinguishing between tasks that are urgent and those that are truly important.

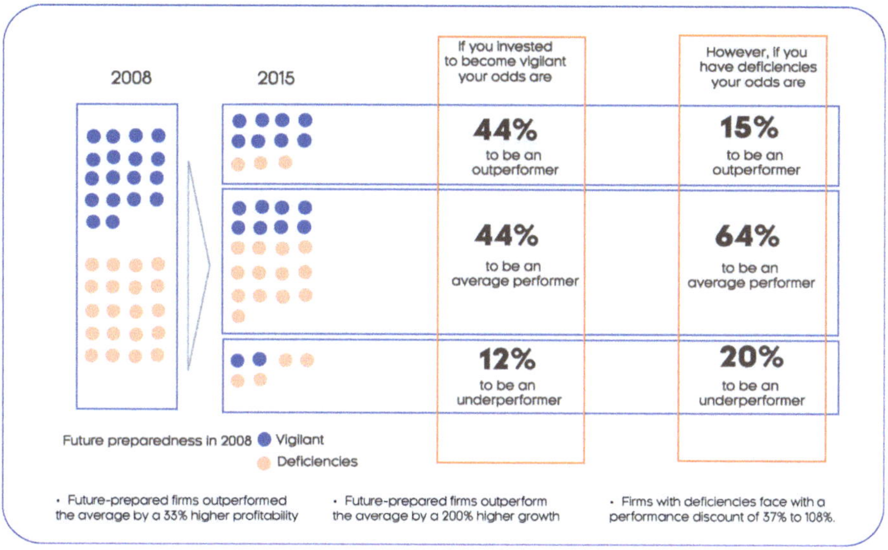

Fig. 2.1 Long-term success rate and foresight

John Kotter, one of the foremost authorities in change management over the past half-century, emphasises that true leaders are not merely planners, problem-solvers, or organisers. Instead, their essential role is to prepare organisations for change and support them in navigating the challenges that arise throughout the process (Kotter 2001). This perspective highlights the essential role of leadership in guiding organisations through the complexities of transformation, rather than simply managing day-to-day operations. The responsibility of leadership, therefore, is primarily to understand the necessary changes and then serve as a support function when these changes need to be implemented. A study on future-oriented leadership identifies three key characteristics of a anticipatory leader as a futurist, strategist, and integrator (Savage and Sales 2008).

- Scanning: They continuously scan the environment to identify relevant changes.
- Sense-making: They ensure ongoing organisational dialogue and learning about the strategic consequence.
- Mobilising: They mobilise resources to create change towards a preferred future.

The point here is much the same, and a suggestion would be to create a list of the tasks you focus on as a manager, dividing them into these three categories. Then, add a fourth category for day-to-day tasks that are urgent but do not contribute to long-term success. Once you've allocated your tasks, consider whether you are spending your time appropriately or if you could delegate tasks in the day-to-day category to generate greater value for your organisation in the long term. Foresight fundamentally involves striking a balance between short-term and long-term perspectives. It requires the ability to address immediate needs and challenges while also keeping a clear vision of future goals and developments. Effective foresight ensures that actions taken today align with and support sustainable success in the future, bridging the gap between present priorities and enduring objectives.

2.3 Approaching the Future with Structure and Strategy

Fundamentally, there are four elements we work with when conducting structured future analysis at the Copenhagen Institute for Futures Studies:

- **MEGATRENDS:** Overarching drivers of change in society.
- **UNCERTAINTIES:** Elements that may have different future outcomes.
- **UNEXPECTED EVENTS:** Potential events that take most people by surprise and can have a major impact on the future.
- **HUMAN BIAS:** Our tendency to be biased when making predictions about the future.

MEGATRENDS

MEGATRENDS Megatrends are overarching forces of change that are set to have a profound societal impact in the coming decades. In an unpredictable world, these trends stand out as one of the few relative certainties we possess. Experienced futurists are quick to emphasise that the future cannot be predicted that it always encompasses multiple plausible scenarios, and that any attempt to make concrete forecasts is, at best, futile and, at worst, misleading and counterproductive. However, not all aspects of the future are equally unpredictable. There are often relatively stable forces of change that influence societal development across various areas—forces that, while predictable, are difficult to alter.

Take Moore's Law, for instance, which posits that the number of transistors on a computer chip doubles approximately every 2 years (Moore 1965). It is frequently cited as an example of predictability in technological development. Although Moore's Law may soon reach its physical limitations, it has largely held true since its proposal in 1975 and has significantly shaped the trajectory of technological progress.

On a broader scale, "megatrends" play a similar role. The term was first coined in 1982 by futurist John Naisbitt (Nasbitt 1982), as a popularisation of a concept previously explored by military strategist and futurist Herman Kahn in the 1970s: overarching drivers of change that will have a significant impact on global society in the coming decades. Due to their vast scale and far-reaching influence, megatrends are often interconnected and typically have a lifespan extending at least 10–15 years into the future.

In an unpredictable world, megatrends appear to be the only relative certainty we have. However, if you trace the historical development of any megatrend, it becomes evident that they do not unfold in a linear manner but often fluctuate, alternately waxing and waning. Take globalisation, for example (one of the 15 megatrends identified by CIFS in our 2022 publication). Viewed over the long term, globalisation—the process by which the world becomes increasingly interconnected through trade, migration, technology, and culture—seems to be a stable trend that has persisted throughout much of modern history. Yet, during certain periods, this progress has encountered obstacles and, at times, even regressions, driven by powerful stakeholders. These setbacks have taken the form of conflicts, trade embargoes, isolationist policies, and trade disputes.

Above is an overview of the 15 global megatrends identified by CIFS (Fig. 2.2). (If you wish to explore the detailed descriptions of each individual megatrend, the full publication is freely available on our website https://cifs.dk/global-megatrends/). By developing a comprehensive understanding of global megatrends, stakeholders and organisations will be well positioned to anticipate how any given phenomenon is likely to evolve, guided by relatively predictable forces of change. I will delve into the defining megatrends and sub-trends for the hybrid office workplace in greater detail later in the book.

UNCERTAINTIES

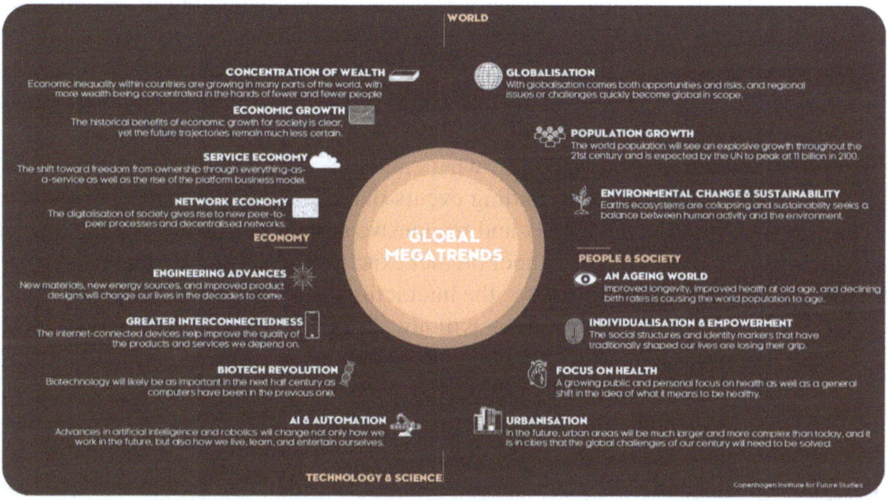

Fig. 2.2 CIFS global megatrends

UNCERTAINTY The challenge arises when greater precision is required—whether in terms of geographical influences or more industry-specific elements. Here, you will find that the more detail you seek, the more questions emerge. This is why managing uncertainty is perhaps the most vital skill in futures studies. For most decision-makers, uncertainty is an uncomfortable irritant. It creates friction in the decision-making process and demands deeper analysis. Many approach uncertainties about the future in the same way they address uncertainties about the past, assuming that sufficient data analysis will lead to the "right" answer. However, there is no "right" answer when it comes to future events. The future does not yet exist, so at best, we can arrive at a qualified answer—one that is more or less probable (hence futurist often use the term anticipate). Even with the benefit of hindsight, there is no definitive "right" or "wrong" estimate.

A qualified answer regarding a potential future can easily be proven incorrect. Yet, if an event is estimated to have a high probability of occurring, its failure to materialise does not invalidate the analysis. For instance, if something is given a 90 per cent probability of happening, it inherently acknowledges a 10 per cent chance that it will not.

The concept of uncertainty often sits uneasily with the worldview of many traditional business leaders, who tend to use machine analogies to explain complex systems and expect leaders to provide clear answers and solutions. However, uncertainties about the future comprise two components:

- The first component of uncertainty stems from a lack of understanding of the dynamics that influence it. This type of uncertainty can often be significantly reduced by developing a deeper understanding through the analysis of historical correlations, among other factors. For example, in analysing future unemployment within the customer service workforce, an understanding of the relationship between economic activity, productivity trends, and technological advancements can help clarify uncertainty. This aspect of uncertainty relates to knowledge, where it is evident that some are better equipped to comprehend these correlations than others.
- The second component relates to what can be termed fundamental uncertainty. This is the uncertainty surrounding events that cannot be predicted because the world is, at its core, a complex and responsive system. If you throw a handful of glass balls into the air, you cannot predict exactly where they will land, and similarly, when attempting to foresee the interaction between a wide range of people, institutions, and technology, there will always be uncertainty. While some models and rules of thumb can help you understand this complexity, the fundamental uncertainty can never be fully eliminated.

The key to managing uncertainty lies in understanding its different components. You should then evaluate how many resources to allocate towards reducing uncertainty, weighed against the potential benefits of that reduction. In this analysis, it is important to recognise that uncertainty can never be eliminated. The real world will always remain complex, meaning we can never make a perfectly accurate estimate—but we can come close. Equally important is the ability to manage uncertainty in multiple ways. We can monitor uncertainty, along with its sub-components, enabling us to detect changes faster than the competition. Alternatively, we can position ourselves in such a way that we are not adversely affected if the outcome is unexpected. This might involve shifting from fixed to variable costs or making strategic investments in different markets or customer segments.

UNEXPECTED EVENTS

UNEXPECTED EVENTS One of the reasons we are constantly surrounded by uncertainty is the frequency and impact of large-scale, unexpected events. The pandemic and its influence on the development of the office workplace is an obvious example. When discussing the workplace of the future, it is difficult to overstate how Covid-19 has reshaped our relationship with physical office attendance, leading to significant changes in workflows, organisational culture, management practices, and customer interactions. Another example is the war in Ukraine, which has brought about historic and lasting shifts in how companies manage their supply chains. By the time you read this, new examples will likely have emerged.

In the book *Fooled By Randomness* (later expanded in his 2007 book *The Black Swan*), Nassim Nicholas Taleb introduced the term "black swan" (Taleb 2005). In Europe, the term was originally used to describe something impossible, until black swans were discovered by explorers in Australia in 1697. Taleb explains how a series of major, unexpected events have fundamentally shaped the course of history, arguing that these events collectively have a far greater influence on history than ordinary, "expected" events. Theoretically, unexpected events are simply uncertainties. However, due to their unpredictability, a different approach to managing them is recommended. While uncertainties can be addressed on a concrete level (e.g. will we have digital tools in the future that better facilitate conversations about innovation in a virtual world compared to a physical one?), you can focus on building resilience into your organisation—culturally, organisationally, strategically, and financially. The success of Taleb's Black Swan theory has inspired the creation of several related terms, often named after animals. One such term is "black jellyfish", which refers to known and normal risks that unexpectedly spiral out of control due to "positive feedback loops". An example might be the relocation of physical premises, where a recognised risk escalates into a series of layoffs, leading to stress-related absences, which in turn threaten a company's very existence. Unlike black swans, for which you cannot prepare, black jellyfish risks can be mitigated through better preparation and heightened awareness of potential dangers. This helps to reduce blind spots, which typically emerge when conventional wisdom no longer applies due to changing circumstances. Blind spots arise from incomplete, outdated, or incorrect assumptions in a decision-maker's understanding of their environment.

This brings us to the final category that is crucial to include in future analysis: human bias (human bias is also discussed and addressed in the preceding chapter).

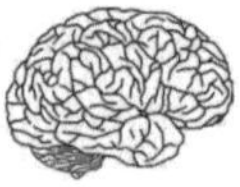

... AND UNDERSTANDING
OUR OWN BIASES

HUMAN BIAS The phrase, "All models are wrong, but some are useful", often attributed to statistician George E.P. Box, aptly illustrates why blind spots are so common. Our brains cannot process the vast complexity of society, so we depend on simplified models to make sense of the world. These models can range from the expectation that an object, like my computer, will fall quickly if I let go of it, to the assumption that the older man before me is likely the boss and the younger woman his assistant, or the belief that our strategy assumes employees are primarily motivated by income. While the first model serves well in most situations, the second is increasingly outdated, and the last can often be misleading.

The key is to rely on models of understanding that lead to better decisions, whether through faster decision-making or more effective outcomes. Equally important is the ability to discard these models when they no longer serve their purpose. The latter can be extremely difficult, not least because we are often unaware of the models we use to interpret the world. For many years, Philip Tetlock has studied the traits of those who excel at predicting future uncertainties—the so-called super forecasters (Tetlock and Gardner 2016). Among other things, he notes their willingness to update their assessments when new information becomes available. These individuals operate in a state of "infinite beta", constantly striving to refine their beliefs and improve their forecasting abilities. They work systematically, employing research, critical thinking, self-reflection, gathering and synthesising diverse perspectives, and re-evaluating their positions. In essence, they actively seek to eliminate their known biases—an essential practice when working with the future.

Pierre Wack, an iconic figure in futures studies, once remarked that the most valuable and challenging task for a futurist is to encourage people to think about the world in new ways (Wack 1985). He coined the term "reperception" to describe how individuals awaken to the possibility that the future may differ from the past. Wack believed that the greatest achievement, and the most difficult for those working with foresight and scenarios, is to facilitate this transformation. He saw reperception as key to opening the minds of executives, enabling them to understand both the risks of disruption to their business and the opportunities that lie in alternative futures. At its core, Wack was addressing the challenge of overcoming the "status quo bias". The issue with this bias is that it resists perceiving change as positive. For various reasons, change is often seen as a threat, particularly by established businesses that have significantly reduced costs in their core processes to enhance competitiveness.

Such businesses have invested heavily in optimising their offerings for efficiency and are often leaders in low-cost markets, typically within a red ocean strategy.

One of the most important tasks for futurists, and working with foresight, is to identify where opinions diverge between those within an organisation and external experts. When external experts hold radically different views about the state of the world compared to internal stakeholders, it is often a sign of status quo bias, which should raise concern. In many cases, the tendency to seek out, interpret, and remember information that aligns with one's own beliefs hinders the ability to choose a better path forward. This "confirmation bias" has been recognised for years, and rules to mitigate it are embedded in the scientific method and in the principles of good scientific practice. However, it remains prevalent in everyday media and politics, and it continues to influence decision-making across many areas of society and business.

As Nobel laureate Daniel Kahneman highlights in his book *Thinking, Fast and Slow*, confirmation bias exerts its strongest influence when we are dealing with emotionally charged issues and deeply held beliefs (Kahneman 2011). In today's media landscape, increasingly shaped by online echo chambers, this bias is reinforced as we gravitate towards spaces where our existing beliefs are readily affirmed by like-minded individuals (among other things reinforcing tribalisation and polarisation). A study published in *Science* in 2018 confirmed that confirmation bias thrives in the fast-paced environment of social media (Vosoughi et al. 2018). The study tracked the circulation of news and found that hoaxes, rumours, and falsehoods consistently dominated discussions on X (formerly Twitter). In fact, stories containing false information spread six times faster than those based on factual accuracy.

For executives and management, confirmation bias most often manifests when they choose to listen only to those who share their opinions. This tendency can be so strong that it becomes a defining characteristic of the organisational culture. As a result, information that contradicts the established narrative may not be circulated or taken seriously. In other words, a form of self-imposed censorship can develop, causing disruptive business models or emerging technologies to be ignored, to the detriment of the organisation.

One of the most observed biases is known as the "optimism bias". Almost without exception, both experts and media commentators tend to believe that change happens more quickly than it does. Kahneman argues that several factors contribute to this, the most significant being that our judgement is influenced by the goals or outcomes we desire. Additionally, we often fail to account for unforeseen events. We plan for what we know, and as a result, most planning is based on best-case scenarios. However, when the unexpected occurs, it usually leads to delays in projects, the adoption of new technologies, and other initiatives. Research has shown that this kind of bias is closely linked to mental well-being, with individuals suffering from depression showing fewer signs of optimism bias (Sharot 2011). The same study also demonstrated that even experts are not immune to this bias: "Divorce lawyers underestimate the negative consequences of divorce, financial analysts expect improbably high profits, and medical doctors overestimate the effectiveness of their treatments", the researchers note.

2.4 Extrapolating Existing Trends Versus Long-Term Futures

Most people tend to approach the future by extrapolating existing trends and analysing how they might influence current conditions. This methodology is typically preferred when the expected changes are incremental and when the foresight exercise focuses on the near-term future, usually within a 0–3-year timeframe. However, this approach imposes several limitations, as thinking incrementally puts you in a position where you must justify why things are changing. As mentioned earlier, history has shown that many significant changes are driven by unforeseen events.

The journey from relying on existing knowledge to embracing a mindset of curiosity represents a profound transition in how we approach challenges and opportunities (Johnson et al. 2020). This shift requires moving from merely improving what already exists to actively developing and creating what is new and innovative (Fig. 2.3).

It is a transformation that goes beyond surface-level enhancements and demands a more radical, open, and forward-thinking perspective and includes:

- Incremental Thinking to Radical Thinking: Instead of simply building upon established ideas, this transition encourages us to think in revolutionary terms. It is about daring to explore uncharted territories and challenging the status quo, allowing for breakthroughs that redefine what is possible.
- Enhancing to Creating: While improvement focuses on refining and optimising existing processes or products, creation is about bringing something entirely new into existence. This shift encourages a mindset that prioritises innovation over mere refinement, fostering an environment where originality flourishes.
- Inside-Out to Outside-In: Moving from an internal, self-focused perspective to an external, outward-looking approach opens up new avenues for inspiration. By seeking insights from the external environment, market trends, and broader societal shifts, we become more attuned to emerging needs and opportunities.

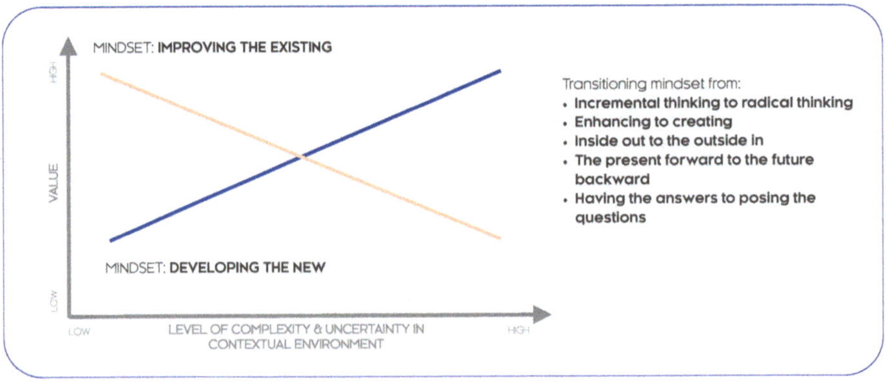

Fig. 2.3 From existing knowledge to curiosity. Source: Lead from the Future, Johnson, Mark W.; Suskewicz, Josh Harvard Business Review Press 2020

- From Present Forward to Future Backward: Instead of solely focusing on extending today's practices into the future, this mindset encourages envisioning the future first and working backward to identify the steps needed to get there. This approach allows for a more strategic and visionary path, ensuring that present actions are aligned with long-term aspirations.
- From Having the Answers to Posing the Questions: Shifting from a mindset of certainty to one of inquiry encourages a culture of curiosity and exploration. Rather than merely relying on established answers, this approach values the power of asking insightful and decisive questions, enabling a deeper understanding of the challenges and possibilities ahead.

This transformation from an existing knowledge base to a curiosity-driven mindset is essential for organisations and individuals who aspire to remain relevant and innovative in an ever-changing world. By fostering this mindset, we open the door to limitless possibilities, driving progress and creating a future that is not just an extension of the past but a bold step into the unknown.

In the "future-back" approach, participants develop a thorough analysis of the potential future environment by once again examining existing trends and drivers of change (Fig. 2.4). However, instead of focusing on how things might change, your emphasis is on envisioning how things might appear. The difference between the two approaches may seem subtle, but in practice, it shifts people's perspectives. It is comparable to the shift in product and service design, where companies realised that by adopting the customer's perspective (rather than an inside-out view), they most likely create far more value for their customers.

If the organisation does not empathise with the future needs of its employees, it will struggle to remain competitive in a fast-changing and complex business environment. Understanding the biases at play when we envision the future is crucial to how we plan for it. Numerous additional biases exist beyond those discussed here (see Chap. 1), and work continues to identify those most pertinent to the field of

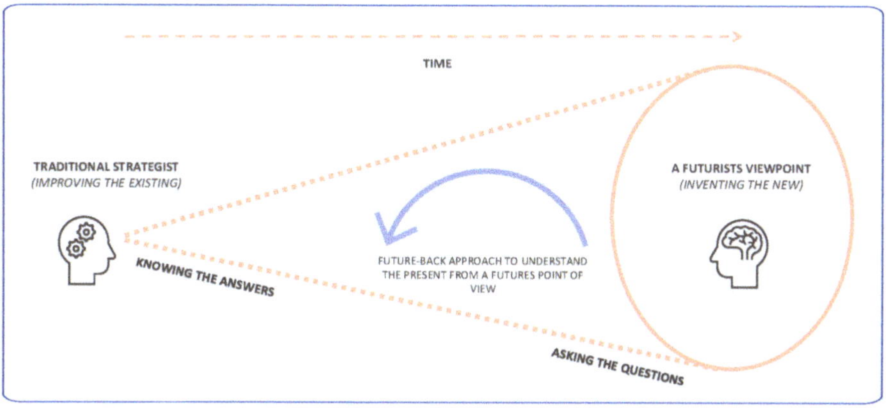

Fig. 2.4 The practice of long-term thinking: creating resilient long-term strategies through future-back thinking. Source Copenhagen Institute for Futures Studies

futures studies and foresight. The fundamental challenge is that if we are unaware of what influences our decisions, we are not well-equipped to make the right ones. The future we will face—whether it be climate change, hybrid workplaces, the well-being of our workforce, the position of our organisations, or indeed our own circumstances—will be shaped by the decisions we make today.

References

(Bar Am, Furstenthal, Jorge and Roth 2020) Innovation in a crisis: why it is more critical than ever. Prioritizing innovation today is the key to unlocking post-crisis growth. McKinsey and Company. Hunger https://www.mckinsey.com/business-functions/strategy-and-corporate-finance/our-insights/innovation-in-a-crisis-why-it-is-more-critical-than-evertime

(Johnson, Suskewicz and Josh 2020) Lead from the Future, Harvard Business Review Press https://store.hbr.org/product/lead-from-the-future-how-to-turn-visionary-thinking-into-breakthrough-growth/10268?srsltid=AfmBOop67fE1skVv-5ItI2LtMjN9Gmss-QuIFh7JsMvmgpxrgiA4tvBy

(Kahneman 2011) Farrar, Straus and Giroux Thinking, Fast and Slow https://www.amazon.com/Thinking-Fast-Slow-Daniel-Kahneman/dp/0374533555

(Kotter 2001) HBR http://fs.ncaa.org/Docs/DIII/What%20Leaders%20Really%20Do.pdf

(Moore 1965) The Future of Integrated Electronics https://www.chiphistory.org/20-moore-s-law-original-draft-1965

(Nasbitt 1982) Ten New Directions Transforming Our Lives https://web.engr.uky.edu/~jrchee0/CE%20401/Megatrends-Naisbitt/megatrends-1982_synopsis.pdf

(Rohrbeck, Etingue Kum 2018) Corporate Foresight and its Impact on Firm Performance: A Longitudinal Analysis https://www.sciencedirect.com/science/article/pii/S0040162517302287

(Savage and Sales 2008) The anticipatory leader: futurist, strategist and integrator https://www.researchgate.net/publication/243462575_The_anticipatory_leader_Futurist_strategist_and_integrator

(Sharot 2011) "The Optimism Bias", Current Biology 2011

(Taleb 2005) Fooled by Randomness: The Hidden Role of Chance in Life and in the Markets https://www.amazon.com/Fooled-Randomness-Hidden-Markets-Incerto/dp/0812975219

(Tetlock and Gardner 2016) Superforecasting https://thedecisionlab.com/thinkers/political-science/philip-tetlock?ref=josephnoelwalker.com

(Vosoughi, Roy and Aral 2018) "The spread of true and false news online"

(Wack 1985) HBR September 1985 Scenarios: Uncharted Waters Ahead https://hbr.org/1985/09/scenarios-uncharted-waters-ahead HBR November 1985 Scenarios: Shooting the Rapids https://hbr.org/1985/11/scenarios-shooting-the-rapids

Part I

The Current State of the Hybrid Office Workplace

The Hybrid Office Workplace Model 3

Abstract

The relationship between work-life and workplace models is deeply interconnected, with each influencing the other. Not all employees have equal access to hybrid working arrangements due to the nature of their roles, which may require physical presence. As a result, workplaces with higher digital integration are more likely to adopt hybrid models compared to those with analogue dependencies. The evolving hybrid workplace model emerged during the COVID-19 pandemic, blending digital and analogue work environments. It offers flexibility, allowing employees to work from various locations while maintaining productivity and work-life balance. However, the term "Hybrid Workplace" may not fully capture the future complexities of work-life integration.

The contemporary hybrid workplace challenges traditional notions of time, place, and space, promoting a work environment that is increasingly agnostic to these factors. Organisations must navigate the development of this model carefully, balancing physical and digital infrastructure with employee behaviour, management practices, and overall organisational culture. The ultimate goal is to enhance sustainable productivity and efficiency, but achieving this requires a holistic approach that considers all elements of the workplace.

The hybrid workplace illustrates the dynamic interplay between these components, highlighting the importance of employees as central to value creation. As digitalisation accelerates, organisations must continuously adapt to maintain a competitive productive and flexible work environment.

C. Sneppen, *The Future (R)Evolution of the Office Workspace*, Future of Business and Finance, https://doi.org/10.1007/978-3-031-85229-9_3

3.1 The Interplay Between Work-Life and Workplace Models

The type of work being done and workplace model design are causally related, and each has the potential to impact and influence the other. In an individual perspective this implies that, not all employees have the same access to hybrid and the same degree of flexible working, as some may have a necessity to be physically present at a specific time, place, and space, while others have the possibility to work independently of time and location (Figs. 3.1 and 3.2). However, when considering the bigger picture, all employees will ultimately benefit from greater flexibility, regardless of any reliance on analogue systems. For instance, the recent advancements in AI have made it possible for employees who depend on being physically present for shift work—such as in factories or caregiving roles—to have their schedules optimised by AI. This allows for the accommodation of individual preferences while still meeting the requirements of their roles (WSJ 2024 and Fortune 2024). In other words, we are witnessing a significant loosening of the rigid, one-size-fits-all post-industrial office approach of the past.

As a result, the hybrid and flexible workplace impacts functions and organisations differently. Highly digitised workplaces have the possibility to be more hybrid compared to workplaces with analogue dependencies, as illustrated in the tables (Fig. 3.3). Additionally, the work-life of an individual employee affects the workplace, and vice versa (These differences are evident in the data, as many sources cover both segments of the labour market, making it difficult to obtain reliable data on the distribution of flexibility among "pure" knowledge workers who have limited analogue dependencies in their work).

We can in a macro perspective consider the causality between work-life and workplace from two distinct perspectives:

- Externalisation of Workplace and Work-life Causality. The nature of the work itself can determine the necessity of performing it at a specific place, time, and

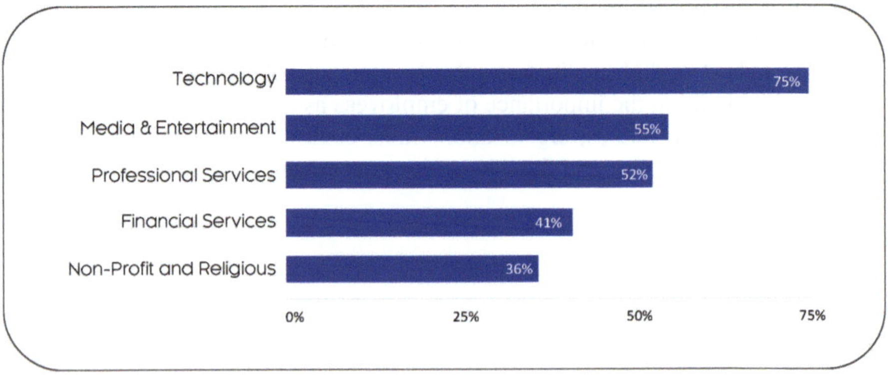

Fig. 3.1 Top five most flexible industries% of companies that are fully flexible. Source: "The Flex Index (flex.scoopforwork.com), Q2 2023 Flex Report"

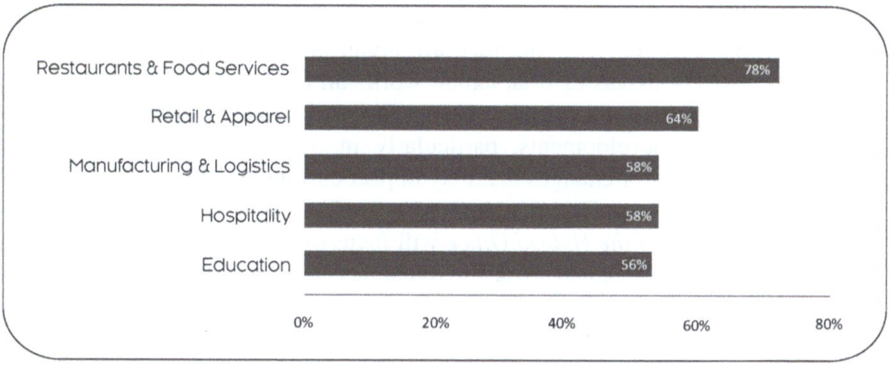

Fig. 3.2 Top five least flexible industries% of companies that are full time in office. Source: "The Flex Index (flex.scoopforwork.com), Q2 2023 Flex Report"

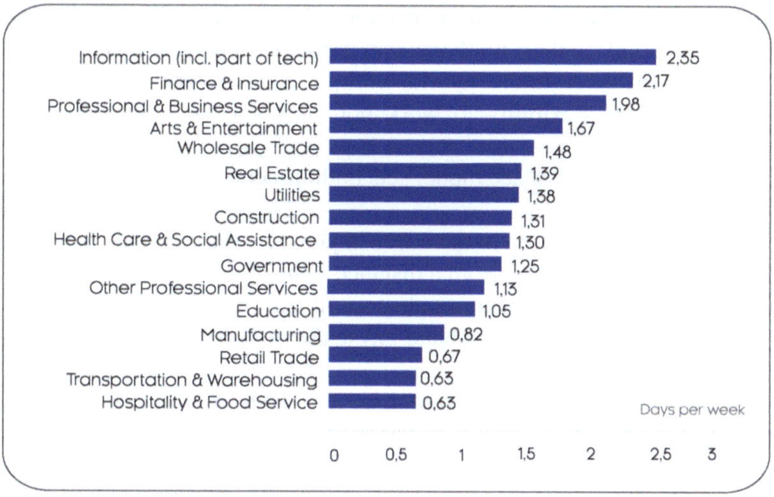

Fig. 3.3 Current working from home: all wages and salary employees. Source: https://wfhresearch.com

space. Regardless of the current causality, the growing digital and technological capabilities will increasingly enable employees to perform work remotely through the use of robots, automation, digital communication, and so on. Tasks that currently demand physical presence may, to a greater extent in the future, be accomplished remotely.

- Internalisation of Workplace and Work-life Causality: The work performed by individuals within a workplace can influence the workplace's environment and culture, while the nature of the workplace can also impact the work done by individuals. For example, a poorly designed or inadequately equipped workplace may negatively affect employees' performance, while a highly motivated and engaged workforce can contribute to a positive and productive workplace. In contrast, disengaged or unhappy employees can create a negative and unproductive workplace culture. Moving forward, organisations need to objectively and comprehensively assess to what extent work can be done remotely or requires in-person attendance at a shared working space. Additionally, organisations must consider future developments, particularly in the digital and technological realms, to prepare for changes that may impact current priorities and choices.

The (R)Evolution of the Hybrid Office will focus on understanding and developing the internal workplace and work-life dynamics and causalities of office knowledge workers.

3.2 The Contemporary Office Workplace Model

The hybrid workplace model is a flexible model designed to support a distributed workforce that simultaneous works in person at the physical office workplace and at a distance. A workplace that simultaneously functions analogue and digital with the best of both worlds. A future hybrid workplace is a work environment where employees have the flexibility to work both remotely and on-site at an office (Fig. 3.4).

The hybrid office workplace model sets both direction and framework for:

- Working and collaboration in the office in person—the analogue workplace.
- Working and collaboration from a distance—the digital workplace.
- Working and collaboration through a combination of interactions and meetings—with simultaneous digital and physical presence.

The widely accepted term at present is "The Hybrid Office Workplace". This shared terminology simply makes it easier for all of us to discuss and shape the future of the workplace and work-life model. Some have named the evolution of the workplace "Working from Home", "Tele Working", "Distributed Working", or "Flexible Working", but it all encompasses the same thing. The name "Hybrid Workplace" is comforting and occupies a middle ground: significant change has occurred, but it is not revolutionary. We have temporarily settled into a semi-static phase, allowing us to cope mentally and view developments as incremental rather than radical. This shift highlights a markedly more diversified approach to where work is conducted, with a clear correlation to the spectrum of flexibility inherently linked to the nature of the work function, as well as the degree of digitisation and automation (Fig. 3.5).

But does Hybrid work really embrace and adequately define the future work-life and workplace? Hybrid basically means a thing made by combining two different elements. In other words, combining digital and analogue work-life simultaneously. That is not new—most office and knowledge workers have been doing exactly that for decades. And are employees working in an office ever not digital and totally unplugged?

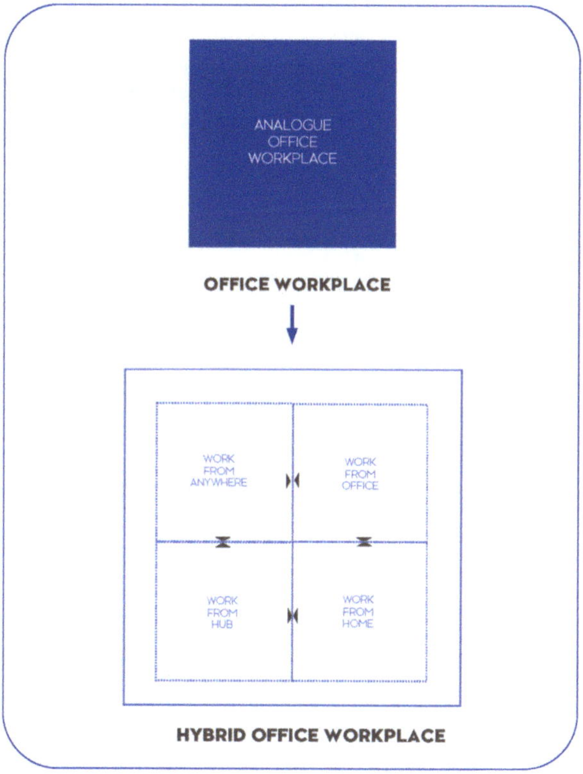

Fig. 3.4 From "Workplace" to "Hybrid" workplace

The name "The Hybrid Office Workplace" will be challenged and most likely be renamed several times before it embraces the full implications of the future workplace for knowledge workers. The answer to the current naming "Hybrid workplace" is basically: "It's what materialised and was broadly accepted during the pandemic, but you are more than welcome to up with a better name". In a hybrid workplace, employees are not bound to a physical office and can work from any location, such as their home, cafe, or a co-working space, as long as they have access to the necessary tools and technologies to perform their job. The hybrid workplace model is becoming increasingly popular as it offers several advantages for both employees and employers. It is a flexible and adaptable work model that can benefit both employees and employers by promoting productivity, creativity, and work-life balance.

The hybrid office workplace, and its associated terms, challenges and redefines traditional, past-oriented understandings and perceptions of working time, place, and space. It provides greater flexibility and freedom to employees in their work and working life, thereby breaking away from the past-oriented mindset (Gratton 2021). The workplace is increasingly becoming agnostic to time, place, and space, as the distributed workforce and digital work continue to expand. This trend enables employees to work from anywhere and at any time. Being workplace agnostic

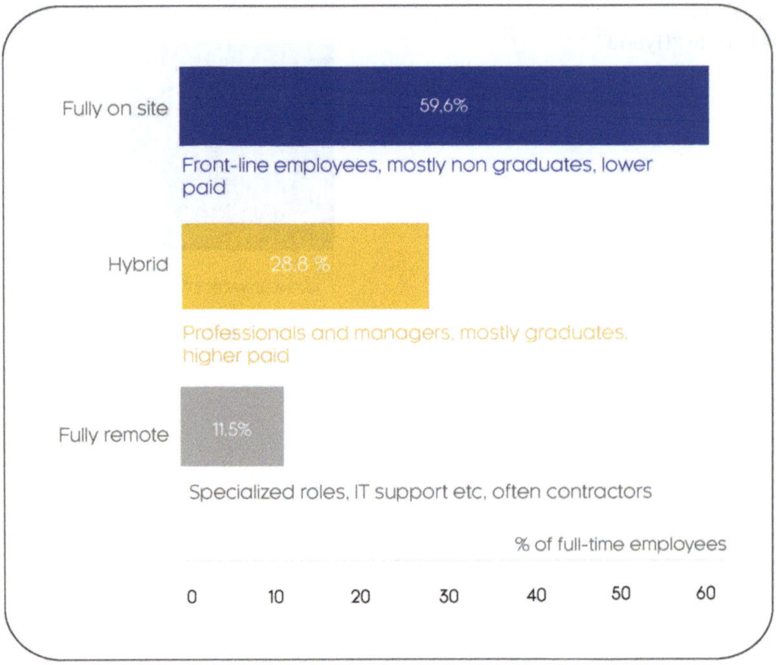

Fig. 3.5 Working arrangements. Source: https://wfhresearch.com

means that when developing the future-ready hybrid workplace, one should not be limited or influenced by specific considerations related to time, location, or physical surroundings. It encourages an open, flexible, and adaptable mindset, allowing for the exploration of ideas and possibilities beyond the traditional constraints of time, place, and physical surroundings in relation to the workplace model.

3.3 Challenge: The Future Office Workplace: Agile Beyond Flexibility

Since the pandemic struck and the concept of the hybrid workplace became widespread, I have stated that it was much more than just flexibility. I now challenge that statement and assert that the hybrid workplace is mainly about the flexibility of the workplace, but in a broad sense it is not merely about employees choosing how much work is done in the office or at home, or opting for different workspaces within a newly designed office based on the activity-based working concept.

The broad scope of development is better encapsulated by the term "Agile Workplace". The terms "flexible" and "agile" are often used interchangeably in the context of organisational behaviour, but they refer to distinct concepts with different implications for how an organisation and workplace operate. A flexible workplace can adapt to changes in its environment with relative ease. Flexibility is a reactive and situational capability. An agile workplace, on the other hand, is built to thrive on change and uncertainty. Agility is a more ingrained, proactive approach that becomes part of the organisational culture, enabling sustained responsiveness and innovation.

The proactive agility of the post-pandemic workplace encompasses all three dimensions: time, place, and space:

Time

- Working agility is defined by non-linear, asynchronous, and asymmetric (hybrid) patterns.
- Time agility also includes seasonally defined periods with more or less work.
- Working time will become increasingly agile as digitisation and technological advancements continue to evolve.

Place

- The workplace can be the office, home, or elsewhere.
- The concept of place will become increasingly agile over time, adapting to the organisation's objectives.

Space

- Activity-based working, work at home, and "home at work" all encompass the agility to choose the space best suited for conducting work. It boils down to individual agility to choose the optimal space.
- Space must become increasingly agile over time, in accordance with the agility of place and time.

The office workplace will increasingly be defined by agility. Previously, we perceived the office and office work as static and implicitly synonymous with linear, synchronous, and symmetrical physical presence in the shared office. But those days are numbered. The execution of knowledge work will be digitally based regardless of where it is carried out—in the office, at home, the local café, or on a beach in Bali. That requires the workplace model to be proactively agile to leverage all the competitive advantages that support the changing objectives of the organisation.

Welcome to the proactive, agile, and dynamic office era, where the office workplace exists wherever the employee is with their personal digital device and unhindered access to their always-present AI assistant. This will be supplemented with in-person interactions and meeting spaces, such as shared agile offices. But rest assured, work remains work whether it is hybrid, flexible, or agile. Nevertheless, throughout the book, I will use the term "hybrid office workplace", with the simple reasoning that it has been widely accepted as the name for the new office workplace model.

3.4 The Hybrid Office Workplace Matrix: A Framework for the Future

The hybrid office workplace model is currently a trendsetting approach, and most organisations are striving to find the optimal design in a rapidly evolving digital realm. But developing a forward-looking workplace model is not a zero-sum game. Instead, it is like playing a "game" with the aim of achieving win-win outcomes, but there is also a risk of ending up with lose-lose outcomes. How can one build an optimal workplace without detailed insight into the value creation of each employee and, crucially, the interactions between employees in everyday work, thereby understanding the overall collaboration matrix of the organisation? The honest and straightforward answer is that one cannot.

To create the best hybrid workplace model for their organisation, management needs to consider that the office workplace is no longer a uniform model in the traditional sense. Instead, value creation in each organisation is uniquely defined by its management. For example, management, employees, work processes, and culture are never identical, even in similar and competing organisations. So why should the workplace model be almost identical? Therefore, the workplace should be tailored optimally to the specific organisation to enhance value creation, rather than the other way around.

Many times, the current discussion about the development of the modern hybrid workplace model tends to focus solely on the methods and process rather than the goal (vision). The ultimate objective of the workplace is to improve sustainable productivity and efficiency. Productivity is ultimately a result of combining speed and time. If the main purpose of the office is to facilitate communication and collaboration, it becomes logical to replace or complement the traditional office with solutions that allow for even greater speed and more efficient use of time (D. Poleg 2023). The distinction between efficiency (the quality = "doing the right things" and "doing things right") and productivity (the quantity = doing a lot in relation to an output target) is consequently important to clarify. Employees, management, and both digital and analogue infrastructure are the key components that together constitute the "engine" of the workplace.

This mindset is reflected and further elaborated upon in *The Skills-Powered Organization*, which addresses the need for organisations to rethink their work models in light of unprecedented global challenges such as advancements in AI, climate change, and geopolitical instability (Kapilashrami and Jesuthasan 2024). The authors argue that the traditional emphasis on jobs must be replaced by a skills-driven approach, enabling organisations to become more agile, resilient, and capable of thriving amidst disruption. They explore how leading companies are reimagining their operations by adopting a skills-first mindset, introducing new capabilities such as AI-powered resourcing and innovative work design. This shift, they contend, is crucial for unlocking productivity, agility, and the long-term success of organisations in a world that demands continuous reinvention. Leaders are urged to align their strategies, talent management, and technology to successfully navigate this transition, carefully balancing the costs, risks, and potential benefits of embracing a skills-based organisational model.

The primary and central component of the office workplace for knowledge workers is not the establishment of digital and analogue infrastructure, but the employees themselves, who form the dominant main element in the "office machine". They are equivalent to the machines in the factories of the industrial society of past centuries (Fig. 3.6).

In this context, the concept of employee well-being (and, by extension, engagement) is functional and intrinsically connected to improving productivity and efficiency (e.g. Bakker and Pal 2010). There can be many means to achieve this goal. The means can be enforcing connection to manager, new guidelines for working from home, a redesigned physical workplace, free seating (Activity-Based Working) with remote desk reservation, new digital infrastructure, new software, distance management, and new ways of meeting, among others. Exploring the critical link between employee well-being and engagement, it is well-documented that engaged employees are consistently more productive. Key engagement drivers—such as having clear expectations, receiving regular feedback, and feeling a strong connection to the organisations mission—are especially vital in boosting the performance of knowledge workers. These individuals, who depend heavily on cognitive processes, collaboration, and problem-solving, benefit significantly when they feel valued and aligned with organisational goals, leading to enhanced focus, creativity, and output.

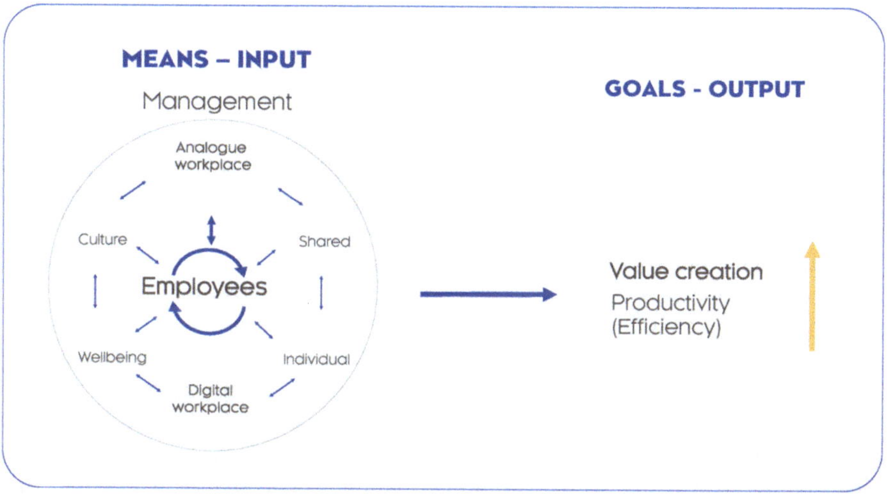

Fig. 3.6 Increased focus on goals and not means: the hybrid workplace model is not a zero-sum game

But what is the optimal balance of physical and digital infrastructure, employee behaviour, management, well-being, and organisational culture? The answer to this question is not widely known, and there is, as previously stated, very limited historical data to draw upon, as all stakeholders, as well as scholars, are navigating uncharted territory when it comes to the sustainable future office workplace model. Nevertheless, this should not deter organisations from developing a contemporary workplace that enhances productivity and efficiency. The greatest risk lies in workplace actors having personal preferences for certain approaches, while lacking a comprehensive understanding of their correlation with actual overall organisational value creation and efficiency. By considering the workplace in a holistic manner, the focus shifts from mere efficiency and operation to a greater emphasis on productivity and untapped potential for value creation associated with the entire workplace model. Some members of senior management express it this way: the priority is not for leaders to feel good about themselves, but to act in the best interests of the organisation. The real reward is a workforce that is more energised, experiences reduced stress, enjoys greater life satisfaction, and is motivated to exceed expectations in their roles (Lederstof 2022).

As Microsoft state in their annual Work Trend Index Annual Report "Great Expectations Making Hybrid Work *Work*": The new "worth it" equation is not a zero-sum game (Microsoft 2022). Employees value flexibility and well-being, and these great expectations create an opportunity for every organisation to reimagine work-life integration as a win-win. Empowering individuals to excel in their work not only benefits them personally but also has a positive impact on the business. To effectively implement hybrid work, leaders must empower managers to maintain the organisations culture, rethink the role of the physical office, foster social connections in a digital-first (not office-first) environment, and establish sustainable practices for flexible work. While technology is important, this moment calls for a fresh mindset. As the world continues to evolve, organisations that prioritise a culture-centric, continuous learning approach will emerge as front runners. Strong employee engagement is closely linked to improved performance, as it is an essential part of the performance equation. To drive overall success, organisations need more than just productivity alone. Think of engagement and productivity as mutually reinforcing, with each aspect amplifying the other: When you are engaged in your work, your productivity increases, and when you are productive, you become more engaged in your work.

Productivity and efficiency are increasing and will continue to rise significantly for knowledge workers. Knowledge workers are relatively cost-intensive, and at the same time, the digital development has reached a tipping point where AI, automation, and the metaverse are becoming more operationalised and available at all levels of the organisation. AI, VR, AR, Metaverse, etc., will all have a profound effect on the design of the hybrid workplace model. Ultimately, more and more tasks can be accomplished remotely. At the same time, in-person attendance at the office will increasingly be used for collaboration and building relationships with colleagues and teams. The future of knowledge work is not limited to a screen but a new reality where we will see continuous changes in the optimal workplace model. A model that persistently aligns management and employees using analogue and digital channels balanced... until the next digital update disrupts the temporary equilibrium.

3.5 Systemic and Structural Change

The flexible and hybrid workplace encompasses all aspects of how management organises employees' working days, combining both analogue and digital elements. We can broadly categorise the flexible workplace into physical, digital, employee-related, and managerial frameworks.

The physical aspects are relatively straightforward, but the hybrid workplace presents various and uncharted possibilities for "soft" design solutions in creating a modern office workplace. For example, in the knowledge society, employees tend to feel more productive when they have the freedom to choose their workspace and surroundings for their work. There is no universal solution that works for everyone, and providing flexibility and variety can significantly boost employee happiness, engagement, and productivity.

Transitioning the office workplace from traditional to hybrid brings forth numerous challenges, opportunities, and potential issues. Developing the hybrid workplace necessitates a re-evaluation of various aspects, such as agile and decentralised organisational structures, distance management, and further digitisation of work processes. Establishing a competitive hybrid workplace is a complex endeavour that can metaphorically open Pandora's box, revealing various complexities and uncertainties.

The hybrid workplace ecosystem is comprised of four main components, each interconnected. Altering one will inevitably impact the others (Fig. 3.7):

- **DIGITAL WORKPLACE**: The digital infrastructure that enables virtual work.
- **ANALOGUE WORKPLACE**: The physical infrastructure supporting traditional, in-person work (at the office, home, or third places).
- **EMPLOYEES**: The organisation of working processes, routines, balancing employee preferences with management's objectives and expectations.
- **MANAGEMENT**: The design and leadership of the hybrid workplace. With the rise of hybrid working, management faces a formidable challenge and is expected to experience the most pressure and transformation.

From an evolutionary standpoint, we are currently witnessing a notable rise in the digital workplace, accompanied by a decline in the importance of the traditional office. This shift is expected to continue as digitalisation and emerging technologies are embraced. Employees have adapted to these new opportunities with surprising speed; however, like management, they are in a transitional phase towards a new, systemic, and structural workplace ecosystem. This is evident when we observe the changing ecosystem caused by the shifting balance (Fig. 3.8).

In essence, the digitalised workplace increasingly facilitates interactions and collaboration between management and employees, while, conversely, the analogue

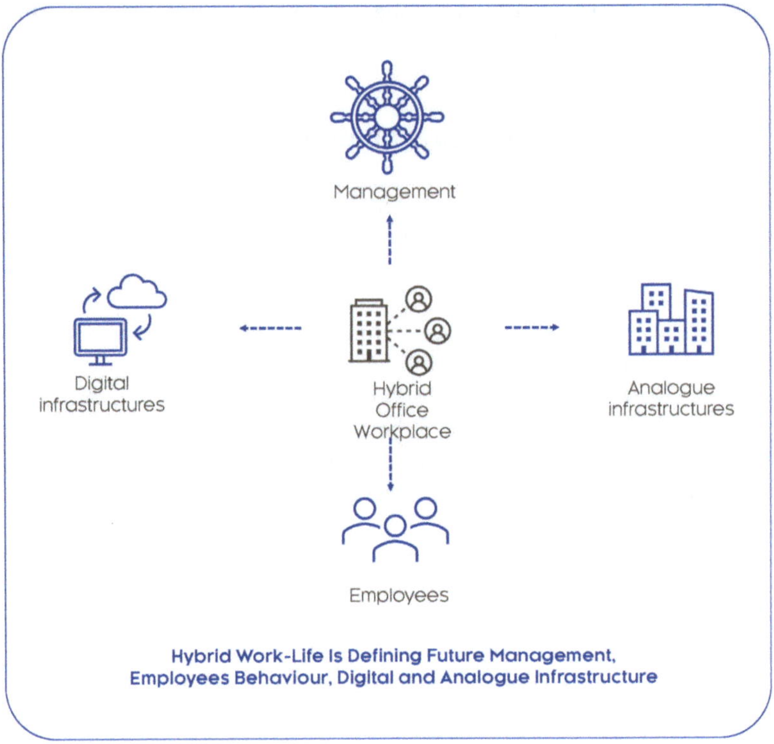

Fig. 3.7 The four defining components constituting the hybrid office workplace

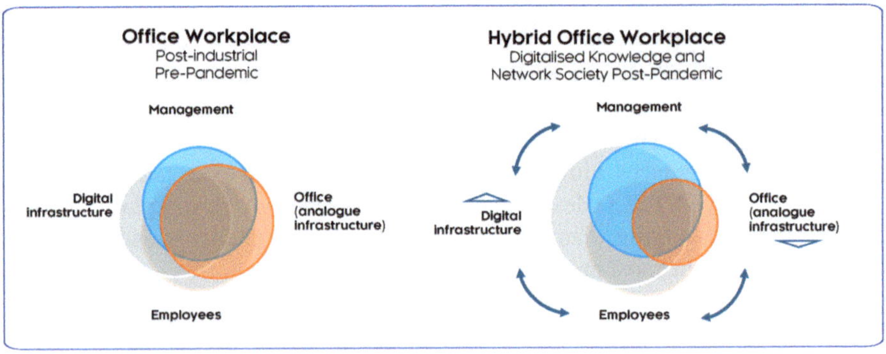

Fig. 3.8 The (R)Evolution of the office hybrid office: changing components and ecosystem of the workplace for knowledge workers

office space plays a diminishing role in such collaboration and interaction. Not included in the model (Fig. 3.8) is the argument that the increasing importance and influence of employees, in line with the rise of the network and knowledge society, further contributes to the complexity of the future hybrid office workplace. The components of the workplace are very much in flux, and organisations are venturing into uncharted territory, with varying degrees of success in keeping pace with these developments.

3.6 The Hybrid Office Workplace Equation

The concept of the hybrid office workplace goes beyond merely reimagining the physical office space. All elements that contribute to the hybrid workplace are interconnected. To help comprehend this, I have devised a very simplistic equation that illustrates how workplace value is generated (Fig. 3.9: Algorithm variables are correlated and/or causal). I invite you to join me in this thought process, allowing you to contemplate the various components and dynamics of the workplace. Although not straightforward, the equation is much simpler compared to the real-life challenge of creating a successful and future-proof hybrid workplace model.

The parameters of the model are interconnected, and any alteration to one variable will have an impact on the others and the ultimate outcome. For instance, if the digital infrastructure is modified, it will influence the analogue aspect, as well as the employees and management, to varying degrees. While it does not precisely mirror reality on a one-to-one basis, it can serve as a foundation for informed discussions concerning the evolution of the hybrid office workplace model.

The office workplace equation comprises of an input and output side. On the input side of the hybrid workplace equation, the primary components are management, employees, physical, and digital infrastructure. All these factors are significant and necessary for the workplace, but their importance varies in relation to one another for value creation, and as such, they are inserted in the equation accordingly.

Employees wield the greatest influence on value creation and act as the primary driver of the workplace. They also typically represent the highest investment and

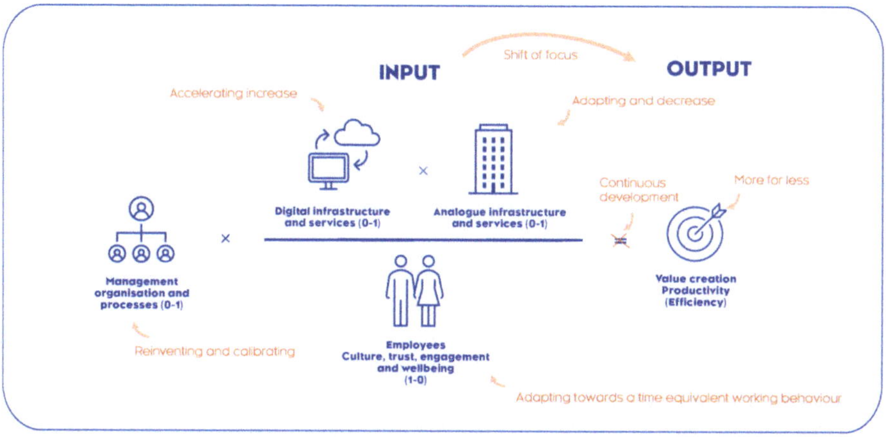

Fig. 3.9 Hybrid office workplace equation (simplified)

cost for the organisation. Hence, they are placed in the denominator of the equation to underscore their significance. It is important to note that employees encompass not only their physical presence but also aspects such as culture, engagement, psychological safety, and well-being, as these directly and decisively impact employee productivity. To elaborate on well-being, studies already indicate that remote work can increase employee satisfaction and their willingness to contribute additional effort at the same pay level (Becchetti et al. 2024). This boost in satisfaction is often attributed to the greater flexibility remote work offers, allowing for a better work-life balance, reduced commuting stress, and increased autonomy. A recent global study conducted by Microsoft revealed a noteworthy positive correlation between high employee engagement and stronger financial performance (Microsoft 2023). We should consider engagement and productivity as mutually reinforcing factors, where each aspect amplifies the other: When employees are engaged in their work, organisations become more productive, and vice versa (e.g. Kim et al. 2023, Smith et al. 2027). As machines and technology increasingly handle trivial tasks and routines, employees' role in value creation has become more significant in the knowledge and network society. Consequently, employees are of utmost importance in shaping the workplace model, recognising their central and decisive role in organisations and, by extension, the workplace model itself.

Initially, the digital and analogue infrastructure has the least influence on value creation. In the previous relatively static workplace model, there has been a dominant focus on these components. The static approach emphasised efficiency and incremental development of the analogue and digital infrastructure in relation to the workplace model. Consequently, the physical and digital infrastructure is placed in the numerator, as it is relatively less significant for the hybrid workplace model.

Management maintains direct control over other components and can, therefore, significantly influence overall value creation. Consequently, management holds a multiplier effect on these factors. However, they are less impactful than employees, who serve as the primary denominator in this equation.

On the output side is the productivity or value creation generated from the input side of the workplace equation. Has the workplace been designed in a manner ensuring that the employees' efforts and hours of labour have created the optimal value?

Numeric intervals: For clarity, arbitrary predetermined numerical intervals have been inserted into the equation for the components. All numerical intervals are set up starting from 0+, where higher numbers result in greater value creation. However, this is not the case for employees who are placed closer to 0, where a lower value indicates greater value creation through a reversed 1 to 0 affirmation (where 1 is the worst and 0.1 is fantastic and 10 times more value creation). It is evident that even small adjustments to the employee component, and to some extent in management, will have a significant impact on the overall value creation. Similarly, a non-optimal digital and analogue infrastructure, which is not well adapted to employees and management, will be clearly reflected in the overall value creation.

Indeed, there should not be an equal's sign in the equation, and it should be set up as an algorithm. The workplace is continuously evolving over time, aiming for ever-increasing and rising value creation. Equal signs might convey the impression that the workplace model is static, which is not the case. We can only obtain short-term snapshots and insights into the optimal workplace model; therefore, we should not work with static workplace models or approaches. The speed of development is accelerating, primarily driven by digitalisation, but it is also influenced by adapted employee behaviour and changing preferences. This puts the analogue workplace and leadership in the position of continuously keeping up with the ongoing changes, both in the short and the long term. This highlights that the prevailing discourse of seeking to define and implement yet another fixed and static office model is a default approach and discourse, as the hybrid workplace model is dynamic by nature.

Once again, the equation is not a direct nor a scientific reflection of the real-life workplace but serves as a mere illustration for reflection and awareness of correlations and crucial workplace components.

References

(Bakker and Pal 2010) Weekly work engagement and performance: A study among starting teachers https://bpspsychub.onlinelibrary.wiley.com/doi/abs/10.1348/096317909X402596

(Becchetti et al., 2024) Becchetti, Leonardo; Salustri, Francesco; Solferino, Nazaria The new industrial revolution: the optimal choice for flexible work companies [42] Published in: Journal of Economic Interaction and Coordination (2024) https://doi.org/10.1007/s11403-024-00418-y

(Fortune 2024) J. Their April 8, 2024' $19 billion Land O'Lakes is halting churn by giving workers flexibility over their schedules: 'It's the one thing all the people can rally around' https://fortune.com/2024/04/08/land-o-lakes-yone-dewberry-flexible-work-schedules-factory-workers/

(Gratton 2021) HBR: "How to do hybrid right" https://hbr.org/2021/05/how-to-do-hybrid-right

(Kapilashrami and Jesuthasan, 2024) The MIT Press, The Skills-Powered Organization The Journey to the Next-Generation Enterprise https://mitpress.mit.edu/9780262049238/the-skills-powered-organization/

(Kim, Kolb, et al. 2023) The Relationship Between Work Engagement and Performance: A Review of Empirical Literature and a Proposed Research Agenda https://journals.sagepub.com/doi/abs/10.1177/1534484312461635

Lederstof 2022) »På skærmen er du nødt til at tro på, at du har folk meddig« https://www.lederstof.dk/paa-skaermen-er-du-noedt-til-at-tro-paa-at-du-har-folk-med-dig

(Microsoft 2022) Great Expectations: Making Hybrid Work *Work* https://www.microsoft.com/en-us/worklab/work-trend-index/great-expectations-making-hybrid-work-work

(Microsoft 2023) The New Performance Equation in the Age of AI https://www.microsoft.com/en-us/worklab/work-trend-index/the-new-performance-equation-in-the-age-of-ai

(D. Poleg 2023) https://www.drorpoleg.com

(Smith et al. 2027) Interplay between performance measurement and management, employee engagement and performance https://www.emerald.com/insight/content/doi/10.1108/IJOPM-06-2015-0313/full/html

(WSJ 2024) G. Guildford March 6, 2024, Flexible Hours Come to the Factory: A Look Inside Land O'Lakes' Plant https://www.wsj.com/business/flexible-working-hours-manufacturing-8af49530?mod=Searchresults_pos1&page=1

Office Workplace Flexibility

4

Abstract

The hybrid office workplace transcends the simplistic notion of flexibility, encompassing a dynamic transformation of how organisations operate. It goes beyond mere guidelines for remote work and physical attendance, heralding a paradigm shift in the balance between digital and analogue workspaces. This evolution demands a fundamental redesign of traditional structures, fostering collaboration, productivity, and inclusivity.

It challenges entrenched hierarchies and encourages co-creation, where tailored solutions replace uniformity, and hybrid models align with unique organisational needs. As "unequal but fair" becomes the new norm, a future-proof hybrid workplace offers the potential for increased productivity, engagement, and innovation, reflecting the diverse needs of modern work-life.

4.1 The Hybrid Office: Beyond Just a Question of Flexibility

As previously stated, the hybrid office workplace extends far beyond merely being a matter of flexibility. Listening to the ongoing dialogue about the hybrid workplace might give the impression that it is solely about flexibility. However, the hybrid office workplace is much more than just remote work guidelines and physical office attendance. In fact, the flexible workplace is just the beginning, as it opens the door to a wide array of possibilities and innovations in the form of the hybrid workplace. This is not a new insight and has been highlighted in numerous studies over time (e.g. Hill et al. 2008).

The hybrid workplace brings forth crucial questions and challenges for all aspects of the workplace. It raises inquiries related to leadership, including distance leadership, organisation, and work processes, fostering collaboration, maintaining coherence and culture, monitoring employee productivity and well-being,

C. Sneppen, *The Future (R)Evolution of the Office Workspace*, Future of Business and Finance, https://doi.org/10.1007/978-3-031-85229-9_4

managing the physical workplace and its services, and optimising the digital workplace and its services, among other factors. All these components require thoughtful consideration and adjustments to ensure the successful implementation of the hybrid workplace model.

4.2 Tailored Office Workplaces

Office workplaces are no longer as uniform and standardised as pre-pandemic. Instead, we witness a considerable increase in diversity and differentiation among workplaces, as knowledge worker organisations move away from the conventional office-first model and embrace their own interpretations of flexibility (Fig. 4.1). This presents both opportunities and challenges for organisations. The positive aspect is that organisations can create unique and tailored workplace models that provide the most value for their specific needs. However, the downside is that each organisation will have to take a proactive approach in designing their individual workplace, considering the three dimensions of time, place, and space to optimise productivity and well-being.

As the evolution of the hybrid workplaces continues, the future physical office workplace is expected to become more flexible, less centralised, and more focused on meeting the specific needs of the organisation and employees. E.g. one current significant organisational goal is to increase the talent pool, attract and retain the right talent and competencies by creating an environment that motivates employees to work effectively regardless of their location (whether alone or together). In response to the new workplace and work-life reality, organisations are increasingly adopting diverse solutions. Overall workplace models will be primarily developed using an employee and team segmentation approach that considers demographics, job roles, individual preferences, and team dynamics, all while aligning with the organisation's objectives and operational processes. This framing and approach will result in each workplace model being tailored to meet the specific needs and goals of both the employees and the organisation.

The uniquely designed workplace model will prioritise supporting the organisation's values, culture, and employee well-being. The bazaar workplace approach of trying to cater to every need and preference through a one-size-fits-all strategy will

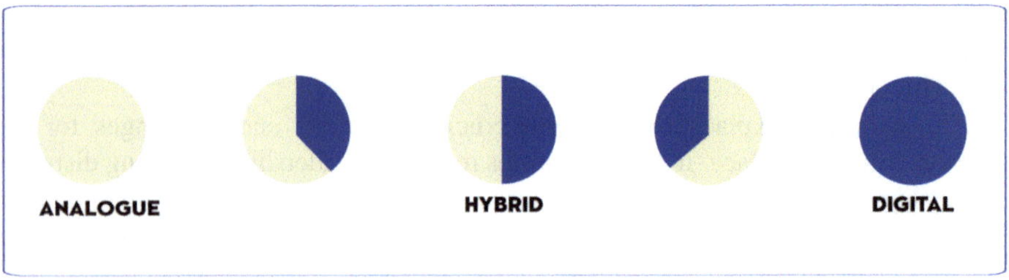

Fig. 4.1 Balancing analogue and digital work-life

diminish as organisations recognise the benefits of tailored workplace solutions. If you attempt to cater to everyone within your office model, you risk serving no one effectively. Workplaces will transition from merely differentiating themselves through minor variations in colours and design choices to becoming true creators of identity and uniqueness, even without relying on visible logos and other traditional design techniques. The focus will be on creating spaces that authentically reflect the organisation's essence and purpose.

Because of this development the analogue workplace will serve the work needs where the digital workplace may have limitations. Rather than being taken for granted, the physical workplace will transform into an intentional choice made by individual employees.

The physical workplace will evolve into a distinct meeting place, with face-to-face interactions at its core. Collaboration, trust-building, and fostering a sense of belonging will be its key strengths (Microsoft 2024). It will increasingly be reserved for important interactions, resolving conflicts, and holding unpredictable meetings where in-person attendance is crucial. Studies have consistently shown that development and innovation thrive in analogue meetings and interactions and suggest that remote and hybrid work modes may inhibit collaboration and innovation (e.g. Gibbs et al. 2024). On the other hand, the digital workplace excels in operational tasks, individual work, and executing established processes.

Those physical office workplaces that fail to implement unique initiatives to motivate employees to attend in person risk losing the rationale for their existence. There will be a wide array of variations in physical workplaces, encompassing size, workstation numbers, collaborations with external organisations, and layouts that facilitate internal value creation while breaking down traditional siloed workspaces. Moreover, the approach to flexibility and the employee's freedom to decide when, where, and how to work will differ significantly.

Unlike the physical office workplace, the digital workplace will increasingly serve as the hub for operational and process-oriented work, characterised by focused concentration and higher predictability. Furthermore, the digital workplace will become more individualised, tailored to the specific needs of each organisation. This trend arises from the necessity of establishing a customised digital environment that fulfils the organisation's requirements regardless of the employee's chosen time and place of work. The physical workplace will not simply imitate other organisations' workplaces. It will also not be a replica of the digital workplace, where tasks and needs can be solved in the same way. Conversely, workplaces will present diverse interpretations of flexibility for employees regarding time, place, and space for work, spanning from fully remote to fully in-office arrangements. Each organisation is unique, and identical workplaces will no longer suffice in creating adequate value. Copying other office workplaces will no longer be a viable approach for the future.

4.3 Challenge: The New Workplace Norm: Embracing "Unequal Is Fair"

Work-life flexibility is for everyone. A work-life defined by differentiated self-determination and perceived as fair by all. But not everyone has the same immediate access to flexibility. This has, in fact, always been the case, but it has become more apparent and evident with certain employee groups gaining access to increased flexibility. A study conducted in the United States revealed that over a third of jobs nationwide can be performed entirely from home, though this proportion varies significantly across different cities and industries (Dingel et al. 2020). Roles suitable for remote work generally offer higher salaries than those requiring on-site presence and collectively account for nearly half of total US wages. When this classification was extended to 85 other countries, it became evident that lower-income economies have a smaller share of jobs that can realistically be performed remotely, underscoring significant global differences in remote work potential. This research highlights the economic benefits that remote-capable jobs provide to wealthier nations, contrasting with the limitations faced by lower-income countries, where fewer jobs afford the flexibility of remote work.

The hybrid office model is based on a balance between individual and collective preferences, and growing individual self-determination of time, place, and space in the work-life. However, not all employees have the same possibilities and preferences for flexibility across the organisation (as stated in Chap. 3). All organisations must therefore grapple with employee flexibility and self-determination over their work-life, while also ensuring that differentiated flexibility is perceived as fair and just by all employees. Unjust and unfair perceptions of flexibility in the work-life can negatively affect productivity, increase burnout, reduce collaboration, and decrease retention.

Acceptance and justification of differentiated employee access to flexibility and hybrid working can be challenging for several reasons:

- PERCEPTIONS OF FAIRNESS: Employees may perceive differential access to flexibility and hybrid working as unfair, particularly if they feel that certain employees or groups are being given preferential treatment.
- MANAGERIAL RESISTANCE: Managers may be resistant to granting differential access to flexibility and hybrid working, either because they believe it will be too difficult to manage or because they worry that some employees will abuse the system.
- LACK OF CLARITY AROUND POLICIES AND PROCEDURES: If policies and procedures around flexibility and hybrid working are not clearly communicated or understood, employees may feel confused or frustrated by differential access.

When discussing this flexibility inequality with employees, the response is often that there is "nothing new under the sun". Ultimately, it comes down to the perception of equality and access to flexibility within the predefined circumstances of each individual's job situation. The prevailing situation will therefore result in what can be summarised by the phrase "Unequal and fair", which will become the new norm in the workplace as the hybrid model continues to evolve. "Unequal is fair" as an increasing forward-looking norm for the workplace, regarding individual employees' access to flexibility in their work-life and workplace, is very much culturally determined. This applies not only in a narrow organisational context but, crucially, also in relation to the broader national work-life culture.

On the other hand, the "unequal and fair" norm can create a much more productive and future-proof workplace model. Flexibility can be interpreted and unfolded in many ways. For instance, in Denmark, AI is now being utilised to create work schedules for employees who typically work fixed shifts in roles that require physical presence. This system considers individual input and preferences, allowing employees to experience greater flexibility and, as a result, higher job satisfaction. A manual worker can achieve greater co-determination and flexibility by, for example, being able to choose periods of heavy work and corresponding longer periods of time off or long weekends. On the other hand, a knowledge worker working on a deep project that is performed alone can choose to work remotely until the task is completed, as I have done in creating this publication. It truly comes down to self- and co-determination over where and when work is performed.

It should be noted that all employee groups will have increasingly greater opportunities for flexibility in the future with digital and technological developments. In other words, technological development will eventually provide all employee groups with a basis for greater remote participation and flexibility. An equal work-life for everyone in the organisation is explicitly impossible with the unfolding and development of the hybrid workplace. Implicitly, employees' ability to be flexible in their work has always been unequal, but now the inequality is becoming explicit as co-determination and flexibility across organisational employees become more pronounced.

Organisations have a significant communicative task in ensuring that all employees across the organisation find that "unequal is fair" and that everyone has understood, accepted, and support this. At the same time, it is crucial to ensure that everyone has equal access to information, support, and opportunities, regardless of where, when, and how employees perform their work.

References

(Gibbs et al. 2024) Gibbs M, Mengel F, Siemroth C. Employee innovation during office work, work from home and hybrid work. Sci Rep. 2024 Jul 24;14(1):17117. doi: 10.1038/s41598-024-67122-6. PMID: 39048695; PMCID: PMC11269655. https://pubmed.ncbi.nlm.nih.gov/39048695/

(Dingel et al., 2020) Jonathan I. Dingel, Brent Neiman, How many jobs can be done at home?, Journal of Public Economics, Volume 189, 2020, 104235, ISSN 0047-2727, https://doi.org/10.1016/j.jpubeco.2020.104235. (https://www.sciencedirect.com/science/article/pii/S0047272720300992)

(Hill et al., 2008) Jeffrey Hill, E., Grzywacz, J. G., Allen, S., Blanchard, V. L., Matz-Costa, C., Shulkin, S., & Pitt-Catsouphes, M. (2008). Defining and conceptualizing workplace flexibility. *Community, Work & Family*, *11*(2), 149–163. https://doi.org/10.1080/13668800802024678

(Microsoft 2024) Working in a phygital world: Why businesses need to rethink their workspace experiences now https://www.microsoft.com/insidetrack/blog/working-in-a-phygital-world-why-businesses-need-to-rethink-their-workspace-experiences-now/

Hybrid Workplace Structure, Rhythm and Routines

5

Abstract

Establishing a future-ready hybrid workplace requires a structured approach that balances flexibility with predictability. As traditional 9–5 office-based work fades, organisations must redefine routines to ensure efficiency and productivity. The hybrid model introduces flexibility across time, place, and space, allowing employees to alternate between remote work and in-person collaboration. This approach requires clear communication and well-defined expectations to maintain alignment.

Organisations will needs to tailor their hybrid workplace policies, considering both individual and collective needs, while adapting to the evolving work landscape. The hybrid model will increasingly blend linear and non-linear work patterns, synchronous and asynchronous interactions, and digital and in-person engagements. As work becomes more flexible, the importance of structure, rhythm, and routines will grow, ensuring sustainable productivity.

Cultural shifts are also essential, as workplace rituals need reinvention to foster community and belonging in a hybrid environment. Effective rituals, whether digital or in-person, will help maintain employee engagement and promote a positive work culture. As organisations navigate these changes, they must create inclusive and meaningful experiences that resonate with employees, regardless of their location. This tailored, flexible approach will shape the future of work, enabling organisations to thrive in a dynamic, hybrid world.

5.1 Enabling Agile Work Life: Making It Work at the Workplace

Establishing a structured workplace with defined rhythms and routines is crucial for developing a future-ready hybrid workplace, as the traditional 9–5 workday in a fixed location is no longer the standard. Having a foundation of predictability is

C. Sneppen, *The Future (R)Evolution of the Office Workspace*, Future of Business and Finance, https://doi.org/10.1007/978-3-031-85229-9_5

widely regarded as essential, as it enhances efficiency and productivity when all employees are on the same page. However, in the hybrid workplace, predictability may look different as employees have varying schedules and locations for work. This requires clear communication, well-defined expectations, and a cohesive approach to ensure everyone is aligned and working effectively towards common goals.

Flexibility in the workplace will continue to expand across all dimensions, encompassing daily, weekly, monthly, and yearly aspects of work execution. This flexibility will be applied to knowledge workers, and it will resemble the seasonal workers in other sectors but with a different focus. In addition to the existing shifts and flexibility in office workers' routines, a new dimension is added, which involves the location of work. Employees will have periods of focused and remote work, followed by periods of in-person collaboration in the office. As holidays or vacations approach, remote work may increase, especially when individual tasks need to be completed amid personal life commitments. On the other hand, in-person collaboration will occur when activities are initiated and developed in the shared workspace of the office, typically in January and after summer vacation. The development of workplace flexibility is an ongoing and irreversible trend, moving towards more multidimensional flexibility for employees in the future. Just like an operating system serves as the foundation for software and applications to run on a computer, a well-implemented hybrid policy establishes the fundamental structure for how an organisation operates. This policy not only defines the rules and procedures for the organisation's primary work practices but also ensures that all employees work from a shared platform and foundation, empowering them to excel. The importance of this framework cannot be overstated, especially given the current high level of uncertainty in the working world. Hybrid work brings much-needed structure and stability. Striking a balance between short-term business needs and the long-term advantages of new scheduling strategies will be key in reaping the benefits for both employees and the organisation.

Looking ahead to the next decade, it is anticipated that work for knowledge workers will become more non-linear and asynchronous. The interactions within the hybrid workplace will also become more symmetrical as technology and behaviour reduce the importance of format, whether it's digital, in-person, or a hybrid blend of both. This evolution will be driven, in part, by the growing trend of younger organisations adopting higher levels of remote work, with many start-ups opting for fully remote setups (Gupta et al. 2024). For example, observations suggest that remote start-ups demonstrate faster scaling and greater productivity growth among software engineers compared to more established firms. As these start-ups mature into larger companies, the emphasis on remote work is likely to spread throughout the economy (Bloom 2023). This shift towards non-linear and asynchronous work, combined with the increased prevalence of remote work, will shape the future of the hybrid workplace.

5.2 Culture Shapes the Possibility Span of the Hybrid Working Model

The current culture of the organisation limits the potential scope of the hybrid working model. Data clearly indicate how flexibility and hybrid workplaces are understood is related to this (the elements are neither comprehensive nor prioritised, and in many cases, they are interrelated):

- Organisational size has a significant impact on flexibility, with mid-sized organisations being less flexible, and smaller ones being the most flexible (Fig. 5.1). Large international organisations with an established distributed workforce, already accustomed to managing and working in hybrid environments, tend to be more flexible and adaptable to hybrid models than mid-sized organisations.
- Private organisations tend to be more flexible than public ones, likely due to the latter's greater bureaucracy and stricter governance. This often results in public organisations adhering more inclined to a post-industrial workplace office model, which is less adaptable to hybrid working practices.
- Established remote management approaches within an organisation tend to demonstrate greater inherent flexibility. This is due to their experience and infrastructure in managing dispersed teams, which allows them to more easily adapt to hybrid working models and evolving work environments.
- Digitisation of an organisation at a high level provides more inherent flexibility.
- A robust organisational protocol for assessing individual and team performance allows for greater flexibility.
- The age and generation of management also influence workplace flexibility, with younger and female top management generally tending to be more open to flexible working arrangements. Older male top management tends to be the least inclined to adopt flexible workplace arrangements (Flynn et al. 2024).
- Organisation with higher expenses on office space, particularly in more costly locations, is more likely to mandate an office-first approach.

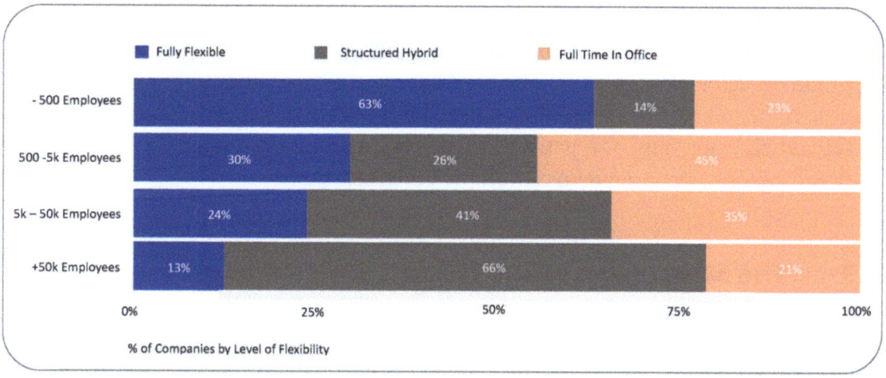

Fig. 5.1 Flex index company office requirements by size. Source: "The Flex Index Q2 2023 Flex Report"

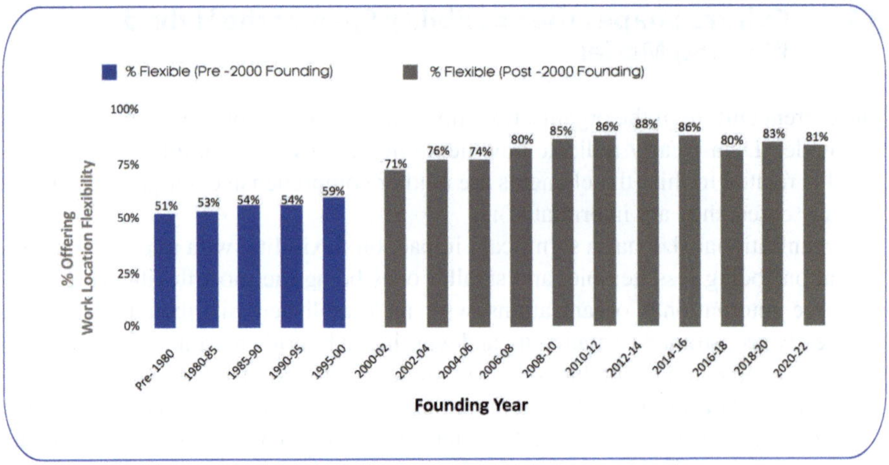

Fig. 5.2 Younger companies have more generous work from home policies. Source: The flex Index www.flexindex.com

- Greater distance between an employee's home and the workplace leads to more flexibility.
- Internationalisation of an organisation tends to increase its flexibility (established remote management and performance matrix practices).
- More recent foundation years of an organisation are significantly associated with more flexibility (Fig. 5.2).
- National and regional cultures significantly shape organisational interpretations of the hybrid workplace and flexibility (Zarate et al. 2024). In the article *"Why Does Working from Home Vary Across Countries and People?"*, cultural individualism accounts for roughly one-third of the cross-country variation in remote working rates. Countries such as Australia, Canada, the UK, and the US rank high in individualism and remote working rates, whereas Asian countries score lower on both. Additional factors—such as cumulative lockdown stringency, population density, industry mix, and GDP per capita—also influence this variation, though to a lesser extent. The study concludes that while technological feasibility plays a role, a multitude of factors determine remote working rates. These culturally rooted variations define the interpretive span of the hybrid workplace, making cultural understanding crucial not only for national organisations but especially for international organisations operating across multiple cultures.

5.3 The Structuring of the Flexible Office Workplace

The structuring of the flexible workplace can be approached in various ways, and finding the right balance is crucial. Since structure forms the foundation for developing and implementing the hybrid working model, it holds significant importance. However, as we are still in the early stages of understanding the hybrid workplace model, there is no universally established common language, including for structuring.

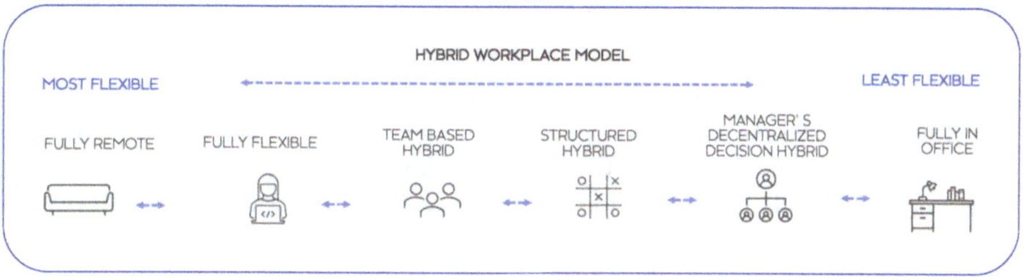

Fig. 5.3 Flexible workplace takes many forms and shapes

One potential approach to gain an overview of flexibility in the hybrid workplace is described in Fig. 5.3. The descriptions are arranged to represent an expected interpretation of flexibility, ranging from "never in the office" to "always in the office," reflecting different levels of flexibility. It's important to note that interpretations of flexibility can vary and may involve a combination of different solutions, tailored to suit individual employees and organisations. Each approach has its own advantages and disadvantages for creating the successful flexible workplace. "Fully in office" and "fully remote" do not represent a hybrid workplace model since they are at opposite ends of the spectrum and do not involve a combination of remote and office-based work. Too often, arguments surrounding different approaches to the office workplace model and flexibility are framed in binary terms—fully remote versus fully in-office—thus overlooking the merits of the hybrid model. This binary approach risks oversimplification and can lead to missed opportunities (Johansen 2020).

The optimal number of on-site office days varies considerably depending on the nature of the role and the type of collaboration it necessitates. For roles that are predominantly independent-where the majority of tasks are undertaken individually and asynchronously (that is, completed separately before being integrated with the work of others)-the current trend suggests that two to three on-site "collaboration days" per week are most beneficial. Notably, the factors influencing this arrangement are neither exhaustive nor ranked in order of importance; rather, they are often interconnected and context-dependent. On the other hand, more collaborative roles naturally necessitate more time working together interdependently, and the correlation between on-site days and employee engagement was particularly significant for this group. Employees in highly collaborative roles exhibited much higher levels of employee engagement when they worked on-site 3 days per week. As the digital possibilities for remote collaboration are expected to increase, this present balance is anticipated to shift towards more remote working flexibility. However, it is important to consider that fully remote work appears to reduce overall organisational performance by approximately 10% to 20% on average (Emanuel and Harrington 2024).

As of the completion of writing this publication in Q3/Q4 2024, market trends suggest that employees and employers may be reaching a tentative middle ground on remote work arrangements. This middle ground does not involve the traditional model of requiring employees to come to the office every day. According to the latest Flex Report from remote work platform Scoop (Flex Report Q2 2024), the majority of companies now offer hybrid work arrangements. The report shows that out of the 4000-plus companies included in the data (USA), 61 per cent implemented hybrid work in Q2, compared to 51 per cent in Q2 2023. This increase in hybrid work is largely due to a decrease in the number of companies mandating full-time on-site work, which dropped from 42 per cent to 33 per cent. The remaining 6 per cent of companies are fully remote (down from 7 per cent in 2023). It is worth noting that there is no evidence to suggest that Return to Office (RTO), as often portrayed in the media, reflects the actual figures—quite the contrary. In fact, there is substantial evidence indicating that stricter RTO policies are predominantly found in employer-dominated markets or segments, where employers hold greater bargaining power in markets with an oversupply of labour (Mckinsey & Company 2021).

According to the Flex Index report, on average, organisations that are working hybrid are now requiring employees to be in the office 2.6 days per week, positioning it between fully remote and fully in-office arrangements (an increase of 0,1 day from a year before) (Flex Index Q2 2023) (Fig. 5.4). Scoop's CEO and co-founder, Rob Sadow, sees this as a sort of truce between employers and employees, where most companies expect employees to be present 2 or 3 days a week. This arrangement is increasingly becoming the norm presently in 2024. Scoop refers to the "structured hybrid" model, which involves setting specific expectations for when employees should work from the office. This model is gaining popularity among large organisations that are neither fully remote nor fully in-office, with 30 per cent of companies adopting this approach. The specific expectations can vary, including requiring a minimum number of days in the office, specific designated days, or a minimum percentage of time employees must be present in the office.

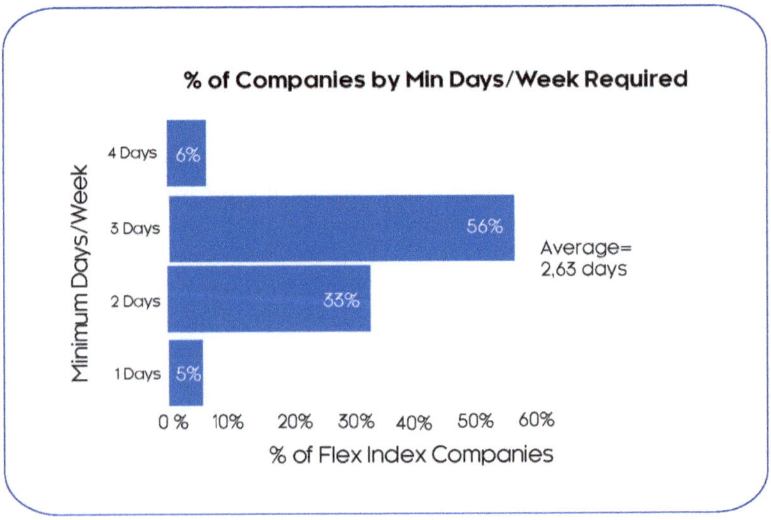

Fig. 5.4 How many days are required among structured hybrid. Source: The Flex Index

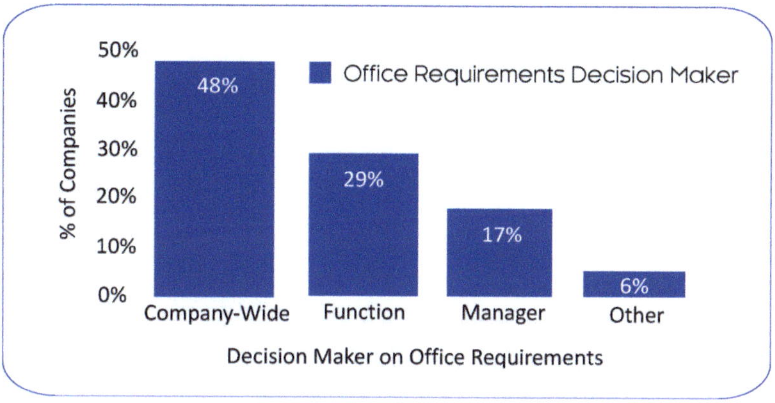

Fig. 5.5 Who decides office requirements? Source The Flex Index

Among these options, the most popular is requiring employees to come to the office for a minimum number of days each week. Looking further ahead, it is anticipated that the balance will shift towards a more remote-oriented distribution as new digital possibilities arise and are adopted, unless digitalisation fails, and the traditional in-person interactions and physical meeting places prove to be the most valuable for both employees and employers.

While the type of policy being established today is certainly important, who ultimately decides and adjusts individual work schedules in the future is even more crucial (Harter et al. 2023). For hybrid workers, responsibility for attendance policies varies across different levels: Organisational top leadership, Team managers, Work teams, Individual employees (Fig. 5.5).

Interestingly, the approach that yields the highest engagement—where teams set their own hybrid work policies—is also the least commonly adopted. Employees report feeling more engaged when their teams are involved in deciding the structure of hybrid work, yet only a small proportion experience this collaborative approach. Including employee input has shown to be highly effective across various areas, from setting shared goals to driving innovation, and now it plays an essential role in shaping hybrid work schedules.

5.4 Daily Structure, Rhythm and Routines

Taking it a step further, the structuring of flexibility in the hybrid workplace can be approached chronologically from a daily, weekly, monthly, or yearly angle. The daily structure of the hybrid workplace requires organisations to consider certain dimensions that have become more relevant than ever before. Hybrid working combines both linear and non-linear, synchronous and asynchronous, and symmetric and asymmetric working and interactions (Fig. 5.6).

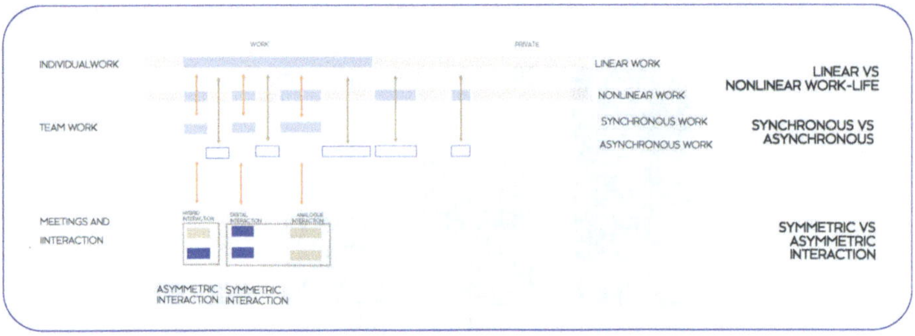

Fig. 5.6 Important daily work-life rhythm indicators: nonlinear vs linear, synchronous vs asynchronous, symmetric vs asymmetric

Organisations must find a future balance between these dimensions to create a work environment that fosters sustainable productivity. (Through a better understanding of these dimensions and the expected future development, we will have the opportunity to achieve increased comprehension of the future hybrid workplace model.) The interpretation and balance of flexibility in the organisation involves reinventing daily workplace routines and finding a balance between individual and organisational needs. This requires answering the question of how working structures correlate with sustainable organisational value creation.

When looking at employee preferences, it is clear that they are not a homogeneous group and can simplified be divided into two categories: "splitters" and "blenders." Splitters prefer a clear separation between work and private life and have a linear approach to work, while blenders prefer a limited separation between work and private life. Depending on segmentation and work profile, they constitute almost equal parts of the workforce. In a 2022 study, it is evident that the profiles of "splitters" and "blenders" differ due to their job functions and life circumstances (Appel-Meulenbroek et al. 2022). This survey-based choice experiment identified two employee segments: those intending to return to the office and those preferring to work primarily from home. Key factors influencing their choices were expected office crowding and the availability of private spaces. Office workers were more likely to be male, highly educated, full-time, with shorter commutes, while home workers were more often female, part-time, in administrative roles, or had longer commutes.

Linear and Non-Linear Working: Linear working is characterised by following a set plan or schedule with a clear separation between working and non-working time. It focuses on processes, procedures, and protocols, with tasks completed in a step-by-step manner, and progress measured in a linear fashion. Linear working is often associated with traditional work environments where employees follow a set routine and work on repetitive tasks. Non-linear working, on the other hand, is more flexible and adaptable, focusing on creativity, innovation, and problem-solving. Tasks are approached in a non-linear fashion, with the freedom to experiment and explore new ideas, and progress is measured by the quality of work produced.

In the non-linear arrangement, employees have the flexibility to perform their jobs outside of the traditional rigid nine-to-five schedule, choosing the time that works best for them. In the past, before digitalisation, non-linear workdays were not very common. However, with the digitalisation, widespread adoption of hybrid and remote working patterns, along with increasing schedule flexibility, non-linear workdays have become more accessible to a larger portion of the workforce. Non-linear workdays shift the focus from merely engaging in activities to achieving desired outcomes. As a result, it is no longer about when or where you work, but rather about completing the work. Managers are responsible for setting goals and providing a vision for employees, but they do not dictate how to accomplish them (BBC News 2022). The non-linear approach aligns with the nature of knowledge work, allowing employees to perform their tasks when they are most creative and productive. It is no longer solely about putting in effort and time but about producing the best results.

Over time, work is expected to become a more deliberate (intentional) mix of non-linear and linear approaches. On a side note, the combination of rigid linear work from 9 to 5 in the office supplemented with extensive non-linear remote work has the potential to be toxic for the well-being of the employees.

Synchronous and Asynchronous Working and Interactions: Synchronous working involves working in real-time, where individuals work together simultaneously and interact with each other in real-time. This type of working is often associated with face-to-face meetings or video conferencing.

In synchronous working, all team members are present and active at the same time, leading to fast-paced collaboration and decision-making. Asynchronous working, on the other hand, involves working without being present or interacting with others in real-time. It allows team members to work at their own pace and communicate through tools like email, messaging, or shared documents, providing more flexibility and autonomy in how work is completed. When working asynchronously, which means having different hours than one's co-workers, employees have the freedom to complete tasks in flexible and focused bursts spread throughout their day. The concept behind this is that employees can design their work schedules around their personal lives, rather than trying to fit their lives into predetermined and fixed working hours. As we progress, it is anticipated that more work will transition to an asynchronous approach.

Symmetric and Asymmetric Working and Interactions: Symmetric interaction refers to collaboration and interaction in the same format, either digitally or in-person. Symmetric interactions ensure a consistent approach to the interaction. Technical symmetry is related to senses and technical abilities, psychological symmetry to a perception of inclusion and participation, and democratic asymmetry where everyone has equal perception of influence, whether the employee is present in-person or participates digitally.

In contrast, asymmetric interactions refer to interacting on different formats, such as having some participants on Teams while others are present in-person at the office in the same meeting room. Asymmetric interactions divide the participants into different possibilities for interaction and collaboration. The asymmetry of hybrid meetings is the very reason why many participants encounter challenges in achieving success (Saatçi et al. 2019).

A study published in HBR (Ranganathan 2023) challenges the common misconception that working synchronously is better for creativity. While synchronous work has its benefits for generating ideas, it also hampers many people's creativity. Many scholars and practitioners believe that synchronous work is crucial for fostering creativity. However, with the rise of remote work and flexible schedules, team members can collaborate on the same project even if they are not in the same time zone or physical office. When team members contribute to a joint outcome but work separately without coordinating over video or phone, we refer to their work as asynchronous. On the other hand, studies suggest that prolonged remote work may hinder collaboration and innovation (Gibbs et al. 2024). Asynchronous teamwork is rapidly gaining popularity and has significant implications for the future of creativity in the workplace. Working synchronously indeed has advantages as it allows individuals to draw inspiration from each other's insights and energy, leading to more and better ideas. It also provides the opportunity to build on each other's feedback and helps workers stay on the same page in a project, reducing coordination costs, which can be substantial in creative endeavours. Additionally, synchronous collaboration exposes team members to a broader range of individuals, leading to fresh insights and information that can spark new ideas. However, the assumption that creativity flourishes in synchronous environments overlooks the social status differences among team members. Studies indicate that women and individuals from marginalised communities are given fewer opportunities to speak and face harsher criticism when they do so in synchronous work settings. Consequently, synchronous teams may discourage women and marginalised individuals from expressing new or risky ideas, resulting in less equality within teams and diminished creative output. Observations suggest that asynchronous working can enhance creativity by allowing greater participation from marginalised individuals. This finding aligns with other studies that indicate that more equality (less hierarchy) in co-creation and collaboration work improves the speed and quality of outcomes.

Over time, all formats of meetings and interactions are anticipated to become increasingly symmetrical, regardless of whether they are digital, analogue, or hybrid in nature. The advancements in digital technology and the levelling of behavioural differences and guidelines will diminish the asymmetry in interactions, regardless of the format used.

5.5 Weekly Structure, Rhythm and Routines

Approaching the topic of workplace flexibility from a weekly perspective, there are various interpretations. Some suggest working remotely for 5 days a week, while others suggest working in-person in the office for 1, 2, 3, 4, or 5 days. In 2023, the predominant arrangement was just over 2 days of remote work for those for whom it is feasible (Fig. 5.7). However, the sharp division of days spent in the office versus working remotely is not entirely accurate, as work is often carried out partially in the office and the remaining time spent working remotely. The current dominant

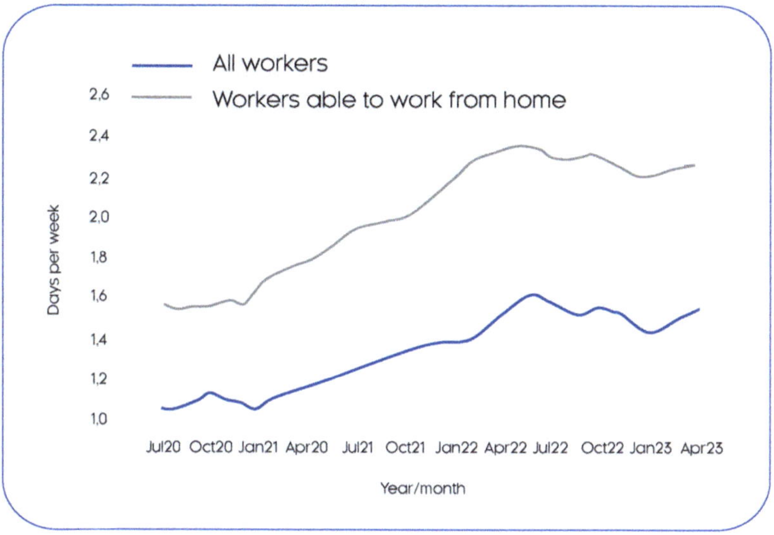

Fig. 5.7 Average days per week working from home: employees plans. Source: www.wfhresearch.com

interpretation of office workplace flexibility among organisations is focused on spending 2 days working remotely and 3 days in the office. Interestingly, management may set this as the flexibility structure, but employees often interpret it as spending two and a half days working remotely and the same amount of time in-person, respectively. In practice, employees rarely spend more time in the office than what management officially specifies in the hybrid workplace model. In general, and quite interestingly, employees tend to take an additional half to 1 day more weekly working out of the office than officially specified. I have coined this observation "Stealth Flexing"—the act of flexing one's work schedule beneath management's radar. (I presume most management and leaders are aware of this phenomenon and generally incorporate it into the overall guidelines for flexibility.)

There is currently no clear pattern indicating which specific days in the office contributed to positive outcomes. Nonetheless, it is observed that individuals generally preferred going to the office on Tuesdays, Wednesdays, and Thursdays (Fig. 5.8). They plan their work accordingly so that Mondays and Fridays are spent working remotely. A sceptical management may claim that this is to take more time off, but a more positive approach would be to assume that employees are optimising their work performance. As a consequence of increased flexibility and remote work, there is a learning process of where and when certain types of work are best performed. Remote work is best suited for digital platforms and in-depth solo work, whereas physical meetings at the workplace increasingly unfold as in-person interactions and collaborations.

Over time, it is expected that weekly structured in-person workdays will become more prevalent as organisations and employees develop proficiency in both digital

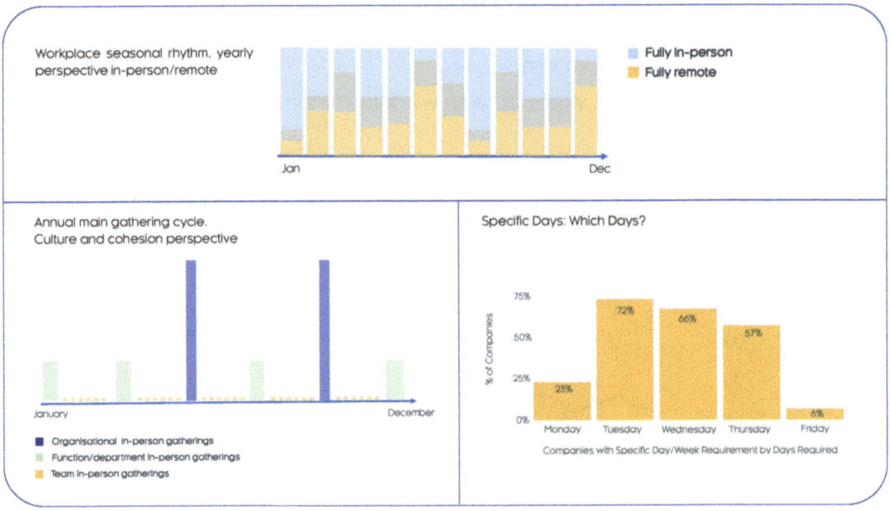

Fig. 5.8 Monthly and yearly rhythm: all together in-person. Balancing analogue and digital work life. Source Specific Days: "The Flex Index, Q2 2023 Flex Report"

and analogue realms. This balance between remote and in-person work will allow for a more productive and efficient approach to work, catering to the specific needs of different tasks and interactions.

A relatively new interpretation of flexibility is the introduction and acknowledgement of a four-day working week, which explicitly provides employees with more consecutive leisure time while raising the daily expectations when working (working intensively and in depth supplemented with intensive and prolonged time off) (4 Day Week Global 2023). The model is being implemented with varying levels of flexibility, ranging from 4 days in the office to 4 days of fully remote work. One could view this negatively as just reducing overall working time and effort by employees. On the other hand, it could be seen as a way to create more satisfied and balanced employees and thus potentially increase productivity.

The near future suggests a practical trend toward a balanced hybrid approach, with employees working both remotely and on-site, roughly split 50/50 across the week. Findings indicated that spending 2 to 3 days in the office each week produced the most favourable outcomes in terms of engagement, well-being, and reduced turnover and burnout. Conversely, working all 5 days on-site, typical of traditional workplace models, led to poorer outcomes for employee satisfaction. Interestingly, full-time on-site presence did not correlate with a stronger sense of belonging to the organisational culture. Although office days are relevant, other factors play a more significant role in influencing positive outcomes.

In the far future, there is likely to be a further shift towards more remote working for knowledge workers. This assumption is based on the expectation that there are no major setbacks in digital infrastructure developments or shifts in priorities towards in-person office work (which are anticipated to occur).

5.6 Monthly and Yearly Structure, Rhythm and Routines

From a monthly and yearly perspective, there is a shaping of structures and patterns for implementing flexibility in the hybrid workplace. On a monthly basis, not all weeks are equally suitable or necessary for in-person presence in the office. Conversely, there will be weeks where full in-person presence in the office is necessary. This rhythm depends on the individual organisation and market, highlighting once again that defining and implementing the hybrid workplace in a specific organisation requires a unique and customised solution.

From a yearly perspective, there is a greater alignment between society's rhythms and structure and the optimal organisational approach and solution for structuring flexibility in the workplace. Typically, leading up to major holiday periods, there will be less presence in the office and more remote work. At the same time, after prolonged periods without in-person presence in the office, there will be an increased demand for in-person presence in the office with the rest of the organisation and colleagues (Fig. 5.8).

According to Prithwiraj Choudhury, a professor at Harvard Business School who has been studying remote work for years, some companies are completely re-evaluating the concept of a permanent office (Choudhury 2020). Some start-ups are recognising that the primary purpose of an office is for socialising, and they are granting employees the flexibility to work from any location. Instead, they arrange occasional in-person meetings throughout the year to facilitate team bonding. For instance, a growing number of companies hold company retreats where all employees are invited to spend a few days together, covering the costs of flights, accommodations, and meals, and organising activities to help colleagues from different departments connect. Gitlab, identified by Choudhury as one of the world's largest remote companies with 1300 employees, allows its staff to work fully remotely but arranges at least one offsite gathering worldwide each year.

5.7 Rebirth of Rituals in a Hybrid Reality

Shared rituals are important in any workplace, including the hybrid workplace, as they create a sense of community and help build relationships between employees. When discussing workplace rituals, the conversation often includes other elements that help define the culture, as in the classic Ed Schein definition of culture rooted in rites, rituals, ceremonies, language, behaviours, and generally accepted norms and values (Schein 1990).

With the shift away from the office-focused workplace for knowledge workers, there is a clear need to reinvent and establish rituals that were present in the traditional in-person office model. Some notable examples include the absence of casual social interactions, the rise of hybrid meetings as a substitute for in-person gatherings, the disappearance of Friday meetings, and the overall sense of community that was fostered by sharing a common in-person workday in the office. Research indicates that effective workplace rituals typically involve two key elements (Mckinsey

& Company 2023). Firstly, there is a deliberate focus on nurturing a sense of community among employees. Secondly, there is often a physical aspect that involves gathering, raising a toast, or engaging in a shared activity. The challenge lies in creating an environment where the sense of belonging and camaraderie arises naturally, rather than feeling like a mandatory obligation.

The aim is to convey that individuals are valued members of the team and that their presence is vital to the collective identity. Striking the right balance can be challenging, but it is essential if the goal is to foster a tightly knit and cohesive team, rather than merely a collection of individuals. Shared rituals can take various forms, depending on whether they are conducted digitally or in person. In the digital realm, regular team meetings serve as an example of shared rituals. It is evident that most digital ritual initiatives have not lived up to expectations, especially as the pandemic has subsided. While communicative initiatives have proven successful in many ways, digital rituals have not achieved the same level of success. In-person settings often provide more conducive conditions for rituals to flourish. These rituals offer a regular opportunity for employees to connect, share experiences, and build relationships beyond their work tasks.

At the management and organisational level, it may be crucial to establish new rituals, such as extended in-depth seminars with mandatory attendance or in-person team-building events to emphasise relationships and trust-building. Shared rituals will foster a sense of continuity and routine, which can be especially valuable for remote employees who may struggle with work-life balance or feelings of isolation. By fostering meaningful shared experiences, organisations can strengthen their sense of community and cultivate a positive work culture, which, among other benefits, aids in attracting and retaining talent (Horn and Moesta 2024). It is expected that meaningful rituals will be reimagined and created to suit the hybrid workplace.

These rituals must be designed in a way that employees are naturally inclined to participate, regardless of their location. In the traditional workplace, where the office was the central hub, it was easier to gather employees and physically close the door to create a sense of unity. In the hybrid workplace, the door is always figuratively open, with fewer physical barriers restricting employees. To foster employee engagement and participation in rituals, organisations will need to be more creative and intentional in their approach.

They should consider using digital platforms and technology to create inclusive and interactive experiences that transcend physical distances. Moreover, offering flexibility and choice in how employees participate can further encourage their voluntary involvement. The goal is to make these rituals appealing and meaningful to employees, whether they are working from the office or remotely.

References

(4 Day Week Global 2023) A Four-Day Workweek Reduces Stress without Hurting Productivity - Scientific American 09.03.2023 https://www.4dayweek.com/uk-full-report-2023

(Appel-Meulenbroek et al., 2022) How to attract employees back to the office? A stated choice study on hybrid working preferences https://www.sciencedirect.com/science/article/pii/S0272494422000299

(BBC News 2022) The non-linear workdays changing the shape of productivity https://www.bbc.com/worklife/article/20220928-the-non-linear-workdays-changing-the-shape-of-productivity

(Bloom 2023) Stanford Professor

(Choudhury 2020) HBR Nov-Dec 2020 Our Work-from-Anywhere Future https://hbr.org/2020/11/our-work-from-anywhere-future

(Emanuel and Harrington 2024) Fully remote working appears to lower average performance by around 10% to 20% https://www.aeaweb.org/articles?id=10.1257/app.20230376

(Flex Index Report Q2 2024) www.flexindex.com https://www.flex.scoopforwork.com/stats?utm_source=press&utm_medium=article&utm_campaign=flex-report-q2

(FlexIndex 2023) Bloom, Nick: https://www.flexindex.com/blog/what-does-work-look-like-in-2030-4-predictions-from-nick-bloom

(Flynn, Ghent and Nair 2024) Determinants and Consequences of Return to Office Policies https://papers.ssrn.com/sol3/papers.cfm?abstract_id=4757876

(Gibbs et al. 2024) Gibbs, Michael; Mengel, Friederike; Siemroth, Christoph Employee innovation during office work, work from home and hybrid work. Scientific Reports (2024). doi: 10.1038/s41598-024-67122-6 https://www.nature.com/articles/s41598-024-67122-6

(Gupta, et al., 2024) Do Startups Benefit from Remote Work? https://drive.google.com/file/d/1G_QQRMIlXhDb8VHXEGKqifseqxxzsFMo/view

(Harter et al. 2023) Ben Wigert, Jim Harter and Sageeta Agrawal, Gallup, Workplace, October 9, 2023, The Future of the Office Has Arrived: It's Hybrid https://www.gallup.com/workplace/511994/future-office-arrived-hybrid.aspx

(Horn and Moesta 2024) HBR Nov-Dec 2024 Why Employees Quit https://hbr.org/2024/11/why-employees-quit

(Johansen 2020) Johansen, Bob. Full-Spectrum Thinking: How to Escape Boxes in a Post-Categorical Future. Oakland, CA: Berret-Koehler 2020. https://www.amazon.com/Full-Spectrum-Thinking-Escape-Post-Categorical-Future/dp/152308751X

(Mckinsey & Company 2021) Hybrid Work After COVID-19: The Future of Work

(Mckinsey & Company 2023): https://www.mckinsey.com/Capabilities/People-and-organisational-Per…Insights/Workplace-rituals-Recapturing-the-power-of-what-weve-lost

(Ranganathan 2023) HBR, Asynchronous Work Can Fuel Creativity https://hbr.org/2023/04/research-asynchronous-work-can-fuel-creativity

(Saatçi, Rädle, Rintel, O'Hara and Nylandsted Klokmose 2019) Hybrid meetings in the modern workplace: stories of success and failure. In Collaboration Technologies and Social Computing: 25th International Conference, CRIWG+ CollabTech 2019, Kyoto, Japan, September 4–6, 2019, Proceedings 25 (pp. 45–61). Springer International Publishing. https://link.springer.com/chapter/10.1007/978-3-030-28011-6_4

(Schein 1990). "Organizational culture". American Psychologist. **45** (2): 109–119. doi:https://doi.org/10.1037/0003-066X.45.2.109.

(Zarate et al., 2024), WHY DOES WORKING FROM HOME VARY ACROSS COUNTRIES AND PEOPLE? Working Paper 32374Pablo Zarate, Mathias Dolls, Steven J. Davis, Nicholas Bloom, Jose Maria Barrero and Cevat Giray Aksoy, http://www.nber.org/papers/w32374

Workplace as a Space for Meetings, Interaction, and Collaboration

6

Abstract

The workplace is undergoing a significant transformation, increasingly evolving into an effective and productive meeting space. The hybrid workplace model, blending digital and analogue interactions, is closely linked to meeting culture, which plays a crucial role in the success of this new work environment. As work becomes more flexible, understanding how to manage meetings—whether digital, analogue, or hybrid—becomes essential.

The workplace functions as a marketplace for collaboration, where knowledge exchange and interaction drive value creation. The rise of digital tools has liberated work from physical constraints, but this shift demands new skills and approaches to meeting management. Effective meeting culture is now more important than ever, as meetings and interactions are central to the development of knowledge and innovation in organisations. As meetings consume a significant portion of work time, their quality and efficiency directly impact productivity. The trend towards shorter, more focused meetings reflects the need for better planning and control, especially in hybrid settings. The future of work will increasingly hold meetings accountable for their value, both to individuals and to organisations, driven by data and artificial intelligence. The traditional meeting overload must be addressed, as it no longer contributes to the competitive advantage of organisations in the hybrid workplace.

6.1 The Meeting Factory: The Production Lines of the Knowledge and Network Society

The workplace will increasingly become a more effective and productive meeting place as we move forward. There is a direct connection and correlation between collaboration, interactions, meetings, and the workplace as a human meeting place

C. Sneppen, *The Future (R)Evolution of the Office Workspace*, Future of Business and Finance, https://doi.org/10.1007/978-3-031-85229-9_6

for work (Fig. 6.1). The future successful hybrid and flexible workplace models are closely tied to a meeting culture where employees comprehend how analogue, digital, and hybrid meetings and interactions are utilised in a busy daily life. To put it plainly, it is challenging to explore the hybrid workplace model without delving into the meeting and collaboration culture.

The workplace is essentially the marketplace for work, where individuals utilised their own work time, where collaborative work takes place, and where the organisation generates value in the market. With digitisation, the office workplace has become hybrid, by enabling digitised meetings, interactions, and collaborations that have freed work and collaboration from physical constraints. This digitisation is still in its early stages, and we are continuously developing the digital and hybrid collaboration and meeting possibilities for the workplace and work-life. Understanding meetings, collaborations, and interactions from an anthropological and sociological perspective can, therefore, help unravel and comprehend the complex challenges around the organisation of working life and the development of the hybrid workplace model. Do the employees have the skills to effectively engage in analogue meetings and interactions? Is the meeting culture in the organisation prepared for the hybrid workplace model? How should meetings and interactions be utilised in a hybrid working environment?

A significant and growing part of workplace collaboration occurs through casual and informal interactions (e.g. Hughes et al. 2018). Addressing casual interactions can be achieved by placing emphasis on fostering weak ties. In the evolving hybrid work environment, weak ties within the workplace are more significant than ever, offering a vital avenue for connection, collaboration, and innovation. Sociologist Mark Granovetter introduced the concept of "weak ties" in social networks, challenging traditional views on how individuals connect and the significance of these connections within social structures (Granovetter 1973). *The Strength of Weak Ties* underscores the importance of casual, less intimate relationships in bridging diverse social networks and accessing new information and opportunities. While strong ties offer emotional support and trust, weak ties are crucial for connecting people to

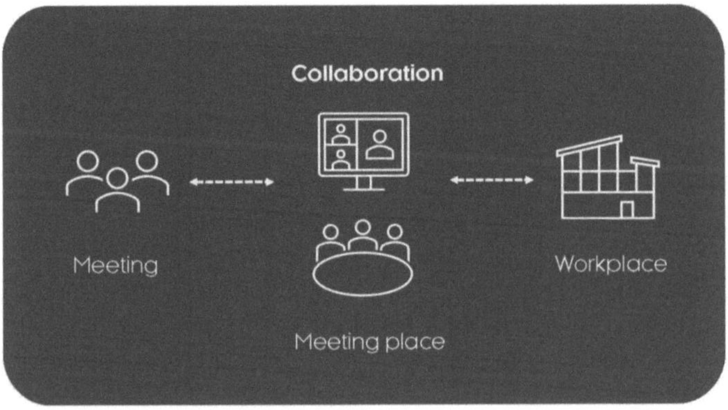

Fig. 6.1 Meeting and workplace correlation

broader social worlds, making them indispensable for fostering innovation, mobility, and social cohesion.

Grundfos, Image credits: HOLMRIS B8

In the knowledge and network society, the production lines to a large extent consist of meetings and interactions between people to facilitate knowledge exchange and the development of new shared knowledge. Employees are increasingly required to co-create with colleagues, stakeholders, and partners to align, coordinate, and generate innovative solutions for the organisation and business challenges. These challenges continuously arise in an environment that is rapidly changing and accelerating in the digital realm.

The percentage of work time spent in structured meetings has been steadily increasing for decades (Cross et al. 2016). They calculated that time spent in meetings had increased by 50 per cent since the 1990s. "Collaboration is taking over the workplace", they wrote in an article in Harvard Business Review. This is not necessarily negative when viewed in isolation, as the rise in meetings and interactions is closely connected to the spread of knowledge and network societies, where value creation largely occurs through human interactions.

The office workplace plays a central role in creating coherence and direction for the organisation. As a meeting place, it serves as a platform to build relationships and trust at all levels and across departments, functions, and tasks. Employee trust is a key indicator positively correlated with three measures of workplace performance: financial performance, labour productivity, and the quality of products or services (Brown et al. 2025). By providing a common meeting place, whether digital or analogue, it enables shared progress to occur more quickly and with higher quality compared to situations where individuals work in isolation with limited opportunities for interaction, meetings, and collaborations. In essence, the workplace as a common meeting place ensures a more efficient workspace with higher productivity for individuals, teams, and the entire organisation.

Continuous generation of new knowledge needs to be considered in collaborations, interactions, and meetings in the workplace moving forward. Below is a small excerpt:

- Collaboration is an increasingly significant, larger, and growing part of our work culture. Collaboration involves interactions, communication, and meetings, which in turn means that meetings are a growing central part of all work cultures.
- Understanding personal profiles and work cultures is crucial for the use and value of meetings, and a one-size-fits-all approach significantly reduces productivity. For example, employees in a competitive work culture experience meetings as 40 per cent less valuable than employees in a collaborative culture (Perlow et al. 2017).
- The rise of non-linear, asynchronous, and asymmetric collaboration amplifies the need to address meeting culture in the hybrid workplace.
- Digitisation creates rapidly accelerated opportunities for digital meetings and interactions. At the same time, our daily behavioural patterns and expectations for interactions and meetings are changing. Digital video meetings are becoming increasingly widespread and are mainly chosen because they are immediately effective. Specifically tailored guidelines for digital meetings significantly increase the value of video meetings.
- Meetings directly related to daily work tasks are generally perceived as more valuable. The further away the meeting content is from the meeting participant's close work tasks, the lower the perceived meeting value.
- Email communication or other asynchrony digital communication is often used as an effective substitute for a brief meeting or phone call. An excessive use of email where we spam each other is also correlated with a meeting culture of low productivity.

It has been established that open office landscapes, as opposed to smaller offices, create an increase of up to 70 per cent in internal emails between employees and a decrease of up to 70 per cent of face-to-face interactions (Bernstein and Turban 2018). We can also observe that changes in physical environments create changes in behaviour and interactions between employees—and not always for the better. The analogue office workplace is overall anticipated to continue to serve an important function as a meeting and interaction space. It has been proven that analogue in-person meetings and interactions are immediately the most effective—and enjoyable—format choice for certain tasks and challenges. On the other hand, other tasks and collaborations are best and most efficiently solved through digital meetings and interactions.

6.2 The Ultimate Digital Meeting Experiment

Even after just a few months of the pandemic, it became evident that meetings would never be the same as it was in the "good old" pre-pandemic days. Organisations and employees became unwitting participants in a grand experiment on conducting and developing businesses remotely through digital meetings. Post-pandemic, we now find ourselves meeting, if anything, even more frequently than before the pandemic sent us from physical workplaces to makeshift home offices. Prior to the pandemic, meetings were mostly held in person. During the pandemic, they shifted primarily to digital formats. Now, with the advent of the hybrid workplace, we meet in person, digitally, and in hybrid formats. This is a development where all stakeholders, without exception, lack knowledge about the future successful meeting place. Decision-makers and actors often have biased approaches to possible solutions, and myths about meetings are not adequately challenged. Development is happening quickly because digital possibilities are the driving force for the future of meetings. We have only seen the beginning of the digital tools that will revolutionise the meeting culture.

Did you miss your colleagues and all the valuable meetings during the pandemic? Most people can answer yes to the first question—that they missed their colleagues. The answer to the second question—whether we miss all the meetings—is more along the lines of a hesitant "Well…", implying that we don't miss all of them—just some. We drown in meetings every day, and a large part of them are assessed by the meeting participants as a waste of time (Bartleby, Economist 2018). And there are still more of them. There are many ways and approaches to enhance the value of meetings and transform the meeting culture within an organisation.

To the best of our knowledge, before the pandemic hit in 2020, no organisations willingly switched nearly all meetings to a digital format for an extended period. Yet, that is precisely what occurred. Consequently, many of us became involuntary participants in the digital meeting experiment. Can we leverage this experience for something positive? Distance work and digital meetings and interactions have highlighted alternative methods of working, interacting, and collaborating while maintaining or even increasing productivity in the workplace. At the same time, it became evident that predominantly meeting and communicating digitally had its limitations, potentially taking a toll on both productivity and innovation. While digital communication offers convenience, it often lacks the spontaneity and depth of face-to-face interactions, which are vital for fostering creativity and driving collaborative problem-solving (e.g. Gibbs et al. 2021, Braun et al. 2019). The rise in remote working and digital meetings also has surged in quantity, potentially hindering both productivity and the overall employee work experience (Whillans et al. 2022). The pandemic and the consequent partial adoption of the hybrid workplace model have emphasised that meetings, interactions, and collaboration are integral to the development of hybrid work-life. It is evident that meetings have considerable room for improvement, and this potential can be harnessed through the development of the hybrid workplace model. The introduction of the hybrid workplace has made employees and organisations more conscious of how meetings and meeting spaces can be optimally utilised. The way we conduct meetings and the design of meeting places are critical elements in the development of the hybrid workplace. They must be aligned with the following considerations, among others:

- How should meetings, interactions, and collaboration be organised when some employees are physically present and others are participating digitally?
- Which meetings, interactions, and collaboration are better suited for digital platforms and which ones are best held in person?
- When and why should employees come together for meetings in any format?

6.3 Where and How to Interact?

Examining the meeting culture and the potential impact of both analogue and digital skills on our future meeting behaviour, I will share a meeting and collaboration model that I developed in collaboration with the think tank Meetings of Tomorrow, including participants from the Universities of Copenhagen and Aarhus. The think tank conducted an explorative study categorising meetings based on insights gathered from over 200 management interviews and questionnaires, examining the purpose, format, and outcomes of planned meetings. As we move forward and become more meeting and collaboration competent, it is anticipated that meeting behaviour will increasingly align with this model and, in turn, co-shape the future hybrid workplace model.

The central outcome of the think tank initial work is summarised in a model that seeks to answer what physical and digital meetings and interactions are suitable for. The model contains insights and recommendations gathered in a bouillon cube that provides a different picture of the meeting landscape and gives a range of new concepts to talk about meetings and interactions from (establishing a common meeting language and vocabulary). The findings are in line with previous studies conducted on face-to-face and meetings and digital communication and collaboration (Wu et al., 2008 and Håkansson et al. 2020).

HQ The Danish Building and Property Agency. *Image credits:* The Danish Building and Property Agency

Meetings and interactions can be divided into three different categories, which we refer to as meeting outcomes. Meeting outcomes cut across the distinctions we normally look at, such as the number of people, short/long, internal/external, physical/digital, etc. All meetings and interactions consist of all three main purposes, but the individual interaction or meeting will have a main focus on one of them.

If we instead solely focus on what the main purpose of the meeting is, we get the following three groupings (Figs. 6.2 and 6.3):

1. **Co-processing Meetings** are meetings and interactions where the main purpose is to ensure progress in a defined process to remove uncertainties. The agenda is predominantly predictable, and no one is really in doubt about their role and delivery. There are not many questions; it is just a process. Co-processing meetings are very suitable to be conducted as digital meetings.
2. **Co-alignment Meetings** are meetings and interactions where the main purpose is to align thoughts, emotions, and behaviour. Often there is a clear hierarchical division, where some people tell others how things should be. There can be many questions that need to be answered, but the goal is always to frame the direction to go. The degree of complexity determines whether a consensus meeting should be held physically or digitally—both can be right.
3. **Co-creation Meetings** are meetings and interactions where the main purpose is for the participants to create something together. It can be a concrete idea or product, and it can be something more diffuse like a sense of community, trust, or corporate culture. These meetings are more complex, and for them to be suc-

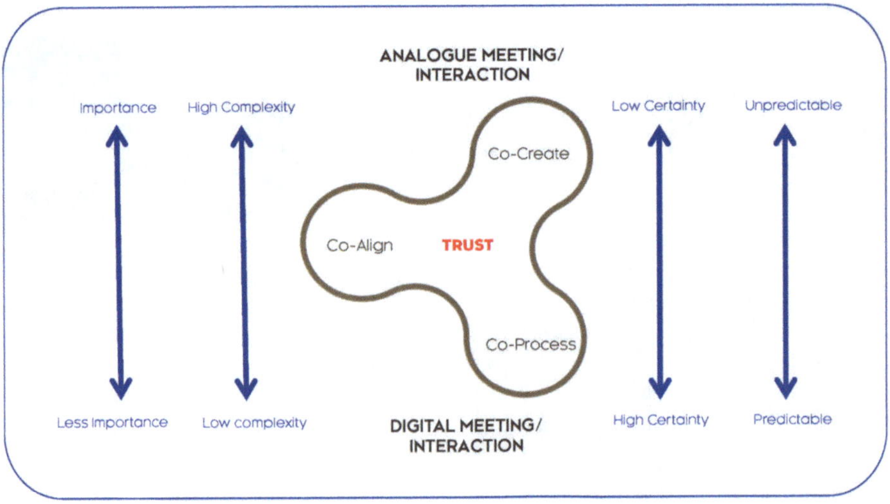

Fig. 6.2 Analogue and digital meeting/interaction model

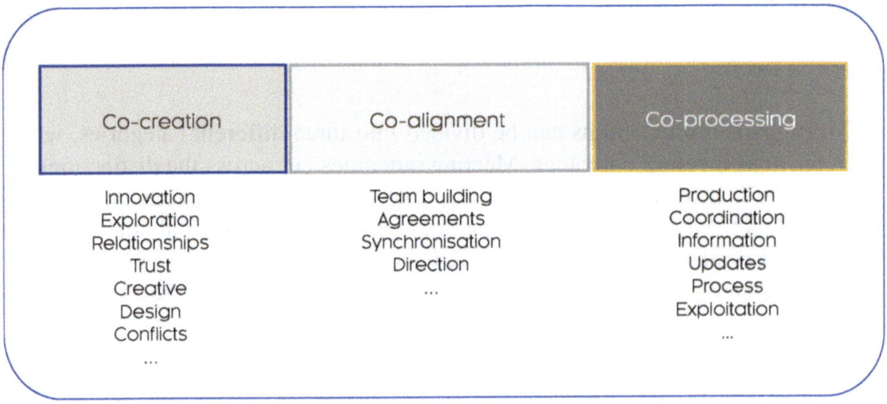

Fig. 6.3 Meeting and interaction purpose typology

cessful, it is crucial that there are no clear hierarchies at play, that all participants actively participate, ask questions, and contribute with answers. Therefore, co-creation meetings are most suitable for being held as physical meetings.

Overall, the following behaviour applies to meetings and interactions in a digitised workplace, and the development of meeting culture is anticipated to reflect this accordingly as the hybrid workplace continues to evolve:

- Digital meetings are particularly suitable for general solutions and processes. Hold digital meetings for what is predictable and focused on coordination and agreements.

- Reduce complexity and uncertainty in digital meetings, possibly by dividing them into several meetings. This makes it easier to ensure activation and involvement of all meeting participants in digital meetings.
- Analogue meetings are particularly suitable for unique needs and solutions—co-creation meetings.
- The quickest and most effective method for developing trust is to meet "face-to-face". Therefore, the valuable digital meeting often relies on meeting participants having met analogously first.
- All meetings are based on trust and psychological safety, and the higher the level of trust between meeting participants, the higher the speed and meeting value. At the same time, a high degree of trust will enable a more challenging and developing digital meeting agenda. In other words, digital meetings can be used to a large extent as a substitute for analogue ones if there is a high degree of trust among all meeting participants.
- The more preparation, the more valuable the meeting—involve and communicate with meeting participants.
- The fewer meeting participants, the higher the meeting efficiency and value—limit the number of participants to the absolute necessary.
- The narrower the agenda, the higher the meeting value.
- The further away the meeting is from present daily tasks of the participants, the shorter the meeting should be.
- The shorter the meeting, the higher the progress.
- The shorter the individual contributions, the higher the value of the meeting.
- The more meeting participants who actively contribute, the higher the value of the meeting.
- The more action-oriented the agenda—with questions that need to be answered—the higher the value of the meeting.
- The more digital and analogue disruptions ("lags"), the lower the value of the meeting.
- The more senses that are activated, the higher the value of the meeting.
- The more data on the quality of the meeting, the higher the value of future meetings.

6.4 Workplace Trust Factor: Digital or Analogue Interaction?

The hybrid office workplace model requires a high level of trust between employees and their managers, as the distance in time, place, and space grows. Managers need to trust that employees are working effectively and efficiently, even when they are working remotely, while employees need to trust that their managers are supporting them and providing the resources they need to be successful (Ozyllmaz et al. 2017). In fact, the trust relationship between employer and employee stands as one of the most crucial factors in employee retention.

But what creates trust in each meeting, interaction, or meeting point in the hybrid workplace? Trust between meeting participants is built on many factors and is a subject for a separate article or book. However, trust in meetings largely depends on the framework of the meeting (what we meet about), the expectations each meeting participant has for the others' competence, decision making and acting power, and credibility, and finally, the current impression and meaning formation during the meeting itself. When we uncover the answer to what creates trust, we implicitly also answer what undermines trust in meetings and meeting points in the hybrid workplace, now and in the future.

The future hybrid workplace and work-life rely on a high degree of trust. Will the leader dare to give employees the freedom to choose where and when they perform their work? Does the leader believe that employees work autonomously, efficiently, purposefully, and productively to solve their own and common challenges and tasks? If the leadership answers with the slightest degree of doubt, the introduction of the hybrid workplace model is challenged, if not impossible. The previous resistance to working from home has had an underlying tone that the employee took a half day off. The leadership did not trust that employees would solve tasks if they were allowed to work from home. As former CEO of Codan, Christian Baltzer, expressed it, "On the screen, you have to believe that you have people supporting you" (Thomsen 2022).

In the context of the hybrid workplace, trust and social capital are closely correlated. Trust refers to the confidence and reliance that individuals have in each other's abilities, intentions, and actions. Social capital, on the other hand, refers to the network of relationships, mutual trust, and shared values that exist within a social group, such as a team or organisation. Trust is an essential component of social capital because it establishes a foundation for effective collaboration, communication, and cooperation among employees in the workplace. When trust is present, individuals are more likely to share information, support each other, and work towards common goals. This leads to the development of stronger social ties, which contribute to the overall social capital within the organisation. Consequently, the hybrid workplace model relies on a higher level of intentional trust and social capital building compared to the predominantly office centred model, where formation occurs more unintentionally and by "accident".

In the hybrid workplace, where employees have a mix of remote and in-person work arrangements, building and maintaining trust and psychological safety (Newman et al. 2017) becomes crucial. In-person interactions, such as meetings and informal conversations, provide opportunities for employees to establish personal connections, read non-verbal cues, and build rapport. These analogue interactions often facilitate the development of trust more quickly and stronger than purely digital interactions (Chai and Freeman 2029). In a hybrid workplace, where remote work and virtual collaboration are prevalent, it is also important to foster trust and social capital through digital means. This can be achieved through regular virtual meetings, video conferences, and platforms that promote communication and collaboration. However, it is no secret that meetings are often perceived as wasteful vacuums, draining employee morale and productivity (Constantinedes et al. 2022).

This is likely due to current technologies falling short in fully supporting a seamless hybrid or virtual meeting experience, leaving participants disengaged and frustrated with the inefficiencies. By creating a supportive and inclusive virtual environment, organisations can strengthen trust and social capital among employees, even in the absence of physical proximity. Trust is thus a prerequisite for creating a hybrid workplace with a dominant share of digital and remote work. The lower the level of trust, the higher the demand for physical presence. At the same time, employees want freedom and flexibility, and in the future, employees will choose a workplace where they work with a high degree of trust between them and their employer. There is therefore pressure to develop the necessary trust framework.

Trust between employees and management in the organisation is also directly related to the network and knowledge economy. The network economy reinforces the widespread trend towards greater independence, more self-management, and fewer management layers. In the network society, the employee is increasingly set free to organise value creation with a focus on immediate task goals in smaller task-oriented teams. In short the freedom associated with the hybrid workplace requires a high level of trust between workplace actors. In the book *Knowledge and Discourse Matters* by Lesley Crane, the author describes how trust is critical if one is to create knowledge and value (Crane 2015). He defines trust as willingness to share, willingness to use, and the experience of receiving useful knowledge.

The future trust-building in meetings and interactions in the hybrid workplace will implicate (in arbitrary order):

- Trust, although the social capital between employees, both bilaterally and multilaterally, with the team and organisation, is built most quickly through face-to-face meetings and interactions.
- By focusing on participation and activation of employees. In co-creation meetings and interactions, there should be a move towards equality and away from hierarchies, while acknowledging that hierarchies can also build trust in alignment. "Creating participation leads to willingness to share and contribute what one possesses".
- By ensuring that each employee finds the purpose important and is confirmed in it. We know that trust develops more when there is more at stake.
- By proximity and sensibility. The closer we are to each other, the more we establish trust—but it is a balancing act considering our individual privacy—being too close too quickly can create distance and erosion of trust. Proximity includes both physical and mental closeness, and building trust is closely related to the exposure that comes from being mentally and physically close (sensory).
- By having exciting and fun meetings and interactions. (It follows from the importance argument that we build trust through increased risk and excitement). Excitement is created by seeking uncertainties, where we are excited about whether we will agree or what new thing we will create together. On an individual level, exposure to uncertainties develops excitement, for example, in relation to how the other meeting participants handle the individual's uncertainty about a problem.

- By strengthening the background of each participant before the meeting or interaction. We all meet each other at contact points and bring our own history in relation to the other participants into the meeting—also called the background. The background and trust of the meeting participant are closely related to personality, knowledge, background, reputation, company, network, recommendations, etc. The background is thus related to knowledge and the experience of access to new knowledge through dialogue with the other meeting participants—which is precisely Lesley Crane's prerequisite for building trust.
- With clear precautions, e.g. frameworks and meeting design. The right precautions create security and reinforce the synchronisation between the participants with the aim of fulfilling the individual and collective purposes of the meeting. Precautions set the direction for the physical and mental meeting design, communication, and the rules that are fundamental to exchanging and developing knowledge together. Rules and design also provide free rein if new solutions to important challenges are to be developed in co-creation meetings.

From a negative perspective, individual employees or parts of the organisation can undermine trust in meetings and interactions by not participating or being mentally present; if the meeting is not important for the individual or the community; if there are strong hierarchies or distance; if the meeting is predictable and boring; if the participants approach each other with scepticism, and if the framework and management of the meeting are lacking. We can all probably recognise that many meetings and meeting places contain elements of trust-eroding behavior.

By concretely working on what creates trust, organisations can effectively increase the perceived—and factual—value of many meetings and meeting points and thus the value of the hybrid workplace model. Are you developing or eroding trust in your workplace through the way the organisation conducts meetings, interactions, and digital and analogue meeting points?

6.5 Accelerated Trust Building at the Workplace Pays Off

By building trust, meeting formats can be transformed from analogue to digital interactions, thereby saving resources and potentially increasing the speed of processes (Fig. 6.4). Naturally, there are significant advantages to developing trust and social capital quickly within an organisation, as increased trust is closely linked to the generation of value. The pace at which trust is built or eroded is accelerating, a consequence of an increasingly digitised reality where time has become the greatest constraint in both work and life. In other words, individuals are quicker to build trust with others, and conversely, they are also quicker to dissolve trust when they meet and interact. In a broader perspective, this is further emphasised by the Pygmalion effect, also known as the Rosenthal effect, which refers to the psychological phenomenon whereby the greater the belief, trust, and expectations placed upon individuals, the better they tend to perform.

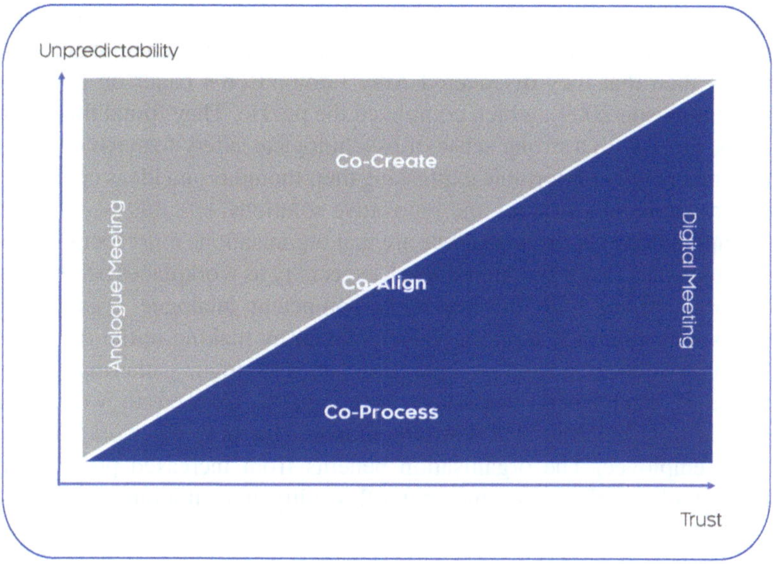

Fig. 6.4 Meeting format and trust/unpredictability

Many high-performing managers emphasise that their top priority is building trust within their team. This is because employee trust fosters alignment and clear communication, unlocking the team's potential for their best work (Lyman 2003). According to the Predictive Index, organisational trust is defined as "having the confidence of your workforce in the actions of your company".

When team members can wholeheartedly trust a company's mission, culture, and actions, they are better equipped to fulfil the vision and feel a part of something greater. Sufficient employee trust leads to psychological safety, a critical element for innovation. Performance and team development are closely linked to the ability to disagree, fail, or make mistakes without fear of punishment—in other words, trust (e.g. Edmondson and Lei 2014).

In Google's Project Aristotle study, teams with psychological safety were found to be "less likely to leave Google, more inclined to leverage diverse ideas from their teammates, generate higher revenue, and were rated as effective twice as often by executives" (Rozovsky 2015). The project sought to identify patterns and behaviours that contributed to high-performing teams. Beginning in 2012, the study spent 2 years examining 250 attributes across 180 teams. Initially, they assumed a successful team would consist of high performers, an experienced manager, and unlimited resources. However, they soon realised this was not the case. Julia Rozovsky, the leader of Project Aristotle, had long been interested in how people work. During her studies at the Yale School of Management, Rozovsky experienced two contrasting study groups: despite both being composed of bright, friendly individuals, one group quickly became dysfunctional. Although the reasons were unclear at the time, her work with Project Aristotle brought clarity. Rozovsky and her team initially identified four key factors for a successful team: dependability, structure and clarity, meaning, and impact. However, they sensed that one crucial component was missing. It was then that they discovered Amy Edmondson's paper on psychological safety (Edmondson 2009), which completed the puzzle. They found that among the 180 teams, those with a strong sense of psychological safety fostered environments where members felt comfortable expressing their thoughts and ideas openly, leading to more productive discussions and innovative solutions.

The implications for the workplace are that organisations must focus on building trust internally at a faster and higher level, especially as workplaces become increasingly hybrid. Along with developing a competent analogue organisation and employees, this approach supports value creation by making initial investments in trust-building initiatives, such as organising larger analogue gatherings and events. Once trust is established, employees can then be allowed to work remotely. Accelerated trust-building is a win-win situation for both the workplace and the individual employee. The organisation benefits from increased productivity and efficiency, while employees enjoy greater flexibility and autonomy.

6.6 The Digitisation of Meeting Culture Has Only Just Begun

Throughout the pandemic, we learned the importance of conducting valuable meetings and interactions in the digital realm. As a result, both digital and analogue meetings will be influenced by the experiences and habits we acquired during those days in a digital meeting reality. For instance, with the widespread adoption of hybrid working, there has been an increase in messaging and video calls, even when all employees are present in the office. This shift demonstrates a move towards more electronic communication and collaboration.

Microsoft Teams is one of numerous popular collaboration platforms used by organisations to communicate and work together. A new feature of Microsoft Teams is the Copilot (2024). Copilot is a virtual assistant that uses artificial intelligence (AI) to help users in Teams meetings. It can perform a variety of tasks, such as taking notes, scheduling meetings, and sending messages. Copilot can also listen in on meetings and provide helpful suggestions based on the context of the conversation. For example, if someone mentions a specific date in a meeting, Copilot might suggest setting up a reminder or calendar appointment for that date. If someone asks a question that Copilot can answer, it might provide a relevant link or resource. Copilot is designed to help teams work more efficiently and stay focused during meetings. It can save time by handling routine tasks and providing relevant information when needed. A recently published study on the use of AI in meetings found varied impacts on time spent in meetings across organisations—some experienced an increase, while others saw a decrease (Microsoft 2024). One hypothesis suggests that AI enhances the value of meetings, transforming them into richer information repositories and accelerating creative processes, such as quickly generating a first draft from a brainstorming session. For certain organisations, the resulting efficiency leads to fewer meetings, whereas others hold more, capitalising on the added value AI brings. As AI capabilities continue to evolve, researchers anticipate this trend to persist—enabling us to reduce time spent in some meetings while making those we hold more valuable.

The pandemic has brought about a radical transformation in the meeting culture and has escalated the demand for a renewed approach to meetings (Tolliver and Sass 2024). These changes in meeting habits not only impact the meeting culture but also have a profound influence on the future workplace and work-life model. The success of a hybrid and flexible workplace model is intricately tied to a meeting culture where employees comprehend how to utilise analogue, digital, and hybrid meetings and interactions in their busy daily routines. On average, office workers and "bureaucrats" or "office warriors" spend approximately 20–40 per cent of their working time in planned meetings (excluding preparation and follow-up time). This percentage may vary depending on factors such as the organisation's size, culture, employee's hierarchical position, public/private sector, industry, and region. As the digitisation of collaboration increases, there has been a significant rise in the use of collaborative tools such as Slack and similar alternatives, which are substituting meetings and other forms of communication. The positive aspects of using these tools in distributed teams include enhanced team awareness, more informal communication, and a reduction in the reliance on email (Stray and Moe 2020) (new generations entering the job market are less likely to use the phone, email, or SMS as their preferred forms of communication).

Post-pandemic, meeting behaviour is undergoing changes, and it is anticipated that the future will be characterised by continuous evolution. These changes in meeting culture will, in many ways, mirror the development of the hybrid workplace. Looking at data from Microsoft in a short-term perspective, some notable trends are emerging (Microsoft Work Trend Index 2022). For instance, meetings now tend to start later Mondays and finish earlier on Fridays, suggesting that fewer employees may be simultaneously present at the shared office during those times (Fig. 6.5). Additionally, there is a decrease in the number of meetings scheduled during lunchtime. While the overall quantity of meetings has increased, their duration has become shorter and more ad hoc. Employees are finding digital alternatives to the spontaneous "drive by" or "hallway conversation", leading to an 8 per cent rise in unscheduled, ad hoc calls in the last 2 years, now constituting 64 per cent of all Teams meetings. Furthermore, meetings under 15 min now comprise the majority (60 per cent) of all meetings and have experienced a 39 per cent increase between February 2021 and 2022, the highest growth rate among meeting lengths.

Data also indicates a shift towards asynchronous work as part of the new normal (Glaveski 2021). The monthly usage of meeting recordings, allowing individuals to catch up on meetings, training, and town halls on-demand, has more than doubled since March 2020. Additionally, new patterns are emerging, such as the "triple peak day", where some individuals are moving away from the traditional 9-to-5 work schedule and adopting a more flexible approach that suits their preferences. Traditionally, knowledge workers had two productivity peaks in their workday: before lunch and after lunch. However, during the pandemic and widespread remote

Fig. 6.5 Meeting habits are changing. Source: Microsoft 2022 Work Trend Index: Annual Report

work, a third peak has emerged for some workers in the hours before bedtime. Microsoft researchers have dubbed this phenomenon the "triple peak day". The movement towards more asynchronous working is aligning with a market trend towards more non-linear working habits with the introduction of the hybrid workplace, leaving more time for in-depth focused working task solving.

6.7 Meetings Are Increasing in Volume and Importance

Over the years, there has been a continuous rise in the total time dedicated to meetings. While advanced communication tools have made it easier to connect with others, they have also brought new challenges in managing demands. A closer analysis of how people allocate their time shows that the lack of uninterrupted focus time, the constant need to search for information, and the overwhelming volume of continuous communication come at a cost. According to a Microsoft survey, 68 per cent of individuals feel they don't have sufficient uninterrupted focus time during their workday, and 62 per cent struggle with spending too much time searching for information (Microsoft 2023). In Microsoft 365 applications, the average employee allocates 57 per cent of their time to communication activities like meetings, email, and chat, and the remaining 43 per cent on creating documents, spreadsheets, and presentations. The heaviest email users spend around 8.8 h per week on email, while the top meeting users dedicate approximately 7.5 h per week to virtual meetings (specifically Teams meetings, not in-person meetings). These figures consider frontline workers as well, but for knowledge workers who heavily depend on digital communication, the percentage of time spent on emails and meetings is notably higher. (According to a local Danish study, office employees spend approximately

15 h a week on communication activities and meetings excluding meeting preparation and follow-up.)

Meetings are a clear example of ongoing productivity challenges (Fig. 6.6). Inefficient meetings are reported as the main disruptor to productivity, with an excessive number of meetings being a close third. Many employees struggle to brainstorm effectively in virtual meetings (58 per cent) or catch up if they join a meeting late (57 per cent). Moreover, the clarity of next steps (55 per cent) and the ability to summarise meeting outcomes (56 per cent) are often cited as problematic. Since February 2020, employees have been involved in three times as many Teams meetings and calls per week (192 per cent) (a statistic clearly correlated to the pandemic). The data clearly indicates the need and desire for better meeting practices, both presently and in the future. Currently, only one in three people (35 per cent) believe that they would be missed in most of their meetings. However, there is a real fear of missing out on important information. When asked what makes meetings worthwhile, the top motivation for employees is receiving information that helps them perform their job better, ranking higher than giving feedback, making decisions, or advancing their career. With the potential aid of AI, meetings can become digital artefacts that allow engagement and interaction at the most convenient time and in the preferred format, whether synchronously or asynchronously.

Bartleby's Law suggests that 80 per cent of the time spent in meetings is wasted for 80 per cent of the people in attendance. A study conducted in 2017 by Harvard Business School professor Leslie Perlow (Perlow et al. 2017) provides further

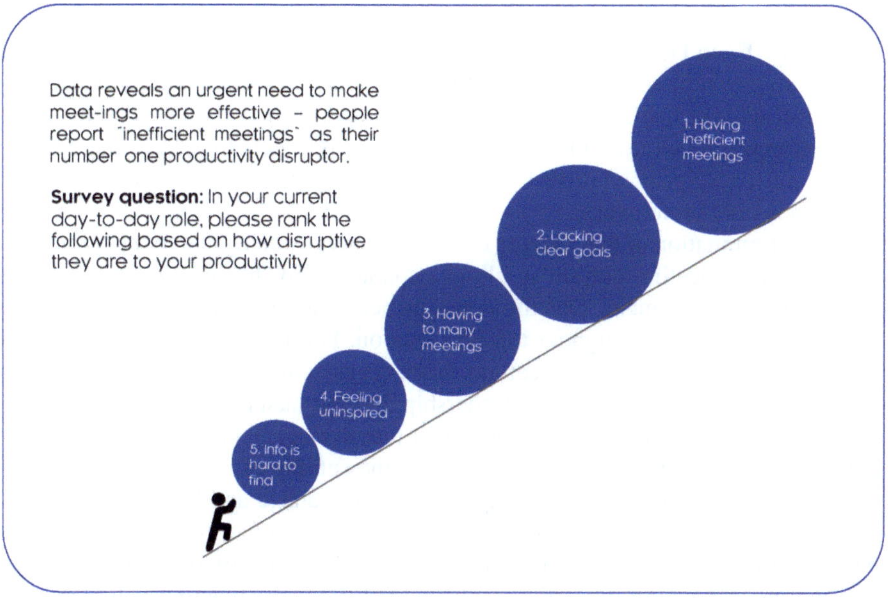

Fig. 6.6 Top five obstacles to productivity. Source: https://www.microsoft.com/en-us/worklab/work-trend-index/will-ai-fix-work

evidence to support this notion, as 71 per cent of senior executives expressed the view that meetings are unproductive and inefficient. Considering these findings, along with the fact that the average person dedicates between 35 per cent and 50 per cent of their time to meetings and is experiencing Zoom fatigue, putting an end to the excessive number of meetings presents a straightforward solution to freeing up people's time (Bloom et al. 2022).

6.8 Challenge: The Meeting Culture at the Workplace Is Presently Habitual Anarchistic

Few organisations and managers consider themselves to be anarchistic, but when it comes to meetings and the organisational meeting culture at the workplace, most behave that way. According to Think Tank "Tomorrow's Meetings", less than 10 per cent of leaders take overall strategic responsibility for productivity and efficiency in the internal meeting culture (Sneppen 2018). It is paradoxical that leaders do not take leadership of the meeting culture and meeting factory when meetings are important but often perceived as a waste of time by the participants.

Meetings are largely determined by the existing ingrained organisational culture and the individual leader's approach to and accumulated experience with meetings. Meetings are reduced to an individual management tool and to control the priorities of the individual meeting leader. Referring to the industrial society's assembly line, this is equivalent to gathering all employees and managers in a building and giving them the task of designing and leading their individual part of the production line. This decentralised approach to the factory and production line had not produced many Ford T's in Detroit in the early nineteenth century. Where the workplace has been relatively centrally organised, the meeting and collaboration culture has been decentralised and habitually anarchistic in its approach. Very few organisations have enforced guidelines for the meeting culture. It is mainly the individual meeting owner and participant who determines the meeting culture, based on their own experiences and preferences.

The determination of the meeting culture is generally delegated to the immediate manager. The meeting culture is closely connected to the individual manager's approach to management, and the consequence is a large difference in meeting quantity and quality throughout the organisation. Is this the optimal approach for creating value from the many meetings in the organisation? One plausible explanation for this paradox may be that leadership and top management are particularly heavy consumers of meetings, to the extent that management is synonymous with meetings, and meetings essentially constitute the entirety of their work during normal working hours (Fig. 6.7). Management often manage and lead through meetings, using them as key milestones. It is important to recognise that different groups have varying levels of access to resources that facilitate meetings. As a result, their perceptions of meeting dynamics, realities, and the corresponding value creation can differ significantly.

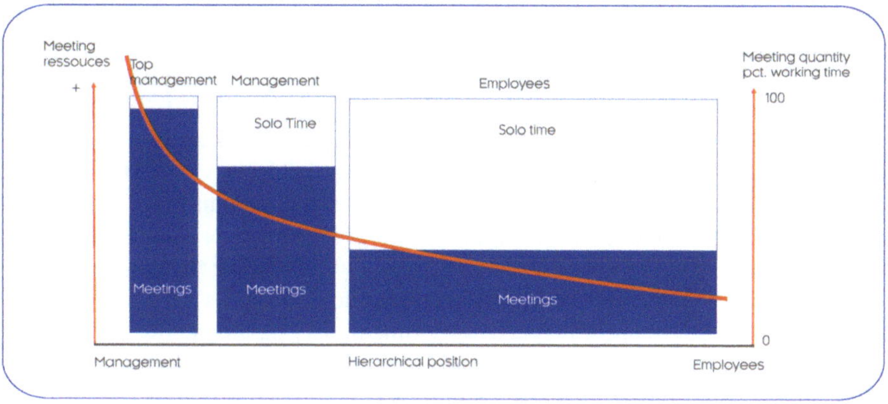

Fig. 6.7 Managers perform management in countless meetings. Employees mainly perform work outside of meetings

As a result, solo work and deep work are increasingly relegated to work outside normal working hours. Why are the meeting culture and meetings that take up almost half of knowledge workers' working time left to be anarchistic? Habitual meeting culture can be an excellent baseline for the individual, but not for the organisation. Is it time to reconsider how we meet and interact in the workplace with the introduction of the hybrid workplace?

An average of 30–40 per cent of meeting time is perceived as fully or partly wasted time that could be better spent solving other work tasks (depending on multiple factors and region). With approximately one-third of the participants describing meetings as an ineffective use of time, the results suggest that many employees are invited to meetings with little personal relevance. Additionally, a significant number of meeting organisers fail to apply essential meeting design practices, contributing to a lack of productivity and engagement during these sessions (Gelmer et al. 2012). In other words, office workers on an average feel that they "lose" approximately one working day every week due to "bad" meetings, or approximately equivalent to 30 perceived lost working days each year. It's no wonder that meetings are often associated with wasted time and are therefore often viewed and framed negatively (Lederne 2017). At the same time, there is a significant positive correlation between the number of meetings attended and daily fatigue, as well as perceived workload. In other words, the more meetings employees attend, the greater their feelings of fatigue and increased workload (Luong et al. 2005).

In 2017, former TV host Charlie Rose asked Bill Gates what the most valuable thing he had learned from his friendship with Warren Buffett was (Forbes 2020). The answer was simple: it wasn't about how to invest money, but how to invest your time. Time is valuable, and as Warren Buffett asserts, he can buy almost anything except time. Time is the most valuable thing we have. In the think tank "Tomorrow's Meetings (Sneppen 2018), the academic participants emphasised early in the process that meetings are ultimately evaluated based on time. The organisation purchases our time, and in turn, we invest our time in work (and meetings). The requirement is that we allocate time effectively for the benefit of the business or organisation. The analogy drawn is that as humans, we have approximately 3 billion heartbeats (unlike most other mammals that have only 1 billion). Therefore, we must consider how we utilise these valuable and irreplaceable heartbeats. The worst thing we can do is squander heartbeats on something that lacks value. This principle applies not only to individuals, but also to businesses and organisations when creating processes and holding meetings that fail to generate value. The researchers in the think tank expressed their nightmare scenario as expending time and heartbeats on something they deem worthless. (As passionate and successful scientists, they enjoy the privileges of spending their work time mostly passionately.)

Once again, we can see that the challenges within the organisation, the workplace model, the culture, meeting culture, and collaboration culture are closely interconnected, and by addressing one, other factors will be involved and affected. As we delve further into this publication, it becomes apparent that the meeting culture, meetings, and collaboration culture are fundamentally influenced by the tension between the heteronomous and autonomous approaches to the workplace model and organisational culture. The fundamental megatrend towards increasingly individualistic behaviour is, in a way, conflicting with the need for community in the expandingly liberated workplace model of knowledge workers.

6.9 Aligning the Meeting Culture and the Hybrid Workplace

As workplaces transition from primarily in-person, linear, synchronous, and symmetrical interactions and collaborations in the office to more non-linear, asynchronous, and asymmetric collaborations, changes in meetings are being observed. Hybrid or purely digital meetings are naturally shorter and require better planning and control. Essentially, digital and hybrid meetings expose meeting culture and overall improve the quality of all meetings. The digital meeting culture and behaviour are impacting traditional in-person meetings.

Overall, there is a decline (to varying degrees depending on the organisation) in repetitive meetings. (Once upon a time, they were the cornerstone of every office worker's routine workweek.) Meetings are becoming shorter, more aligned with work tasks, with fewer participants and a stronger focus on teamwork. The digital development will concurrently provide access to a significant and explosive amount of automatically generated data about meetings, interactions, and meeting culture within each organisation. This will include data at the individual, group, and organisational levels. The collection and access to data will have implications for meetings before, during, and after their occurrence.

In the future, meetings and meeting culture are anticipated to be fundamentally transparently and increasingly be held accountable for two cost-benefit questions: did the meeting create value for the individual participant, and did the meeting create value for the team and/or organisation? This will be achieved through visibility and immediate assistance through artificial intelligence and feedback, as well as passively through the awareness that behaviour and actions are being translated into shared data. The full extent of these changes is not yet fully understood, but one significant factor could be that meetings are increasingly intentional and more focused since participants are no longer in the same physical location or timeframe as in the "old" office days. Therefore, there is a shift from default meeting planning to considering the necessity and benefits of a planned meeting. It's one thing to gather four colleagues for a Teams meeting, but it's another task to call in participants for an in-person meeting in the office. The hybrid workplace model challenges the traditional management-by-meetings approach, and management must consciously or unconsciously contemplate, evaluate, and redesign the meeting culture to adapt to the new ways of working with a distributed workforce. These changes regarded in isolation contribute to more action-oriented, productive, and effective meetings and collaborations as the hybrid workplace model is unfolded and developed.

On the contrary, in the short to medium term, we can expect meetings and interactions to undergo rising complexity, with non-linear, asynchronous, and asymmetric working and interactions, resulting in decreased meeting productivity and efficiency. In the long run we anticipate that with the development of a structured and more mature hybrid workplace model, with more balanced approaches to work task execution, access to valid data, and incorporation of artificial intelligence, there will be a significant improvement in meeting culture.

References

(Bartleby, Economist 2018) Tortured by meetings https://www.economist.com/business/2018/06/30/tortured-by-meetings

(Bernstein and Turban 2018) The impact of the 'open' workspace on human collaboration https://royalsocietypublishing.org/doi/10.1098/rstb.2017.0239

(Bloom, Han and Liang 2022) How Hybrid Working From Home Works Out https://www.nber.org/papers/w30292

(Braun et al. 2019) Braun, S., Hernandez Bark, A.S., Kirchner, A., Stegmann, S., & van Dick, R. (2019). Emails From the Boss - Curse or Blessing? Relations Between Communication Channels, Leader Evaluation, and Employees' Attitudes. *International Journal of Business Communication, 56*, 50–81. https://www.semanticscholar.org/paper/Emails-From-the-Boss-Curse-or-Blessing-Relations-Braun-Bark/cdce555eaae91dfd9caac9261cbeff137a574261

(Brown, Gray, McHardy, and Taylor, 2025) Employee trust and workplace performance https://www.sciencedirect.com/science/article/pii/S0167268115001365

(Chai and Freeman 2029) Temporary colocation and collaborative discovery: Who confers at conferences https://onlinelibrary.wiley.com/doi/full/10.1002/smj.3062

(Constantinedes, et al 2022) The Future of Hybrid Meetings https://dl.acm.org/doi/abs/10.1145/3533406.3533415

(Crane 2015) Knowledge and Discourse Matters: Relocating Knowledge Management's Sphere of Interest onto Language https://www.wiley.com/en-us/Knowledge+and+Discourse+Matters%3A+Relocating+Knowledge+Management's+Sphere+of+Interest+onto+Language-p-9781119079316

(Cross, Rebele and Grant 2016) HBR Collaborative Overload https://hbr.org/2016/01/collaborative-overload

(Edmondson 2009) Psychological Safety and Learning Behavior in Work Teams https://web.mit.edu/curhan/www/docs/Articles/15341_Readings/Group_Performance/Edmondson%20Psychological%20safety.pdf

(Edmondson and Lei 2014) Psychological Safety: The History, Renaissance, and Future of an Interpersonal Construct https://www.annualreviews.org/content/journals/10.1146/annurev-orgpsych-031413-091305

(Forbes 2020) The Most Important Lesson He Learned From 10,649 Days Of Warren Buffett's Friendship https://www.forbes.com/sites/carminegallo/2020/08/30/bill-gates-the-most-important-lesson-he-learned-from-10649-days-of-warren-buffetts-friendship/

(Gelmer, et al 2012) Meetings at work: Perceived effectiveness and recommended improvement https://www.sciencedirect.com/science/article/abs/pii/S0148296315000879

(Gibbs, Mengel and Siemroth 2021) Gibbs, M., Mengel, F. & Siemroth, C. Work from home and productivity: Evidence from personnel and analytics data on information technology professionals. *J. Political Econ. Microecon. 1*(1), 7–41 (2023).https://www.researchgate.net/publication/351446108_Work_from_Home_Productivity_Evidence_from_Personnel_Analytics_Data_on_IT_Professionals

(Glaveski 2021) HBR Remote Work Should Be Mostly Asynchronous https://hbr.org/2021/12/remote-work-should-be-mostly-asynchronous

(Granovetter 1973) American Journal of Sociology, The Strength of Weak Ties. https://snap.stanford.edu/class/cs224w-readings/granovetter73weakties.pdf

(Håkansson et al., 2020) Håkansson Lindqvist M, Mozelius P, Sundgren M, Jaldemark J, Öhman P. (2020). Building a network for collaborative support in professional development In: de Laat M, Ryberg T, Bonderup Dohn N, Børsen Hansen S, Hansen JJ (Eds.), Proceedings of the 12th International Conference on Networked Learning. Vol. 12. Aalborg university. 2020; pp. 108–111 https://journals.aau.dk/index.php/nlc/article/view/8643

(Hughes, et al., 2018) Innovative Behaviour, Trust and Perceived Workplace Performance https://onlinelibrary.wiley.com/doi/abs/10.1111/1467-8551.12305

(Lederne 2017) Møder og Mødekultur

(Luong et al 2005) *Meetings and More Meetings: The Relationship Between Meeting Load and the Daily Well-Being of Employees.* https://psycnet.apa.org/buy/2005-02475-005

(Lyman 2003) Building trust in the workplace http://thepeoplegroup.com/wp-content/uploads/2008/04/article-building-trust-in-the-workplace.pdf

(Microsoft 2023) Will AI Fix Work? https://www.microsoft.com/en-us/worklab/work-trend-index/will-ai-fix-work

(Microsoft 2024) 2024 Work Trend Index Annual Report https://www.microsoft.com/en-us/worklab/work-trend-index/ai-at-work-is-here-now-comes-the-hard-part

(Microsoft Work Trend Index 2022) https://www.microsoft.com/en-us/worklab/work-trend-index/great-expectations-making-hybrid-work-work

(Newman et al. 2017) Psychological safety: A systematic review of the literature https://www.sciencedirect.com/science/article/abs/pii/S1053482217300013

(Ozyllmaz, Erdogan, Karaeminogullari 2017) Trust in organization as a moderator of the relationship between self-efficacy and workplace outcomes: A social cognitive theory-based examination https://bpspsychub.onlinelibrary.wiley.com/doi/abs/10.1111/joop.12189

(Perlow, Hadley and Eun 2017) Stop the Meeting Madness https://hbr.org/2017/07/stop-the-meeting-madness

(Rozovsky 2015) Google's Project Aristotle https://psychsafety.co.uk/googles-project-aristotle/

(Sneppen 2018) Morgendagens møder 2017–2019 https://www.linkedin.com/company/morgendagensmoeder/?viewAsMember=true

(Stray and Moe 2020) Understanding coordination in global software engineering: A mixed-methods study on the use of meetings and Slack https://www.sciencedirect.com/science/article/pii/S0164121220301564

(Thomsen 2022) På skærmen er du nødt til at tro på, at du har folk med dig« | Lederstof 02.05.2022 https://www.lederstof.dk/paa-skaermen-er-du-noedt-til-at-tro-paa-at-du-har-folk-med-dig

(Tolliver and Sass 2024) HBR June 2024 Hybrid Work Has Changed Meetings Forever https://hbr.org/2024/06/hybrid-work-has-changed-meetings-forever
(Whillans et al. 2022) Results from a pre-registered experiment https://drive.google.com/file/d/1uQaxpErEWkZQucqs7BCMT6cIyG094oeM/view
(Wu, Waber, Aral, Brynjolfsson, and Pentland, 2008) Mining Face-to-Face Interaction Networks using Sociometric Badges: Predicting Productivity in an IT Configuration Task https://papers.ssrn.com/sol3/papers.cfm?abstract_id=1130251

Part II

Office Workplace Trends and Future Developments

Hybrid Office Workplace Evolution or Revolution?

7

Abstract

Workplace models have evolved significantly over the years, shaped by shifts in technology, human behaviour, and organisational needs. The digital age has transformed traditional office setups, introducing flexibility and decentralisation into the professional environment. While early models, influenced by industrial processes, focused on efficiency through rigid structures, modern workplaces prioritise adaptability and employee-centric designs. The rise of hybrid working, propelled by advances in technology, signals a departure from the conventional 9–5 model. Employees now demand greater flexibility in where and how they work, challenging organisations to rethink their approach. This transformation, however, is not without challenges. Many companies have responded with temporary fixes rather than a strategic overhaul, risking future competitiveness. As workplaces continue to evolve, they must align with the shifting needs of the workforce, prioritising well-being, collaboration, and productivity. Ultimately, the future of work will depend on organisations' ability to embrace change and reimagine the workplace as a dynamic, evolving environment.

7.1 The Eternal Quest for the Optimal Office Workplace Model

Workplace models are continually evolving in response to changes in knowledge, tools, technologies, product requirements, and human behaviour (Fig. 7.1). These changes lead to adaptations, improvements, and the development of new models (production models). This dynamic process has always been the norm and will continue to shape the future of work.

Believing that the digital possibilities and changes in employee behaviour will have limited effects on the office or management is an example of static, first-order

C. Sneppen, *The Future (R)Evolution of the Office Workspace*, Future of Business and Finance, https://doi.org/10.1007/978-3-031-85229-9_7

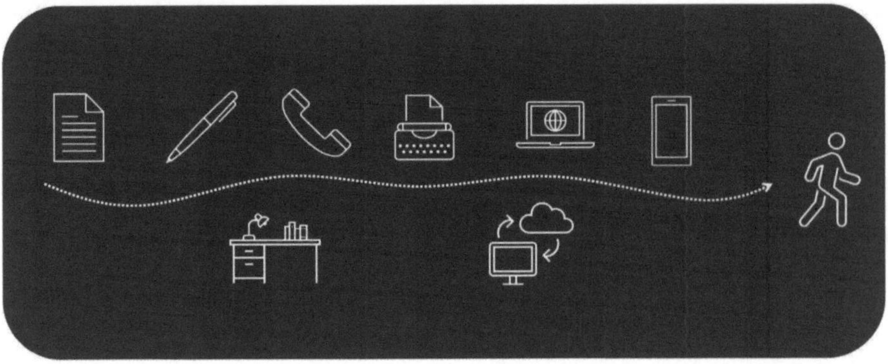

Fig. 7.1 Technology is over time work-life and workplace defining

thinking. First-order thinking assumes that when one thing changes, everything else will largely remain the same. This approach may simplify decision-making and navigation, but it does not accurately reflect the reality of the profound shifts currently taking place in the workplace of knowledge workers. The changes are immense and transformative, impacting every aspect of how we work and interact in the professional sphere.

Before industrialisation, work retained a certain degree of flexibility, allowing individuals to structure their tasks around daily life. However, the rise of industrialisation fundamentally challenged traditional conceptions of work behaviour (Zuboff 1982). The employer's goal to harness the steam engine as a centralised power source, combined with the imperative to closely supervise workers and accelerate production, led to increased collectivisation and synchronisation in the workplace. This shift not only restricted personal autonomy but also imposed new structures and rhythms that aligned with the demands of mechanised production, profoundly altering the relationship between workers and their labour. A lot has happened since the beginning of the 1900s when the industrial society logic unfolded with the introduction of scientific management (Taylor 1911, Weber 1920): a system where individual work was broken down into specific basic tasks and distributed among specialised job functions where each employee performed a set of actions. This model was introduced in the office and reflected the assembly line's focus and approach to efficient value creation. The repetitive specialised approach, combined with the subsequent widespread understanding and acceptance that bureaucracy was the most effective way to run large organisations, formed the basis for how the workplace model and office have evolved up until the pandemic hit the world in 2020.

In *The City of Tomorrow and Its Planning*, Le Corbusier writes, "The city that can achieve speed will achieve success. Work today is more intense and conducted at a faster pace. The faster the intercommunication can be established, the more efficiently business will be carried out. Therefore, it is likely that the working day in skyscrapers will be shorter … the workday may end shortly after noon. The city will empty as if taking a deep breath" (Le Corbusier 1920). In other words, Le Corbusier

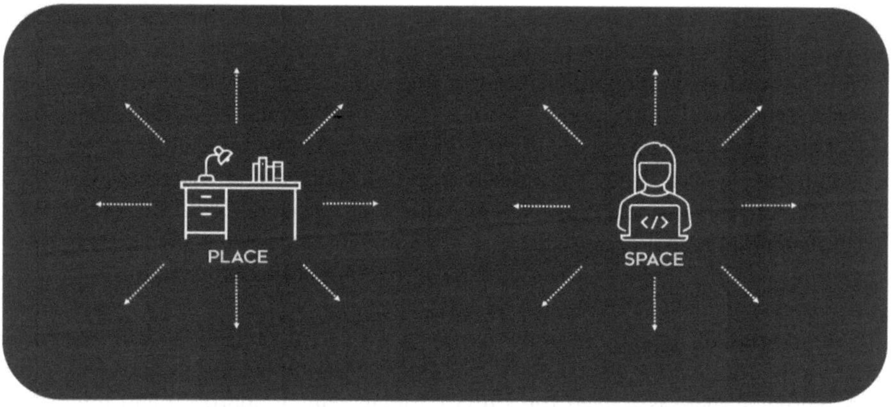

Fig. 7.2 The desk has long been replaced by the computer as the primary work tool for office employees

predicted that once information can flow faster, urban offices would be vacant for half of the time. He was eventually correct, but not in the way he intended.

It is an evolution of the workplace defined by a network approach, where the organisation's needs increasingly must be balanced with the needs of knowledge workers. Behavioural economics has shaped a workplace model where the employee increasingly is at the centre. It is a workplace model where the office adapts to the employee and not just the other way around. The modern office workplace is no longer defined by a desk but rather by our digital screens. This was predicted by Phillip Stone and Robert Luchetti in an article in *HBR* in 1985 with "your office is where you are" (Stones and Luchetti 1985). The computer has presently become a priority over the desk, as we are all busy and constantly managing our time: from checking our phones in the morning to falling asleep with them at night. In this digital reality, there is a constant demand for our attention, and we must carefully consider how we spend our time. Although there are benefits to meeting in the office, the daily commute may not always be the best use of time. Often, our habits, expectations, and outdated requirements govern our decisions, rather than what adds the most value to our work and organisation.

The desk was—and is—designed mainly for writing (now on a personal computer). As technology has progressed, our working habits have also evolved, allowing us to work from various devices like mobile phones, iPads, or laptops (Fig. 7.2). This shift in digital development and employee behaviour has already seen significant progress, but we anticipate that this is just the beginning. The workplace is undergoing constant change and must be continuously adjusted and redesigned to keep pace with the ever-evolving digital landscape and the way we work. In the future, the optimal workplace model will be in a perpetual beta development version state. Much like the digital desktop on a computer, which receives ongoing updates and enhancements to boost efficiency and productivity, the physical workplace will mirror this adaptability. It will constantly evolve and adapt to the changes in the overall ecosystem, accommodating the preferences and needs of employees.

This agile approach will ensure that the workplace remains relevant and effective in supporting the ever-changing demands of the modern workforce. Our working reality has undergone a significant transformation with the advent of the digital age, yet our office workplace model has been slow to catch up. Over the years, many adaptations have been made to office workplaces, from individual cells to open and collaborative spaces, from fixed desks to hot-desking and activity-based layouts. However, these traditional office setups, which were once like customised factories, are no longer practical or optimal in our digital realm. Instead, a new working life is emerging, where employees have greater freedom and flexibility in terms of time, place, and space.

Yet, despite this evolution in the workplace, many organisations still attempt to address the future hybrid workplace model using traditional approaches and mindsets. Perhaps, there is a need for a revised management approach and mindset to adapt to the structural and systemic changes happening in our workplaces. Embracing flexibility and adopting innovative strategies will be essential for success in this new era of work.

The new reality and the initial response to the introduction of the hybrid workplace model resulted in many organisations adopting a band-aid approach to hybrid work (P. Kirschner 2023). They hastily implemented minimum viable tools and behaviours to recreate the atmosphere of the pre-pandemic workplace, attempting to replicate a not-quite-perfect work culture and workplace that was stuck in outdated work processes. In a midterm perspective organisations are now at a crossroads, and in many cases, it is left to individual employees to undertake the challenging task of actually rewiring how employees collaborate, how teams and leaders communicate, and how business processes are executed and visualised.

Everyone may have an opinion, but not all opinions are based on valid knowledge and insights that embrace the hybrid workplace of tomorrow. Most are in fact based on habitual experience and preferences. To create a successful and effective workplace model, we must rely on evidence-based insights, data-driven decisions, future anticipated trend implications, and an open-minded approach that considers the diverse needs and preferences of the workforce. By embracing the evolving nature of the workplace and staying informed about the latest trends and developments, organisations can navigate the path towards a more productive, efficient, and employee-centric future.

7.2 Is It Necessary to Alter the Workplace Model?

Incremental or radical change of the workplace? Revolution or evolution of the workplace? (hence the title of the book). Why change and prioritise a change of the workplace model when it continues to work and has proven its worth over the past several decades? Can't organisations just continue to make minor evolutionary adjustments and thus build slowly on the existing workplace model foundation?

The anecdotic "in the good old days" approach to the pre-pandemic office workplace is in reality just that, namely anecdotic. The previous and pre-pandemic prevalent office workplace model wasn't flawless, in fact far from it (Medium 2023). The culprit behind the open-plan office is Frank Lloyd Wright, at least according to those who curse open-plan offices and hold a grudge against the man who allegedly introduced the concept (Wedel 2019). This happened in the Larkin Building in New York in 1904, where owner and architect Frank Lloyd Wright removed walls and eliminated private offices to accommodate the entire workforce in a single room, promoting open communication and collaboration among employees. The aim was to foster a more egalitarian environment and provide employees with a sense of what he called a "meeting place for the family". The concept gained significant popularity in the USA during the 1960s, inspired by the German Bürolandschaft approach, which involved grouping employees into small teams in an open landscape to ensure efficient workflow. The European development followed suit, and over the past decades, open office layouts have become the standard, aiming to support contemporary work processes where knowledge sharing and feedback are key elements. The flaws of the "old" open workplace model centred around the analogue office are numerous and include (Otterbring 2019) the following.

Commuting The daily commute to and from work was often cited as one of the most stressful and time-consuming parts of the workday. Long commutes in heavy traffic or crowded public transportation could lead to frustration, anxiety, and a loss of valuable time. Another renowned study by Nobel Prize winner Daniel Kahneman revealed that commuting is the most disliked activity of the day, even more so than work itself (Kahneman et al. 2004). This insight helps explain why the average employee places such high value on working from home—it not only saves hours of unpleasant weekly commuting but also offers the flexibility to live further from the workplace.

Office Politics Workplace politics, such as gossip, favouritism, and power struggles, can create a negative work environment and cause stress and tension among employees. Many workers feel that office politics can be a major source of distraction and can hinder productivity.

Distractions In an open-plan office, it can be difficult to concentrate due to noise, interruptions, and distractions from colleagues. Many workers reported that they struggled to stay focused on their work, particularly when they were trying to complete complex or challenging tasks.

Lack of Flexibility For many workers, the traditional 9–5 office schedule doesn't provide enough flexibility to balance work and personal life responsibilities. Employees with caregiving responsibilities, for example, may find it difficult to work fixed hours and may need more flexibility to manage their schedules.

Lack of Autonomy Some workers feel that they have limited control over their work and are unable to make decisions independently. This can lead to feelings of disengagement and dissatisfaction, particularly among those who value autonomy and independence in their work.

Predominately Linear Work Many workers had to cope with the demanding schedule of linear work in the office from 9 to 5, while also trying to fulfil non-linear and asynchronous tasks at home. This situation led to heightened stress and decreased well-being. It was referred to by some as the work-life blender.

Another study found an increased use of asynchronous communication, such as email, among employees in open-plan offices. Specifically, the study found that employees in open-plan offices spent 73 per cent less time engaging in face-to-face interactions, while email and messaging usage increased by over 67 per cent (Bernstein 2018). Based on surveys conducted among 2000 knowledge workers in the USA and UK, a commercial report reveals that online workers are exhibiting behaviour reminiscent of traditional cubicle warriors from the past (Stillman 2022). The report laments missed opportunities during the pandemic-induced workplace transformations. "The dramatic workplace shifts of the pandemic gave organisations a once-in-a-lifetime opportunity to reshape how we work forever. We could have restructured work to be asynchronous, allowing us to build work around our lives, but we failed. Now, our research shows we're falling back into old habits—ones that should have been cast aside when we had the chance". In practical terms, this behaviour manifests as remote workers participating in videoconferencing meetings; they know to be unproductive, strategically responding to emails at specific times, or engaging in other forms of ostentatious online presence to give the impression that they are working long and hard enough. Research indicates that this form of digital presenteeism consumes an average of 67 min per day for remote workers. This represents a significant amount of time wasted on what the report terms "productivity theatre" and the fear of missing out (FOMO) (Jin et al. 2024). A similar phenomenon in the office is physical presenteeism, where employees are present but not fully productive, often due to illness, burnout, or disengagement. Absenteeism, by contrast, is simply not showing up without a valid reason. "Ghost presenteeism" is an even more degenerate form, where employees swipe in but are not truly working—merely performing the appearance of productivity. While absenteeism is easier to measure, presenteeism in all its forms is more subtle and damaging.

Focusing on the physical layout of the office and the possibility for each individual employee to feel like themselves, there is a direct correlation between stress and the lack of opportunity to be oneself (as opposed to pretending and adopting behaviour that is not in line with how the employee perceives themselves) (Ballisager 2023). The feeling of psychological safety is ensured in the relationship with colleagues and can be influenced through the design of the office. While some employees feel secure in an open office environment, others feel the opposite in a more isolated location in the office. Employees are not identical, and, in the future, they will need to be accommodated individually. Alternatively, the organisation should target the workplace model to a defined and segmented target group of potential employees who specifically demand the model that the organisation has established. Do your colleagues feel like themselves at work? The short and most likely answer is that is not all bad to change for an updated workplace model. The introduction of the hybrid workplace model is partially a response to the above employee objections towards the "old" model. All models have a flip side, and we are currently encountering and learning about the challenges of the hybrid workplace.

7.3 Challenge: The Inept Post-industrial Office and Mice

Before delving into the defining trends driving the hybrid workplace revolution in the next chapter, it is worth asking this: what exactly went wrong with the post-industrial office? To unravel this question, one might draw inspiration from an unexpected source—a renowned half-century-old experiment involving mice. In the 1960s and early 1970s, behavioural researcher John B. Calhoun conducted an experiment famously known as the "Universe 25" study—a study that continues to spark debate (Calhoun 1973). This experiment simulated utopian conditions for mice, including abundant food, water, and shelter. However, the population eventually succumbed to social collapse, driven by overpopulation, social stratification, and behavioural aberrations. Parallels between the outcomes of this experiment and the dynamics of the post-industrial office are striking. In Calhoun's experiment, some mice became "beautiful"—isolated, self-serving, and disengaged—while others exhibited asocial or aggressive behaviours. Similarly, the post-industrial office often fosters environments that impede productivity, creativity, and well-being due to systemic and structural flaws. Here are two key manifestations:

1. Isolated Strongholds of Power: In both mice and humans, hierarchical structures can breed isolation. In many traditional offices, strong employees or leaders isolate themselves in defended "strongholds", such as executive offices that are inaccessible to the broader workforce. Gatekeepers and rigid hierarchies further amplify this divide, stifling collaboration and the free flow of ideas.
2. Asocial Behaviour in Crowded Spaces: Overcrowding—whether physical or psychological—inevitably leads to dysfunction. In the workplace, this manifests as:
   - **Office Theatre:** The performative culture of endless presentations and appearances without substantive contribution.
   - **Pretend Collaboration:** Forced teamwork that lacks genuine cooperation or trust.
   - **Commute Overload:** The mental and physical toll of congested commutes, draining employee energy before the workday begins.
   - **Meeting Fatigue:** An overabundance of poorly structured meetings that erode focus and productivity.
   - **Proximity Isolation:** Ironically, even colleagues sitting in close proximity may fail to connect meaningfully due to asynchronous workflows and over-reliance on digital communication tools.

7.4 Transforming the Basic Office into a Competitive Advantage Workplace Model

The factors that define a competitive office workplace model are evolving, and organisations that delay the development of a hybrid workplace model risk losing their competitive edge. By putting off necessary changes, these organisations open themselves up to a future where workplace transformation will not be a gradual and steady process, but rather a sudden and disruptive revolution. The choice before them is clear-cut: either embrace the hybrid workplace model and actively participate in shaping its development or face the inevitable demand for radical change.

From a futurist's perspective, the pace of present office workplace transformation is simply too rapid for organisations to remain passive. Taking proactive initiative is essential to stay ahead of the curve and ensure long-term competitiveness. The hybrid workplace is not just a passing trend but a fundamental shift in how work is done and experienced. Embracing this change will empower organisations to co-create a workplace that optimises productivity, employee satisfaction, and overall success. In contrast, those who hesitate risk being caught off guard and facing significant challenges in keeping up with the rapidly changing demands of the modern workforce and the future of work.

The office workplace has been traditionally viewed, and is largely still seen, as a static cost and instalment for organisations. Investments, developments, and changes are often approached with a strong emphasis on efficiency and a mindset of achieving "more for less". However, the future evolution of the workplace underscores the importance of not considering it merely as a marginal cost, especially in organisations where knowledge workers play a prominent role. Taking a holistic perspective and shifting the focus from mere efficiency and day-to-day operations to unlocking untapped productivity and value creation potential are essential. Instead of seeing the workplace as an expense, it could, and should, be recognised as a key investment in securing the organisation's objectives. The workplace plays a critical role in supporting and enabling the workforce, which, in turn, drives the organisation's success. Recognising the workplace's strategic significance will enable organisations to make more informed decisions and leverage the workplace as a powerful tool for achieving their objectives. Emphasising productivity and unrealised value creation potential shifts the workplace from being a mere cost centre to becoming a valuable asset in shaping the organisation's future competitive success. The office workplace has been continuously evolving since the widespread establishment of massive office buildings during the early nineteenth century's industrialisation. However, the digitisation of the workplace in the latter part of the twentieth century introduced a new dimension. This dimension was characterised by the advent of the Internet and later the cloud, providing employees with the flexibility to work, meet, and communicate from anywhere, whether in real time or asynchronously. The integration of digital technologies transformed the traditional office space into a dynamic and interconnected environment, blurring the boundaries between physical and virtual workspaces. Employees gained the ability to collaborate seamlessly with colleagues, clients, and partners, breaking free from the constraints of a fixed location. This digital transformation opened opportunities for remote work, enabling employees to engage in their tasks and responsibilities outside the traditional office setting. As a result, the workplace underwent a profound shift, embracing both physical and digital elements. This evolution continues to shape the modern office landscape, where employees can choose from a range of work settings, from traditional desks and meeting rooms to virtual platforms and online collaboration tools. The integration of digital technologies has revolutionised how work is conducted, fostering greater flexibility, efficiency, and connectivity for employees across various locations and time zones.

With the advent of the hybrid workplace, organisations are confronted with a significant paradigm shift in their approach to the workplace and the working life of knowledge workers. While the workplace still maintains a connection to the physical office, it is no longer solely dependent on it. The concept of the workplace has evolved from a mere physical location (where we physically reside) to a more abstract notion of a workspace (where we mentally operate). This transformation has shifted the focal point of the workplace from the traditional office to the individual employee. It is now the employee's mental space that takes precedence over the physical bricks and mortar. In this new reality, the workplace is no longer confined to static real estate records but rather revolves around the dynamic nature of the employee's presence. It recognises that the true essence of work lies in the thoughts, ideas, and contributions of the individual, rather than just their physical presence at a particular location. As a result, organisations are reimagining the workplace as a more flexible, adaptable, and inclusive environment. The hybrid workplace model accommodates the diverse needs and preferences of employees, allowing them to seamlessly transition between physical and digital workspaces. The focus is on empowering employees to be productive and innovative, regardless of their physical location, and fostering a work culture that prioritises mental engagement and well-being. By embracing this shift from a rigid, location-centric office to a more dynamic, employee-centric workspace, organisations can unlock the full potential of their workforce and drive greater collaboration, creativity, and efficiency in the modern work landscape.

The absence of continuous, up-to-date changes in the workplace can significantly impact the working lives of knowledge employees. This stagnation may result in the emergence of various concepts and trends that mirror employees' dissatisfaction and frustrations, as they devise individualistic solutions to manage their work-life balance. Some of these concepts include Quite Quitting, where employees silently disengage from their work and organisation; Loud Quitting, where employees voice their grievances and reasons for leaving; Goblin Mode, where employees disengage from work while still physically present; Great Resignation, where there is a surge in employees leaving their jobs by the hordes; Great Reshuffle, where employees seek better opportunities and re-evaluate their career paths; Great Reset, a framework proposed by the World Economic Forum, that suggests a fundamental rethinking of global systems in the wake of COVID-19 (Schwab et al. 2020); Great Breakup, where employees demand more autonomy and control over their work-life balance; and Donut Effect, where there is a hollowing out of talent at various levels

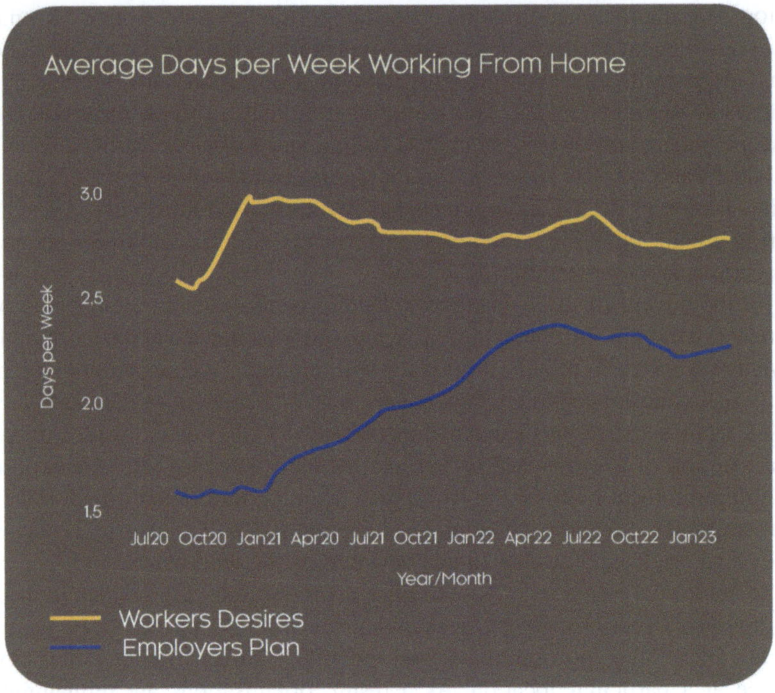

Fig. 7.3 Gap between how much employees want to work from home and employers plan. Source: Barrero, Jose Maria, Nicholas Bloom, and Steven J. Davis, 2021. "Why working from home will stick", National Bureau of Economic Research Working Paper 28,731 www.wfhresearch.com

within the organisation (Akan et al. 2024). Coffee Badging, or Badge Pirating, refers to the practice of briefly going into the office to "show face"—perhaps having coffee with colleagues or attending a meeting—before leaving to work remotely (e.g. *Wall Street Journal* 2023). These concepts and trends are likely to be replaced and supplemented by new ones as the workplace model fails to adapt to the changing needs and preferences of employees. As employees continue to seek more flexibility in their work arrangements, the gap between employers' and employees' expectations regarding remote work will likely decrease over time (Fig. 7.3).

The trend will move towards fulfilling employees' preferences for flexibility, as organisations recognise importance of accommodating their workforce to attract and retain talent. As a response to this development, another emerging workplace trend has been observed in Denmark with the introduction of discretionary or well-being days (BT 2024). Such initiatives, much like Henry Ford's original introduction of the five-day working week, are designed to attract and retain talent while simultaneously boosting engagement and well-being, thereby enhancing both productivity and efficiency. Most organisations strive to embrace ongoing changes and adopt a future-oriented workplace model that prioritises flexibility, employee well-being, and collaboration. In doing so, they can foster a more engaged and productive workforce, while building a positive work culture that aligns with the expectations of knowledge workers in an evolving world of work.

References

(Akan et al. 2024) https://wfhresearch.com/wp-content/uploads/2024/03/Americans-Now-Live-Farther-From-Their-Employers.pdf

(Ballisager 2023) Kandidat analysen 2023 https://ballisager.com/webinar-morten-ballisager-kandidatanalysen-2023

(Bernstein 2018) The impact of the 'open' workspace on human collaboration https://royalsociety-publishing.org/doi/10.1098/rstb.2017.0239

(BT 2024) Dansk gigant med tiltag: Giver sine ansatte 12 ekstra fridage om året

(Calhoun 1973) John B. Calhoun, Proceedings of the Royal Society of Medicine, Page 80–87, "Death Squared: The Explosive Growth and Demise of a Mouse Population,"

(Jin et al., 2024) Jin, W., Li, P., Ma, H. *et al.* The impact of communication software usage on work engagement in remote work: the mediating role of distraction and FOMO. *Curr Psychol* **43**, 23156–23177 (2024). https://doi.org/10.1007/s12144-024-06035-z

(Kahneman et al., 2004) A Survey Method for Characterizing Daily Life Experience: The Day Reconstruction Method https://www.science.org/doi/10.1126/science.1103572

(Le Corbusier 1920) The City of Tomorrow and Its Planning, In The City of Tomorrow and Its Planning, https://mitpress.mit.edu/9780262620178/the-city-of-tomorrow/

(Medium 2023) The Truth About the Office and Why Your People are Resisting Return https://medium.com/@mikeprzytula/the-truth-about-theoffice-and-why-your-people-are-resisting-return-f0fbf46a11ce

(Otterbring 2019) Storrumskontorer kan nedsætte arbejdsglæden https://bss.au.dk/aarhus-bss-nyheder/business-1/2019/storrumskontor-kan-nedsaette-arbejdsglaeden

(P. Kirschner 2023) blog/phil-kirschner-crafting-the-future-of-work-at-mckinseyco

(Schwab et al., 2020) Schwab, Klaus and Therry Malleret: Covid-19: The Great Reset. Geneva: Future Forum Publishing, 2020 https://www.weforum.org/stories/2020/07/covid-19-the-great-reset/

(Stillman 2022) INC Remote Workers Are Wasting More Than an Hour a Day on Productivity Theater https://www.inc.com/jessica-stillman/productivity-asynchronous-remote-work.html https://language.work/research/killing-time-at-work/

(Stones and Luchetti 1985) HBR "The office is where you are" https://dl.acm.org/doi/10.5555/5080.5081

(Taylor 1911) Taylor Frederick. The Principles of Scientific Management. New York: Harper 1911

(*Wall Street Journal*, 2023) Bosses Aren't Just Tracking When You Show Up to the Office but How Long You Stay https://www.wsj.com/lifestyle/careers/attention-office-resisters-the-boss-is-counting-badge-swipes-5fa37ff7

(Weber 1920), The Theory of Social and Economic Organisations

(Wedel 2019) Storrumskontorer kan nedsætte arbejdsglæden https://bss.au.dk/aarhus-bss-nyheder/business-1/2019/storrumskontor-kan-nedsaette-arbejdsglaeden

(Zuboff 1982) New worlds of computer-mediated work. https://hbr.org/1982/09/new-worlds-of-computer-mediated-work (Harvard Business Review)

8 Future Hybrid Workplace Trends and Dynamics

Abstract

The future of work, particularly for knowledge workers, hinges on the balance between in-office and remote work. Simplistically viewed, the development of workplace distribution can take on various speeds and outcomes, represented as a metaphorical "distribution" between office- and home-based work. This concept suggests a movement towards either a stable, gradual change in workplace dynamics or a more radical shift towards digital and remote work environments. In one scenario, the physical workplace undergoes gradual changes, maintaining its relevance while integrating more digital elements. This scenario anticipates that physical workspaces will continue to exist but will evolve to focus on collaboration, well-being, and productivity in a more digitised environment.

Alternatively, a more kinetic development suggests that workplaces which successfully integrate digital advancements with physical spaces will thrive. Here, the physical workplace might shrink in size but gain importance in complementing digital workspaces, creating a balanced hybrid model. In the most radical scenario, the digital workplace dominates, leaving physical offices largely redundant. This shift, accelerated by technological advancements and societal changes, positions remote work as the primary mode, with physical spaces serving niche purposes.

Overall, the future workplace model will be shaped by megatrends like digitalisation, societal norms, and individualisation, requiring organisations to navigate and balance both digital and analogue processes to build resilient and adaptable hybrid office workplaces.

C. Sneppen, *The Future (R)Evolution of the Office Workspace*, Future of Business and Finance, https://doi.org/10.1007/978-3-031-85229-9_8

8.1 Three Future Distributions Between the Office and Remote Work (Knowledge Workers)

If we consider the development simplistically and from the perspective of where office work will be conducted in the future, whether in-office or remote, we can see various speeds of development and possible outcomes. In the model we use the term "distribution" as a metaphor for the future balance of working at the office and home (distance). There is thus a movement (the slope of the line) that indicates how fast the development is going, and a plateau that indicates where the distribution balance lies (Fig. 8.1).

This is inherently a simplistic way of portraying future developments, as we have hardly seen the end of new technologies and changed behaviour patterns that, when they occur, will again, cause imbalances. Distribution will vary according to function, organisation, individual preferences, personal profile, management, market, culture, etc. Building on this simplistic approach—yet overall likely development—I have outlined three potential future scenarios for the distribution between office-based and remote work.

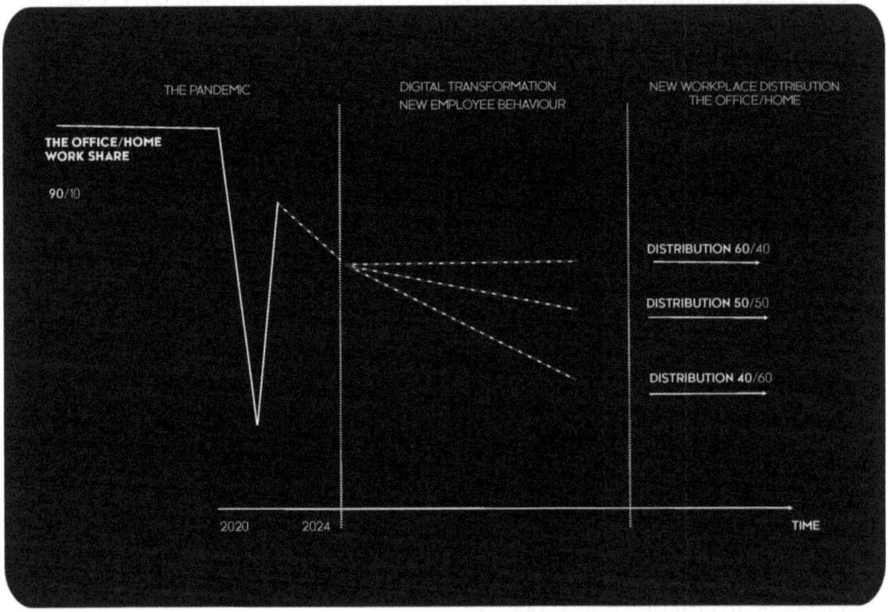

Fig. 8.1 Three future projected distributions between the office and remote work for knowledge workers

Resilient Physical Office Workplace (stabilised development): For the physical workplace, this scenario means that there will only be gradual changes in the relationship between digital and analogue working life. Few physical workplaces are reduced, but also developed and adapted. However, the need for interior design, location, and space has changed, at the same time as the workplace has become increasingly digitised. The limitation in productivity increases has meant that development has proceeded gradually. At the same time, investments have been made in models for physical workplaces, which are more collaborative and give employees more well-being and cooperation. Organisations have managed to make the physical more "physical", react proactively to developments and adapt. The COVID-19 crisis has "cleaned" out less well-functioning concepts, developed new concepts, and there is renewed optimism around the physical as an attractive force for efficient and productive working life.

Kinetic Conditions for Office Workplace (projected development): The workplace winners have been those who have seized the opportunities in digital development and combined and integrated it with the physical workplace. Part of the success is based on being able to constantly adapt the layout and adjustment of the physical workplace based on digitalisation and changed employee behaviour. The decrease in volume of the physical workplace has been significant, but it has become complimentary, balanced, and equal to the digital workplace. The physical workplace has been consolidated and further polarised. This means that there are now many different models for workplace design which are uniquely adapted to the individual organisation. The digital workplace has become even more value-creating, which has given further impetus to development and moved the bar for where work can be done from.

Radically Changed Digital Office Workplace (exponential development): The physical workplace has been hit hard and is left with a lot of empty leases, which must be converted to other uses such as office, warehouse, distribution, production, and housing. A number of offices have become co-working spaces, but this has not been able to compensate for the decline. The pandemic crises and digitalisation have accelerated the development radically, and the workplace for knowledge workers is now predominantly digital and from a distance. There are still physical workplaces that function as cultural identity creators, meeting place for the selected and special events. Employees mainly work digitally from home or local hubs, because it is both cost efficient, more convenient, more sustainable, and provides a higher level of employee well-being. There are a few new physical workplace concepts that have proven to be sustainable, but only because they focus on the completely unique physical meeting places they can create in terms of relationships and development.

8.2 The Tension Field for Future Office Workplace Models

The future is shaped by workplace actors and technological advances. The model (Fig. 8.2) illustrates the tension field of future workplace development, encompassing the following five levels:

- **Megatrends**: Irrevocable trends defining the overall direction of development
- **Sub-trends**: Trends influencing the pace and nature of development
- **Enablers and Blockers**: Factors that can either accelerate, decelerate, or alter the direction and speed of development
- **Work-Life**: Implications for work-life
- **Workplace**: Implications for the workplace

The model is dynamic, reflecting hierarchical effects and correlations, and can be interpreted from the inside out or in reverse. The future workplace model is neither predetermined nor fixed; it is the outcome of future actor behaviour. To understand it, begin by considering the broader perspective, starting with dominant trends and then moving towards specific interpretations of the workplace model. By studying the model and comparing it to the specific reality of each organisation, it becomes clear that there are numerous possibilities and future development scenarios for each individual office workplace model.

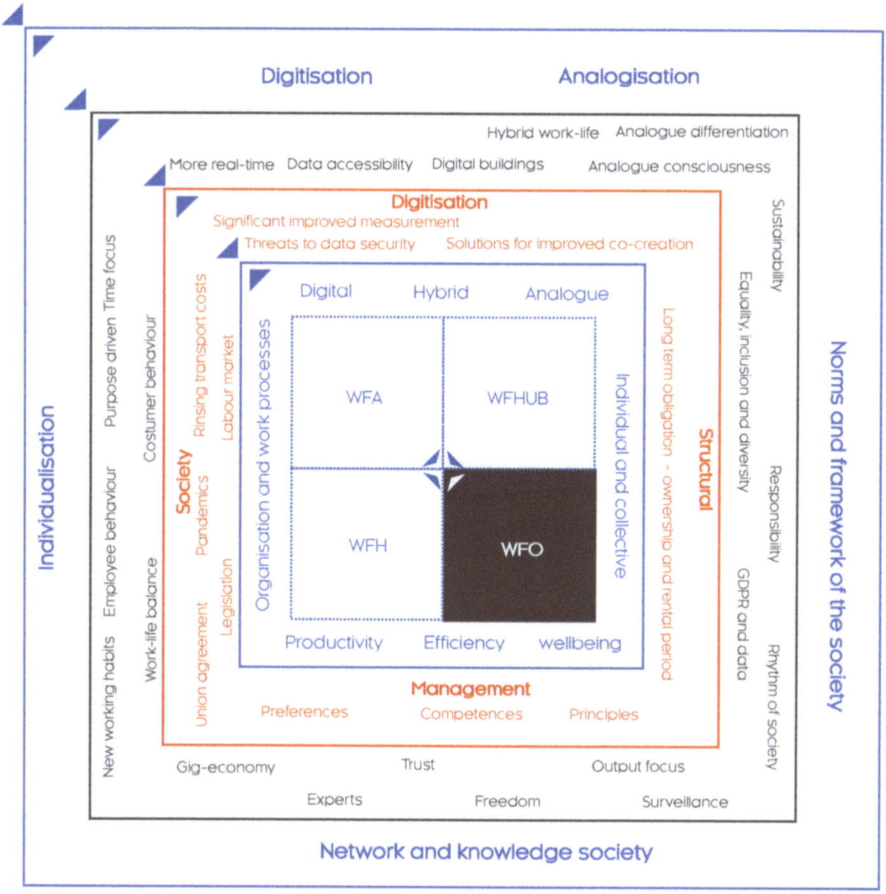

Fig. 8.2 The tension field for future workplace office model

8.3 Office Workplace Megatrends and Sub-trends

8.3.1 Digitalisation

The most notable and significant trend in the evolution and transformation of workplaces is digitalisation. Catalysed, for example, by the pandemic, it has had a profound influence on labour relations and, consequently, on organisational structures within organisations (Palàez Erro-Garcés et al. 2021). In the future, we can anticipate a surge in digital opportunities that will profoundly impact efficiency, productivity, and employee well-being. For reflection, I often ask organisations whether they believe that digitalisation will continue and whether it will have a significant impact on how we work. Without exception, they all agree that it will. I then ask to what extent they expect this to influence the office. This question often prompts a long pause for reflection, followed by a series of responses aligned with first-order thinking. One must, however, remain measured amidst the current wave of digitalisation, which combines, on the one hand, ongoing trends in the analysis of the information or knowledge-based society, and, on the other, significant breakthroughs whose scope and impacts require careful assessment to avoid a regression into technological determinism (Valenduc and Vendramin 2017).

The world is currently experiencing a transformative phase. With the advancements in digitalisation and the emergence of AI, everyday objects are becoming more intelligent, and our interactions are shifting from purely physical to virtual and hybrid experiences. Additionally, physical spaces are becoming contextually aware environments. This influence of AI and digital technology is propelling the world towards a smart future, capable of providing transformative experiences across all aspects of business operations and the daily lives of consumers.

The workplace is on a path of rapid digital transformation, and a growing number of employees will have the opportunity to work digitally and remotely. This shift will lead to a self-reinforcing trend, with more employees preferring remote work. Work and the concept of the workplace are evolving from being primarily shaped by the physical office, its design, and surroundings, to being increasingly shaped by digital elements. In the past, work revolved around the physical workplace, with digital interactions as a supplement. However, the workplace of the future will be centred on digital work-life, with physical touchpoints and interactions serving as valuable additions to the overall experience.

The hybrid workplace has become a reality, where work is accessed through both traditional means and digitally, based on the preferences and opportunities of individual employees and organisations. The conventional understanding of the office workplace is being challenged and transformed by the growing digitalisation. This shift brings about increased complexity, as well as new opportunities and potential threats. The workplace is becoming less uniform and more customised to suit the needs of each individual organisation. In the future, it is anticipated that there will be a considerable decrease in the number of employees working in shared physical workplaces (Fig. 8.3). This trend will lead to a reduction in the size and importance of traditional offices. The anticipated decline of physical workplaces will have significant implications for the commercial real estate market, resulting in office consolidation and concentration in specific areas and ecosystems. Many workplaces will be eliminated and repurposed for other uses. The digitisation of the workplace and work processes is predicted to undergo exponential growth, akin to Moore's Law, and will introduce new technologies that offer increasingly greater opportunities for digital work, freeing employees from the constraints of a physical, synchronous, and linear workplace.

The trends in digitalisation encompass various ground-breaking technologies and digital solutions, such as augmented reality, virtual reality, artificial intelligence, drones, robots, and expanded automation. The increasing integration of technology in the workplace will have widespread effects and will involve aspects such as employee redundancy, liberation from the need for physical presence, and restructuring of functions and tasks that were previously tied to being physically present.

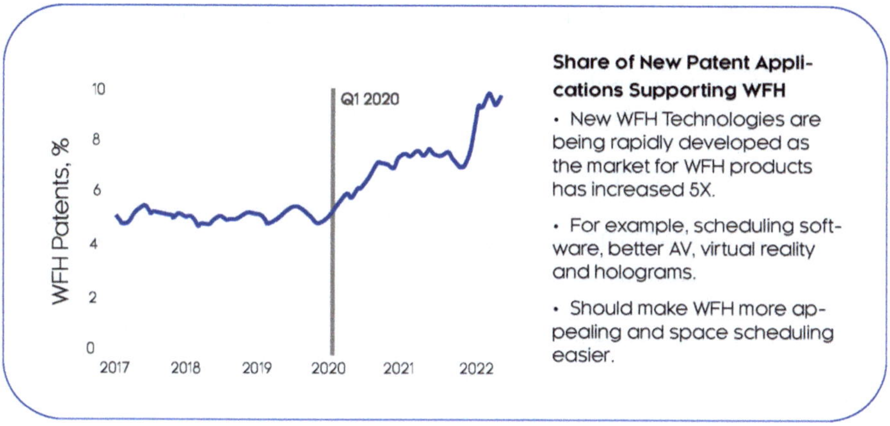

Fig. 8.3 Technology builds WFH momentum. Source: Barrero, Jose Maria, Nicholas Bloom, and Steven J. Davis, 2021. www.wfhresearch.com

As a result, there will be a need for the reorganisation of functions and tasks, upskilling of employees, and other adaptations to accommodate the changing landscape. It will entail various changes, including:

- The future of work is moving towards an increasingly hybrid model, where there will be a seamless integration of both analogue and digital work. Employees will have the flexibility to access the same work and resources regardless of their location, whether they are working in the physical office or remotely. This fusion of analogue and digital work will allow for greater efficiency, productivity, and work-life balance, providing employees with more opportunities to thrive in the evolving workplace landscape.
- As technology advances and access to the cloud becomes more prevalent, everything is moving towards real-time interactions. This shift towards real-time access to information and resources will lead to increased transparency in various aspects of work and life. Employees will have greater immediate accessibility to data, updates, and collaboration tools, enabling them to make more informed decisions and work efficiently. This real-time connectivity will foster a more dynamic and agile work environment, where teams can collaborate seamlessly regardless of their physical location. As a result, the workplace will become more interconnected and responsive, enhancing productivity and driving innovation.
- As digitalisation advances, there will be an increase in the availability of data on employee productivity and value creation, both at the individual and group levels. This shift towards data-driven insights will lead to a decreased focus on tracking the quantity and specific details of how each individual works, but instead, there will be a growing emphasis on the results they achieve. The wealth of employee data will also provide opportunities to monitor and assess employee well-being, including their mental and physical health. With access to digital tools and data, organisations will be better equipped to support their employees'

overall wellness and identify any potential issues that may arise. Overall, the integration of data analytics and digital technologies in the workplace will pave the way for a more results-oriented and employee-focused approach, enhancing productivity and promoting a healthier work environment.

Digitalisation is fast. Whilst people and organisations may, at times, appear slow, they are invariably orchestrated in synchronised, though time-shifted, patterns. Amara's Law, applied to the workplace, highlights the classic issue of both overestimating and underestimating technological development. Often, there is a lack of understanding about the true potential of technology, leading to the emergence of myths and misconceptions about its capabilities. Biases based on individual optimism or pessimism about new technologies also play a role in shaping perceptions. At the onset, people tend to overestimate the impact and potential of new technologies. However, over time, they tend to underestimate the profound impact these technologies can have on their lives and the workplace. As behaviour and new technologies evolve rapidly, it becomes easy to misjudge the speed of change. All stakeholders in the workplace must acknowledge that previous approaches to the digital workplace might not have fully harnessed its potential. Studies have, for example, demonstrated that nearly half of software licences are unused (Nexthink 2024). It is essential to consider Amara's Law when integrating technology and digitalisation into the organisation's future office workplace strategies (Fig. 8.4).

Examples of Digital Game Changers:

- Artificial Intelligence (AI): The integration of artificial intelligence into the daily work environment is set to bring about a profound transformation in the work-

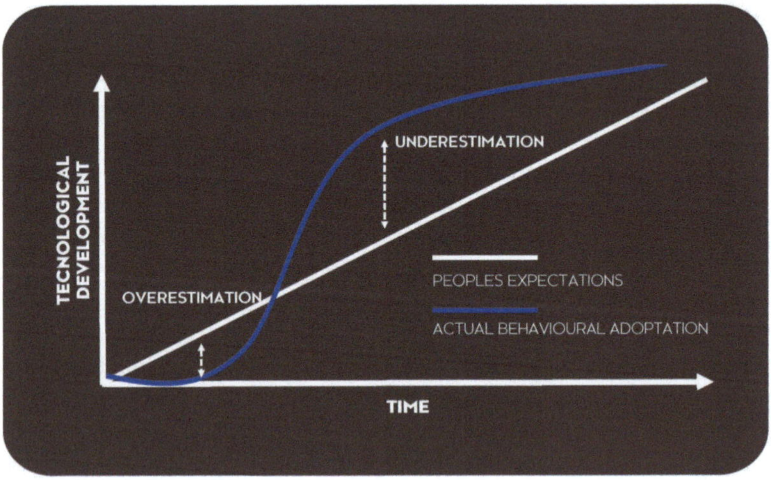

Fig. 8.4 Amara's Law: behaviour and technology. Source: Susan Ratcliffe, ed. (2016). *Oxford Essential Quotations*. Vol. 1 (4th ed.). Oxford University Press. https://doi.org/10.1093/acref/9780191826719.001.0001

life and workplace for knowledge workers. This widespread impact will touch every knowledge worker, as AI takes on the role of supplementing or even replacing various tasks and job functions. Consequently, the workplace will naturally experience adaptive changes to accommodate this shift. AI will seamlessly become an integral part of work-life, readily available on commonly used digital platforms. This accessibility empowers employees to enhance productivity significantly, liberating valuable resources that can be directed towards more value-adding tasks.

- For instance, with the likes of ChatGPT and Microsoft Office Copilot, individual employees will have access to a wealth of value-creating resources at their fingertips, facilitating decentralised problem-solving. The introduction and proliferation of AI are heralding a workplace revolution. The application of numerical and linguistic algorithms, much like the analogy of Gyro Gearloose, provides every employee with a "Little Helper"—a loyal and omnipresent digital companion and assistant to tackle tasks and challenges. This transformation promises to redefine the way work is approached and accomplished, offering unprecedented support and efficiency in the work environment.
- As a young university student, when questioned by a journalist about the reasons for using AI to cheat on exams, he replied, "In my perspective, we must prepare ourselves to compete in the job market, and I believe that all companies in the future will utilise AI if it can complete tasks more efficiently and effectively" (TV2 Denmark 2023).
- Metaverse Workplace: The rise and widespread use of digital metaverse work environments will pose a challenge to the conventional workplace setup. These metaverse platforms empower employees to create personalised digital workspaces that cater to their specific needs, with tasks being accomplished through the utilisation of AR and VR technologies. Additionally, metaverse environments will foster the development and preservation of distinct workplace cultures, gradually diminishing the necessity of a physical workplace as a primary driver of identity and culture. Imagine it as a virtual reality rendition of the present-day Internet (Purdy 2022).

8.3.2 Analogisation

The physical workplace will not simply mimic the digital workplace, as it will have a distinct focus on in-person interactions and support the increasingly vital digital work environment. Rather than serving the same functions, physical workplaces will differentiate themselves as unique meeting places, offering incentives for physical attendance.

Standardised physical workplaces are transitioning towards becoming a luxury and a choice, requiring proactive selection by individual employees. Both organisations and employees are becoming more aware of the value of in-person interactions. The hybrid office workplace is expected to adopt a differentiated approach to analogue and digital work situations based on specific work needs (Bird 2021). The decision to opt for in-person or digital interactions will be carefully reviewed, considering the context and work requirements. In-person workplaces will excel in co-creation, trust-building, and fostering a sense of unity. They will be used for important and unpredictable meetings, collaborations, and tasks that demand physical presence. On the other hand, digital interactions will be favoured for operational and process-oriented work with a higher level of predictability.

As automation and digitisation take over repetitive tasks, employees will be increasingly engaged in non-routine and collaborative tasks, leading to a greater need for interactions, including in-person meetings. The use of the analogue and digital workplace will be an extension of the hybrid workplace concept, with meetings being consciously labelled as digital, analogue, or hybrid depending on their purpose and participants' relationships. The process of analogisation will simultaneously be reinforced by the automation and digitisation of tasks that have previously involved employees.

Consequently, it is expected that employees will increasingly be utilised for non-repetitive or non-routine tasks, which will progressively be taken over by technology. Artificial intelligence is an example of how pervasive this development will be and how work and employees will be affected in the near future. It is a development that, all things considered, will imply that employees will collaborate more and have a rising need for interactions, including analogue in-person meetings.

Examples of Analogue Game Changers:

- Face2face: Work is best in a shared synchronised, linear, and symmetric physical office workplace. Research has shown that the shared physical office workplace outperforms the digital one in terms of productivity, efficiency, management support, and employee well-being. However, this doesn't imply that the digital workplace won't gain more prominence; it simply means that the physical workplace will continue to hold a dominant position.
- Stability and routines: The analogue workplace provides a stable structure and serves as the primary foundation for managers and employees. It remains highly desirable for talent, playing a crucial role in attracting and retaining valuable employees. While the workplace will naturally undergo more digitalisation, it will largely maintain its current form and structures. In essence, the physical workplace has proven to be resilient and remains the best solution for ensuring the competitiveness of organisations and companies in both the short and long terms.
- Network and knowledge society and value chains: With the emergence of the network society, the workplace undergoes a transformation from being centred around physical desks to being centred around the network. Instead of being oriented towards the closest colleagues in the same department, the focus shifts towards building relationships that are relevant and crucial for specific tasks, regardless of time and location. This means a greater emphasis on connections and collaborations across the entire organisation. The concept of the network society, coined by the Spanish sociologist Manuel Castells, refers to a society where communication happens independently of time and place (Castells 2000).

In this networked society, social structures are formed around digital communication and interactions, often occurring over the Internet and transcending national borders. As the workplace becomes increasingly digitalised, it is expected to profoundly influence how relationships, communication, and value creation occur both within and outside organisations. Access to and connections with essential resources are becoming more valuable than the physical proximity of individuals. The sense of community is moving away from departmental boundaries and towards task-based collaboration in organisations, fostering increased collaboration and co-creation across the organisational hierarchy.

- The emergence of the network society further strengthens the prevailing trend towards greater autonomy, self-leadership, shared-leadership, and reduced layers of management. In this networked society, employees are increasingly liberated, giving them the opportunity to organise value creation with a focus on the immediate goals of their tasks. The development results in a growing demand for specialists and neo-specialists, while there is a noticeable decline in middle management and the traditional workforce (Mikkelsen and Martin 2019). This reduction in the regular workforce is a direct outcome of automation, robotisation, and the implementation of artificial intelligence. The network society is propelling the workplace into a deeper transformation, moving away from analogue-based models like activity- and experience-based design to a hybrid and digitally driven network-based model. In this model, employees can work freely without being bound by time and location. The network-based approach revolves around the digital workplace and is supplemented by the physical workplace, converging in the hybrid workplace.
- The workplace is experiencing profound transformations driven by the emergence of the network and knowledge society. In this modern era, the emphasis on value creation is shifting away from the traditional focus on efficiency, epitomised by methodologies like Lean, and moving towards collaboration and innovation. This shift is propelled by the necessity to meet the ever-changing market demands for updated solutions and services. In this new society, to foster value creation, it becomes crucial for value chains and the process of value creation to prioritised co-creation and collaboration. Consequently, the establishment of frameworks for collaboration will play a vital role in designing and shaping the hybrid workplace. In the short and medium terms, the physical workplace will remain crucial for fostering relationships, collaborations, and co-creation. However, in the long term, technological advancements are anticipated to facilitate digital alternatives for building relationships, collaborating, and engaging in co-creation activities.
- As we constantly move forward, a new approach to collaboration, value chain creation, and processes is required, both internally and externally. As a result, collaboration between individuals is a central and increasingly vital element of value creation within organisations and businesses. This aligns with the increased focus on innovation facilitated through, e.g., collaboration and trust (e.g. Dovey 2009). Rigid, top-down management has struggled to adapt to distributed work environments, with leaders often more concerned about where work takes place

than about developing their leadership to meet the needs of an evolving workforce (Upwork 2024). Innovators, on the other hand, bring a product mindset to drive improvements within their organisations, not just externally. They understand that internal ways of working must evolve, or risk being left behind. A key factor highlighted in Upwork's study is how these innovators align with Nassim Nicholas Taleb's concept of anti-fragility: "These organisations gain an edge over those clinging to outdated notions of stability or merely reacting to external pressures—because in a world where stability is elusive, resilience isn't enough, and reaction is simply too slow. To succeed, businesses must be proactive in their evolution, using disruption as a catalyst for change rather than viewing it as a threat to be managed". The report emphasises that clinging to the traditional mindset of the workplace as a value chain is no longer viable. It introduces the concept of Kaizen—continuous improvement, made famous in manufacturing and supply chains—into internal work processes.

Understanding analogisation and its implications is central to determining the system and structure for the development of the hybrid office workplace. Analogisation implies that organisations must balance and navigate the use of both digital and analogue work processes. The ability of both organisations and employees to effectively utilise digital and analogue approaches is, therefore, a crucial element in constructing a successful and future-proof hybrid office workplace model. An analogue competent organisation understands the different interaction formats and channel choices available and empowers employees to make informed decisions about their daily workplace and tasks accordingly. This approach ensures that neither employees nor the organisation waste valuable time in interactions that could have been more productive and efficient employing other formats. In essence, the future hybrid organisation demonstrates proficiency in both digital and analogue strategies.

DIGITAL DEXTERITY Digital dexterity refers to an employee's ability to work effectively with digital tools and technologies, such as email, video conferencing, project management software, and other digital platforms. In a hybrid workplace, employees must be able to communicate and collaborate effectively in a digital environment to ensure that projects and tasks are completed on time and with the desired quality. Extreme digital dexterity can be observed in fully remote workplaces, where employees are compelled to develop efficient work habits in order to thrive (e.g. Pozen et al. 2021).

ANALOGUE DEXTERITY Analogue dexterity refers to an employee's ability to work effectively in an analogue environment, such as in-person meetings, face-to-face conversations, and other non-digital interactions. In a hybrid workplace, employees may need to attend in-person meetings or collaborate with colleagues in the office, requiring strong interpersonal skills and the ability to work effectively in an analogue environment (Bolino and Phelps 2024, Ferguson et al. 2022).

Previously, analogue interactions and meetings were the unconscious and preferred choice, and the digital meeting was considered an option (and thus a conscious choice to avoid analogue meetings and interactions). The digital format for meetings and interactions was often selected for its efficiency and was sometimes seen as less important. However, with the introduction of the hybrid office workplace, the situation has been reversed, and the digital work and collaboration format is now the standard, while the analogue format is a more deliberate choice and upgrade.

The analogue competent organisation understands when and how to use analogue collaboration, meetings, and interactions and does not default to a particular format. Analogue competence involves upgrading meetings or interactions from digital to analogue when appropriate, not the other way around. In practice, this means that most meetings can be conducted digitally, but there are certain situations where analogue meetings are preferred for what is best suited, even if they cost more in time and money. To be analogue competent, employees must be digitally competent from the outset. The organisation and its employees must be able to navigate seamlessly between unplanned, planned digital, hybrid, and analogue meetings and interactions, and design their workday accordingly, whether they attend the office or work remotely.

The analogy to flipped classrooms in pedagogy is striking and can be almost directly applied to the analogue competent workplace model (Nechkina 1984). In the flipped classroom concept, the traditional approach of in-class lectures and homework assignments is reversed. Students watch pre-recorded video lectures or read instructional materials before coming to class, usually at home or outside the classroom. The in-class time is then utilised for interactive activities, discussions, and problem-solving exercises that reinforce the concepts taught in the pre-recorded lectures or readings. The aim of the flipped classroom is to create a more active and engaged learning experience for students (further inspiration, e.g. Trede et al. 2019). Similarly, in the analogue competent workplace, employees have the flexibility to engage in individual tasks and prepare for meetings digitally before coming to the office or participating in hybrid interactions. The office or physical workplace is then used for collaborative activities, discussions, and relationship-building, maximising the value of in-person interactions.

To become proficient in both analogue and digital skills and be prepared for the future development of the hybrid workplace and work-life, it is essential to have a clear understanding and effectively differentiate between digital and analogue behaviours concerning time, location, and space.

- Digitalisation of Workplace Behaviour: The most obvious and largest trend for the development of meetings and interactions is the increasing digitalisation. In the future, there will be an explosion of digital opportunities with great positive implications for efficiency and productivity. Digital meetings and interactions are generally best and most effective for operations and alignments in established processes. Digital meetings and interactions will, therefore, increasingly be used for work that is operation- and process-oriented with a higher degree of predictability for the outcome of the interaction. Digital and virtual meetings are not a direct reproduction of analogue in-person meetings but have their own characteristics and rules of play. All the small errors and shortcomings that participants can get away with in face-to-face meetings and interactions are all amplified and more evident in digital formats. If participants are not aware of the differences between analogue and digital meetings in their approach to digital meetings, the value is lowered. Digital meetings generally curb creative idea generation (Brucks and Levav 2022).

- Conversely, organisations and employees through mastery of digital meetings will experience that they can use digital meeting competencies to create better analogue meetings.
- Analogisation of Workplace Behaviour: Parallel to our expanding digitisation, we will increasingly become analogised: we become aware and competent in using the analogue meeting differentiated from the digital meeting (e.g. Atkin et al. 2022). The analogue meeting is best for co-creation (Brucks and Levav 2022), building trust, and creating a sense of belonging, and will growingly be used for important interactions, frictions, and unpredictable meetings where participants need to meet face-to-face. Studies have indicated that development and innovation happen better and faster in analogue collaboration where participants are equal.
- Hybrid Behaviour and Workplace: The approach to hybrid collaboration, meetings, and interactions is quite simple. All hybrid meetings should basically be approached as digital meetings to avoid splitting meeting participants into A and B teams depending on whether they participate physically or digitally at a distance (asymmetric interaction). In a fully remote setting, meetings are conducted on Teams/Zoom, well-documented, and recorded, following a turn-based approach. However, in-person meetings can become more informal and free-flowing, with less documentation and structure. Combining both without intentional rules can lead to a situation where individuals in the conference room speak over those on videoconferencing. To maintain a productive hybrid meeting environment, it is essential to establish clear rules for taking turns and making space for remote attendees, which relies on employee trust. Additionally, it requires a significant level of psychological safety for remote workers to speak up, especially when the majority of their team is physically present in a conference room (Tan 2024).
- From a broader, team-oriented perspective, hybrid project management approaches have been found to be as effective as fully agile methodologies, significantly enhancing stakeholder success compared to traditional project management approaches, all while maintaining similar outcomes in terms of budget, time, scope, and quality (Gemino et al. 2020). These findings suggest that the hybrid model is emerging as a leading strategy in project management.

8.3.3 Society Norms and Frameworks

The workplace will increasingly be influenced by new societal norms and frameworks. These norms will play a significant role in shaping the future hybrid workplace, transitioning from being a "NICE" to a "NEED" for organisations. This impact will be driven partly by rising expectations and changing societal norms, as well as the introduction of new legislation and guidelines. The COVID-19 pandemic has heightened the focus on mental and physical health, and there is also a notable shift towards society taking a stronger stance in safeguarding against external influences.

An inflexible office workplace model undermines the organisation's Environmental, Social, and Governance (ESG) ambitions. You can't blow and have flour in your mouth. The same applies to the hybrid workplace model and ESG aspirations. Organisations can't wholeheartedly pursue ESG goals while simultaneously clinging to an office-centric pre-pandemic and post-industrial workplace model. There is substantial evidence that ESG aspirations promote the hybrid workplace model and increased flexibility if it is implemented thoughtfully (and not the reverse). In simpler terms, constraining flexibility and insisting on a predominantly office-bound approach hinder an organisation's ESG compliance.

The hybrid workplace contributes to the organisation's environmental ambitions, making it more prepared for the future. In the analysis of various work scenarios, individuals' behaviours, and sources of emissions, researchers discovered that transitioning from on-site work to full-time remote work could reduce a person's carbon footprint by over 50 per cent. Hybrid schedules, where individuals work remotely for 2 to 4 days a week, could also lead to emissions reductions ranging from 11 to 29 per cent, according to the study. However, the researchers in the study cautioned against assuming that any level of remote work would automatically benefit the environment (Tao et al. 2023).

Simultaneously, hybrid workplaces observe that a more flexible work environment enhances the social and engagement (DEI: inclusivity, diversity, and equality) dimensions of ESG within the organisation (e.g. Hu and Tambe 2023 and Badal et al. 2013). For instance, employees with disabilities, older individuals with reduced working hours, or families with caregiving responsibilities will find it advantageous to have the option to work remotely. Especially women, families with children, and marginalised employees are more likely to be attracted to and retained by hybrid workplaces (Wiswall and Zafar 2018, Le Barbanchon et al. 2021, Bergemann et al. 2023). Harvard University professor Claudia Goldin, a Nobel Prize laureate in economics (2023), has conducted research demonstrating that "remote work" has historically been a crucial factor in enabling women to contribute to the economy (Goldin and Katz 2011). With the advent of the industrial era, which drew workers into factories and offices, women's participation in the formal economy began to decline. However, in the pre-nineteenth century, when more work took place in the home, a greater number of women were involved. From this perspective, the remote work during the pandemic era is not an "aberration", as some CEOs have described it, but rather a return to the historical norm. Goldin's additional research has shown that women's wages increase when work is restructured to provide both flexibility and substitutability. A classic example she cites is that of pharmacists. In the past, when more pharmacies were independent, pharmacists had to be always on call, and the majority of pharmacists were men. However, with the emergence of chain drug stores, pharmacists could work in shifts, substituting for each other as necessary. The outcome is that today, pharmacists have one of the smallest gender-wage gaps among high-earning professions, and it is now a field in which the majority of professionals are female.

From a macro perspective, a Danish study examining the impact of remote work has demonstrated that an increase in remote working yields substantial overall positive socio-economic benefits (Wilken and Joergensen 2020). In other words, it is highly beneficial for society to support flexible working arrangements. These advantages include saved commuting time, reduced transportation costs, decreased congestion, and less pollution. Additionally, the study indicates that increased remote work can also contribute to an increase in the labour supply and GDP, although the findings are associated with a degree of uncertainty. If we consider the critical frameworks set by society for the standards and regulation of the factors within which the office workplace is developed and interpreted, we can reasonably expect that society will increasingly establish frameworks that allow for a more progressive interpretation of the hybrid and flexible workplace. Quite simply, society as a whole stand to benefit from this (Bloom 2024). The results provide an indication that increased remote work can be a socio-economic advantage, and the future legislation will promote further flexibility. However, it is important to note that the potential overall societal benefits do not necessarily guarantee that all actors will benefit from these changes. In reality, that is far from being the case. The impact of increased remote work can vary widely depending on individual circumstances and industries. Some may reap substantial benefits, while other stakeholders and organisations might face challenges or disadvantages due to the transformation in work dynamics.

I anticipate workplaces and organisations to be developed with a growing emphasis on sustainability and environmental concerns, as well as on promoting mental and physical health, fostering equality, inclusion, and diversity. Workplace actors will be increasingly expected to demonstrate a sense of social responsibility and contribute positively to the community. These evolving societal norms and frameworks will profoundly influence the development of workplace efficiency, productivity, and employee well-being. As organisations align themselves with these values, they are likely to create more meaningful and supportive work environments, leading to enhanced overall performance and employee satisfaction.

The societal norms and framework trends include:

- Sustainability: UN Sustainable Development Goals, ESG regulatory requirements, and market-promoting initiatives that are attractive to employees and customers.
- Health—mental and physical well-being: Mental health is becoming an important factor in business—increasing productivity and efficiency as well as attracting and retaining employees.

- Equality, inclusion, and diversity (DEI): The workplace should be inclusive and able to accommodate all employees—with differences—to thrive and perform in the workplace.
- It is good for the workplace and good for the community and society.
- Corporate social responsibility: If you are not part of the solution as a workplace, then you are part of the problem. All workplace actors must actively participate in solving community challenges—and this applies to workplaces even though society bears a large part of the responsibility. It is a common challenge, and the community and society will play a growingly prominent role in the design and operation of the workplace moving forward.
- GDPR and data: Collection and use of data on employee behaviour, productivity, efficiency, and mental and physical health will increasingly be subject to restrictions through new guidelines and legislation.

Examples of Society Norms Game Changers:

- Commuting CO_2 emission becomes the employers' responsibility, and they will be held accountable. The workplace will take full responsibility for employees' total CO_2 emissions related to work-life, including daily commuting and transportation between workplaces. Employers and workplaces will be accountable for the overall CO_2 impact, and they will seek to limit commuting by offering more remote work opportunities or establishing smaller HUB satellites closer to employees' homes.
- Carpooling, cycling, and public transportation will be promoted to reduce individual commuting. Air travel and other forms of transportation will also be significantly reduced. As a result, the physical workplace will be considerably smaller, while the digital workplace will expand significantly. The implementation of total employee transport CO_2 responsibility is already in progress, driven by the introduction of ESG (Environmental, Social, and Governance) legislation in the EU. Envision a future city and infrastructure with reduced rush hour traffic and less commuting. Such changes will create more space, lessen environmental impact, and improve living environments for people.
- The shared economy is reshaping office workplaces with carpooling, co-working spaces, and activity-based working (ABW) models. Together, these trends promote sustainable, adaptable, and socially connected work environments, aligning with modern expectations for flexibility and resource sharing.
- Gluttony of office space becomes a climate sin. In the future there is a concerted effort to eliminate excessive use of office space. Offices with excessive square footage per employee will be subject to surcharges or other public sanctions. The public perception of large office spaces will also shift from being a sign of success to being seen as wasteful and sinful. Many workplaces currently maintain their size despite low occupancy rates on a daily basis. By reducing the square footage, the proportion of people working remotely will be strengthened, assuming all other factors remain constant.

- Cities and districts change. The shift away from the traditional physical office workspace is expected to bring significant transformations to cities and urban areas. The pace of these changes remains uncertain, but looking ahead, we can anticipate significant effects. As history has shown, developments like the emergence of the hybrid workplace can be unexpected yet impactful.
- Exhausting employees will be considered ethically reprehensible. In the evolving society, with an ageing population and increasing strain on the public economy, organisations are taking on a more comprehensive responsibility for the health of their employees. As a result, the workplace is becoming a focal point for addressing both the mental and physical well-being of its workforce. The emphasis is shifting from individual and societal responsibility for health to a shared responsibility between employees and employers.

8.3.4 Individualisation

"Never bet against a megatrend", as we frequently emphasise at the Copenhagen Institute for Futures Studies, and few things are as true or pervasive as the megatrend of individualisation and its implications for the future of the workplace. In our view, individualisation is often underestimated and should be considered just as crucial to the evolution of the office workplace as the megatrend of digitalisation. Since Anthony Giddens, in the context of late modernity, identified how traditional social structures such as family, religion, and class have become less rigid, allowing for greater personal freedom—a shift he referred to as individualisation—this trend has only become more prevalent in modern society (A. Giddens 1994). Giddens argued that in late modernity, individuals are increasingly reflexive, continually questioning and reassessing their beliefs, behaviours, and identities. This shift is driven by the rapid pace of social change, greater access to information, and the waning influence of traditional authorities. Individuals now craft their own sense of self through personal choices rather than being defined by fixed social categories. As a result, people are expected to create their own life stories, managing careers, relationships, and lifestyle decisions, which can offer greater freedom but also bring about anxiety and uncertainty. Employees are increasingly expecting personalised and tailored solutions that cater to their productivity, efficiency, and well-being preferences. As a result, future employers must adapt to a labour market where organisations unnecessarily attract and retain the most suitable talents and skills. The design of the future hybrid workplace will be significantly influenced by employee behaviour and preferences. Employers who adhere to traditional approaches may face challenges in attracting and retaining employees and may be more vulnerable to negative outcomes.

The de facto scarcity of qualified labour creates a competitive market where employers must vie for qualified employees. All employees, including those who were previously seen as requiring physical presence, will now be digitised. The shift in employee behaviour and preferences is not only specific to certain generations but is a structural change that spans across age, gender, personal profiles, and education levels. The transformation towards a more digitised workforce is universal and affects employees from all walks of life.

Employee behavioural trends include:

- **New habits and behaviour:** The pandemic has created new habits and experiences that will permanently change employees' approach to the workplace. There will be an increasing preference for remote work. With the prolonged pandemic, employees' habits have changed significantly, and this development is expected to continue. Some employees recognise that remote work is convenient, while others prefer the physical workplace.
- **Work-life balance:** Employees will increasingly prioritise work-life balance. Maslow's hierarchy of needs and well-being should not be compromised at the expense of workplace well-being and health. Mental health is increasingly becoming integral to good business practices, leading to enhanced productivity and efficiency, as well as improved employee attraction and retention.
- **Purpose-driven:** "Why" is increasingly determining employee productivity and efficiency. Purpose is strongly driven by a desire to make a significant and preferably significant difference for customers and society.
- **Gig economy and specialists:** More and more employees take responsibility for their own development and life by becoming specialists or experts with a constant career path. The freer expert-nomad is a growing proportion of employees and will be defining for the future hybrid workplace.
- **Freedom and surveillance:** Employees will increasingly insist upon and establish limits on the extent to which they are subjected to monitoring. Data collection has reached a juncture where it is the employees who define the boundaries, as opposed to technology dictating the extent of surveillance (and to what degree will we be monitored?).
- **Competition for talent:** The competition for talent intensifies as the labour market becomes more employee-focused. Organisations and workplaces will compete with each other to be the workplace model that provides tailored solutions that fit each individual employee.
- **Polarisation and tribalisation:** The dynamics within society and social cohesion—and thus the sense of community—pose challenges to the workplace, much as they do in other shared public spaces. This challenge arises from growing polarisation, requiring the office environment to address and balance a multitude of individual—and often opposing—approaches to working life and collaboration (this dynamic is examined in depth later in the book, specifically in relation to balancing autonomy and heteronomy).
- **Collective agreements:** Collective agreements will be made that place fewer restrictions on the number of remote working days and distance work. This will free employees from the physical workplace as the cornerstone of the hybrid workplace for large and organised employee groups.
- **Employees decide—organisations adapt:** An increasing number of employees and groups will de facto determine their workplace model—and organisations will adapt the model to attract and retain these important and decisive employ-

ees. It will have a waterfall effect on the entire workplace model and accelerate the development towards a more individual, flexible, and hybrid workplace model.

8.4 Challenge: Employees Now Switch to a Four-Day Week

Germany has become the latest testing ground for a four-day week, with a new pilot project involving 45 companies set to commence in 2025 (Euronews 2024). The COVID-19 pandemic initially rekindled discussions on the four-day workweek, prompting both workers and employers to reassess the significance of workplace flexibility and benefits. The concept is straightforward: employees work 4 days a week while receiving the same pay and benefits, maintaining their full workload. For organisations reducing their workweek, this would likely mean fewer meetings and a greater emphasis on independent work. Lauded as the future of employee productivity and work-life balance, proponents of the four-day workweek argue that its implementation leads to increased worker satisfaction and productivity. In Belgium, employees have had the right to a four-day week since November 2021, following regulations drafted by the Belgian government earlier that year (Euronews 2022). This makes Belgium the first country in the European Union, and only the third globally after Iceland and New Zealand, to formally offer the four-day workweek as an option for employees. However, according to Belgian media, the reception has been mixed among both employers and employees. Companies express concerns about potential organisational challenges posed by the condensed working week, while unions worry it could result in a heavier workload for employees on their working days.

8.5 Future Hybrid Office Workplace Enablers and Blockers

Workplace actors play a crucial role in development, and through actions and behaviours, they can influence and create the workplace of the future. To clarify workplace development at a societal level, there are several critical "enablers" and "blockers"—potentially decisive factors that either push or hinder development trends towards the hybrid workplace, and thus the balance between digital and analogue work-life.

Examples of Critical Game Changers for the Future Development:

SOCIETY

- Legislation and new regulatory guidelines regarding the workplace: Introduction of provisions for remote work, entitlement to access a physical workplace, updated rules for the workplace, 4 days of working weeks …. (As a footnote: Regulation and legislation are largely shaped by politicians with a close eye on voters—primarily employees. Since both society and employees benefit from increased flexibility, this could well serve as a powerful catalyst for accelerated change.)

- Assessments, introduction of 360-degree sustainability responsibility for employees' total CO_2 emissions, increased demands for equality, inclusion, and diversity, changed taxation and tax deductions for remote work, changed insurance conditions, etc.
- Collective agreements aimed at ensuring equal conditions for remote workers, supporting a sense of justice, securing access to a fixed workplace to retain positions, introducing economic employee compensation for the establishment and operation of remote workplaces, etc.
- Shift from an employee market to an employer market, either through reduced demand or through increased supply of employees.
- Continued presence of pandemics—the threat of the continuation of coronavirus or new ones—and thus a prolonged impact on the workplace.
- Escalating conflicts between nations influencing the populations' daily work rhythm and work-life priorities (in Europe there is presently a full-scale regional war between Russia and Ukraine).
- Prolonged and deep economic recession, where there is a significant shift from an employee-dominated to an employer-dominated labour market for all employee groups.
- Changing day rhythm of services provided from society such as childcare, education, and public services.
- Major disasters accelerating the demands for sustainability and remote working.

DIGITISATION

- New solutions for significantly greater co-creation through the development of improved opportunities for innovation, development, relationships, etc.
- New solutions for significantly greater automation and use of artificial intelligence.
- Digital opportunity for significantly better hybrid interaction (mix of analogue and digital presence).
- Digital opportunity for significantly better measurement of individual and team productivity, efficiency, and well-being—with even greater focus on output and less focus on input.
- Threats to digital data and network security—increased threat of attacks on the digital infrastructure or data.

STRUCTURAL

Long-term commitments to lease agreements and ownership of physical workplaces can hinder the development towards a more digitised workplace as actors cannot reduce operating expenses quickly enough. It is expected that there will be a reduction in office demand, and thus an expanding supply of rental properties, increased conversion to other uses, or new office collaborations in a growing renters' market.

MANAGEMENT
Management maintains the existing workplace model based on, for example, preferences, skills, or principles for the solution that management considers optimal for the organisation and value creation.

8.6 Challenge: Generation Z and the Workplace

Using the generational angle to forecast the future development of the hybrid office workplace, we can focus on Generation Z as an indicator of what is to come in the short to midterm perspective. Generation Z refers to the demographic cohort born between the mid-1990s and mid-2010s, following the Millennials. As they start entering the workforce, their expectations and preferences are different from previous generations. As always, rigid generational labels should not be used to categorise behaviour based solely on birth year, but rather as indicators of age-related changes and tendencies, particularly in relation to approaches to the workplace and work-life balance. In other words, generations are more alike than we often assume, yet more distinct than we might prefer. However, it is important to recognise that generations are also a product of their time and upbringing. An example of why the next generation has been shaped the way they are can be exemplified by a parent's statement about spending time and considerable resources to buy a highly hyped new energy drink for their son (an energy drink that was only available in limited quantities): "I think it's silly and overhyped. But what wouldn't you do to keep your children satisfied and happy?" (TV2 2023). My primary purpose of considering generational aspects and developments in the context of the evolving workplace is to foster reflections on the progression and potential implications for the hybrid office environment. Ultimately, the next generations of the workforce are not only better prepared for the future of work but naturally also have a longer expected lifespan than the current senior leadership. As a result, they play a key role in co-defining the successful workplace model of the future.

Historically, leadership has been critical of the preferences and behaviours of new generations entering the labour market. It has always been so, so why should it change now? Indeed, Generation Z are overall characterised by question everything and hold strong opinions, being a direct product of their upbringing (I, for one, plead guilty in relation to my offspring), and the myriad opportunities and challenges characteristic of their era.

By 2025 they will represent almost 30 per cent of the labour force in the world. Here are some of the expectations that Generation Z has for the work-life and workplace (e.g. Brower 2024, Mckinsey & Company 2023 and Forbes 2024). It can be described as a generation that gets straight to the point, and in many ways, it is a generation that feels it has nothing to lose. Instead of dismissing them as naive and attributing their idealistic vision of work and society to being a prolongation of the "Generation Snowflake" (referring to individuals born between 1980 and 1994, suggesting they have an exaggerated sense of uniqueness, unwarranted entitlement, or are overly emotional, easily offended, and unable to handle differing opinions),

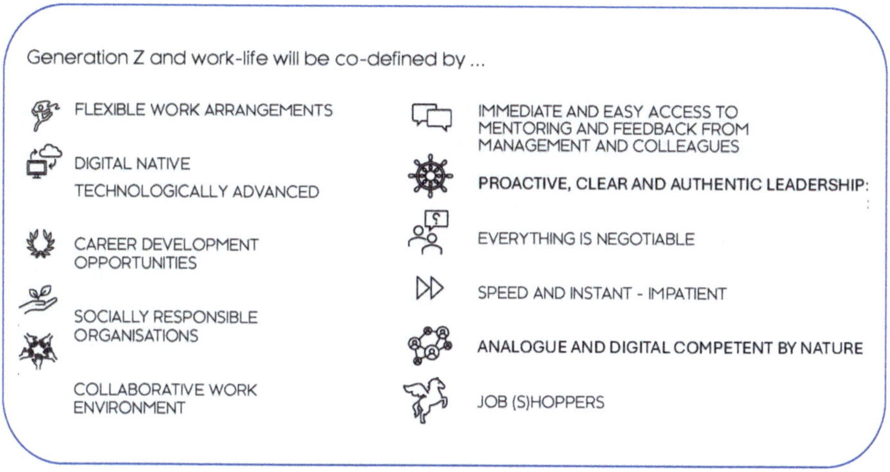

Fig. 8.5 Generation Z and the workplace

organisations should contemplate the implications they will have for the future workplace (Fig. 8.5).

FLEXIBLE WORK ARRANGEMENTS Generation Z places a strong emphasis on work-life balance and seeks flexible work arrangements that offer autonomy over their schedules. They value the ability to set their own hours or have greater self-determination in how and when they work. Organisations that offer options for remote working and flexible hours are particularly attractive to this generation. Their focus is increasingly on maintaining a balance between their personal and professional lives, with a growing tendency to prioritise private life over work-life. For Gen Z, the ability to integrate work around their personal commitments is a key factor in choosing an employer.

TECHNOLOGICALLY ADVANCED WORKPLACE Generation Z is the first generation to grow up entirely in the digital age. As such, they expect their workplace to be technologically advanced, with the latest tools and software. They prefer organisations that leverage technology to streamline frictionless work processes and enhance collaboration.

CAREER DEVELOPMENT OPPORTUNITIES Generation Z is ambitious and seeks growth opportunities in their careers. They widely believe that they are their own maker of their destiny. They look for organisations that offer clear paths for advancement and training programmes to help them develop their skills and advance in their careers. This implies clearly defined roles and processes where individual employee productivity is quickly ensured, given the increasingly shorter expected employment durations. At the same time, it is important to note the rising polarisation within Generation Z, as individualism grows and values are increasingly expressed as identity markers, with a stronger emphasis on goal-orientation (the polarisation is particularly evident in the differing approaches between genders).

SOCIALLY RESPONSIBLE ORGANISATIONS Generation Z places a high value on social responsibility and expects their employers to contribute positively to society. They are drawn to organisations that prioritise environmental sustainability, diversity, equity, and inclusion. This generation seeks workplaces that not only operate ethically but also have a clear and meaningful "why" behind their actions—organisations that are committed to addressing significant social, environmental, or cultural challenges. For Gen Z, aligning with an employer that embodies these values is not just desirable but often essential, as they seek purpose and impact in both their professional and personal lives.

COLLABORATIVE WORK ENVIRONMENT Generation Z is used to working collaboratively and values teamwork. They seek out organisations that foster a culture of collaboration and have a flat organisational structure that allows for open communication and the sharing of ideas. This also signifies governance transparency, with a clear, honest, and reasonable internal playbook. This generation can navigate intuitively in games and networks, and conversely, they reject unclear and difficult-to-interpret governance. To make the collaborative work environment, employers must facilitate strong internal interpersonal social capital, as social and professional networks are prioritised as essential.

IMMEDIATE AND EASY ACCESS TO MENTORING AND FEEDBACK FROM MANAGEMENT This includes continuous guidance and recognition of employee's work affirming the individual on a person level as well as a worker delivering value. Easy access to systematic mentoring is a key reason why Generation Z prefers in-person office attendance (anticipated to change as they become more senior).

PROACTIVE, CLEAR AND AUTHENTIC LEADERSHIP Generation Z is a purpose-driven cohort that values transparency and seeks leaders who can provide both clarity and guidance. They want to understand the "why" behind their work and prefer to operate within well-defined frameworks, where their contributions have clear direction and purpose. This generation appreciates leaders who communicate openly and authentically, fostering an environment of trust and collaboration. They are less likely to be motivated by traditional hierarchical structures and more inspired by leaders who demonstrate integrity and a genuine commitment to shared values. In the context of the workplace, providing clear expectations and offering opportunities for meaningful contributions are key to engaging and empowering this generation. This style of leadership not only aligns with their desire for transparency but also supports their need for personal growth and purpose in the workplace.

EVERYTHING IS NEGOTIABLE This mindset is a direct result of the individualistic approach many experienced growing up, especially within the educational system. Over time, this has fostered a culture where nearly every decision or outcome is open to discussion and negotiation. At its extreme, it can be traced back to parenting styles that offer children multiple choices for even the simplest everyday matters. From choosing what to wear to deciding what to eat, children are often encouraged to express preferences and make decisions from an early age, which cultivates a sense of autonomy and personal agency.

As adults, this upbringing has translated into an expectation that flexibility and negotiation are the norms, not just in personal life but also in the professional world. Whether it's negotiating working conditions, career paths, or even project approaches, individuals are more inclined to see options as fluid rather than fixed, making the workplace a space where adaptability and open dialogue become essential leadership tools.

SPEED AND INSTANT Generation Z was born into the digital age and has grown up in an online world where immediacy and transparency are the norms. They are accustomed to receiving and processing information quickly, and they expect the same rapid, straightforward responses from the world around them. This generation has a heightened ability to see through corporate jargon and empty promises, making them quick to analyse and form own conclusions based on their experiences and observations. It's increasingly common to hear Generation Z asking for specific sources of information presented to them. Their digital fluency enables them to sift through large volumes of information with speed and accuracy, giving them a keen sense for authenticity and efficiency in communication and action.

JOB (S)HOPPERS As Millennials they will shift jobs in order to enhance career and staying in pursuit of their goal for a successful work-life. This generation Z is predicted to have an average of over 20 jobs throughout their career (Szczepanek 2023). They view employers in the same way that employers view them, as mutually beneficial relationships where both parties seek to gain something. For Generation Z, there is no turning back. For younger employees, flexibility, mobility, and the freedom to be entrepreneurial are absolute requirements. In the coming year, 58 per cent of Gen Z individuals are contemplating changing jobs, compared to 43 per cent of the overall population (Mckinsey & Company 2023). Additionally, 58 per cent are considering transitioning to hybrid work, as opposed to 53 per cent overall, and 56 per cent are contemplating a shift to remote work, compared to 49 per cent overall.

ANALOGUE AND DIGITAL COMPETENT BY NATURE Generation Z employees instinctively navigate between on-site and offsite work, naturally adapting to both analogue and digital formats. While they are highly conscious of the differences between these modes of work, this doesn't necessarily mean they are proficient in specific digital workplace tools and processes—far from it. However, their comfort with technology, combined with their fast learning capabilities, allows them to quickly adapt and master new digital tools and systems when necessary. This dual competency in understanding the value of both physical and digital workspaces positions them to thrive in hybrid environments, even as they continue to build proficiency in the technical aspects.

Generation Z expects their workplace to be flexible, technologically advanced, socially responsible, and to offer opportunities for career development and collaboration. In short, they want to—and expect to—be engaged. To emphasise the point that generations are, in many respects, similar yet different due to the distinct periods in which they developed and matured, I have included Fig. 8.6. The overarching question for organisations is whether their workplace is prepared to embrace and adapt to the behaviours and preferences of both new and older generations, or if their approach remains rooted in the notion that employees, regardless of generational and age-related tendencies, must conform to existing norms.

To those who explicitly express concerns about Generation Z, and any forthcoming generations, I have three final points regarding generational perspectives. Firstly, it is not new for older generations to critique younger ones; such criticisms have been documented since the time of ancient Greece. Secondly, the older generations have directly influenced the development of the younger ones, so in a sense, they share responsibility for the outcome. And finally, it is far more strategic to embrace the changes brought by new generational approaches to work than to resist them. This resistance is exemplified by a US study from 2023, which found that 40% of employers avoid hiring members of Generation Z in favour of older

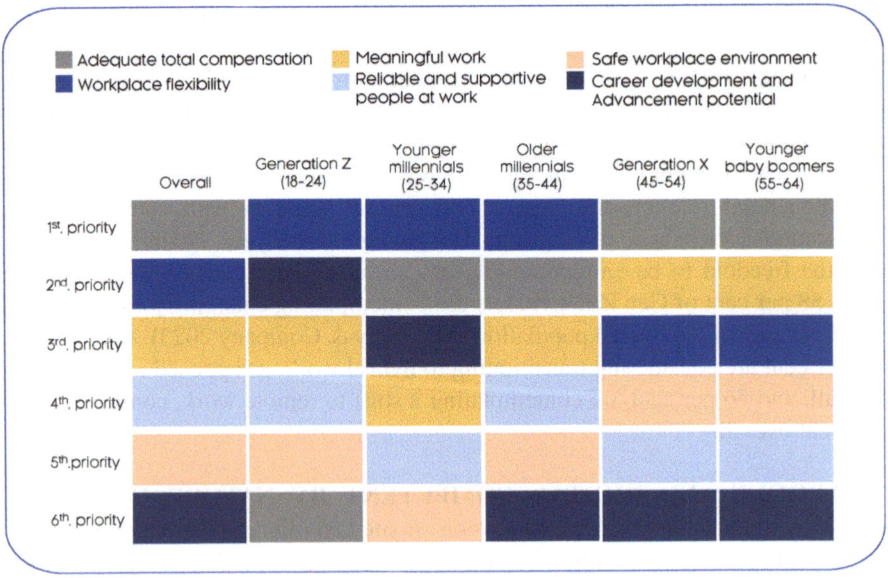

Fig. 8.6 Top reasons why respondents chose to stay in current job, by age group. source: Mckinsey and Company https://www.mckinsey.com/capabilities/people-and-organizational-performance/our-insights/gen-what-debunking-age-based-myths-about-worker-preferences

workers, primarily because 58% indicated that recent college graduates are unprepared for the workforce (Intelligent 2023). To put it bluntly, if management cannot lead this new generation, perhaps it is time to question whether that management should be leading at all.

References

(Atkin et al., 2022) The returns to face-to-face interactions—knowledge spillovers in silicon valley https://www.nber.org/system/files/working_papers/w30147/w30147.pdf

(Badal et al, 2013) Gender Diversity, Business-Unit Engagement, and Performance https://journals.sagepub.com/doi/abs/10.1177/1548051813504460

(Bergemann et al., 2023), There and back again https://population-economics.committee.socialpolitik.de/sites/default/files/2024-01/Bergemann_wp_december23.pdf

(Bird 2021) MIT Sloan Management Review "Remaking the Workspace to Boost Social Connection" https://sloanreview.mit.edu/article/remaking-the-workspace-to-boost-social-connection/

(Bloom 2024) IMF September 2024 Working from Home Is Powering Productivity https://www.imf.org/en/Publications/fandd/issues/2024/09/working-from-home-is-powering-productivity-bloom

(Bolino and Phelps 2024) HBR April 2024 3 Challenges to Hybrid Work - and How to Overcome Them https://hbr.org/2024/05/3-challenges-to-hybrid-work-and-how-to-overcome-them

(Brower 2024) Forbes The Gen Z Effect - And How The Youngest Employees Are Shaping The Future https://www.forbes.com/sites/tracybrower/2024/04/09/the-gen-z-effect/

(Brucks and Levav 2022) Virtual Communication Curbs Creative Idea Generation https://www.gsb.stanford.edu/faculty-research/publications/virtual-communication-curbs-creative-idea-generation

(Castells 2000) Contemporary Sociology Vol. 29, No. 5 (Sep., 2000) Toward a Sociology of the Network Society

(Dovey 2009) The role of trust in innovation https://www.emerald.com/insight/content/doi/10.1108/09696470910960400/full/html

(Euronews 2022) Workers in Belgium can now switch to a four-day week - but they won't be working fewer hours https://www.euronews.com/next/2022/11/21/workers-in-belgium-can-now-switch-to-a-four-day-week-but-they-wont-be-working-fewer-hours

(Euronews 2024) Four-day week: Which countries are embracing it and how is it going so far? https://www.euronews.com/next/2024/02/02/the-four-day-week-which-countries-have-embraced-it-and-how-s-it-going-so-far

(Ferguson et al. 2022) Ferguson, S., Lai, K., Chen, J. *et al.* "Why couldn't we do this more often?": exploring the feasibility of virtual and distributed work in product design engineering. *Res Eng Design* **33**, 413–436 (2022). https://doi.org/10.1007/s00163-022-00391-2

(Forbes 2024) The Gen Z Effect - And How The Youngest Employees Are Shaping The Future https://www.forbes.com/sites/tracybrower/2024/04/09/the-gen-z-effect/

(Gemino et al., 2020) Agile, Traditional, and Hybrid Approaches to Project Success: Is Hybrid a Poor Second Choice? https://journals.sagepub.com/doi/abs/10.1177/8756972820973082

(A. Giddens, 1994) Stanford University Press **Reflexive** modernization: Politics, tradition and aesthetics in the modern social order

(Goldin and Katz 2011) The Cost of Workplace Flexibility for High-Powered Professionals https://www.researchgate.net/publication/258125340_The_Cost_of_Workplace_Flexibility_for_High-Powered_Professionals

(Hu and Tambe, 2023) Offering remote work helps attract underrepresented groups https://faculty.wharton.upenn.edu/wp-content/uploads/2016/11/Hsu-Tambe-Remote-Work.pdf

(Intelligent 2023) 40% of Employers Avoid Hiring Gen Z Workers, Survey Says https://www.intelligent.com/nearly-4-in-10-employers-avoid-hiring-recent-college-grads-in-favor-of-older-workers/.

(Le Barbanchon et al., 2021) Gender Differences in Job Search: Trading off Commute against Wage https://academic.oup.com/qje/article/136/1/381/5928590
(Mckinsey & Company 2023) Gen what? Debunking age-based myths about worker preferences https://www.mckinsey.com/capabilities/people-and-organizational-performance/our-insights/gen-what-debunking-age-based-myths-about-worker-preferences
(Mikkelsen and Martin 2019) The Neo-Generalist: Where You Go is Who You are https://www.amazon.com/Neo-Generalist-Where-You-Who-Are/dp/1910649554
(Nechkina 1984) "Increasing the effectiveness of a lesson".
(Nexthink 2024) Nexthink Insights, SOFTWASTE: How Much Does IT Waste on Unused Software Licenses? https://nexthink.com/resource/unused-software-licenses
(Palàez Erro-Garcés, Garcia, and Kiriakou, 2021) Working in the 21st Century. The Coronavirus Crisis: A Driver of Digitalisation, Teleworking, and Innovation, with Unintended Social Consequences https://www.mdpi.com/2078-2489/12/9/377
(Pozen et al., 2021) R.C. Pozen and A. Samuel. Remote, Inc.: How to thrive at Work… Wherever You Are. New York: Harper Business, 2021 https://www.amazon.com/Remote-Inc-Thrive-Work-Wherever/dp/0063079372
(Purdy 2022) HBR How the Metaverse Could Change Work https://hbr.org/2022/04/how-the-metaverse-could-change-work?ut…sider_activesubs&utm_content=signinnudge&deliveryName=%20%20DM186314
(Szczepanek 2023) 83% of Generation Z workers are job hoppers (2023 Report) https://resumelab.com/career-advice/generation-z-and-work
(Tan 2024) Why trust is important on a hybrid team (and how managers can build it) https://hypercontext.com/blog/communication/trust-at-work-core-to-high-performance
(Tao, Yang, Jaffe, Amini, Bergen, Hecht and You 2023) Residential Energy Consumption Survey https://www.bls.gov/cex/cecomparison/recs_profile.htm
(Trede et al, 2019) Workplace Learning as a Hybrid Space. Education for Practice in a Hybrid Space: Enhancing Professional Learning with Mobile Technology, 19–31. https://www.researchgate.net/publication/331482859_Education_for_Practice_in_a_Hybrid_Space_Enhancing_Professional_Learning_with_Mobile_Technology
(TV2 2023) https://nyheder.tv2.dk/samfund/2023-06-17-jeg-synes-det-er-fjollet-siger-far-om-prime-hype-ekspert-kalder-det-pragteksempel-paa-markedsfoering-med-penge-i-ryggen
(TV2 Denmark 2023) Studerende snyder til eksamen med ChatGPT: - Jeg erkender fuldt ud, at jeg bryder reglerne https://nyheder.tv2.dk/samfund/2023-06-20-studerende-snyder-til-eksamen-med-chatgpt-jeg-erkender-fuldt-ud-at-jeg-bryder-reglerne
(Upwork 2024) Kelly Monahan and Gabby Burlacu, Work Innovators: A Playbook for Innovation in an Uncertain World, https://www.upwork.com/research/work-innovator-report-2024
(Valenduc and Vendramin 2017) Digitalisation, between disruption and evolution https://journals.sagepub.com/doi/abs/10.1177/1024258917701379
(Wilken and Joergensen 2020) Kraka, Store gevinster ved mere hjemmearbejde
(Wiswall and Zafar 2018) Preference for the Workplace, Investment in Human Capital, and Gender womenhttps://academic.oup.com/qje/article-abstract/133/1/457/4095201

On the Verge of a White-Collar Productivity Revolution

9

Abstract

The rapid adoption of generative AI tools is raising new questions about their impact on work, including whether they might lead to a significant productivity revolution. While the long-term effects are still uncertain, early studies suggest these technologies are already affecting many job tasks. For instance, GPT language models could impact up to 80% of the US workforce, with some workers seeing half of their tasks transformed. The potential for AI to reshape work extends beyond productivity gains, prompting comparisons to past transformative technologies like the printing press and steam engine. However, the speed and ease of AI integration, as well as its reliance on natural language, make it distinct from earlier innovations. This shift could lead to unintended consequences, such as increased administrative burdens, and may redefine work itself, requiring new skills and potentially altering traditional job roles.

9.1 Artificial Intelligence and Knowledge Work

The recent widespread adoption of generative AI tools has sparked new (and revived some old) questions about technology and work. How significant will their impact be? Are we on the cusp of a major productivity boost—a "productivity revolution", perhaps? Will jobs be displaced on a large scale, or will changes occur only at the margins? While it's too early to fully assess the long-term effects of these technologies, studies indicate that they are already making a measurable impact. Research from Stanford University's Digital Economy Lab found that 80% of the US workforce could have at least 10% of their work tasks affected by GPT language models, with 19% of workers potentially seeing at least half of their tasks impacted (Rock 2023). The study also reveals that approximately 15% of all daily work tasks in the country could be completed "significantly faster" at the same quality when workers

C. Sneppen, *The Future (R)Evolution of the Office Workspace*, Future of Business and Finance, https://doi.org/10.1007/978-3-031-85229-9_9

have access to large language models (LLMs). Remarkably, when additional software and tools built on these models are considered, this figure rises between 47% and 56% of all work tasks. While the researchers are cautious not to assign a specific timeline to their predictions, the study concludes that GPTs (generative pretrained transformers) should be regarded as "general-purpose technologies"—innovations with potentially significant economic, social, and policy implications.

Looking to the past might help us understand the potential for change, although comparisons are challenging because technological advancements in the workplace often lead not only to quantitative changes in output but also to qualitative shifts in the nature of work. If the most ambitious expectations for generative AI prove accurate, artificial intelligence could join the ranks of historically transformative technologies—like the printing press, power loom, steam engine, electricity, conveyor belt, automobile, computer, and Internet—that have fundamentally altered how work is performed and by whom. Such technologies have been central to previous industrial revolutions, leading to the automation of human labour, reducing the cost of producing goods and services, creating economies of scale, and generating new types of work and employment patterns. These industrial revolutions reshaped economies and labour markets and had profound impacts on the political, cultural, and social fabric of society. The first revolution initiated the shift from agrarian to urban industrial society; the second gave rise to mass politics and suburban life; the third saw the migration of much of the workforce from factories to offices. Crucially, the tipping points that triggered these revolutionary effects didn't stem solely from the invention of new technologies but from their widespread application. For instance, the invention of the mechanical loom or sewing machine in the 1700s did not immediately change much, but once these tools were widely adopted, low-skill textile workers could produce clothing faster and more cheaply than artisans, leading to a cascade of effects. The textile industry boomed, garment prices dropped, global labour markets shifted, new industrial districts emerged in cities, and novel markets for textile goods and consumer cultures developed. Countertrends like the Arts and Crafts movement even emerged in response to mass production, with "handmade" becoming a mark of quality. Technology has always impacted human work. While past waves of automation have eventually led to a new equilibrium, with the creation of new jobs, industries, and ways of life, these societal changes have often been painful. Mechanisation and industrialisation in the past sometimes resulted in violent clashes between displaced workers and their former employers, as famously seen when English textile artisans protested against manufacturers who replaced them with cheaper, lower-skilled workers using machines. These artisans formed militias and destroyed textile machinery in a desperate attempt to protect their livelihoods. It is unlikely that displaced office workers today would resort to similar measures against technology encroaching on their jobs. However, the significant profits of tech companies have understandably led to concerns about how the potential benefits of a productivity boom will be distributed. Just as the mechanical loom put downward pressure on the wages of skilled artisans, there is a risk that specialised knowledge workers may also face wage suppression as their skills become automated. Thus is the argument that in an increasingly complex and fast-changing world, generalists—those with broad knowledge and varied skill sets—are better equipped to succeed than specialists who focus narrowly on one field (Epstein 2019). One possible outcome could be the widespread "proletarianisation" of the white-collar workforce, with digital automation displacing skilled white-collar workers in a manner like how mechanisation displaced skilled artisans in the past.

As an aside, the same dynamic applies to the capacity of generative AI tools to influence the creation of cultural products—such as fiction, art, and music. Much will depend on our willingness to consume AI-generated content once its novelty wears off. Will we want to read novels or social media posts without a human author? Will we be satisfied with procedurally generated playlists, or will we prefer the human touch, despite its imperfections and slower pace, over the seamlessness of AI? Will cheap, instant, and "good enough" content fulfil 99% of our needs, leaving the artisanal, time-consuming, and costly products of human labour to occupy the remaining 1%? Might "human-made" in cultural products become akin to "handmade" in physical products?

The introduction of computers into the workplace from the end-twentieth century might seem comparable to the current rise of AI software, given that both targeted white-collar knowledge work rather than manual labour. However, there are notable differences, one being the speed at which AI software can be deployed compared to the physical, expensive, and skill-dependent hardware of early computers. ChatGPT, for example, reached 1 million users in just 1 week in 2022 and hit 100 million registered users within 2 months (Reuters 2023). Its public release sparked an arms race among tech providers, with Google quickly scrambling to offer their own generative AI tools to users. In contrast, it took decades for computers to have a significant impact on productivity, as was the case with the mechanised loom centuries earlier. These technologies also required extensive retraining and mental adjustments to use. Generative AIs, by contrast, are built on existing digital infrastructure and operate on hardware already accessible to knowledge workers.

The speed of proliferation and adoption of these new technologies has greatly accelerated compared to past transformative technologies. This adoption is made easier by the tools' reliance on natural language, significantly increasing their intuitiveness. Another factor complicating comparisons is that new technologies not only change work in ways that can be measured, such as through productivity output, but they can also lead to unintended consequences and a reshuffling of work tasks in unforeseen ways. As the late anthropologist David Graeber pointed out in his writings, while computers revolutionised office work, they did not necessarily reduce the amount of work we have to do (Graeber 2018). On the contrary, they sometimes increased the administrative burdens they were meant to alleviate: "Just as the invention of new forms of industrial automation in the eighteenth and nineteenth centuries had the paradoxical effect of turning more and more of the world's population into full-time industrial workers, so has all the software designed to save us from administrative responsibilities turned us into part- or full-time administrators. [...] We all spend increasing amounts of time punching passwords into our phones to manage bank and credit accounts and learning how to perform jobs once done by travel agents, brokers, and accountants." It's a case of labour adapting to the technology at hand rather than the other way around. This illustrates that estimating the impact of generative AI based solely on productivity would miss the point. What will be far more interesting is how these technologies may eventually contribute to transforming work as we presently perceive it.

There is an increase in productivity (represented by the slope of the line), which indicates the pace of development—its impact is contingent upon how swiftly we adapt, as illustrated in Fig. 9.1.

The illustration is, by nature, a simplified depiction of future productivity trends, as we are yet to witness the culmination of new technologies and evolving behaviour patterns that, when they emerge, will once again create imbalances. Productivity growth will vary depending on function, organisation, individual preferences, personal profile, management, market, and culture. The primary driver of productivity increase will be the ability to digitalise work processes.

That's all in the long term. While we cannot rule out the possibility that AI and other digital automation technologies could eventually transform white-collar work into something unrecognisable today, there are other potential scenarios that may be more plausible in the near term. The most obvious scenario is what we are already beginning to see: a more deeply integrated collaboration between humans and AI. The AI surpasses the human in experience (achieved through deep learning) and can work at greater speed, but the human understands the meaning of the task and the quality of solutions in a way the machine cannot—unless it becomes sentient.

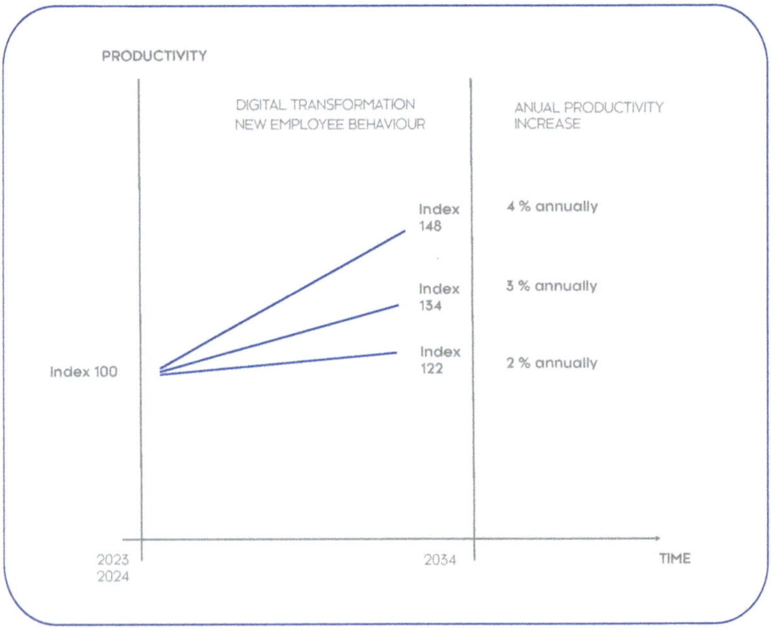

Fig. 9.1 AI: three future productivity projections of knowledge workers

Medical work provides examples of this dynamic today; a deep learning AI may surpass a single radiologist's ability to correctly diagnose cancer from X-rays, but a human radiologist and an AI working together has been demonstrated to be a far more effective combination because their strengths complement each other's weaknesses.

A more likely near-term future than wholesale transformation sees AI handling the grunt work of white-collar jobs, with humans defining the parameters and putting the finishing touches on the output. Since attention will remain a finite resource, no matter how much content AIs can churn out, this might spell bad news for copywriters, editors, marketers, and social media managers—or good news, if you are among the select few who will oversee and manage the work of computers. In such a scenario, we would likely see a broad need for reskilling, assuming there are new jobs to reskill into. If not, we may have to reconsider whether our definition of "work"—as something that takes place from 9-to-5 at the behest of an employer—is sufficiently broad. Housework, child-rearing, volunteering—if we are willing to let go of conventions, work in a more AI-dominated future could include anything that positively contributes to society or the lives of those around us. In Fig. 9.2, people were asked to envision work in 2030 within the context of AI (source: https://www.microsoft.com/en-us/worklab/work-trend-index/will-ai-fix-work). They indicated

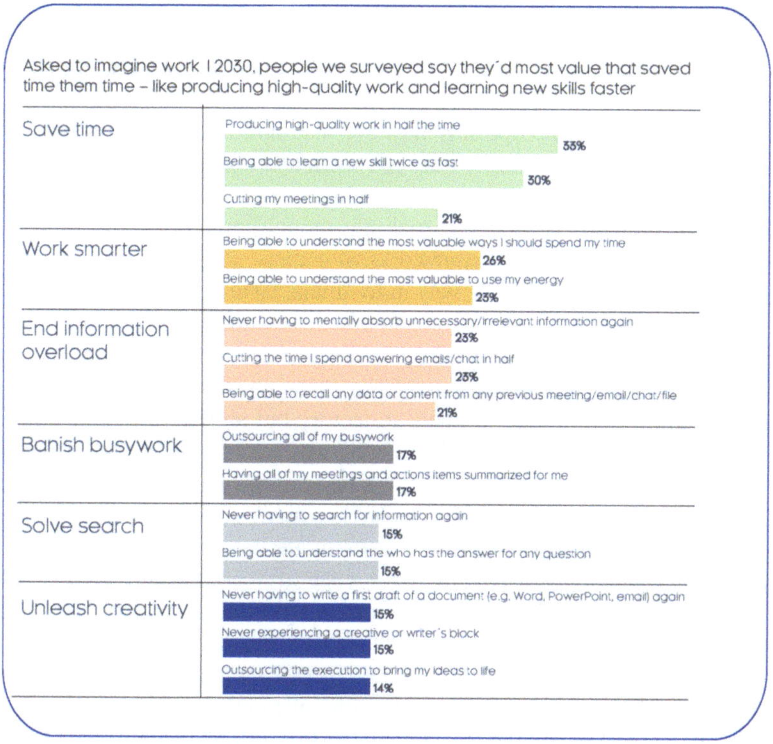

Fig. 9.2 Work in 2030: what people want

that they would most value AI for its ability to save them time, such as by producing high-quality work more efficiently and facilitating faster learning of new skills.

People tend to fear the unknown and readily accept the familiar (Castro and McQuinn 2015). A "mass moral panic" arises when one segment of society distrusts or fears the choices of others, believing these choices pose a threat to society as a whole (Tierer 2011). Extending this concept is the notion of a "techno-panic", which occurs when a segment of society fears a particular aspect of technological change. Often, these fears focus on anticipated problems that ultimately fail to materialise at various points in history; it was believed that reading novels could corrupt "the morals of many a promising youth", that movies might lead children to "dissolute lives", and that the telephone could make people lazy (Sadge 2006). Although society eventually overcomes these techno-panics, they can significantly slow technological progress, imposing real costs on society in the process.

If history is a guide, sudden technological changes can be both frightening and disruptive, but there will likely always be meaningful work for humans to do. We may just have to prepare for the future of work to be stranger than we have come to expect.

9.2 Challenge: Imagine an Office Day Automatically Tailored to You: Every Single Day!

Artificial Intelligence is no longer the distant promise of a future era; it is here, advancing at an unprecedented pace and reshaping the very fabric of our working lives. Soon, it will redefine not only how we lead and manage our office environments but also the delicate balance between work and life itself. No longer relegated to the background, AI has emerged as a transformative force—one that challenges our traditional methods of decision-making, reconfigures our daily routines, and even questions the established frameworks of society. Its influence is not confined to isolated tasks but extends to the way individuals, businesses, and entire industries operate. While it is widely acknowledged that AI will dramatically alter the nature of work, few have truly grasped its full potential to revolutionise the office—the very domain of the modern knowledge worker. The landscape has irrevocably changed: progress is no longer a linear trajectory but an adaptive, real-time evolution. Traditional workplace services are giving way to systems that learn, adjust, and continuously reshape themselves with every interaction. The era of designing offices based on the familiar patterns of the past is over; the "good old days" of the conventional office have been superseded by a new, dynamic paradigm. Among the most groundbreaking developments is the emergence of Workplace Agent as a Service (AaaS). This novel paradigm marries the autonomy of AI agents with the scalability and flexibility of cloud-based services, offering a transformative solution that spans customer service, work organisation, and beyond. In a recent vision articulated by Satya Nadella, CEO of Microsoft, the traditional model of Software as a Service (SaaS) is being supplanted by integrated platforms with AI at their core (AaaS) (AP News 2024). This shift promises to revolutionise conventional tools and workflows, ushering in an era of intelligent applications that adapt to the evolving needs of the modern workforce. The transition to hybrid and more flexible working arrangements for knowledge workers has introduced an unprecedented level of complexity. Organisations are compelled to rethink workflows, infrastructure, and employee engagement to balance the demands of remote and in-office work. AaaS offers an elegant solution to this complexity by automating routine processes—from scheduling meetings and analysing data trends to generating reports—thus liberating valuable human resources for strategic endeavours. For instance, as of mid-January 2025, ChatGPT has unveiled a beta version of an independent agent known as Task Management Assistance, which, when integrated with personal digital assistants, promises to revolutionise individual planning and task prioritisation. Parallel to these technological advances is the evolution of Activity-Based Workplace (ABW) design—a concept that has been evolving since its inception in the 1990s. Today, we stand on the threshold of what might be termed ABW 3.0—a sophisticated iteration that seamlessly integrates modern technologies and hybrid working. While many organisations are in the early stages of embracing ABW, the necessity to align workspace design with the diverse tasks of the modern employee is becoming ever more apparent.

Key Characteristics of ABW 3.0

1. Hybrid and Digital Integration: Modern ABW models effortlessly accommodate hybrid work arrangements, allowing employees to transition between physical offices and remote environments. Smart technologies, such as IoT devices and intuitive apps, monitor space utilisation and guide users to available workstations, enhancing both efficiency and convenience.
2. Human-Centric Design: Today's office design places the employee experience at its core, prioritising psychological safety, health, and inclusion. Contemporary layouts offer a variety of spaces—from quiet zones and creative hubs to areas for relaxation—catering to a wide spectrum of needs.
3. Data- and AI-Driven Decisions: Continuous improvements in workspace design are increasingly underpinned by data analytics. AI tools predict and adapt to user demands, ensuring that office capacity and layout evolve in real time to reflect emerging trends.
4. Sustainability at the Core: There is a growing commitment to reducing energy consumption and waste. The use of circular materials and modular furniture underscores a dedication to environmental responsibility, while also supporting diversity, equity, inclusion, and overall employee well-being.
5. Adaptation to Generational and Life-Stage Needs: ABW 3.0 is designed to meet the demands of a multigenerational workforce. It provides flexible, inclusive environments that adapt to the evolving needs of early-career professionals, mid-career leaders, and those later in their careers—each with distinct priorities ranging from collaboration and social interaction to focused leadership and mentorship.
6. Workplace as a Service (WaaS): Increasingly, the office is viewed as a service platform, offering bespoke solutions to meet individual and team needs. This approach fosters both productivity and satisfaction by ensuring that workspace design is continually responsive to organisational goals.

Looking Ahead: ABW 4.0 on Digital Steroids

The next phase—ABW 4.0—promises an individualised, scalable, and flexible office environment, enhanced by advanced digital capabilities. In this vision, the boundaries of time, space, and location blur, enabling seamless collaboration across both digital and physical realms.

- Intelligent Digital Systems: Advanced analytics, IoT sensors, and AI converge to create environments where data-driven insights optimise user experiences and operational efficiency. Automated adjustments in lighting, climate, and resource allocation ensure that the workspace adapts in real time to the needs of its occupants.
- Seamless Hybrid Environments: By integrating advanced technologies and flexible policies, hybrid work models break down traditional barriers. Real-time collaboration, equitable resource access, and synchronised workflows empower employees to choose where and how they work most effectively.
- Revolutionary AI-Powered Assistants: Digital assistants are set to manage workspaces, schedules, and resources with unprecedented precision. Balancing individual preferences with organisational needs, these AI aides are poised to transform productivity and enhance workplace cohesion.

In essence, the future of office design lies in a delicate balance between technological innovation and the enduring human need for connection and purpose. As organisations navigate this ever-changing landscape, the challenge will be to harness these advancements while preserving the autonomy and control that employees value. The promise of ABW 4.0 is not just about a more efficient office—it is about crafting a workspace that truly empowers individuals, teams, and entire organisations to thrive in a knowledge-driven world.

References

(AP News 2024) Microsoft pitches AI 'agents' that can perform tasks on their own at Ignite 2024 https://apnews.com/article/microsoft-artificial-intelligence-ai-agents-copilot-agentic-ignite-2024-782119423e28a7d88e4a27c12ce4e11f

(Castro and McQuinn 2015) ITIF September 2015, The Privacy Panic Cycle: A Guide to Public Fears About New Technologies https://www2.itif.org/2015-privacy-panic.pdf

(Epstein 2019) Epstein, David: Why Generilsts Triumph in a Specialized World. New York: Riverhead Books, 2019. https://www.amazon.com/Range-Generalists-Triumph-Specialized-World/dp/0735214484

(Graeber 2018) "Bullshit Jobs"

(Reuters 2023) ChatGPT sets record for fastest-growing user base

(Rock 2023) Stanford GPTs are GPTs: An Early Look at the Labor Market Impact Potential of Large Language Models https://digitaleconomy.stanford.edu/publications/gpts-are-gpts-an-early-look-at-the-labor-market-impact-potential-of-large-language-models/

(Sadge 2006) "The Culture War," Wired, April 2006, http://archive.wired.com/wired/archive/14.04/war.html

(Tierer 2011) "Techno-Panic Cycles (and How the Latest Privacy Scare Fits In)," the Technology Liberation Front, February 24, 2011, http://techliberation.com/2011/02/24/techno-panic-cycles-and-how-the-latest-privacy-scare-fits-in/

Part III

Anticipated Office Workplace Implications

10 The Successful Hybrid Office Workplace Model Is Ambidextrous

Abstract

The shift from an industrial to a knowledge-based society is reshaping traditional workplace models. Forward-thinking organisations are moving towards a hybrid workplace model that emphasises flexibility, employee well-being, and collaboration, creating environments that are better aligned with the needs of modern knowledge workers. This trend reflects a departure from desk-centric workplaces towards network-based models, where value creation happens through collaboration across the organisation. The transformation allows greater autonomy for employees, fostering engagement and aligning with modern work-life expectations. However, the pressure to adapt is intensifying, and management passivity is no longer an option. Organisations that fail to embrace these changes risk falling behind. Ultimately, the future office workplace will be a dynamic, flexible space—constantly evolving to meet the demands of a changing world.

10.1 The Workplace and Work-Life Changes Are Real

Is your boss physically located at the workplace, able to exert control? Is your workplace primarily designed from the perspective of employees or management? The future physical workplace must be designed based on employee value creation and not based on managerial preferences.

Management and employees fundamentally have different perspectives on the physical workplace. Managers often see it as an organisationally structured cobweb, with central actors exerting control. Physically, it appears as an analogue workplace divided into departmental areas centred around managers and middle managers. On the other hand, employees generally view value creation as happening through networks across the organisation. These networks contribute to solving concrete work challenges and tasks. Physically, it manifests as a flexible workplace where

C. Sneppen, *The Future (R)Evolution of the Office Workspace*, Future of Business and Finance, https://doi.org/10.1007/978-3-031-85229-9_10

employees can freely choose between physical, digital, or hybrid workspaces, independently of immediate management. In the network society, the workplace undergoes a transformation from being desk-centric to being centred around the network. Instead of being focused on physically close colleagues or managers, the workplace becomes more oriented towards relevant relationships that are essential for a given task. This shift allows for greater flexibility in terms of time and location and enables work to take place across the entire organisation.

In the network-based model, work is organised around the digital workplace, with additional support from the analogue workplace. Collaboration occurs at the "middle" of the hybrid workplace. In the network society, the social structure is built around digital communication and interaction as the primary means of connection. The increasing digitisation of the workplace is anticipated to have a significant impact on how relationships, communication, and value are shaped within organisations in the future. The sense of community is shifting from departmental communities to task-based communities, requiring more collaboration and co-creation across the organisational structure. The network society further reinforces the growing trend towards increased autonomy, self-management, and reduced hierarchical layers of management. In this context, employees are given more freedom to organise value creation with a focus on specific task goals. In the workplace of the future, task-based communities become more crucial than physical proximity, and this applies to management as well. At the same time, it is important to address that different employees have different work preferences. Additionally, the conflict between fixed routines and behaviour patterns is challenged by the flexible workplace without fixed workstations.

The pressure from the environment to change the workplace is growing. It requires that the management and the individual organisation take a proactive stance on how the future-proof workplace model should be designed. If the answer is "no" to the fact that you haven't experienced major sustained change and adjustments to the workplace model, then we anticipate that it will most likely happen soon. Either because the workplace is being rethought and redesigned or because you are changing to a new workplace with a more up-to-date workplace model (the workplace model, including the degree of flexibility, is crucial for attracting and retaining employees). If the answer is "yes" to you experiencing changes, then we predict that in the future you will experience a continuous adaptation of the workplace. The workplace is no longer a static "workplace" but dynamic "workspace"—and increasingly freed from time and place through changed employee behaviour and digitisation.

10.2 Passive Management Is No Longer an Option

Are you employed in a workplace that seems like a living museum of post-industrial work practices, with rigid 9-to-5 schedules and an overwhelming number of meetings? Does your workplace appear to be stuck in outdated ways of organising and designing work? How does your management view the concept of a hybrid workplace? Can your organisation afford to ignore the potential benefits of embracing the hybrid workplace model? The questions are boundless, and the pivotal future development of the hybrid workplace is depicted in Fig. 10.1. The tension field and balance point for the future evolution of the hybrid workplace can be simplified and illustrated by the following diagram, which portrays the essential trends and currents. The defining components of future hybrid workplace balance will be further elaborated and discussed in depth later in this publication. The points presented are neither exhaustive nor complete and will be explored in greater detail in the subsequent chapters.

A top manager emphasised in an interview, "My clear and strongest advice to workplace actors and decision-makers: 'Don't do nothing. Just do something.' Don't believe that you have to get it right, but the alternative is highly dangerous, which is being in a state of waiting. Not moving forward and prolonged contemplating will eventually mean moving backward." Management is accountable for the workplace, and thus has a significant impact on how the individual organisation establishes a successful hybrid workplace. Choosing not to develop the hybrid workplace is also a decision, but all trend indications and factors strongly suggest that it is not a wise and viable option. The individual organisation doesn't necessarily have to be at the cutting edge of development. However, partially or entirely rejecting the hybrid workplace model is tantamount to hindering progress, or at the very least, the maintenance of competitiveness. In a competitive marketplace, it's not about being the fastest or being at the forefront of hybrid workplace model development. It's about avoiding being left behind and losing out to competitors. Organisations don't have to be the fastest; they just need to match or outperform competitors. Developing a workplace model that optimises value for the organisation is a lengthy process. It must occur concurrently with ongoing changes in digitisation and employee behaviour.

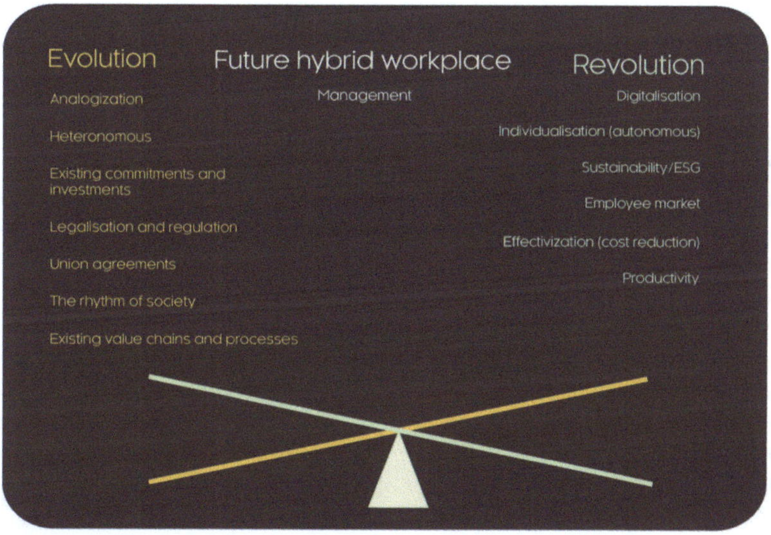

Fig. 10.1 The decisive future hybrid workplace development balance

Workspace Case: Danish Building and Property Agency

The Danish Building and Property Agency is the largest government real estate agency in Denmark, responsible for providing workplaces for universities, courts, police, ministries, and governmental agencies throughout Denmark, the Faroe Islands, and Greenland. The agency employs around 370 specialists in asset management, construction project management, and facility management, working out of offices in Copenhagen and Skanderborg.

Both of these offices are entirely activity-based, featuring free seating for all employees, including top management, and are divided into different activity zones—such as quiet zones, focus zones, active zones, and drop-down zones—providing ample space for both open and private meetings and knowledge sharing. The agency actively supports remote work and is equipped with modern AV facilities to facilitate hybrid meetings across all meeting rooms.

The agency fully implemented the activity-based workplace (ABW) model in 2019 following pilot projects in both offices. This implementation was accompanied by an ambitious change management process to adapt to new working methods, including developing competencies in leading remote teams within a free-seating workplace. As a result, the agency was well-prepared for the COVID-19 lockdown, as well as the more permanent increase in remote working that followed the pandemic.

The Hybrid Activity-Based Workplace Is Here to Stay

Our vision for the workplace is to be a living showcase of modern, activity-based, hybrid office environments. In doing so, we aim to inspire and advise our clients on optimising their organisations and office spaces. The advantages in terms of flexibility, workspace optimisation for various types of work, sustainability, and cost savings far outweigh challenges relating to cohesion and culture, as these challenges can be addressed through improved management with a focus on outcomes (value creation) rather than input.

The potential for optimising governmental office workplaces is enormous. By implementing the activity-based, hybrid workplace within our own organisation, the Danish Building and Property Agency has improved its space efficiency from 23 m^2/FTE in 2019 to 12 m^2/FTE in 2024. A similar potential for optimisation exists among our customer organisations located within our 4.5 million m^2 portfolio, where space efficiency is currently estimated to be around 30 m^2/FTE (Full-Time Equivalent employee).

Many of The Danish Building and Property Agency's office clients are already motivated to modernise their office spaces. However, the existing portfolio of governmental office buildings, combined with an outdated rental model, does not provide the necessary flexibility and incentives for a comprehensive transformation. The Danish Building and Property Agency is currently developing several multi-customer office hubs that will deliver this flexibility, and we are working on updating the lease model and multi-customer office hub facility management solutions to facilitate the transformation.

HQ The Danish Building and Property Agency. *Image credits:* The Danish Building and Property Agency

Recommendations

- *Recognise that change management is even more crucial than the office's interior programming and design.*
- *Ensure top management is actively involved in the transition and operates on equal terms with staff.*
- *Implement fully digital work processes and provide state-of-the-art ICT (Information and Communication Technology) hardware.*
- *Allocate some of the savings for reinvestment into creating an attractive workplace environment.*
- *Be prepared to evaluate and adjust according to experience.*
- *Avoid over-programming your office space with inflexible solutions, as you may need to make changes in the future.*

10.3 The Organic Office Workplace

As previously stated, walls and buildings will no longer define work life as they once did. The future physical workplace will revolve around plasticity, meaning it will be a mouldable and adaptable digital and analogue workspace and place. To succeed, one should aim for where the target will be, not where it currently is, just like a skilled hunter aiming at a leaping hare. The significant difference with the hunting analogy is that the future hybrid workplace means the workplace will be a constantly moving target for the foreseeable future.

To succeed in the present and future workplace, actors must adopt a long-term mindset. The developments and changes are too significant to be addressed by focusing solely on the current situation. This poses a major challenge for office workspace actors and decision-makers. They must shift from a relatively stationary and comfortable approach to continuously adapting the office and overall workplace model development to accommodate significant changes and advancements, in order to create the most optimal hybrid workplace. As the workplace transforms into a dynamic and organic ecosystem, the ability to respond and adapt must increase.

The successful hybrid workplace model is expected to involve instant remodelling and adjustability, figuratively speaking, evolving daily. To draw an analogy, the future workplace can be likened to baking bread. My wife is a passionate bread baker and continuously works with the right mix of ingredients and preparation techniques. It is a highly organic process where various factors come into play, such as the age of the flour, the sourdough, room temperature, humidity, proofing time, oven, mixer, and so on. She frequently uses old, dried bread that contains all the mentioned ingredients from a previous process. The result is that the process of making each loaf of bread is dependent on and constantly adjusted to achieve the optimal outcome.

10.4 Ambidextrous Office Workplace: Simultaneously Exploiting and Exploring

The office model of the future needs to continuously balance between moments of efficient utilisation—exploitation—of the model to ensure productivity and effectiveness, and on the other hand, constantly be exploratory and seeking new ways to develop the office model to complement management, employees, and digital advancements. A workplace model and organisation that balances the present exploitation and optimisation of employees' working lives, while simultaneously exploring and developing the model, is referred to as the ambidextrous hybrid workplace model (Tushman and O'Reilly 1996).

The central workplace that once stood as a castle and manifestation of organisational success is increasingly giving way to the workplace in constant beta—an organic workplace that functions in symbiosis and adapts with its users and surroundings. As we move forward, the "old" office is transforming, and the development means that the static overconsumption of physical space is a thing of the past. Instead, intelligent use of square metres based on the sharing economy is the future. At the same time, the digital workplace and infrastructure are evolving at a revolutionary pace. The office model is though now functioning like a piece of software in continuous development, always in a beta version. It's an office model where solutions are implemented but subject to correction and improvement in increasingly shorter intervals. This poses a challenge for organisations to be ambidextrous, capable of developing and leveraging the workplace simultaneously. It requires constant optimisation while allowing room for experimentation.

The ambidextrous hybrid workplace represents a departure from the traditional approach to the workplace, where elements were approximately permanent. The workplace in constant beta poses challenges for management and challenges the previous approach to the workplace as a static entity. The old model, which still exists to varying degrees in organisations, was simpler, less complex, and more predictable. The successful future ever evolving hybrid workplace raises practical questions for management: How can we establish a process that ensures continuous development? How should we allocate responsibility and resources to achieve this?

A central and crucial question within the ambidextrous hybrid office model is how to balance sustainable productivity with the framework of organisational rules, regulations, and allowances for mistakes. This balance is highly relevant across all levels—from individuals and teams to departments, organisations, and society as a whole. Where is the optimal balance point between sustainable productivity and the rules and guidelines that shape the workplace model? The concept in question is encapsulated in Michael Power's notion of the Audit Society, introduced by the British sociologist in his seminal 1997 work, *The Audit Society: Rituals of Verification* (Powers 1997). Power's central argument is that contemporary societies, particularly advanced industrial nations, have developed an increasing preoccupation with audits, evaluations, and assessments across various domains. This phenomenon reflects a broader cultural shift towards accountability and transparency, though it also brings with it significant consequences.

Regarding the strict governance, I have coined this "The Regulatory Dilemma" of the hybrid office model. While it is possible to distinguish between the volume and quality of rules, they can generally be summarised as the organisational workplace regulatory framework. Different sectors and segments of the workplace have varying regulatory frameworks, as governance naturally varies. For instance, a hospital will have far more rules than a digital start-up. Inherent in these differences are significant challenges for organisations with strong governance structures and extensive rules, as every organisation—regardless of size or industry—must experiment with the ongoing development of the modern hybrid workplace model. This brings us back to the culture of the organisation, which will ultimately shape the workplace model approach. Within any given organisation, there exists an optimal balance point where sustainable productivity intersects with an appropriate level of rules and guidelines. An overly restrictive or extensive set of rules, coupled with rigid frameworks, will inevitably lead to lower productivity and on the positive side reduced room for short sight errors. On the other hand, too few rules or guidelines may result in diminished cohesion, collaboration, coordination, and the pursuit of shared goals and an abundance of errors. In the context of the hybrid model, this becomes a question of where the optimal point lies—both qualitatively and quantitatively—in terms of the structured hybrid workplace model's regulatory framework.

The ambidextrous hybrid office workplace aligns with Dave Snowden's Cynefin Framework, a decision-making model that categorises challenges into four domains: simple, complicated, complex, and chaotic (Snowdon and Boone 2007). Each domain requires a different approach, and the hybrid workplace model increasingly operates within the complex domain:

- In the simple domain, solutions are clear, and best practices are applied (the post-industrial office model).
- In the complicated domain, expertise and analysis lead to workable solutions.

- In the complex domain, outcomes are unpredictable, and experimentation becomes essential. This domain is where the hybrid workplace thrives: organisations must probe, sense, and respond, allowing small experiments to reveal emergent solutions.
- In the chaotic domain, rapid action is required to restore stability.

The present hybrid office workplace exists primarily in the complex domain, where cause and effect are not immediately clear. It requires leaders to create environments that encourage safe-to-fail experiments, where failure is not seen as an endpoint but as an opportunity to learn and iterate. It is likely, in this context, that the current discussion and partial shift towards a return to the office (RTO) should be seen quite simply as an attempt to reduce complexity. However, is this approach truly viable, and does it represent the most competitive solution?

When debating regulatory framework within the ambidextrous hybrid office workplace model, the acceptable room for error—and thus experimentation—comes into focus. Here, too, there is an optimal point for sustainable productivity, particularly in relation to an organisation's approach to mistakes. Workplace rules and guidelines serve many purposes, one of which is to minimise errors and prevent unproductive or counterproductive use of resources. Where is the optimal balance point for the ambidextrous office workplace model between exploration and exploitation? Implicitly, this raises the question of the balance between mistakes and productivity. A very low—or in the extreme zero—tolerance for mistakes in a dynamic environment will lead to lower sustainable productivity, just as an overly high tolerance for errors will do the same. This is what I refer to as the "error dilemma" for the hybrid office model. Both dilemmas are rooted in a fundamental departure from the post-industrial static office model, moving towards a more dynamic, agile, knowledge-, and network-based approach.

The hybrid office model signifies a profound transition from the static, post-industrial workplace to a dynamic, agile, and network-driven model. Leaders must acknowledge and embrace the complexity inherent in this transformation, recognising that failure is not the antithesis of success but an essential step on the path towards it. This perspective presents a particular challenge for operational workforce, and workplace functions traditionally prioritise minimising mistakes and ensuring seamless operations and processes.

References

(Powers 1997) Oxford University Press, The Audit Society: Rituals of Verification

(Snowdon and Boone 2007) Dave Snowdon and Mary Boone, HBR November 2007 A Leader's Framework for Decision Making, https://hbr.org/2007/11/a-leaders-framework-for-decision-making

(Tushman and O'Reilly 1996) Michael L. Tushman and Charles A. O'Reilly III *California Management Review: "Ambidextrous Organizations: Managing Evolutionary and Revolutionary Change,"* https://web.mit.edu/curhan/www/docs/Articles/15341_Readings/Organizational_Learning_and_Change/Tushman_&_OReilly_1996_Ambidextrous_Organizations.pdf

Future Hybrid Work: Employee Behavioural Dynamics

11

Abstract

The optimal workplace design must consider employee value creation and interactions in the networked, knowledge-based society. As workplace models evolve, they will increasingly prioritise networks, collaboration, and individualisation. The hybrid workplace, offering flexibility and catering to both individual and collective needs, is likely to prevail. Employee motivations for coming to the office vary, including mandatory presence, social interaction, development opportunities, task necessity, and effectiveness. Employers must adapt to the changing landscape, as the employee experience and preferences will significantly influence workplace models. The hybrid workplace should balance individual work focus with long-term investment in collective goals.

Organisations that succeed in offering accommodating hybrid models will attract and retain the best talent, ensuring continued value creation and competitiveness. Emphasising psychological safety, flexibility, and a strong sense of belonging will be crucial in shaping the future of work. Ultimately, employees will increasingly dictate the terms of workplace models, making it essential for organisations to understand and respect their needs, ensuring a mutually beneficial and productive work environment.

11.1 The Current Reasons for Coming to Work In Person Are Changing

Why do employees physically go to the office? What can the physical workplace offer that justifies employees daily commute from home? The old-fashioned and past-oriented manager will dismiss this question with a simple answer: Because the employee gets paid for it. However, this is being challenged by studies showing that employees are increasingly willing to accept a reduced salary in exchange for more

C. Sneppen, *The Future (R)Evolution of the Office Workspace*, Future of Business and Finance, https://doi.org/10.1007/978-3-031-85229-9_11

flexibility (Mas and Pallais 2017; Bagga et al. 2024). These findings indicate a shift in priorities, where workers value the ability to manage their work-life balance more than higher pay, particularly in hybrid or remote work environments. This trend highlights the growing demand for flexibility in the modern workforce, which organisations will need to consider as they shape their future workplace models. No one knows the exact framework for a good future work-life and workspace, but everything points to the fact that the hybrid workday is here to stay. Employees have different motivations for physically coming in person to the office workplace. Based on numerous workshops held, five main motivations have crystallised (Fig. 11.1):

- Mandatory: It is a requirement and rule that the employee follows. A motivation that will come under increasing pressure as the hybrid workplace model develops and is implemented in society.
- Social: Relationships with colleagues create a framework for social security, engagement, and well-being.
- Development: Physical presence creates a breeding ground for development and innovation—a lack that is often highlighted after long periods of working from home during the pandemic.

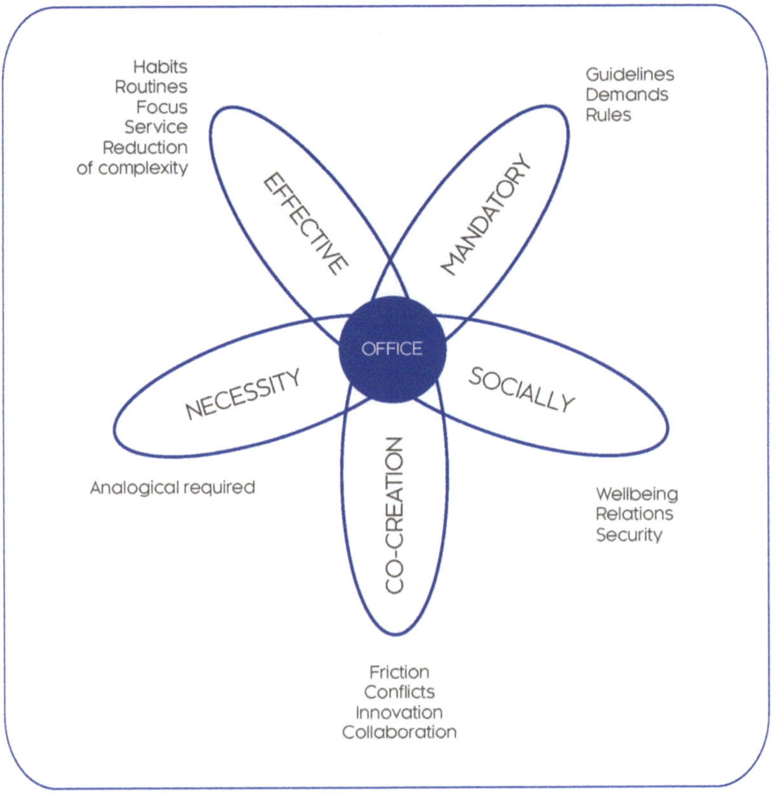

Fig. 11.1 Why do employees physically go to the office?

- Necessary: Functions and tasks that require physical presence to be solved. Distance work is just not possible.
- Effective: Physical presence creates focus on solving tasks—without distractions.

The prevailing motivation brought forward differs depending on the individual. Overall, generally it is one main motivation, of all the above, that is being brought forward as the most prevailing when individuals argue for a less flexible workplace model. And the other motivations are subsequently included in the overall justification for why the employee physically shows up to work—and thus take the consequence not to work remotely. A more nuanced and personal employee perspective can be observed in Fig. 11.2, where the two predominant responses centre around collaboration and work-life/personal boundaries.

The motivations are not fully representative, but they paint a clear picture of how employees differ based on several crucial parameters such as demographics, personal profile, and function. The combination possibilities of motivations are almost endless and leave organisations with a challenge: How should the workplace and work model be thought of and designed based on different employee preferences and motivations? Employers must be aware that the work model will be a crucial parameter for employees when choosing a workplace in the future. Employers may have the illusion that it is management that sets the framework and determines the work model.

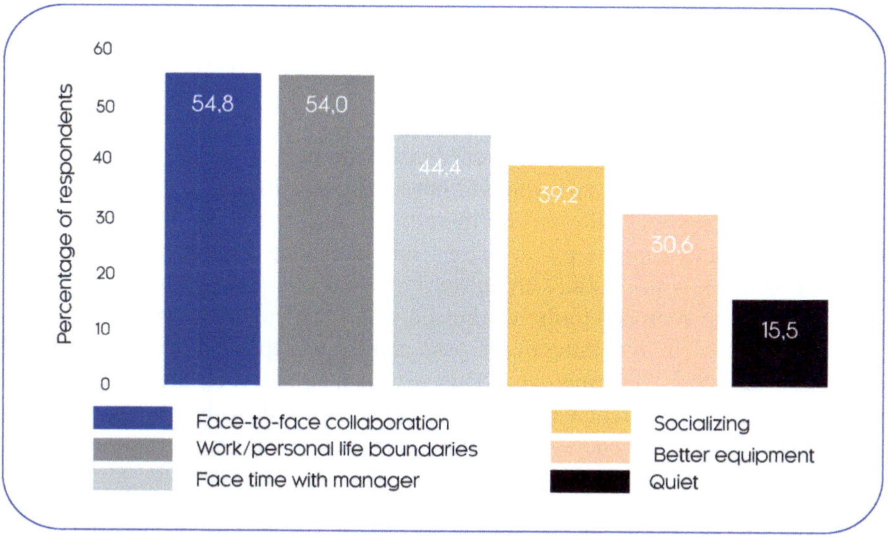

Fig. 11.2 What are the top three benefits of working on your employer's business premises? Source: Barrero, Jose Maria, Nicholas Bloom, and Steven J. Davis, 2021. "Why working from home will stick," National Bureau of Economic Research Working Paper 28731. www.wfhresearch.com

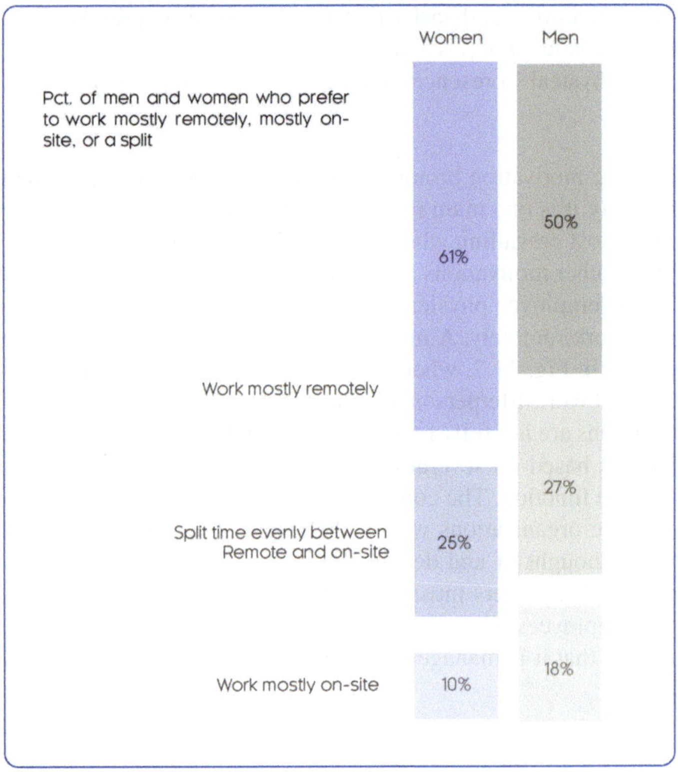

Fig. 11.3 Women are far less likely than men to want to work mostly on-site. Source: McKinsey & Company: Women in the Workplace 2022

But in a labour market with heightened competition to attract and retainvaluable employees, it is the employees who will have a decisive influence on the model for the hybrid workplace. Employers will therefore be under growing pressure to create understanding and support for decisions that influence employees' freedom to choose how work is structurally organised.

The industrial approach to the workplace with identical linear and synchronous solutions is increasingly a thing of the past, and the workplace will increasingly be tailored to the individual employee. This will happen based on the understanding that employees are different and that workplace design is directly correlated to individual employees' efficiency, productivity, and well-being and the corresponding unique organisational culture. It has simply become too expensive to approach employees as a homogeneous entity and not as consumers. The "one-size-fits-all" approach is not optimal, and inherently contradictive to flexibility, and better models will prevail in the future. One example of this is evident between genders, as men and women may experience flexibility differently in relation to interference (Brulin et al. 2023). Consequently, employers aiming to reduce interference for employees should consider gender norms and individual needs (Fig. 11.3).

11.2 Employees Act: Organisations and Employers Adapt

Employees are currently, and will increasingly become, the driving force in shaping the workplace model and the interpretation of the hybrid workplace. This is largely due to the scarcity of qualified employees and the significant impact that engaged, thriving employees have on an organisation's cumulative value creation. Employee support for their organisation's remote work strategy plays a crucial role in turnover rates, with this relationship being influenced by factors such as burnout and feelings of inclusion (Kim et al. 2023). Valuable employees will be, if not already, a "scarce resource" that employers must attract, retain, and develop.

The scarcity of valuable employees and talent mass will have a ripple effect on all other employees, as organisations will strive to create an inclusive workplace and culture. Economic challenges will not dampen the demand for highly talented employees; instead, organisations will seek such skills to ensure value creation during times of market changes and challenges. Recruiters predict that talent will continue to have the upper hand for at least another 5 years, according to a LinkedIn survey (LinkedIn Business 2024). As the expected tenure of each employee in the organisation decreases, the quest for talent attraction development, and retention becomes even more critical.

Employees are becoming increasingly mobile and more self-oriented in their loyalty. According to the most recent data available from the Bureau of Labor Statistics (USA), the average worker today stays at each job for 3,9 years, but the expected tenure of the youngest employees in the workforce is about half of that (Bureau of Labor Statistics 2024). This means they could potentially have 15–20 jobs over the course of their working lives! In the future, employees will increasingly choose the workplace model that best caters to their well-being as individuals. Simultaneously, they will also select the workplace model where they can be most productive and efficient for the organisation. These approaches to employees and human needs are not contradictory but rather mutually reinforcing. Employees who thrive in their work environment tend to be significantly more productive and efficient. Allowing employees to have a say in shaping the workplace model holds significant potential value—a potential that should not be ignored.

The preferences of employees are highly diverse and sometimes conflicting. Location-agnostic working is an approach that allows employees to choose where they want to work on a day-to-day basis. For some individuals, the idea of working from home is highly appealing, while others may prefer a more vibrant office environment or lack a suitable home office space, making it less ideal for them. For these employees, working from a convenient co-working space could be a better option. A pre-pandemic study by Stanford found that 55% of respondents want to spend some time in the office and some time at home, while 25% want to work from home full-time and 20% only want to work in the office (Bloom 2020). The study also found that some employees who tried working from home found it too lonely while others became addicted to distractions such as television, the fridge, or the bed, and ended up returning to work in their office. Even small permanent shifts in employees' preferences can have a significant impact on the workplace model, given the increasing demand for qualified labour. Employers need to adapt to an employee market where organisations compete to attract and retain the right talents and skills. Employee behaviour and preferences will thus play a crucial role in shaping the future hybrid workplace.

Some employers might mistakenly believe that their decisions alone will determine the development of the hybrid workplace. However, in the long run, digitalisation and employee behaviour and preferences will define the workplace models. Employers who adhere to a traditional approach may find it challenging to attract employees and be more susceptible to negative developments. The scarcity of qualified labour creates a market where employers must strive to attract and retain skilled employees. The workplace must increasingly adapt to employees' preferences and behaviours. In the hybrid office workplace model, it should be customised to suit individuals' work from a flexible perspective, as well as to address the broader aspect of meeting employees as social beings with needs for relationships, interactions, and collaboration. The primary focus is on ensuring the well-being, engagement, and sense of psychological security of the employees.

The introduction of the hybrid workplace has further emphasised the importance of psychological safety in an ever more complex and unpredictable work environment. Consequently, the traditional setup of having employees come to the office every day and work from assigned desks, where they sit next to the same people day after day, does not necessarily allow them to effectively build relationships and connections with the right and task-related optimal colleagues. Value is created through networks and collaboration with colleagues relevant to the work task, not necessarily the ones sitting next to the employee. Adapting a more flexible setup where individuals can co-locate with the many different teams and people they work with is therefore a core enabler of helping teams build value. The physical office, in that regard, should mirror the digital workplace and platform where networks form the foundation for value creation (Fig. 11.4).

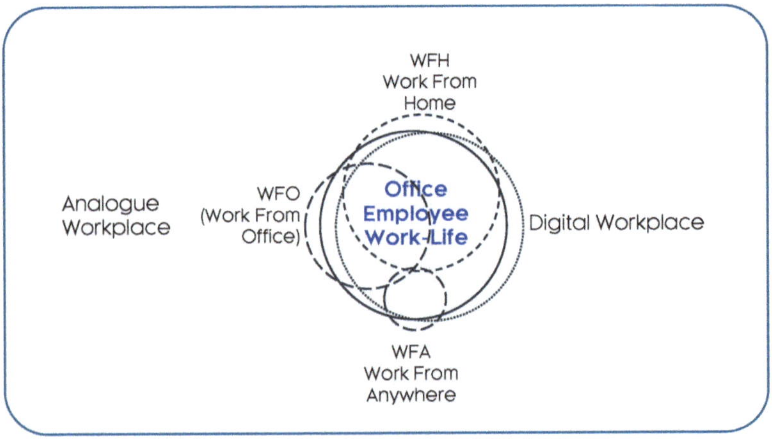

Fig. 11.4 The hybrid office: navigating employee work-life realities

The workplace model will be a crucial factor for employees in terms of employment in the future. A workplace model that offers distance work and flexibility will be a decisive parameter for a soaring proportion of employees. If there is a lack of flexibility and a high demand for physical presence, the employer must be aware of the risk of being a "deal-breaker" in the job interview. If competitors have a more accommodating approach and better meet employee preferences, they will win the battle for talent. In the end, the organisations with the largest talent pool to recruit from will succeed, and those with the largest talent pool are the ones that have the most accommodating hybrid office workplace model.

11.3 Challenge: Can Organisations Have Success If Segments of Employees Are Opting Out?

Individuals are now more inclined to prioritise their health and well-being over work than they were before the pandemic. Moreover, employees are acting upon these newly embraced priorities. 'The boss may command our time, but never our soul, for the existential meaning of life is to be found elsewhere,' an executive stated during an interview for this book.When looking at the overall picture of how much work occupies employees' time in the Western world, the trend over the past decades has been progressively less, with the exception of the USA. But despite countries like Denmark, where employees on average work about 25% less than in the USA, there is also a shift here in how we want to prioritise and structure work in life (Figs. 11.5 and 11.6).

In a survey from Microsoft (2022), 17% of people left their jobs, and the trend is expected to continue. The top five reasons employees quit were personal well-being or mental health (24%), work-life balance (24%), risk of getting COVID-19 (21%), lack of confidence in senior management/leadership (21%), and lack of flexible work hours or location (21%). Somewhat surprisingly, "not receiving promotions or raises I deserved" ranked seventh on the list at 19%, further illustrating the shift in priorities. The data also shows that the Great Reshuffle is far from over. In the upcoming year, 51% of hybrid employees say they will consider switching to remote work, and even more remote employees (57%) say they'll consider a switch to hybrid work. Meanwhile, 43% of employees are somewhat or extremely likely to

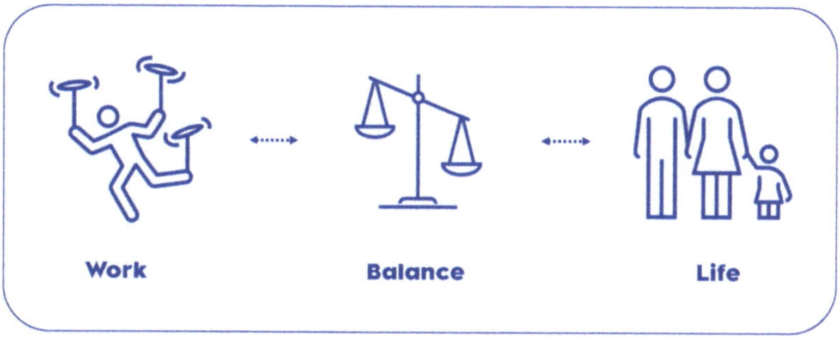

Fig. 11.5 From work-life balance to life-work balance

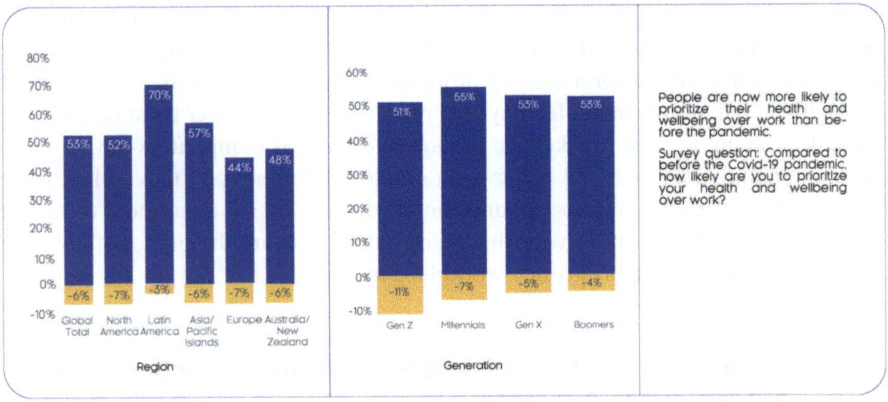

Fig. 11.6 Employee priorities have shifted. Source: Microsoft 2022 Work Trend Index

consider changing jobs in the coming year, slightly up from 41% compared to the previous year.

Certain generations are even more inclined to change employers—over half (52%) of Generation Z and Millennials combined may change jobs in the year ahead, a 3% increase since last year. In comparison, only 35% of Gen X and Boomers say they're considering a job change (Microsoft 2022). The desire for flexibility extends to leadership as well, as 47% of leaders are likely to consider applying for jobs that are not near their homes in the next year. An example of this development and shift can be seen in the increasing number of employees opting out of career jobs in the central administration in Denmark in the aftermath of the heavy workload during the pandemic (TV2 DK 2023). Over a quarter of employees resigned from ministries in Denmark in 2022. In 2022, 27% of the staff left various departments in ministries in Denmark. This figure is the highest in the past 10 years and 29% higher than in 2021. The number of days of absence due to long-term sick leave is also the highest in the 10-year period for which the media has obtained information. Officials report a work culture where they are constantly busy and expected to be available at all times. Former and current officials report instances such as being called to work even when they are sick with a concussion or on maternity leave. Another person shares their experience of working with their work computer on their lap while attending their best friend's bachelorette party.

11.4 Challenge: Are You a Lucky Chosen Potato at Your Workplace—Or Do You Feel Like a Mashed Potato?

The workplace as a central focal point for working life is breaking up for knowledge workers. The workplace is no longer a place, but an activity. Many employees demand an increasingly individually adapted model for where, how, and when work is done (Owl Labs 2023). It challenges the organisation, management, and not least the physical workplace as an entity for working life.

In a recent report on work-life and workplace development within the Danish market, it is concluded that the conventional notion of the workplace as the primary focal point of professional life is diminishing for knowledge workers (Ballisager 2023). This aligns with the overall trend observed in the Western Hemisphere. The workplace is no longer defined by a physical location, but by the activities performed there. Many employees are growingly demanding individually tailored models for where, how, and when work is done. This poses challenges for the organisation, management, and especially the physical workplace as a concept.

Many organisations spend almost unimaginable resources on selecting the right and most value-creating employees, to then ensure that they uniquely adapt their work processes to the organisation and the existing workplace model. In populist terms, the right and best "potatoes" are selected so that they are then transformed into "mashed potatoes" by forcing the individual into a rigid organisation of working life and the workplace. But is it the future optimal approach to ensure the attraction, development, and retention of knowledge workers in an increasingly individualised and knowledge-heavy labour market? Does it provide the greatest possible value for the organisation? There is obviously and self-evidently great potential in selecting the right knowledge workers, and subsequently individually adapting work processes so that the employee's value potential is realised for the organisation.

Employees who are happy and motivated, and look forward to their work, are simply far more value-creating and long-lasting. In a personal dialogue a Danish CEO found that there was great unrealised potential in giving employees more freedom and that precisely through the development of a more up-to-date workplace model, they worked focused on realising employee potential. The individually adapted workplace model requires trust between employee and organisation. It also requires a management that has the skills to lead an increasingly differentiated and heterogeneous workplace model. Why spend so many resources on finding the right employees, and then manage them based on the basic premise that they must be closely managed and monitored? Does the management not trust that the individual employee works focused on solving assigned tasks? This is precisely the point that Director Rasmus Brandt Lassen of the Danish Building and Property Agency made during dialogues about the development of the office workplace model of the future. "It does not make sense to spend energy on selecting and hiring the most competent knowledge workers, only to then not have confidence that they can solve their daily tasks without in-person supervision."

11.5 The Future Behaviour of Employees Is as Consumers of Time

Welcome to the new era of employee consumerism. Nowadays, employees devote their work time to creating value in an omnichannel reality. Just as you comprehend what motivates your customers, do you understand what motivates your employees? Is your workplace ready for the new behaviour of employees, where they "shop" for work time that is no longer restricted by traditional constraints of time, place, and space?

We live in a productivity-focused age where the culture of being "always on" means work often spills into our personal time. Parenting feels more demanding, and our friends, hobbies, and interests are just a tap or swipe away on our phones, 24/7. In Fig. 11.7, Ultimately, it comes down to how we as individuals—consciously and unconsciously—choose and prioritise to spend the 3 billion heartbeats that, on average, make up a human life.

In the 1980s, Paul Virilio, a professor at Ecole Speciale d' Architecture France, defined the growing significance of speed in the social-economic dynamics of modern culture with the concept of "Dromocracy" (Virilio 1986). Speed continues to increase with technological advancements, becoming a fundamental element of innovation and driving ongoing exploration of the relationship between space and time. The "high-speed society" where our way of life is characterised by rapid movement, communication, and production. This has given rise to an era in which technical speed has accelerated all aspects of social existence. Speed has permeated collective dynamics, influencing private life, work, and transportation. It achieves simultaneity with networks and data transmission, erasing distances and temporal barriers, thereby emphasising the importance of the present in both individual and collective experiences. The acceleration of social change is tied to the ever-rising rapidity in the dissemination of major innovations. For instance, it took around 40 years for radio, a late nineteenth-century invention, to reach 50 million listeners. On the other hand, television, introduced in the first half of the twentieth century,

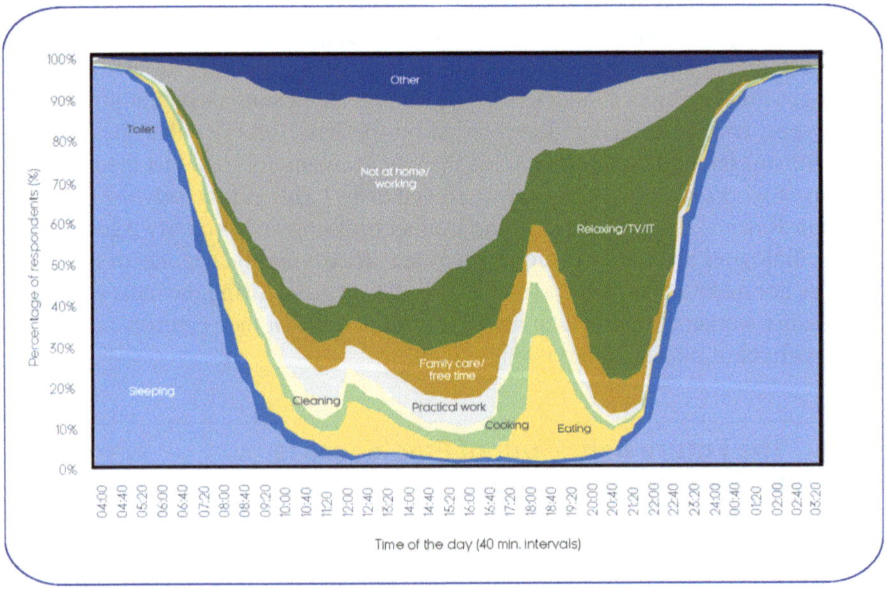

Fig. 11.7 Human consumption of time is illustrated in 24 h. Source: Hans Skifter Andersen: BUILD Rapport 2021:1. Boligen i samfundet. Viden fra boligforskningen

achieved the same level of diffusion in just 13 years. Even more remarkable, it only took 4 years for the Internet to connect its first 50 million users. ChatGPT broke this record by reaching 200 million users well within the two first months of its launch. Speed cannot be dissociated from time and space. As time undergoes exponential compression, a reflection on the implications of this evolution becomes implicitly intertwined with the characteristics of space in all its forms, ranging from individual living spaces to workplaces and towns. The escalating speed of movement alters our relationship with space, our experience of living, and our perception of time.

Contemplating contemporary workspaces today involves pondering how to accommodate and embrace rapidity, envisioning new patterns of utilisation and continual changes. The increasing complexity of relationships is mirrored in the processes that generate new workspaces and redefine existing ones. Conventional borders are being constantly blurred and dissolved, leading to a proliferation of overlapping areas of existence. Different workplaces increasingly coexist within the same space, merging together in the hybrid workplace model. Employees are growingly seeking to optimise their work time as well as their overall time. If you ask any employee if they have spare time, the resounding answer is no. Time is a scarce resource in a world filled with endless opportunities for productivity and entertainment. Mobile phones are always within reach, and even the smallest pockets of free time are utilised to maximise short-term productivity. This trend is positive for organisations and workplaces that create an environment and culture where employees constantly strive to achieve the highest possible output within the given time. However, organisations that primarily focus on input of work time face challenges with the emergence and expansion of a distributed hybrid workforce.

Employees have simply adopted an individualistic and self-centred behaviour learned from the opportunities and offerings available to all consumers in today's market. It's referred to as the horizontal displacement of expectations, where individuals transfer demands and expectations between different sectors, services, and products. As consumers, employees now have instant access to products and services tailored to their needs and desires.

Consequently, organisations are increasingly expected to adapt to these market forces. When employees, as consumers of their own personal time, have optimised their use of on-demand TV, dating apps, shopping, and package deliveries, this mindset extends to the workplace regarding meetings and work approaches. The main expectation becomes "don't waste my time", based on personal experiences and perceptions of the work reality. This poses a challenge for management and the organisation to align collective goals while ensuring individual employees feel they are utilising their work time effectively.

In the spring of 2023, yet another interesting employee phenomenon has emerged. It is called "Bare Minimum Mondays"—employees are advocating for a more relaxed start to the workweek (The Guardian 2023). Instead of facing a barrage of meetings, tasks, and work pressure right from the beginning, they believe Monday should be a softer transition. This reflects employees' desire for a workplace that takes responsibility for their mental health and overall well-being. From a positive perspective, any initiative that improves employee well-being while still ensuring value creation is beneficial. However, from a negative perspective, this initiative could be seen as a reduction in work time and input, potentially leading to less individual and collective value creation. The conflict between these two perspectives highlights the tensions between focusing on input and output, on the one hand, and individual and collective approaches to the workplace on the other. All of this occurs within the context of value creation. The perception of not having enough time is significant for organisations and the design of the workplace model because time pressure affects how people explore and respond to uncertainty.

How does time pressure influence exploration and decision-making? A study explored this question through several experiments involving four-armed bandit tasks, where the study manipulated expected reward, uncertainty, and time pressure (limited vs. unlimited) within subjects (Wu et al. 2022). When time is limited, individuals have fewer opportunities to engage in costly computations, which alters the cost-benefit balance of different exploration strategies. Through behavioural analysis, reinforcement learning (RL), reaction time (RT), and evidence accumulation analysis, the study discovered that time pressure affects how people explore and respond to uncertainty. Specifically, participants engaged in less uncertainty-directed exploration under time pressure, displayed reduced value-directed behaviour, and repeated choices more frequently. Since the analysis linked uncertainty to slower responses, it demonstrates a resource-rational shift towards simpler, lower-cost strategies under time pressure. These findings provide insights into how people adapt their exploration and decision-making strategies in response to externally imposed cognitive constraints.

However, how should we approach the design and leadership of office workplaces and work-life in the future in order to balance increased exploration and innovation? How can we ensure that employees optimise their "shopping" for work time in a way that maximises the organisation's overall value creation and ability to renew itself continuously?

11.6 Time Poverty and the Quest for Balance

Time poverty refers to having the perception of enough discretionary time. Discretionary time is the amount of time available to engage in activities that enhance social and human capital, such as spending quality time with loved ones. However, discretionary time is affected by the need to dedicate significant portions of life to necessities like sleep and work responsibilities (both paid and unpaid). There are a lot of data and studies into the subject, and as mostly the case the findings are not conclusive. Feeling time-poor? There has been a significant increase in offers on how to utilise time (Zheng et al. 2022). It's a constant battle for your time and attention because ultimately, time is money, and where individuals spend their time, money can be made. Whether it's on Netflix, social media, shopping malls, recreational activities, or work, assessing employees' time poverty is crucial because it has a negative impact on well-being and work engagement. This, in turn, can result in various financial and psychological costs for both individuals and organisations.

Research in today's fast-paced world reveals that a growing number of people consistently feel "time poor" to an extent that it could be described as an epidemic (Lashbrooke 2022). While some may view time poverty as less significant than material poverty, it carries considerable negative implications for well-being, physical health, and productivity that warrant attention. The concept of *money affluence* versus *time affluence* highlights the experience of having sufficient time to fulfil obligations, a degree of control over how to spend that time, and enough free time to engage in meaningful, enjoyable activities. Despite this pervasive sense of time scarcity, many continue to work long hours, often sacrificing valuable time with loved ones in an attempt to keep up with their busy schedules. Delving deeper, a study by Etkin and Mogilner demonstrates that the impact of variety on happiness depends on the perceived length of the time period in which activities occur (Etkin and Mogilner 2016). For longer spans of time, such as a day, variety tends to increase happiness. However, for shorter timeframes, such as an hour, variety can actually decrease happiness. This shift is due to the sense of stimulation and productivity associated with time: while filling longer periods with varied activities enhances stimulation (and thus happiness), packing too much variety into short periods makes the time feel less productive (and reduces happiness). More recent research (Sharif et al. 2021) has shown that having 2–5 h of free time per day is optimal for enhancing happiness. However, when free time falls below 2 h or exceeds 5 h, happiness levels decline. This aligns unsurprisingly with the shift we're seeing in response to "time poverty" (or "time hunger") as some employees, increasingly affluent in terms of money, seek ways to reclaim time. Ultimately, time poverty can lead to feelings of overwhelm, with too many tasks to accomplish in too little time. Balancing necessary tasks with discretionary time often creates a constant pressure to make difficult decisions, forcing individuals to prioritise certain areas of life over others.

Time poverty can also have a negative impact on work performance (Giurge, Whillans and West 2020). Research indicates that time-poor individuals experience reduced productivity at work. This not only affects the employee's potential but also has consequences for employers. Employees who are time-poor may not work effectively, resulting in a negative impact on both the employee and the employer's benefits. The reality is that we have never had more time, and most employees have never worked fewer hours compared to the past. Despite the fast-paced, multitasking, constantly connected lifestyle many Americans lead today, the 48% who claim they don't have enough time to do what they want is not significantly different from the 47% average over the past 14 years. In fact, this percentage is slightly lower than it was in the 1990s according to another study (Newmann 2019). From 1965 to 2003, the average working week for Americans actually decreased by 3 h, while leisure time increased. Moreover, in many developed countries, the working week has become even shorter since then. In a study involving over 7000 working Australians, researchers concluded that the perception of time pressure is an "illusion". They compared the amount of time required for essential activities such as paid work, housework, and personal care to the actual amount of free time people had in their schedules. The researchers noted, "Those who feel the most overworked, who have the least 'free time,' largely bring it upon themselves." In other words, we could potentially spend fewer hours earning money, doing household chores like vacuuming and washing dishes, or cooking and eating, and still manage without feeling overwhelmed.

I anticipate that the future will bring even greater prioritisation and focus on the factual and perceptual consumption of time. Employees will growingly attempt to avoid "time poverty", which is not the same as they will succeed.

11.7 Hybrid Working Wins for the Employees

In short, the main benefits for employees working in a hybrid and more distributed and flexible office workplace model are increased flexibility, autonomy, work-life balance, and individual performance (Chafi et al. 2022; Peprah 2023). This leads to improved employee well-being and job satisfaction. Reversely the major challenges of predominantly remote working were social aspects such as lost comradery and isolation. Hybrid work was perceived to provide the best of both worlds of remote and office work, given that employees and managers develop new skills and competencies to adjust to new ways of working.

A study conducted in the USA found that on average, employees highly value the hybrid working model, resulting in a 33% decrease in attrition and an improvement in job satisfaction measures (Dam et al. 2022). Non-managers were more likely to volunteer for the hybrid experiment, work from home on eligible days, predict positive impacts on productivity, and reduce attrition rates under hybrid. On the other hand, managers were less likely to volunteer, work from home on eligible days, predicted negative impacts on productivity, and saw increased attrition rates under hybrid.

Another study conducted in the USA found a substantial decrease in time spent working in a hybrid workplace model (Bloom et al. 2022). Although there was an increase in working from home, it only partially offset the decrease in hours worked away from home. These findings are in line with previous studies on commute times, which found that employees spent fewer total hours in paid employment despite allocating 40% of their saved commute time to work. Commute time is often seen as unproductive time, and in the future, organisations must make sure that the time spent commuting is worthwhile for both the employee and the organisation. In short this has been coined "Earn the Commute" (Han and Peng XU 2023).

In the USA (and Denmark), the average daily commute time is just under 1 h (Statista 2023), which is equivalent to approximately 1 month for employees working full-time yearly. The results from another study suggest that there is a notable increase in leisure time and sleeping with a hybrid workplace model (Fig. 11.8) (Aksoy et al. 2023). Younger employees reported spending more time at social events, eating at restaurants or bars, and exercising, while older age groups tended to allocate more time to nonmarket work, such as activities related to childcare, household maintenance, repairs, and meal preparation.

Employers may perceive a reduction in overall working time as potentially jeopardising productivity. But as previously stated in this publication, the opposite is

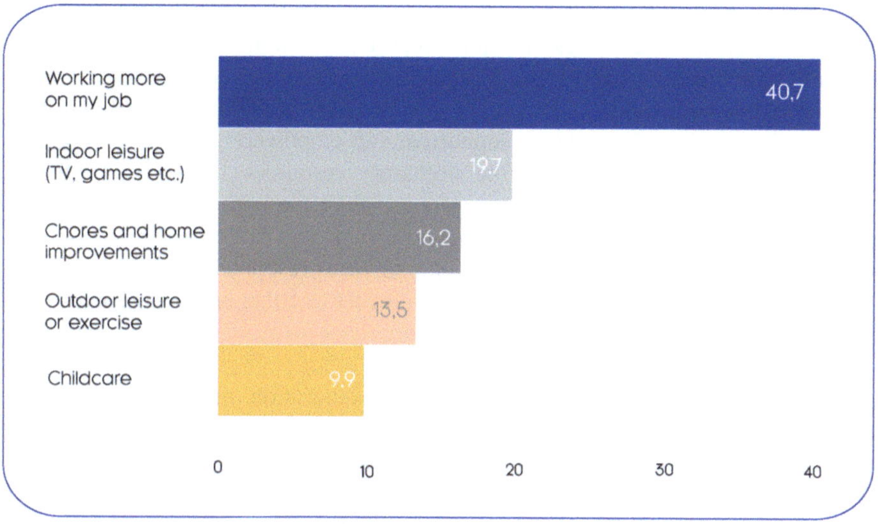

Fig. 11.8 How did you use the commuting time you saved by working from home? (percentage)

true. The organisation is—if applied cleverly—more productive in a hybrid model because autonomy and flexibility more than compensate for the overall decrease in working time. It also suggests that the optimal place to work for the employee is not limited to one location but is situational and correlated to the given work assignment and task. Another benefit of a hybrid workplace model is a reduction in sick days (especially among families with younger children), among other things. Working from home isolates employees, reducing social contact and the hassle of commuting, which may contribute to fewer sick days taken while preforming work.

11.8 Challenge: Want a Better Office Workplace? Stop Ignoring the Employees Preferences

Cease wasting employees' valuable time with unnecessary "noise". Employees are primarily dedicated to their individual tasks, not activities that detract from their core work objectives. Most employees are motivated, engaged, and focused on their responsibilities, avoiding any misuse of their working hours. If this isn't the case, then the organisation faces a more pressing challenge than simply transforming the workplace into a hybrid model. Either the work is poorly organised or the organisation has hired the wrong employees.

McGregor's Theory X and Theory Y present two contrasting views on management and human motivation, which can be reflected in how employers perceive employee engagement (McGregor 1960). According to Theory X, managers assume that employees inherently dislike work and will avoid it if possible. As a result, managers with this mindset believe that strict control, supervision, and even coercion are necessary to ensure productivity. These managers tend to micromanage and believe that employees need constant oversight to complete their tasks effectively. In contrast, Theory Y assumes that employees are self-motivated and view work as a natural and fulfilling part of life. Managers who adopt this approach believe that employees can be trusted to take initiative and perform well without constant supervision. They focus on creating a supportive and empowering work environment, delegating tasks, and providing the necessary resources for success. Overall, McGregor argued that Theory Y managers are more likely to foster a positive and productive workplace culture, while Theory X managers risk creating a more negative and restrictive environment. This dichotomy still resonates in modern management, where employers might categorise employees as either engaged (Theory Y) or disengaged (Theory X), influencing their approach to leadership and workplace dynamics.

An illustrative example lies in examining collaboration, meetings, and interactions anew. When there is a misalignment between employer and employee objectives, it can lead to disengaged behaviours during meetings, such as taking phone calls, texting, or working on other tasks. In such situations, employees often prioritise their individual work and create value independently, sometimes opting not to attend or to limit their active participation in meetings. Meeting organisers and organisations must recognise the hierarchy of value creation in relation to how employees use their time. When employees appear unfocused, it is frequently a result of the organisations or managements shortfall in designing an effective work-life and workplace model. While employees can take responsibility and initiative in managing their time well, the ultimate accountability rests with management.

The hierarchy of employees' work-life values can be effectively summarised by categorising their work priorities into four levels (Fig. 11.9). The foremost priority is fulfilling high-priority work objectives; the more time diverted from core tasks and specific skill development, the more distracted, detached, and unfocused employees may feel. The second priority revolves around colleagues and

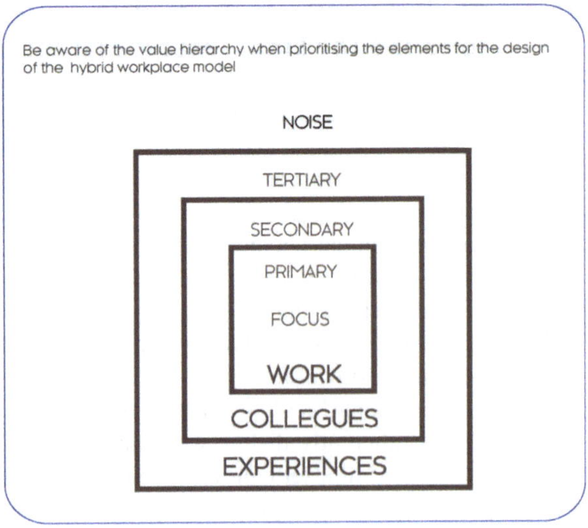

Fig. 11.9 Employees focus primarily on work—design accordingly

collaboration recognising the importance of team synergy. Once again it is important to note that positive social connections at work can increase productivity by improving how employees work together to get the job done (Work Design Principle). The third priority centres on sensory and shared experiences. This is partly driven by a desire for self-fulfillment and recognition, but, more importantly, by the understanding that shared workplace experiences cultivate relationships, foster a sense of belonging, and build trust among colleagues and with the organisation. Such interactions not only enhance personal satisfaction but also strengthen employees' ability to tackle work tasks effectively. The fourth category, in contrast, is not a priority at all; rather, it serves as a "garbage bin" for activities employees perceive as distractions, noise, or simply a waste of time. As noted, approximately 30–50% of scheduled meeting time is often perceived as unproductive or misaligned with individual employees' priorities (it is important to note that perception does not always equate to reality, but any responsible employer would be wise to take these perceptions seriously).

Employees' emphasis on prioritising their individual tasks reflects the broader trend of individualisation, where there is a short-term focus on personal preferences and needs. However, this focus often conflicts with the increasing value generated through networks and collaborative interactions, especially in a knowledge-driven society. Employees seek environments where they can efficiently address their immediate tasks—whether in an activity-based workspace, on a digital platform, or, crucially, where the right colleagues and management are accessible for the task at hand. From the perspective of time and resource investment, the hybrid workplace model must balance catering to individuals' focus on their own tasks with ensuring that employees invest in networks and relationships with colleagues for organisational value creation. The hybrid workplace must foster incentives to encourage long-term commitments to the collective "we", sustaining shared value creation over time. Currently, the analogue office remains the most effective space for building relationships and fostering interaction with colleagues, reinforcing its relevance in a hybrid model. When we shift our focus to the analogue office workplace and consider the motivational reasons for being at the office, the picture changes. Analogue dexterity becomes increasingly apparent, as more employees—and especially the most successful ones, along with high-performing teams—attend the office primarily for teamwork, secondarily for individual work, and thirdly simply to sit alongside colleagues (Gensler 2024).

The pandemic and economic crisis have intensified the demand for a positive sensory experience for employees. However, organisations should recognise that a narrow, touchpoint-focused approach to sensory experiences is not a universal solution for addressing employees' evolving preferences and behaviours. While enhancing specific interactions can contribute to a better work environment, a broader, more holistic strategy is essential to meet the complex needs of the workforce in a sustainable and meaningful way (WTW 2021). (As opposed to the holistic and overall employee experience, referring to the overall perception an employee has within an organisation, employee sense of belonging and contribution pertains to the employee's feeling of being a part of the organisation and making a meaningful impact). Employees expect to have positive sensory experiences when they interact with their workplace, whether in person or digitally. A positive sensory experience-has become a standard expectation, even when the organisation is under pressure due to the pandemic and economic challenges. Employees respond quickly and negatively when their experience does not meet their expectations and will as we progress increasingly quit their employment. The experience economy has been growing continuously since Pine and Gilmore formulated experiences as the future economic growth engine in 1998 (Pine and Gilmore 1998). Experiences have been a significant explicit economic driving force for over 20 years and have had a crucial impact on customers' and employees' valuation of services. Entire industries and sectors have been created and developed based on the experience economy, and service design with carefully planned touchpoints is now a prerequisite for developing the future workplace. Positive experiences are by now expected in all aspects of life, from unique experiences in stores and theme parks to commuting and coffee shops. When everyone strives to deliver the ultimate experience to customers, partners, and employees, the experience economy can be said to have both won and lost—resulting in a Pyrrhic victory. Good sensory employee experiences are no longer a differentiator or an economic growth engine. They have become a hygiene factor, just like expecting hot and cold water from a tap. Who wants to have a meeting in a workplace that delivers a bad experience? Who want to work at a workplace that is a bad experience? Negative experiences will immediately be rejected. In the future, employees will growingly respond promptly and negatively to bad experiences. Therefore, organisations can only establish a genuine basis by providing good workplace experiences. By delivering negative experiences, organisations are undermining their own value creation. (Much of the current office redesign stems in part from a desire to eliminate negative experiences).

The proposed work-life value hierarchy aligns with the broader trend of "back to core", reflecting a strategic shift where organisations refocus on the essential functions, capabilities, and values that define their business. This approach has gained momentum as organisations recognise the need to streamline operations and concentrate on activities that drive core business objectives. Within the workplace, this shift is evident in the way organisations now approach hybrid and remote work policies. Rather than offering unlimited flexibility or an abundance of perks, businesses are grounding their strategies in elements that directly support productivity, collaboration, and organisational culture. From an employee and workplace perspective, the "back to core" trend brings a renewed emphasis on clarity, purpose, and stability. For employees, this often results in a more focused and streamlined work environment, where roles and expectations are better defined, thereby reducing ambiguity. It also means that their efforts are increasingly aligned with the company's central mission, making work feel more purposeful and impactful. In essence, the "back to core" trend may provide employees with a sense of stability and a clearer sense of purpose, as organisations anchor their strategies in what truly adds value, striking a balance between flexibility and consistency. In summary, this shift in employee experience represents a return to purposeful engagement, with a sharper focus on what truly matters.

The value hierarchy work-life model is oversimplified and is presented solely to emphasise that employees are primarily focused on completing their work tasks. However, this does not mean that purpose, brand, personal development, etc., are not also prioritised. It pays off to prioritise employees' overall experience when making strategic decisions about the workplace (e.g. Morgan 2017). In conclusion, I recommend designing a future-proof hybrid workplace that respects employees' working time in accordance with the employees' hierarchy of work-life values. A great hybrid workplace that is characterised by all employees being naturally, fully, and sustainably engaged in shared objectives.

11.9 Crafting a Successful Workplace Model with Employee Flexibility

The Gig-economy with external gig workers, project-based staff, and temporary employees will increasingly notice that organisations are leveraging their services specifically to enhance flexibility. Full-time employees are predominantly engaged in project work, and for those who aren't, their roles are likely to evolve due to technological advancements such as AI and automation. The focus is no longer on whether organisations should be flexible, but rather on how they can implement flexibility effectively. A study conducted by McKinsey & Company confirmed that 9 out of 10 workplaces recognise the importance of adopting flexible work practices (McKinsey & Company 2021).

Internally within organisations, the conversation surrounding remote working is often framed as a conflict between managers and employees. This narrative does not accurately represent the true driving force behind the desire for flexibility in the future of working life. The real demand for flexibility is coming from the organisations themselves, particularly in response to the changing nature of capitalism (Poleg 2023). The traditional approach of industrial capitalism, which relied on detailed long-term planning for workforce and office needs, is becoming increasingly outdated. The traditional model of office-centric workplaces with rows of desks is gradually being replaced by a more flexible way of working, where time, place, and space are, to varying degrees, freed from rigid constraints. This trend is anticipated to continue to gain momentum as the economy becomes more focused on creativity, knowledge-intensive tasks, and reliance on networks. Instead of organisations with rigid structures and hierarchies, we will see the rise of networks comprised of specialists and knowledge workers who come together to collaborate and achieve goals. In other words, organisations are shifting their emphasis from measuring labour input to focusing on output. It's no longer solely about the number of hours worked or tasks completed, but rather the results and accomplishments achieved.

The discourse that centres employee flexibility solely around remote working is fundamentally flawed. Organisations that see flexibility as a point of contention with their employees are missing the larger challenge: navigating the growing uncertainty and unpredictability of the business landscape. Forward-thinking organisations address this challenge by embracing flexibility as a strategic approach to achieve their crucial objectives, such as attracting and retaining top talent. The role of management is to figure out how to implement flexibility in a way that suits their specific market and organisation, rather than attempting to revert to the pre-pandemic office-first workplace model.

References

(Aksoy, Barrero, Bloom, Davis, Dolls and Zarate 2023) Time Savings When Working from Home https://www.aeaweb.org/articles?id=10.1257/pandp.20231013

(Bagga et al. 2024) https://www.eief.it/eief/images/Violante.pdf

(Ballisager 2023) Kandidatanalysen 2023 https://ballisager.com/kandidatanalysen/

(Bloom 2020) How working from home works out https://siepr.stanford.edu/publications/policy-brief/how-working-home-works-out

(Bloom, Han and Liang 2022) How Hybrid Working From Home Works Out https://www.nber.org/papers/w30292

(Brulin et al., 2023) Brulin, Emma; Bjärntoft, Sofie; Bergström, Gunnar; Hallman, David M. Gendered Associations of Flexible Work Arrangement and Perceived Flexibility with Work–Life Interference Gendered Associations of Flexible Work Arrangement and Perceived Flexibility with Work–Life Interference: A Cross-Sectional Mediation Analysis on Office Workers in Sweden https://www.researchgate.net/publication/370605488_Gendered_Associations_of_Flexible_Work_Arrangement_and_Perceived_Flexibility_with_Work-Life_Interference_A_Cross-Sectional_Mediation_Analysis_on_Office_Workers_in_Sweden

(Bureau of Labor Statistics 2024) Employee Tenure in 2024 https://www.bls.gov/news.release/pdf/tenure.pdf

(Chafi, Hultberg and Yams 2022) Post-Pandemic Office Work: Perceived Challenges and Opportunities for a Sustainable Work Environment https://www.mdpi.com/2071-1050/14/1/294

(Dam, Melcangi, Pilossoph, and Toner-Rodgers 2022) What Have Workers Done with the Time Freed up by Commuting Less? https://libertystreeteconomics.newyorkfed.org/2022/10/what-have-workers-done-with-the-time-freed-up-by-commuting-less/

(Etkin and Mogilner 2016) Jordan Etkin, Cassie Mogilner, Does Variety Among Activities Increase Happiness?, *Journal of Consumer Research*, Volume 43, Issue 2, August 2016, Pages 210–229, https://doi.org/10.1093/jcr/ucw021

(Gensler 2024) GLOBAL WORKPLACE SURVEY 2024 Moving beyond employee presence to workplace performance https://www.gensler.com/doc/research-global-workplace-survey-2024.pdf

(Giurge, Whillans and West 2020) Why time poverty matters for individuals, organisations and nations https://static1.squarespace.com/static/5e270ffe949f6c4d0d0fcc55/t/5f77c04124f75f5a9d823ba6/1601683526489/Why+time+poverty+matters+-+giurge+whillans+west.pdf

(Han, Peng XU 2023) The Effect of Commuting Time on Quality of Life https://www.ncbi.nlm.nih.gov/pmc/articles/PMC9819363/

(Kim et al., 2023) Kim J, Dirks A. Is Your Organization's Remote Work Strategy "Working"? Exploring the Impact of Employees' Attitudes Toward Flexible Work Arrangements on Inclusion and Turnover Intention. Ther Innov Regul Sci. 2023 Nov;57(6):1209-1216. doi: 10.1007/s43441-023-00549-7. Epub 2023 Jul 17. https://pubmed.ncbi.nlm.nih.gov/37458899/

(Lashbrooke, 2022) Barnaby Lashbrooke This Is The Key To Achieving 'Time Affluence' Forbes Sep 23, 2022 https://www.forbes.com/sites/barnabylashbrooke/2022/09/23/this-is-the-key-to-achieving-time-affluence/

(LinkedIn Business 2024) The Future of Recruiting https://business.linkedin.com/talent-solutions/resources/future-of-recruiting?trk=bl-po&veh=FoR_Launch_Post

(Mas and Pallais 2017) Valuing Alternative Work Arrangements https://www.aeaweb.org/articles?id=10.1257/aer.20161500

(McGregor 1960) Theory X and Theory Y. Organization Theory

(McKinsey & Company 2021) What executives are saying about the future of hybrid work

(Microsoft 2022) Work Trend Index : Annual Report 2022 https://www.microsoft.com/en-us/worklab/work-trend-index/great-expectations-making-hybrid-work-work

(Morgan 2017) Wiley 2017 Employee Experience Advantage: How to Win the War for Talent by Giving Employees the Workspaces they Want, the Tools they Need, and a Culture They Can Celebrate https://www.amazon.com/Employee-Experience-Advantage-Employees-Workspaces/dp/111932162X

(Newmann 2019) Why You Never Seem to Have Enough Time https://greatergood.berkeley.edu/article/item/why_you_never_seem_to_have_enough_time

(Owl Labs 2023) State of work including in-office, hybrid and remote 2023. https://owllabs.com/state-of-hybrid-work/2023

(Peprah 2023) Hybrid workplace: current status, positives, negatives, challenges, and team learning. The Learning Organization, (ahead-of-print). https://ouci.dntb.gov.ua/en/works/ldV1zBD7/

(Pine and Gilmore 1998) The experience economy: past, present and future

(Poleg 2023) https://www.drorpoleg.com/its-the-company-stupid/

(Sharif, Mogilner and Hershfield 2021) Sharif, M. A., Mogilner, C., & Hershfield, H. E. (2021). Having too little or too much time is linked to lower subjective well-being. *Journal of Personality and Social Psychology, 121*(4), 933–947. https://doi.org/10.1037/pspp0000391

(Statista 2023) https://www.statista.com/statistics/1427497/workers-average-daily-commute-length-united-states/

(The Guardian 2023) Bare Minimum Mondays: a perfect start to the week – or a recipe for disaster? https://www.theguardian.com/money/2023/feb/08/bare-minimum-mondays-a-perfect-start-to-the-week-or-a-recipe-for-disaster

(TV2 DK 2023) Over en fjerdedel sagde op i ministerierne sidste år https://nyheder.tv2.dk/politik/2023-05-01-over-en-fjerdedel-sagde-op-i-ministerierne-sidste-ar

(Virilio 1986) Speed and Politics -Essay on Dromology

(Work Design Principle) Work Design Principle #3: Improve social relationships in the workplace. The Work and Well-Being Initiative: A Joint Harvard and MIT Collaborative https://workwell-beinginitiative.org/module-4-moderating-work-demands

(WTW 2021) 2021 Employee Experience Survey

(Wu, Schultz, Pleskac and Peekenbrink 2022) Time pressure changes how people explore and respond to uncertainty https://www.nature.com/articles/s41598-022-07901-1

(Zheng, Zhang, Li and Wu 2022) Being busy, feeling poor: The scale development and validation of perceived time poverty https://www.researchgate.net/publication/361954468_Being_busy_feeling_poor_The_scale_development_and_validation_of_perceived_time_poverty

12 Future Management of the Hybrid Office Workplace

Abstract

Management has a critical role in embracing and shaping the hybrid workplace model, which is still in its developmental stages. This model, integral to future work design, demands a long-term strategic approach, as it will outlast current management and significantly impact an organisation's success in a digitalised world. The hybrid workplace requires collaboration among HR, IT, and facilities management, with some organisations appointing a Chief Hybrid Officer to oversee its development.

The hybrid model's success hinges on management's ability to adapt and ensure a workplace that caters to employees' preferences, fostering productivity, engagement, and well-being. As employees increasingly influence workplace models, especially in competitive job markets, organisations must prioritise flexibility to attract and retain talent. The hybrid workplace model is not just about offering remote work; it involves a strategic balance between autonomy and structured collaboration, tailored to individual and organisational needs.

Management must also consider various factors, such as communication, culture, digital dexterity, and employee well-being, to create a sustainable hybrid environment. As this model evolves, the emphasis will be on agility, continuous learning, and aligning work processes to ensure long-term organisational success.

12.1 Management Under the Spotlight

The hybrid workplace model places significant pressure on management to recalibrate and develop the best-suited interpretation of hybrid work life for their specific organisation (e.g. Flassak et al. 2022). The workplace is no longer a standardised model as value creation within each organisation is uniquely defined by its management. Therefore, the workplace must by management be optimally tailored to

C. Sneppen, *The Future (R)Evolution of the Office Workspace*, Future of Business and Finance, https://doi.org/10.1007/978-3-031-85229-9_12

support value creation, rather than expecting value creation to conform to a rigid workplace model. Management has though the opportunity to harness the potential of organising and designing the ideal combination of infrastructure and employees, as well as determining how this is led. This, among other factors, must be balanced with employees' increasing desire for meaning and value in their overall lives capable of thriving in uncertain and dynamic environments (Hastings et al. 2020). Organisations must enhance the sense of purpose and value in both work and the workplace. Studies measuring employees' motivation and attachment to their work confirm this, with salary, flexibility, development, and meaning ranking as the top four priorities across various segments (as of 2024) (e.g. Ballisager 2023).

Simultaneously, the dynamic and ever-evolving approach to organising and performing work poses an equally significant challenge for management. Merely developing a flexible and flexible hybrid workplace model is not sufficient; they must also continually adapt and refine it to maintain competitiveness. Management must possess the ability to make ongoing adjustments and changes, all the while ensuring that employees can consistently carry out their work in a focused and seamless manner. This is encapsuled in the below brief list of anticipated trends shaping the future of work, which workplaces and, by extension, leadership will need to navigate in the coming years (Fig. 12.1). The list is neither exhaustive nor prioritised, and the trends are interrelated and overlapping. All of these points are addressed and elaborated upon throughout the book.

- *Increasing individualisation:* Personalised approaches to work, reflecting unique employee needs.
- *Increasing digitalisation:* Greater integration of digital tools into daily workflows.
- *Growing ESG compliance:* Enhanced focus on environmental, social, and governance standards.
- *Growing focus on DEI (Diversity, Equity, and Inclusion):* Emphasis on creating fair, inclusive, and diverse workplaces (as part of the ESG compliance).

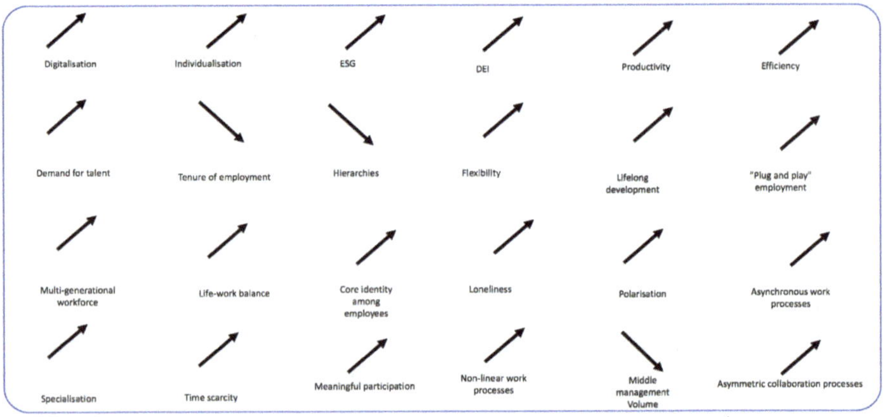

Fig. 12.1 Are management aligning with or resisting the trends of the office workplace?

- *Increasing productivity:* Pressure to deliver more output with the same resources (as always).
- *Increasing efficiency:* Streamlining processes for faster and more effective results (as always).
- *Rising demand for talent:* Increasing competition to attract and retain top talent.
- *Shortening tenure of employment:* Employees staying for shorter periods in companies.
- *Flattening hierarchies:* Reduced layers of management, encouraging more direct communication.
- *Decline in middle management:* Fewer managerial roles due to automation and flatter structures.
- *Increasing flexibility:* Greater demand for adaptable working hours and locations.
- *Growing emphasis on lifelong development:* Continuous learning and skill development throughout employees' careers.
- *Increasing prevalence of "plug and play" employment:* Ready-to-contribute employees with minimal onboarding required.
- *Increasing multi-generational workforce:* Diverse age groups working side by side in organisations.
- *Growing emphasis on life-work balance:* Prioritising personal well-being alongside professional responsibilities.
- *Increasing focus on core identity among employees:* Stronger alignment between work and personal values.
- *Growing sense of loneliness:* Remote work leading to feelings of isolation and disconnection (e.g. Fortune 2023). Loneliness correlates with declining job performance (Ozcelik and Barsade 2018).
- *Increasing polarisation:* Greater division in opinions and work-life approaches among employees.
- *Increasing asynchronous work processes:* Teams collaborating across different times, not requiring simultaneous work.
- *Growing specialisation:* Increased focus on niche expertise and specialised roles.
- *Increasing time scarcity:* Perception of insufficient time to meet growing demands.
- *Rising demand for meaningful participation:* Employees seeking greater influence and input in decision-making.
- *Increasing non-linear work processes:* Complex workflows, moving away from traditional step-by-step approaches.
- *Growing asymmetric collaboration processes:* Uneven contributions across teams, driven by diverse skills or roles.

12.2 The Short-Term vs. Long-Term Dilemma

The external environment is evolving at an unprecedented pace. Societal expectations, technological advancements, and workforce dynamics demand that the office model remain both adaptive and relevant. However, to achieve this, management must balance two competing forces:

- Incremental improvements: Small, ongoing changes that sustain day-to-day operations.
- Radical innovation: Bold steps that reimagine the workplace to meet the demands of tomorrow.

The challenge lies not only in finding this balance but also in determining the *speed* at which innovation is implemented. Too fast, and organisations risk disruption; too slow, and they risk obsolescence. This is where office workplace strategy and vision become crucial. While short-term adjustments will always be necessary, the long-term perspective must take a defining role in shaping the future office workplace. Without this foresight, organisations may find themselves implementing fragmented solutions that fail to sustain long-term success.

A forward-thinking office strategy considers:

- How external forces will shape work culture and employee behaviour.
- The evolving technological and environmental landscape.
- The need for flexibility without compromising on sustainability and productivity.

To contextualise this shift, it is worth revisiting the insights of Clayton Christensen, the renowned Harvard Business School professor and author of *The Innovator's Dilemma: When New Technologies Cause Great Firms to Fail* (Christensen 1997). Christensen's work explains that incumbents often fail not because they are incompetent, but because they are too competent in the established ways of working. Their success in the old era makes it difficult to pivot emerging, disruptive innovations. This phenomenon resonates deeply in the context of the hybrid office evolution:

- Organisations are still overly competent at managing traditional office models and structures, built for pre-digital, location-based work.
- The shift to hybrid and distributed workplaces represents a disruptive transformation that challenges these long-held competencies.

Christensen highlights a sobering fact: 98% of companies fail to meet disruptive challenges over time because adapting to change is inherently difficult. The same risk exists for organisations that fail to evolve their office models to align with the needs of the digital, hybrid reality. The ability to overcome this challenge lies in:

- A willingness to unlearn outdated practices.
- Investing in new capabilities that support flexible, omnichannel, and employee-centric workplace strategies.
- Recognising that disruption does not signal failure but rather an opportunity for reinvention.

12.3 Challenge: Cutting Through Office Complexity—Streamlining the Modern Hybrid Workplace

Organisational complexity is increasing at an alarming rate, threatening competitiveness and sustainability. This challenge extends to the modern office workplace, particularly in the context of hybrid work. The evolution of the office model into a hybrid, distributed framework has undeniably added layers of complexity. While this approach allows for greater flexibility and adaptability, it also exposes systemic and structural inefficiencies. Incremental adjustments are insufficient—they merely amplify internal complexity and place organisations under even greater pressure. A radical rethink of how we approach knowledge work is required to navigate this transformation successfully.

The September 2011 Harvard Business Review article "Smart Rules: Six Ways to Get People to Solve Problems Without You" by Yves Morieux (BSG) highlights the growing challenge of complexity in organisations (Morieux 2011). Organisations today face a more intricate world shaped by globalisation and rapid technological advancement. Customers are increasingly demanding, competitors are more agile, and what works today may fail tomorrow. This external complexity is mirrored internally within organisations.

Key Observations:

1. Proliferation of performance goals: Organisations now pursue an average of 25–40 performance imperatives compared to just 4–7 in the 1950s. Many of these goals conflict, such as the need for both customisation and standardisation, or innovation and efficiency.
2. The double-edged sword of complexity: Organisations are caught in a dilemma. Addressing external complexity without a strategy to manage internal complexity risks overwhelming the system, leading to inefficiency and burnout.

The hybrid office workplace exemplifies this dilemma. While it responds to external demands for flexibility and innovation, it exacerbates internal challenges. Uncoordinated adjustments to hybrid work practices increase complexity disproportionately, resulting in:

- Fragmented collaboration: Distributed teams often struggle with misaligned workflows and communication gaps.
- Overburdened systems: The reliance on multiple digital tools can overwhelm employees and hinder productivity.
- Increased managerial pressure: Leaders face the dual challenge of addressing external complexity while mitigating its internal repercussions.

The hybrid office workplace is both an opportunity and a challenge. By addressing external complexity thoughtfully while actively reducing internal complexity, organisations can build sustainable competitiveness in an ever-changing world. This requires a deliberate approach that combines strategic simplification, technological integration, and cultural transformation. "You are damned if you don't accommodate to the rising complexity of the exterior, and you are damned if you do, as it increases the internal complexity disproportionately." The solution lies in finding balance. How will management navigate this office complexity to emerge stronger in the hybrid work revolution?

12.4 Initial Management Response and Hybrid Workplace Hacks

Many leadership teams and organisations have initiated preliminary responses to the shift towards a more flexible and hybrid workplace model.

One observed reaction is the attempt to return to the pre-pandemic office model, often labelled the RTO (Return-to-Office) movement. Upon closer examination of the market reaction, it is notable that some management teams have used employees' desire for flexibility to impose RTO mandates as a tactic to encourage voluntary resignations, thereby reducing workforce numbers at a lower cost. Furthermore, some organisations may be driven to mandate RTO due to the sunk cost fallacy: those bound by office leases feel compelled to justify the expense through in-person attendance. Similarly, the hybrid management fallacy comes into play, where there is a reluctance or inability to adopt the new management styles essential for remote and flexible working. Delving further into the present Return-to-Office (RTO) debate (2024), studies have shown that some organisations and managers use RTO mandates as a way to reassert control over employees, even blaming them for poor company performance (Ding and Ma 2023). Interestingly, there is little evidence to support the notion that managers impose these mandates because they believe RTO increases company value. Additionally, research highlights significant declines in employee job satisfaction following mandates, without corresponding improvements in financial performance or company value. A further downside of RTO mandates is that there are indications they can lead to significant brain drain, as senior employees choose to leave. This poses a potential risk to the productivity, innovation, and competitiveness of the firm as a whole (Dijcke et al. 2024).

The more widespread initial initiatives embracing hybrid work life are, at their core, operational in nature and have been broadly adopted by various organisations as practical solutions to guide a more structured evolution towards a modern, flexible, and dynamic hybrid office model. They are grounded in the first and immediate responses of organisations to this ongoing transformation:

Hotelification, Homefication, and Office Upgrades *Organisational challenge: Employees are not attracted to the office, and management prioritises to support in-person attendance. Solution: Make commuting worthwhile and in-person work at the office more attractive, pleasant, and convenient.* Office hacks:

- Enhanced and more personalised services (hotelification).
- Home at work—making the office more homely (homification).

- Higher quality food options.
- Enhanced options for optimised individual workspaces through Activity-Based Working (ABW) (e.g. Oygür et al. 2022; Liang 1997; Wholers 2015).
- Widespread introduction of office workplace desk ratio.
- Optimised facilities and spaces for individual digital meetings.
- Increasing the number of meeting spaces, while reducing their size.

Meeting and Communication Culture *Organisational challenge: Assumptions that meetings are not effective and productive enough with the increase in digital, hybrid, and analogue formats. Solution: Develop a more contemporary meeting and electronic communication culture to increase productivity and simultaneously improve employee satisfaction.*

Meeting and communication culture hacks:

- Meeting-free time slots.
- Explicit meeting frameworks—enhance skills, define consequences, and calibrate practices regularly.
- Explicit email frameworks—enhance skills, define consequences, and calibrate practices regularly.

Culture and Community *Organisational challenge: Lack of shared culture and community results in lower employee retention, social capital, innovation, and collaboration. Solution: Introduce new initiatives and interventions to accelerate the formation of interpersonal social capital.* Culture and community hacks:

- Increase off-site gatherings. Studies suggest that well-planned events can significantly enhance internal connectivity, with over a 100% increase in employee communication. Meeting in person, even just once a quarter, generates a lasting boost in employee connectivity (Sevcenko et al. 2024).
- Reduce onsite gatherings in number but increase in significance.
- Enhance focus on augmentation of interpersonal social capital, though facilitating trust and collaboration regardless of time, place, and space.
- Enforce onboarding and mentoring programmes (Klinghoffer et al. 2024).
- Shift from experience management to community management—focus on building community rather than individual experiences.
- Condense office space as fewer people are present daily; empty offices do little to encourage daily commuting or in-person attendance.

Flexibility *Organisational challenge: Balancing employee expectations and preferences with organisational value creation. Solution: Increase structured and enforced systemic flexibility.*

Flexibility hacks:

- Flexibility quotas.
- Work-from-anywhere time slots, allowing prolonged periods where employees can work from any location.
- Discretionary days where employees can choose to work from home or take a day off without a reduction in salary.

Leadership *Organisational challenge: Management and leadership are under great strain as employees increasingly work non-linearly, asynchronously, and asymmetrically. Solution: Equip management, particularly middle management, to handle the hybrid workplace model.*

Culture and community hacks:

- Increase offsite gatherings.
- Reduce onsite gatherings in number but increase in significance.
- Enhance focus on augmentation of interpersonal social capital, though facilitating trust and collaboration regardless of time, place, and space.
- Enforce onboarding and mentoring programmes.
- Shift from experience management to community management—focus on building community rather than individual experiences.
- Condense office space as fewer people are present daily; empty offices do not attract daily commuting.

These initial responses to the evolving landscape merely scratch the surface of how the ultimate, future-proof hybrid office model will and should unfold. As the process continues, more significant and fundamental leadership questions and dilemmas inevitably come to the forefront.

12.5 Challenge: Who Holds Responsibility for the Hybrid Office Workplace?

Management has a unique opportunity to take a significant digital leap into the twenty-first century and align their approach to digitalisation by embracing the hybrid workplace model. Regardless of the specific approach management chooses and prioritises, the hybrid workplace model will have a defining impact on how work is designed and managed in an increasingly digitised reality. Many organisations are currently in a state of limbo, caught between their existing workplace model with its infrastructure, culture, and management practices and their desire for a more up-to-date model.

The elements of the workplace model, such as buildings, digital infrastructure, work organisation, and culture, are inherently long-term and demand substantial investment and organisational changes for development. Once established, a workplace will endure long beyond the current management's tenure. To exaggerate and simplify, most organisations' existing workplace models—comprising fundamental components such as buildings, infrastructure, and culture—have a lifespan that far exceeds that of any individual employee, leader, or even the organisation itself. The decrease in the expected lifespan of organisations is particularly significant (Garelli 2016). It highlights the fact that adaptability, innovation, and reinvention are essential for modern organisations to survive and prosper. Those that fail to evolve or keep pace with rapid technological advancements and shifting market dynamics are more likely to experience shorter lifespans. However, individuals, whether in management or as employees, consistently exhibit a bias towards short- to mid-term outcomes and preferences. As a result, organisations may face considerable investments and challenges if they seek to modify or update their workplace model once it has been established.

In the development of the hybrid workplace, there are multiple stakeholders involved and a reduced number of primary responsible workplace actors within the organisation. The workplace model impacts everyone and can generate passionate, diverse, and polarised discussions and opinions. But who is truly responsible for the hybrid workplace? Does your organisation have an overall responsible party for the workplace and work life? Or is the responsibility fragmented and shared among different internal actors? As we delve further into the value chain, the question of organisational responsibility for the hybrid workplace arises. From a collective perspective, there seems to be uncertainty regarding who should be responsible for the process of implementing and overseeing the ins and outs of hybrid work.

Which function should hold the overall responsibility for the hybrid workplace? The CEO, COO, CFO, CTO, CHR, CFM, or should there be a dedicated role such as the Chief Hybrid Officer (CHO) or Chief Remote Officer (CRO) (Fig. 12.2). While some employers have taken an ad hoc approach, others are being proactive by appointing high-ranking leaders solely dedicated to ensuring the success of remote work throughout the organisation. These chief remote officers may have different titles, but they are each assigned with addressing the complex issues that arise from new ways of working and future-proofing businesses' post-pandemic operating models. Figuring out remote work has been a challenge for employers, whether they choose a hybrid working model or fully distributed teams. In response, some companies have created new positions to help navigate the evolving work landscape. This trend has been particularly prominent in the tech industry, which has a higher proportion of remote workers and companies that prioritise digital-first processes. Advancing a level, the board of directors should not leave the development of the hybrid workplace solely in the hands of top management, as it is essential to maintain a long-term perspective. The board bears a critical responsibility in providing strategic direction for the ongoing development and implementation of the hybrid workplace model. Ultimately, this workplace model will likely outlast the tenure of any current management team.

Based on our anecdotal experience at the institute, four out of five organisations have divided workplace responsibility among IT, HR, and facilities management (FM), with each function predominantly represented in top management by the

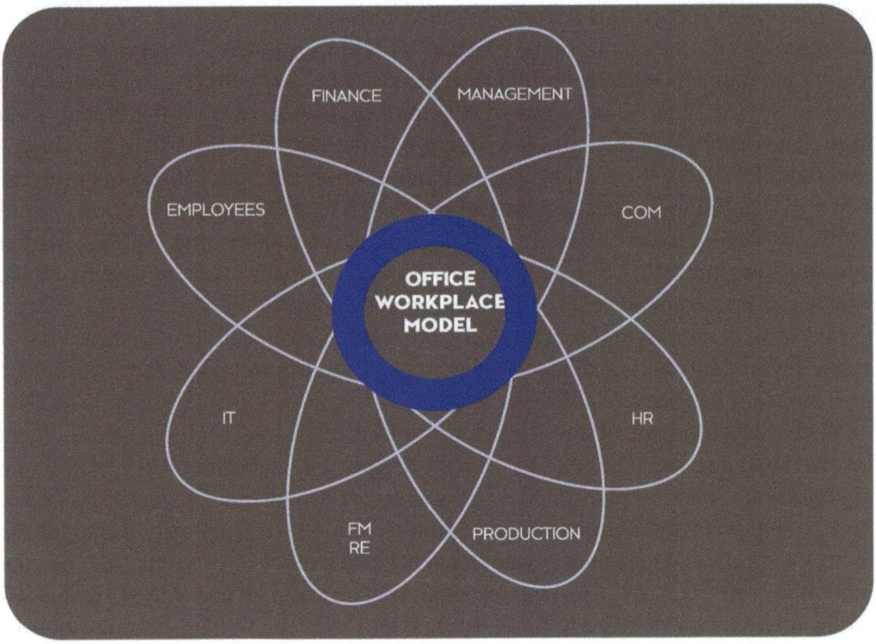

Fig. 12.2 Ownership of the future-proof hybrid office workplace model?

CIO, CHRO, and CFO, respectively. However, is this the optimal organisational and process design for developing the hybrid workplace? The current approach to the workplace is incremental, with ownership and responsibility for the overall workplace model consequently divided among different stakeholders. This divided approach is operationally based and allows for incremental adjustments. Nevertheless, as the workplace undergoes radical structural development with the introduction of the hybrid workplace, the organisation needs to address the challenges and opportunities of a more value-creating workplace. Regardless of the division of overall hybrid workplace responsibility, Facilities Management (FM), IT, and HR must collaborate closely in order to realise the competitive potential of the hybrid workplace. A successful workplace and employee experience strategy requires, at the very least, a committee consisting of HR, IT, and FM. This committee should share information and align their efforts towards enhancing the employee experience (Atlassian 2022). However, during a prolonged period of significant change and experimental learning, it is objectively more effective to have a dedicated Chief of Hybrid Workplace or a similar role. This dedicated executive would be responsible for the hybrid workplace, with actual budgetary authority and the ability to influence various aspects, such as the physical environment, technical policies, digital workplace, and workstyles. This workplace representative would be held accountable for the overall development of the hybrid workplace model.

In some organisations, the CHRO (Chief Human Resources Officer) may fill this role, although their title is continually evolving. However, the problem arises when HR, FM, and other teams can be pulled in different directions during times of crisis or competition (Kirschner 2023). This can result in losing sight of the importance of the total value creation of the workplace and hinder the ability of teams to collaborate effectively.

We return to the fundamental question of how important the workplace model is for the sustainable competitiveness of the organisation. In the most successful hybrid organisations, it is our experience that the responsibility has been delegated to one function to ensure a coordinated strategic approach to the implementation of resources. We therefore anticipate that organisations that prioritise the development of the hybrid workplace will increasingly have a dedicated individual or role with the mandate, organisation, structured processes, and resources to oversee this initiative effectively.

There is a need for a hybrid workplace vision and plan. The workplace model for knowledge employees is crucial to the organisation's value creation, and it is also forward-looking, dynamic, and continuously evolving in response to changing environments. Apart from disrupting the traditional setup of static workplaces, it now requires a strategic framework for the development of the hybrid workplace. (As mentioned earlier, maintaining the static and traditional workplace model might be easier for current leadership, but it can have significant implications for mid- and long-term competitiveness.) Based on our observations and discussions, the most successful hybrid organisations have taken a deliberate and thoughtful approach, allowing them to act quickly with a long-term perspective and a solid foundation (drawing on Daniel Kahneman's ideas). In other words, these successful organisations have developed a clear vision for the hybrid workplace, which is supported by a well-crafted plan anchored in top management. On the other hand, organisations that lack a clear vision and plan for the hybrid workplace may not prioritise its development or recognise its significance for future value creation in the organisation.

Taking a wait-and-see approach to the hybrid workplace is akin to waiting for the perfect digital workplace product before implementing it, even though most users only utilise a small fraction of the digital capabilities in existing products, and digital development is continuous and ongoing. An example of hasty and habitual thinking is the widespread post-pandemic redesign of the physical workplace. As we transition from a traditional and less flexible office to a more hybrid workplace model, there has been a significant emphasis on creating socially appealing offices with comfortable furniture and expanding the use of space for informal and formal interactions (shifting the analogue office towards the principles of a marketplace for work).

As futurist, I inherently view this approach as biased and habitual, as it may not necessarily align with the daily, present, and future preferences and behaviours of employees, who primarily focus on accomplishing individual work tasks with the help of relevant colleagues for the current work task. Instead, it seems to be primarily driven by management's desire for more collaboration and cohesion in the office, as the thesis is that employees lose their connections and attachment to the workplace and organisation while working partly remote. In this binary approach to the workplace, the desk quickly becomes an obstacle, while the sofa and social areas become the solution. In reality, it's not the desk itself, but rather the person sitting next to the employee and the extent to which they genuinely contribute to each other's specific tasks. Simply installing sofas and recreational areas will not necessarily bring the individual employee closer to the relevant colleague. The desk, in fact, remains a marvellous invention as a working station in the hybrid work model, as long as the people physically next to you are perceived as important for collaboration. However, it can be observed that many of the immediate design initiatives implemented to promote socialisation are left unused for a significant portion of the time. To put it bluntly, in many cases, these unused initiatives only serve as artefacts of management's desire for collaboration without actually fulfilling their intended purpose. From another perspective, this is yet another example of first-order thinking. The office is not being used to the same extent anymore; therefore, we must make the office more attractive, and thereby partly solve the challenge of the hybrid workplace. And again, this can be seen as part of the experimental approach to the workplace, which constitutes a vital element of a successful hybrid office model.

12.6 Hybrid Workplace Maturity and Capabilities

When assessing the organisational capabilities and maturity in managing the hybrid office, the question ultimately comes down to: How Resilient is your office workplace model in standing the test of time? The question can also be framed as assessing its true agility, highlighting the conflict between the solid bricks and mortar of the physical office and the digital collaboration and work life. It all boils down to how mature your organisational approach is to the hybrid workplace model. Do you see the post-industrial office as central to your organisation both now and in the future? Or are you inclined towards an ever more digitally founded approach to the evolution of the hybrid workplace? Office workplace models are no longer a one-size-fits-all solution, and ostensibly comparable organisations will increasingly have significantly different approaches and interpretations of the optimal workplace model.

Drawing a parallel to measuring maturity in how organisations work and incorporate the customer experience into their internal structures and processes, we can apply the same mindset to how organisations approach the internal employee experience at the workplace.

This naturally raises the question of how much insight and focus the organisation has on the internal employee experience compared to the external customer experience. In the vast majority of organisations, the understanding of the external customer experience far surpasses that of the internal employee experience. This is reflected in processes, systems, and structures that are primarily in the early stages of establishment and development to support the evolution of the hybrid workplace. In other words, most organisations are still not mature in developing and implementing a hybrid workplace model. Fundamentally, management needs to reflect on the priority and importance they assign to the workplace model in the future.

The hybrid office workplace maturity scale is not clear-cut and is solely presented to create reflection (listed from immature to mature) (Fig. 12.3):

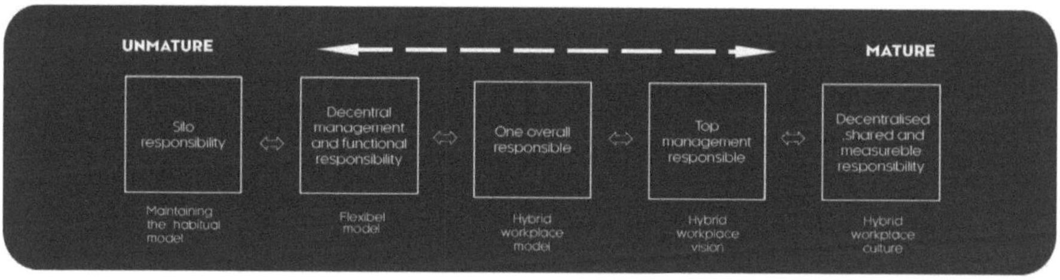

Fig. 12.3 Organisational maturity scale for the hybrid workplace model

- Silo responsibility: Each function has responsibility for a fragment of the workplace model, and there is limited and relation-based collaboration between departments. The organisation is working with preserving and maintaining the "old" workplace model, and focuses on minor adjustments, adaptations, and incremental development.
- Decentralised management and functional responsibility: Functions are still individually responsible, and there is a level of structured and systemic collaboration. Most organisations working and experimenting with widespread flexible working arrangements have entered this level of maturity.
- One overall responsible: The organisation is working in a structured and systematic manner with the hybrid workplace model by assigning one overall responsible person within the organisation. This person has objectives, a mandate, and a budget to unleash the potential of the hybrid workplace model.
- Top management responsible: With the responsibility assigned to top management, the organisation prioritises and is able to fully unleash the potential of the hybrid workplace model. Most of the early and successful organisations working with the hybrid workplace model have had top management taking ownership of the process.
- Decentralised and measurable responsibility: Everyone is responsible and accountable for the hybrid workplace and employee experience. The parallel to the current state of customer experience management in organisations is evident.

An operational and indicative assessment of the organisation's maturity approach to the hybrid workplace model for knowledge workers is looking at seven key indicators. The below maturity scale can very much indicate an "immature" approach to the hybrid workplace as optimal, without it being inherently negative or positive (Fig. 12.4). However, it is crucial that this is a deliberate choice made on a solid foundation, and not merely an extension of the post-industrial approach to the workplace by mindlessly copying the market. All else being equal, a higher level of organisational maturity in approaching and continuously developing the hybrid workplace will ensure sustained competitive advantage. In essence, the hybrid workplace scale can help you understand how advanced your organisation is in leveraging the full potential of the hybrid workplace, and how well-prepared you are for inevitable changes in the future. Generally, the greater the maturity, the more significant markers will be positioned towards the right. These markers are

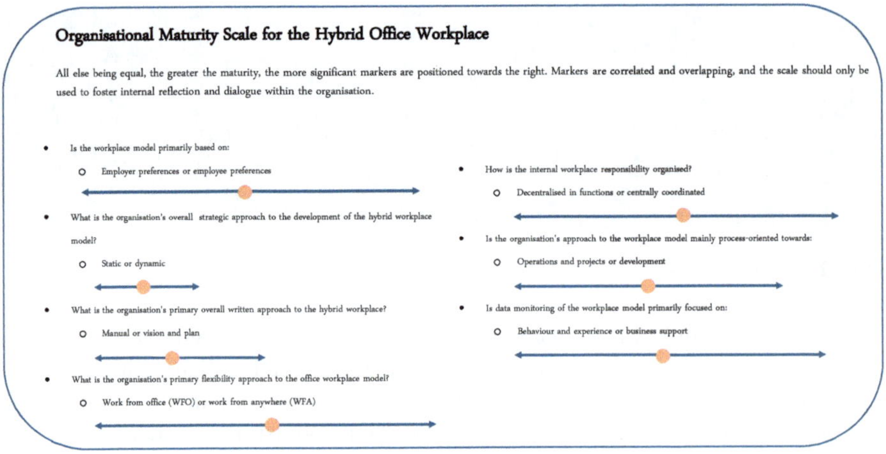

Fig. 12.4 Organisational maturity scale for the hybrid office workplace

correlated and overlapping, and the scale should be used solely to foster internal reflection and dialogue within the organisation.

1. *Is the current workplace model primarily based on* management preferences or employee preferences?
2. *What is the organisation's primary approach to the employee flexibility in the workplace model?* Work from office (WFO) or work from anywhere (WFA)?
3. *What is the organisation's primary approach to the workplace model dynamics?* Static or dynamic?
4. *What is the organisation's primary overall written approach to the workplace?* Manual or visionary and plan?
5. *How is the internal workplace responsibility organised?* Decentralised within functions or centrally coordinated?
6. *Is the organisation's approach to the workplace model mainly process-oriented towards* operations and projects or business development?
7. *Is data monitoring of the workplace model primarily focused on* behaviour and experience or business support?

In a recent study (2022–2023) 50 major organisations responded on 12 key components of forming the hybrid workplace (McKinsey and Company 2023). The study revealed that most organisations by large still are struggling to adapt to the model dynamic hybrid workplace model. The 12 measuring points (practices or capabilities) are one—and in my opinion quite qualified—yardstick to measure the "maturity" of the organisations' approach to the development and implementation of the hybrid workplace mode. The A-C represent that the answers fell into three situational categories. Almost one-third of the capabilities, such as gathering employee sentiment data and considering sustainability, are consistently being applied (A). Another third of behaviours that we have identified as best practices, such as leveraging advanced workplace technology and creating work-from-anywhere systems, were reported to be adopted by a smaller number of companies (B). The remaining third of best practices, including implementing a test-and-measure system and documenting processes, are eluding even the most progressive workplaces (C).

A. Consistently being applied

1. Employee sentiment and well-being are actively incorporated into workplace experience decisions.
2. We understand the virtual and in-person moments that matter for our employees.
3. We consider environmental sustainability and climate risk in workplace experience decisions.
4. We use advanced workplace technologies to enable seamless working from anywhere.

B: Adopted by a smaller number

5. Our physical workplaces support our business requirements and are responsive to change.
6. We empower our employees, wherever they work, through best-in-class benefits and amenities.
7. Our workplace experience strategy is informed by a wide range of interconnected datasets.
8. We train individuals and teams how to manage by measurable results, not physical presence.

C: Eluded in even the most progressive workplaces

9. Our workforce and workplace experience strategy has a clearly defined North Star vision.
10. We have a dedicated executive accountable for workplace experience with a string budget influence.
11. We have iterative processes in place to test and measure new work experience concepts.
12. We have unified, easily accessible, and up-to-date playbook documenting how we work.

12.7 Present and Future Level of Hybrid Workplace Maturity

We are naturally in the early stages of developing the hybrid workplace model, and organisations are undergoing a steep learning curve to fully understand and implement it. As a result, different organisations are at different stages of development in adopting the hybrid workplace.

Based on observations and dialogues with stakeholders, we estimate that organisations can be categorised as follows:

- Fully hybrid workplace model: 10–20% of organisations embrace the hybrid approach and are at the forefront of experimenting, understanding, and implementing the hybrid workplace model. These early adopters are motivated primarily by the potential for increased competitiveness and immediate benefits. Typically, these are organisations that had the resources and foundation to establish a hybrid work environment.
- Partial hybrid workplace model: 30–40% of organisations are in the initial phases of developing the hybrid workplace. These followers are taking the first steps towards increased flexibility while attempting to maintain a functioning workplace model alongside the newly introduced hybrid model. They are usually not driven by an urgent need but are in the process of clarifying objectives and assessing the potential consequences for the organisation.
- Contemplating hybrid workplace model: 40–50% of organisations are considering and hesitating for various reasons, including being objectively unsuited for a partially remote working arrangement and increased flexibility.

As we move forward, there will be a significant shift towards more organisations deeply engaging with the hybrid workplace model, resulting in a reduction of organisations in the partial hybrid and contemplating stages, ultimately becoming fully hybrid workplace organisations. As previously stated, we anticipate that the structured team-based hybrid workplace model will become the prevalent approach to organise the work life of distributed knowledge workers.

12.8 Challenge: Management Is Deluded If They Think They Alone Decide

Can the management, if self-willed, succeed in determining the hybrid office model? My immediate answer is a soft "yes", but diffidently only in the short term, and a clear and solid "no" in the long term. Apart from external factors influencing management's determination of the workplace model, such as legislation, regulations, and societal norms, the most important element of the hybrid workplace and any organisation consisting of knowledge workers is the employees.

In the short term, management can obviously determine the framework of the hybrid workplace model, but a model perceived as out of sync with employees' expectations will, over time, have profound negative consequences for the organisation. In a narrow workforce context, this will primarily occur either through additional direct salary costs to compensate for an unattractive workplace model or through indirect costs due to the loss of existing or potential employee talent, as the workplace and organisation struggle to attract and retain valuable individuals.

Basically, most employees have a very strong preference for flexibility and the ability to define their individual work life—and this preference is increasing. In an employee-dominated labour market, which is the dominant situation in most markets and labour segments, employees hold the advantage in the hybrid workplace model. In employer-dominated segments or regions of the labour market, the answer is a bit more ambiguous, but ultimately, talented employees still hold significant co-decisive power. Consequently, management cannot self-willedly determine the hybrid office model in the long run. This is because all organisations are increasingly striving to attract and retain talent, regardless of the current market situation, and failing to do so will severely impact their competitiveness. Employee talent cannot be ignored without significant consequences. In short, understanding the hybrid workplace is more about understanding the employees than understanding management.

The employees are the central actors as they form the core of the workplace, and most of the advantages of implementing the hybrid workplace model come from empowering the employees. The employees' freedom to choose a flexible work life is based on trust and relies on the organisation, work processes, digital tools, and physical environment supporting a hybrid and flexible workplace. This workplace allows work to be done where it potentially enhances productivity, efficiency, and well-being for both individuals and the team.

Employers may believe that management has the authority to establish the framework and determine the future workplace model. However, in a competitive job market, it is the workers who will increasingly hold decisive influence over the hybrid workplace model. As a result, employers will face mounting pressure to gain understanding and support for decisions that affect employees' freedom to choose how they structure their work. The risk of losing flexibility is that employees may seek out other workplaces that offer more flexibility in a job market where sought-after talents and skills are in high demand. Every management team must ask themselves whether the organisation can afford to lose valuable employees by maintaining a restrictive approach to remote work in the short term, rather than developing and implementing a hybrid workplace model in the long term. In a straightforward manner, employers must either empower their employees with greater freedom or risk losing them to more flexible opportunities elsewhere.

Flexibility requires that management is open to exploring the boundaries of employees' choices regarding their workplace, whether it's the office, cafe, or home, depending on the circumstances. Phil Kirschner emphasises that management should listen to employees and involve them in the decision-making process (Kirschner 2023). He suggests that there won't be a one-size-fits-all solution to the flexible or hybrid work dilemma. Leaders must provide authentic, transparent, and empathetic responses to employees, such as saying "I don't know, let's all figure it out together." Instead of jumping to conclusions, the focus should be on the challenging task of adapting processes to give employees the flexibility they need while assuring employers that things are heading in the right direction.

12.9 Challenge: Employees Who Do Not Fit in

There are always individuals who do not fit in or thrive in a given workplace model, and such employees must either adapt or ultimately seek new opportunities elsewhere.

Existing office workplace models have always inherently been tailored to suit certain types of employees, and naturally, many have managed to adapt to them to a significant extent. Conversely, there have always been groups of employees who have struggled to fit into, and adapt to, the prevailing office workplace model of the time. In essence, the current office model is more suited to some employee profiles than others. As these models evolve and develop, they cater to different and changing profile groups. This has been the case, whether the office model was grounded in the traditional 9-to-5 office hours, fixed workstations with designated personal desks, cellular offices, open-plan offices, or as is the case now, with increased flexibility regarding where the work is carried out, activity-based workplaces, and in some cases the option to book a desk via an app. Some employee profiles inherently thrive best in an open-plan office, while others are more comfortable in cellular offices. For someone who prefers and thrives in a small cellular office with a fixed workspace, the rigorous implementation of yet another new workplace model where everyone can work from anywhere could be tantamount to a nightmare, potentially leading to dissatisfaction.

With the advent of the hybrid workplace, organisations now have the opportunity to tailor work environments more closely to individual employees, thereby increasing the likelihood that the workplace will meet the most crucial individual expectations, no matter how varied they may be. Naturally, this presupposes that management is prepared to allocate resources and prioritise accordingly, with the aim of enhancing the organisation's overall competitiveness. Ultimately, it comes down to a cost-benefit analysis and whether individual and organisational needs can be met simultaneously. In essence, unlike previous post-industrial office workplace models, the hybrid model provides an increased opportunity for a larger population of employees to thrive, thanks to its embedded enhanced degree of flexibility.

12.10 Management's Balance of the Autonomous and Heteronomous Office Workplace

In a hybrid workplace model, the management balance of autonomous and heteronomous refers to the balance between self-directed and externally directed work approaches within an organisation that combines remote and onsite work arrangements.

As the megatrend suggests, employees are expected to become more individualistic in their approach to work, while digitisation simultaneously offers greater opportunities for freedom and flexibility. Employees tend to prioritise short-term focus on specific tasks and are inclined to collaborate and build relationships with those who can assist in resolving the current work task. However, a significant portion of value creation still occurs through collaboration and cooperation with others.

Management is, therefore, confronted with a significant cultural and communicative challenge to encourage employees to prioritise collaboration and interactions from a broader perspective. This will lead to increased engagement and strengthen the overall culture and the organisation's ability to retain and develop employees (Bolino and Phelps 2024). The more autonomous, free, and flexible employees become, the higher the likelihood that particularly those with low seniority may seek opportunities elsewhere. Organisations risk losing certain groups of employees if they lack flexibility and hybrid work arrangements, while, on the other hand, they may lose other employee groups if they are too flexible and hybrid. How management addresses and optimally balances the challenge and dilemma between autonomy and heteronomy will be crucial for the organisation's future competitiveness.

Organisations that are observed to be further along in the hybrid workplace maturity process place an increasing focus on the "we vs. me" relationship. They proactively and intentionally work to influence employee behaviour towards a balanced approach where "we" is prioritised more strongly than if the employee is solely left to prioritise. This is typically achieved through an approach that combines both rewards and consequences—with clear policies, ongoing communication, a reward structure, and the threat of potential consequences. During the pandemic, we largely succeeded in creating value remotely through the digital workplace by leveraging the established social capital built in the physical workplace. As the pandemic prolonged, it became increasingly clear that the social capital was not inexhaustible, particularly for employee groups where it was not especially strong (such as new employees) or for individuals who relied on constant maintenance and building through interactions in the physical workplace.

The key question in the post-pandemic era is how to craft a hybrid workplace model that effectively fosters and sustains social capital while providing employees with the flexibility they desire. It is once again a delicate balance between autonomy and heteronomy, weighing the needs of the community against those of the individual. As organisations grow, individuals tend to experience greater detachment from workgroups and communities, a challenge exacerbated by the increasing individualisation of employee behaviour. This shift towards individualism makes it more difficult to foster a sense of belonging and cohesion, particularly in larger or expanding teams. The hybrid model, therefore, needs to carefully address these dynamics, ensuring that employees remain connected while still enjoying the flexibility they desire. In the future, it is expected that management partly will address this polarisation between the individual and the community by establishing and reinforcing smaller group dynamics where participation and influence will result in greater group responsibility and increased engagement in solving common challenges. Therefore, the hybrid workplace model with greater individual autonomy goes against engaging employees in smaller groups with greater responsibility and a focus on the group rather than the individual. Large groups essentially foster individualism and reduce willingness to invest time in relationships that are not directly linked to egocentric needs. It should be noted that the individualistic demand for maximum flexibility is not necessarily what benefits the individual in the long run. All employees thrive best and produce most effectively in organisations with strong communities. In other words, what employees demand is not always what benefits them the most, and increased distancing from the workplace can ultimately lead to dissatisfaction, disengagement, and lower efficiency and productivity for the individual, the team, and the organisation. More flexibility has a tipping point of value creation for both the individual and the organisation.

Historically, the post-industrial office was primarily centred on organisational optimisation, structured around the traditional organisational chart with its departments and silos. This centralised approach, often referred to as the "office-first" or "office-only" model, was rooted in a belief that productivity stemmed from physical presence and rigid structures. The goal was clear: to create efficiency and value at the organisational level. At the other end of the spectrum is the fully remote model, or approaches where employees are given full autonomy to choose their working patterns. This approach prioritises individual optimisation—providing flexibility to accommodate personal productivity styles, preferences, and work-life balance. The hybrid model seeks to merge these two paradigms. By blending flexibility with physical presence, the hybrid workplace has the potential to:

- Optimise individual productivity through flexibility and autonomy.
- Enhance team collaboration through intentional, face-to-face engagement.
- Drive organisational value creation by aligning productivity strategies with overarching goals.

In this context, Activity-Based Working (ABW) office design emerges as a potential potent tool to increase both individual and team value creation. By designing office spaces to accommodate specific activities—such as focused work, collaboration, brainstorming, or social engagement—organisations can:

- Enable individuals to work effectively on tasks that require deep focus or autonomy.
- Provide teams with spaces that enhance collaboration, problem-solving, and creativity.
- Align physical spaces with the broader organisational goals of innovation, culture, and productivity.

When thoughtfully implemented, activity-based design transforms the office into a dynamic hub that serves as a complement to flexible, remote work. Rather than forcing employees into a one-size-fits-all model, it recognises the diverse needs of individuals and teams while supporting organisational objectives.

The hybrid model must not be contradictory—pitting individual needs against team collaboration or organisational goals. Instead, it should be complementary, creating a synergistic relationship between these three levels of productivity:

- Individual: Flexibility that empowers focus, creativity, and well-being.
- Team: Spaces and opportunities for cross-functional and functional team collaboration, cohesion, and shared value creation.
- Organisation: Structures and systems that align productivity, culture, and overall collaboration with strategic goals.

The idea behind Fig. 12.5 is straightforward: the better a workplace model can simultaneously facilitate individual, team, and organisational work dynamics, the greater the value creation, all other factors being equal. The larger the area depicted, the greater the potential for value creation. Achieving this requires deliberate design, clear communication, and continuous adaptation to ensure that the hybrid workplace is not only sustainable but also transformative (leadership, organisation, systems, structures, and interventions). The concept of balancing and harmonising individual, team, and organisational perspectives aligns closely with the evolving nature of knowledge work. Increasingly, work is conducted horizontally across the organisation rather than confined to vertical structures within departments. This shift reflects a dynamic environment where teams and projects are continually reconfigured to meet changing demands and priorities. This figure is not specific to any particular organisation or work processes; rather, it is designed to demonstrate the potential outcomes when these elements are thoughtfully integrated. In the end, it depends on the specific job function, performance metrics, organisation, and other relevant factors.

Figure 12.6 provides a detailed description of four distinct office workplace models along with the potential areas representing the value creation possible through a thoughtful application of the balance between individual, team, and organisational perspectives in the office workplace model.

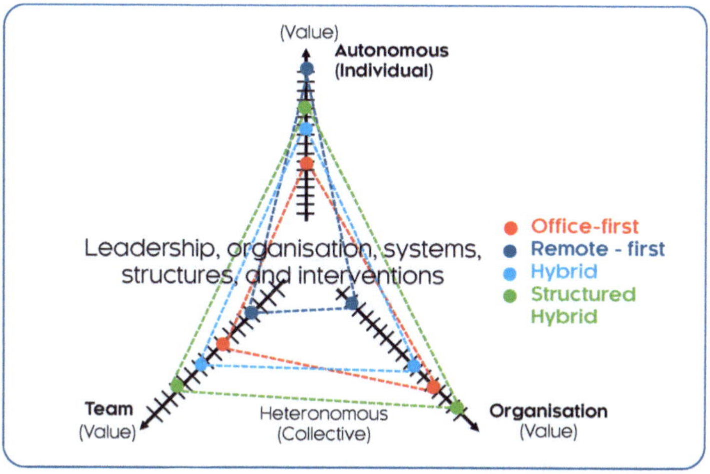

Fig. 12.5 Balancing office work value between autonomy, team, and organisation

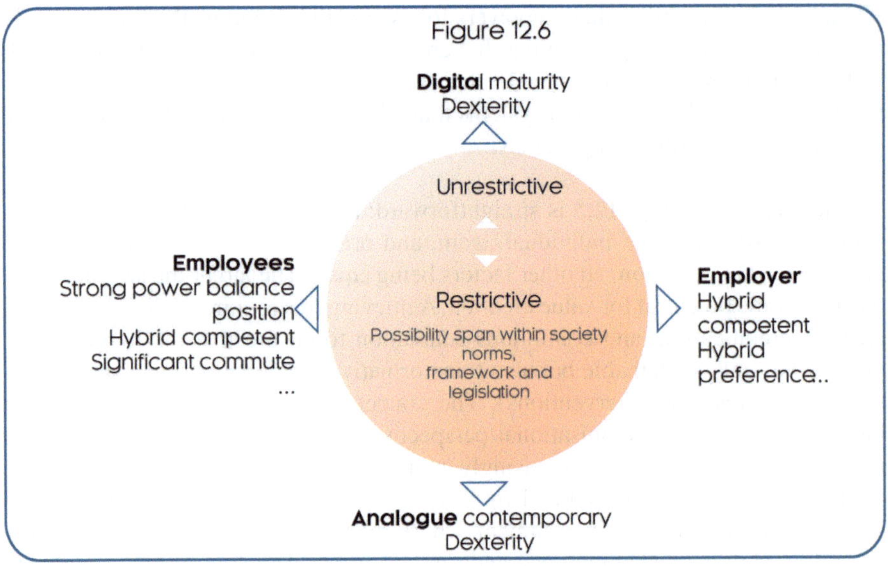

Fig. 12.6 Office-first, remote-first, hybrid, and structured hybrid

There are many areas where the existing approach to the workplace model will fall short.

There are places where attempting to solve challenges within the existing structures and systems will be confronted with the fact that management approaches do not adequately address the challenges or unlock the potential. The challenge going forward is twofold: on the one hand, identifying the management structures and systems that need to be either de-prioritised or strengthened, while simultaneously utilising existing or exploratory approaches and solutions in the development towards the balanced and dynamic hybrid workplace model. A hybrid workplace that balances the five key challenges of the hybrid workplace dilemmas, namely "we/me", "plugged/unplugged", "synchronous/asynchronous", "development/utilisation", "closeness/distance", and enables the maximum sustainable value creation for employees, the organisation, and ultimately the customers/market (see Chap. 20).

12.11 Logical Variations Between Seemingly Comparable Organisations

Some organisations adopt an "office-first" model, while others embrace true flexibility, and a few opt for either fully remote or fully in-person setups. (This polarisation and differentiation of workplace models has been extensively elaborated upon earlier in the book.) Each interpretation of the workplace model carries significant implications for both digital and analogue infrastructure, management practices, and, perhaps most crucially, the employees, altogether ultimately shaping the competitiveness of the organisation.

Consequently, questions arise, such as "What are the decisive organisational factors that define the hybrid workplace model in a given organisation?" Or formulated a slightly different "What decisive factors determine the range of interpretations of the hybrid workplace model?" In the following, I will endeavour to shed some light on the factors determining the range of interpretation possibilities of the hybrid workplace model based on personal observations and a background of knowledge on the current evolution of the hybrid workplace model.

The power balance between employee and employer is perhaps the most decisive factor in determining the interpretation of the hybrid workplace model. Essentially, it comes down to employees seeking flexibility while employers aim to maintain the status quo and the current successful workplace model. In situations where employers hold more power (with an abundant supply of employees and talent), there tends to be a clear preference for an office-first approach to the workplace model. In more extreme cases, an office-first or mandatory full-time office approach may be used to lay off surplus employees, resulting in them leaving the organisation at a lower cost than through layoffs. Conversely, in situations where employees have more power, there is increasingly greater freedom in how work is carried out, regardless of location, space, and time. In other words, there is a significant correlation between the current power balance between employee and employer and the interpretation of the hybrid workplace model.

The pivotal aspect of the workplace model, the power balance between employee and employer, is a natural consequence, as employees are the driving force behind flexibility post-pandemic. It's worth noting that employee preference for flexibility is closely linked to commute distance, with distances longer than 15 min significantly increasing the desire for greater flexibility and a more unrestricted hybrid workplace model. Diving a bit deeper the hybrid workplace dynamics there are five major categories of forces and underlying factors at play in the interpretation of the hybrid workplace model (Fig. 12.7). It is important to note that the defining factors of the evolution of the hybrid workplace have a built-in self-reinforcing effect as the development continues. Organisations with a restrictive approach will maintain current trends, while those that are more experimental will experience a reinforcement of potentially future competitiveness-enhancing factors such as analogue, digital, employee, and management dexterity. Nothing is without consequences, and this is particularly true for the unfolding and determination of the evolving hybrid workplace model.

Society norms, framework, and legislation Regulatory and legislation factors have a decisive impact on the interpretation of the workplace model, and many cultural and regional differences in the interpretation of the workplace model can be correlated to them. The more restrictive the legislation, the more restrictive the hybrid workplace model, and vice versa.

Digital maturity and dexterity There is a positive correlation between the level of organisational digital maturity and dexterity and the interpretation and implementation of the hybrid workplace model. Organisations with lower levels of digital matu-

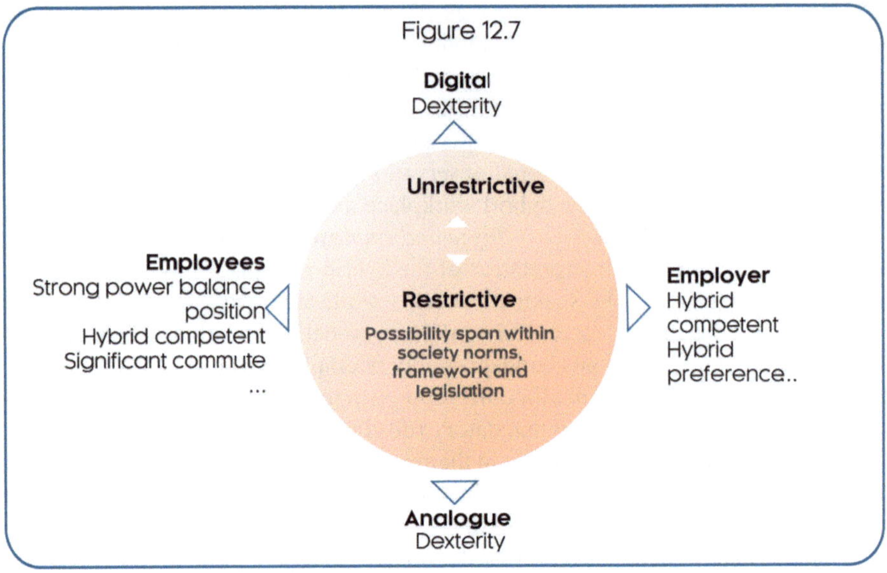

Fig. 12.7 Interpretation span of the hybrid workplace model

rity and dexterity tend to have less flexibility and a more restrictive hybrid workplace model, whereas those with higher levels of digital maturity and dexterity tend to have greater flexibility. This correlation also encompasses analogue-dominant work processes that presently require in-person presence to conduct the work effectively.

Analogue contemporary dexterity Analogue contemporary dexterity essentially refers to an organisation's overall ability to effectively utilise analogue interactions and behaviours within a digital context. In other words, it involves navigating, using, and leveraging analogue touchpoints only when they are more productive and efficient than their digital counterparts. There is a positive correlation between an organisation's level of analogue contemporary dexterity and its interpretation and implementation of the hybrid workplace model. Organisations with lower levels of analogue contemporary dexterity tend to have less flexibility and a more restrictive hybrid workplace model, whereas those with higher levels of analogue contemporary dexterity tend to exhibit greater flexibility.

Employee hybrid dexterity The behavioural aspects of the interpretations of the hybrid workplace model cannot be overestimated—and are in fact quite often neglected and left for the individual employee to solve on the go. The higher level of hybrid dexterity the employees pose the higher level of workplace model flexibility.

Management hybrid dexterity Ultimately, management appears to be the decisive factor in defining the hybrid workplace model. However, this is merely apparent, as it is ultimately the competitive forces of the market that will, over time, determine the success of organisations with the greatest competitiveness, and taking into consideration that the hybrid workplace model plays a significant role in overall competitiveness, as organisations increasingly differentiate themselves through their models. The greater the competence of management in hybrid practices, enabling them to effectively lead and manage irrespective of time, location, or space, the more flexible the workplace model becomes. Many management teams' preference for an office-first model is partly driven by their limited competencies in hybrid management dexterity. This leads me to assert that many current management teams still have untapped potential to develop their hybrid management skills, to fully realise the future competitive advantages.

In my view, a decisive current obstacle and limiting factor to a successful contemporary workplace model is the hybrid leadership capabilities of management (implicitly connected to a robust employee assessment matrix that enables effective management, even when employees are "out of sight"), and conversely, the potential greatest asset is the liberated and motivated employees, to fully unleash all the potential current and future competitive advantages of the hybrid workplace.

The hybrid workplace model places significant pressure on management to develop the best-suited interpretation of hybrid work life for their specific organisation. With the widespread introduction of the hybrid workplace model, management is essentially undergoing a long-awaited paradigm shift from default management to intentional management. Remote management is no longer a secondary skill but a defining capability of leadership, and this will increasingly be the case. The shift from default to intentional management is naturally driven by changes in the broader ecosystem, and we can expect this transition to establish a new norm. This new equilibrium will bring routines and habits that enable all workplace participants to focus on tasks rather than on the constant adaptation to change. By repeating intentional actions consistently, they will eventually become second nature and form a habit.

In the old model, with a linear and synchronised, symmetrically shared analogue office work life, it was possible to manage by default in a shared space. Essentially, management largely interacted with employees through sensing ("management by sight" or management by default). As the workforce increasingly conducts work non-linearly, asynchronously, and asymmetrically, management is required to lead and manage intentionally and structurally regardless of time, place, and space to ensure cohesion and progress for the organisation (e.g. Meyer 2010).

The management approach to the hybrid workplace model is naturally and implicitly defining on multiple levels for the specific organisation's interpretation. On an initial level, management obviously and ultimately defines, and is responsible for, the organisational workplace model. On a deeper level, management's approach and capabilities to organise and conduct the management of a more distributed workforce are very defining. To a certain extent, management's abilities to conduct hybrid management are the predominant defining factor for the design of the workplace model in the specific organisation. On the one hand, the current hybrid leadership capabilities are defining, as top management must take current competencies into consideration when defining the hybrid workplace model, but the dilemma and central question are whether the current model is the best one for progressing towards a more digitalised and individualistic reality.

Alternatively, leadership may opt for a very restrictive approach towards flexibility to make management easier. Many organisations opt in fact for the easy route to adapt to the shortcomings of hybrid leadership abilities and the willingness to manage intentionally by simply defining a hybrid workplace model based on the present shortcomings of hybrid management capabilities, in other words, settling for a less hybrid and flexible model.

12.12 Middle Management Caught in a Tight Spot

As previously stipulated, between top management and employees, middle management finds itself in a pressured and precarious situation caught between the expectations and demands from both sides in fulfilling the potential of the hybrid workplace. The pressure is particularly high on middle management in those organisations where top leadership has delegated the main and operational responsibility for defining the hybrid workplace model to middle managers. They need to navigate the balance between in-person and remote work dynamics. They must effectively lead and manage teams that may be physically dispersed or working remotely.

Top management inherently conducts strategic and tactical management intentionally, but middle management, being closer to the operational level, has historically primarily conducted management by default (by sight). Consequently, middle management is under immense pressure, as previously mentioned, and in many organisations, it is evident that middle management is struggling with the transition from management by default to management by intention. In the most extreme cases presently, middle management is left to handle the transition to more intentional management themselves without structured and systemic support from top management.

A study has revealed that most managers found their roles as remote managers to be more challenging, requiring them to work longer hours (Ipsen et al. 2022) (Fig. 12.8). The data indicates that managers received the most support from their own employees and fellow managers, while administrative support was generally insufficient. Furthermore, the study shows that the majority (67%) of managers prefer to manage from the office. However, they are also willing to continue managing remotely, if necessary, after the pandemic. Therefore, if an organisation intends to offer hybrid work options, enhancing support from top management and in-house support functions would be beneficial in maintaining or improving managers' satisfaction and effectiveness. Moreover, both employees and managers consider their work during the pandemic to be more challenging than usual. The data suggests that managers worked longer hours, leading to extended workdays. There could be various explanations for this, including additional organisational tasks, difficulties in conducting online leadership, and challenges in coordinating and collaborating with remote employees. Managers reported these factors as the main challenges they faced while working as distance managers from home.

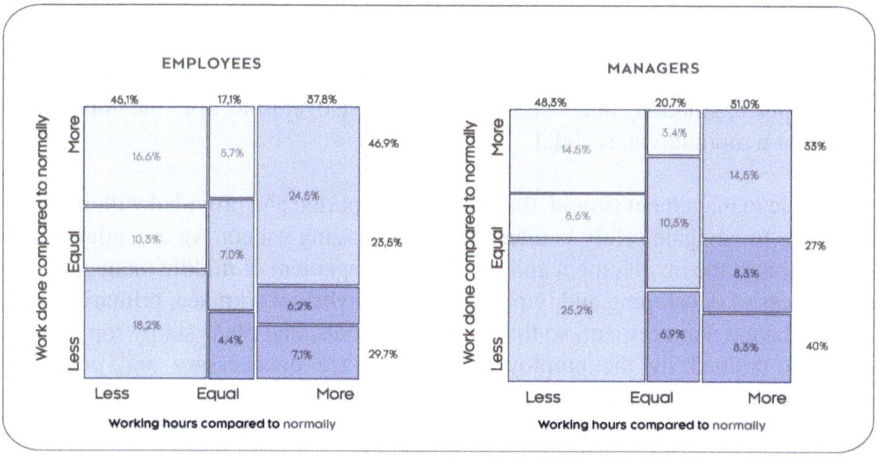

Fig. 12.8 Working hours compared to work performed working remote

Apart from more hours and more demanding tasks some of the reasons brought forward to why managers and management may oppose hybrid working are:

- *Control:* Some managers may feel that they lose control over their team when they are working remotely. They may feel that it is difficult to monitor productivity, manage projects, and ensure that employees are meeting deadlines when they are not physically present in the office.
- *Communication:* Communication can become increasingly challenging in a hybrid work environment, where managers may struggle to maintain effective communication with their team members and other stakeholders when working remotely. This can lead to misunderstandings and delays, with team cohesion proving even more difficult to uphold (Bartsch et al. 2020).
- *Culture:* Hybrid working can make it difficult to maintain a company culture and build team spirit. Managers may worry that employees who work remotely will feel disconnected from the company and its values, leading to lower morale and decreased productivity.
- *Leadership:* Leadership is becoming increasingly task- and relationship-oriented as employees gain greater autonomy (Bartsch et al. 2020).
- *Training:* Some managers may feel that it is more challenging to train and onboard new employees when they are working remotely. They may worry that new employees will not have the necessary support and guidance to succeed in their roles.
- *Technology:* Hybrid working requires the use of technology to facilitate the workplace beehive communication, collaboration, and project management. Some managers may not be comfortable using these tools or may worry about cybersecurity and data privacy issues.
- *Productivity loss:* Managers and employees have a significant disagreement regarding crucial aspects of working from home. Specifically, managers hold the

belief that working from home decreases productivity, whereas employees strongly believe that it significantly enhances productivity. Interestingly, data demonstrates that managers, who initially show resistance towards a hybrid workplace, gradually adapt and become positive over time, after the implementation of a more flexible model.

Middle management should, therefore, be supported and provided with increased resources to navigate safely in uncertain and changing waters. An essential component of this is the involvement and proactive engagement of middle management in the process of developing and implementing the hybrid workplace, primarily focusing on change management, so that the vision, goals, and plans set by top management, co-defined by the employees, do not face unnecessary and potentially derailing resistance and lack of support in the actual middle management interpretation of the hybrid workplace. The considerable autonomy granted to employees introduces a potential built-in paradox for middle management. The more autonomy employees gain, the less need there is for middle management, as it would naturally be expected to lead organisations towards becoming less hierarchical. However, this is evolving, as the current hybrid transformation has placed middle management in a pivotal and essential role.

12.13 Redefining or Recalibrating Management

What does the hybrid office workplace model mean for management and leadership? From a narrow workplace perspective, management, HR, IT, and facilities management (FM) face a unique opportunity and challenge to future-proof the workplace for an increasingly digitised and hybrid reality. These functions are critical in shaping a flexible, efficient, and supportive environment for employees in this evolving landscape. However, in a wider perspective, the widespread adoption of the hybrid workplace could act as a pivotal catalyst for the broader evolution of post-pandemic management practices (Lagowska et al. 2020). This shift has the potential to redefine leadership, organisational structures, and the very nature of work itself, as businesses adapt to the new demands of a hybrid, technology-driven ecosystem. Much like the pandemic accelerated changes in the office workplace model, it has not fundamentally altered the nature of management but has rather hastened the development of the competencies required for a more digitalised working life. I, therefore, anticipate a long-tail recalibration of leadership and management practices in response to the radically transformed ecosystem of office work and work life for knowledge workers. One example of this can be observed in the many organisations that have today adopted hybrid or decentralised models, encouraging cross-functional collaboration, agility, and adaptability (McChrystal 2015). As with general behaviour, management practices will gradually adapt, although technological advancements often outpace behavioural changes. Over time, however, these will converge, with leadership evolving to meet the demands of this new workplace reality. The hybrid model is likely to reshape how leaders engage with their teams, fostering new approaches to collaboration, performance management, and organisational culture.

The implementation of the hybrid workplace is a catalyst for introducing a more dynamic and agile organisational and work process, and it is one of the many components that contribute to developing a contemporary management approach where human beings, behavioural insights, and employees are at the centre of value creation. The hybrid workplace highlights contemporary leadership approaches and internal work processes while exposing previous dominant approaches where daily physical synchronous and symmetric presence of both leaders and employees was a prerequisite for maintaining efficient value creation for the organisation (Fig. 12.9).

Over the past few decades, self- or shared-managing groups or teams have become a ubiquitous organisational principle in workplaces. The prevailing management philosophy can be articulated as follows: By granting employees freedom, demonstrating trust in each individual, and ensuring psychological safety, organisations can unlock a fuller spectrum of their potential—both as individuals and as cohesive teams. And through increased responsibility, the employee simultaneously gains greater influence over the management processes within the organisation, not only pertaining to their own work within the organisation but also across the organisation (Kirschner 2023). The transition to a hybrid workplace model is filled with pitfalls, dilemmas, and challenges for management that can be summarised by the fact that the sum of challenges is constant regardless of which workplace model the organisation develops moving forward. For example, Professor Niles Foss at Copenhagen Business School, based on a study, writes that flattening the organisational structure risks more detailed control of employee (Lederstof 2022).

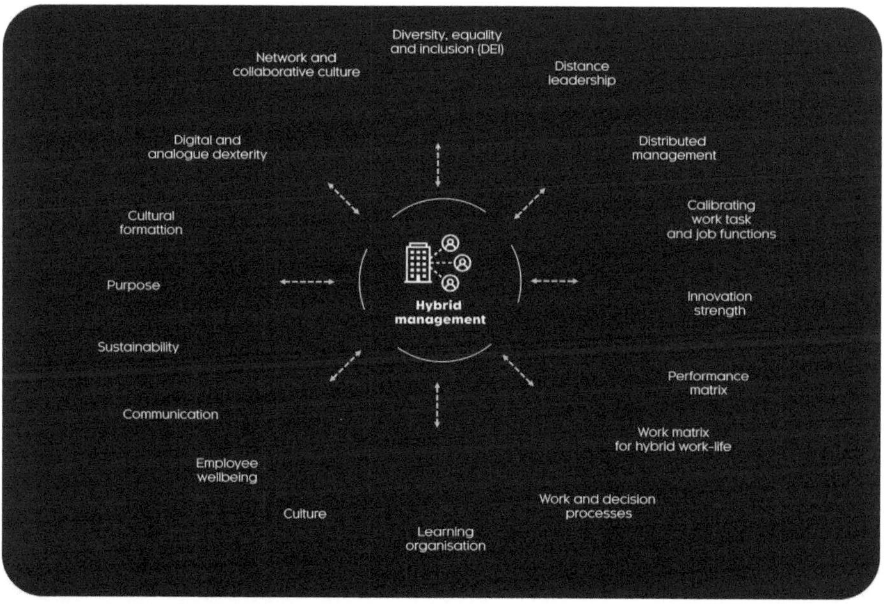

Fig. 12.9 Adapting management to a future hybrid management of work

The hybrid workplace model, all things being equal, enlarges the distance between employees and management, as employees gain more freedom and influence over their work lives. The flip side of the coin is that employees have a greater responsibility for delivering value regards of time place and space. Simply because the significance of the office as a meeting place for the organisation decreases, and employees become more autonomous. Free employees, who have a large say in their own workday, give for most employee's greater job satisfaction and well-being. But to what extent are management and the organisation ready to give employees the freedom to choose time, place, and space for work execution? And to what extent are employees able to deliver on the extended freedom? And to what extent can and will management do it? In 2024, there are still managers and leadership who equate remote work with a partial day off, and therefore are not inclined to give employees the freedom to manage their work execution to a greater or lesser extent.

As the hybrid workplace continues to evolve, employees are enjoying greater autonomy in shaping their working lives. Concurrently, management and leadership are adapting to this new paradigm by providing clear and unambiguous guidance, establishing robust frameworks and objectives, and granting employees the freedom to execute their tasks within these parameters. This balanced approach promotes a more collaborative, team-oriented culture, enhances access to support and feedback mechanisms, and fosters an environment of recognition—aligning with the expectations of contemporary generations in the workplace. Consequently, the importance of effective leadership will hypnotically intensify, with growing demands placed on leaders and a sharper distinction between strong and weak leadership becoming evident. This contrast is particularly pronounced when compared to the traditional "office-first" model, where weaker leadership was often compensated for by the physical office environment.

The continued development and implementation of the hybrid workplace model mark a shift from a predominantly unipolar view of work-life and workplace dynamics—where work and personal time were perceived as distinctly separate (even if this division was illusory for many knowledge workers before the hybrid workplace concept emerged)—to a more multipolar perspective. In this new model, time, place, and space are increasingly defined by individual preferences and needs. This evolution introduces both opportunities and challenges for individuals, organisations, and, most critically, for management.

Historically, a unipolar and binary perception of work-life and workplace simplicity reduced complexity and uncertainty for management. However, this approach also limited the potential benefits and opportunities that a more nuanced and flexible hybrid workplace model can offer. In contrast, the future of managing knowledge workers will be characterised by a more autonomous and decentralised workforce. The hybrid workplace model will redefine management strategies, requiring leaders to embrace complexity and cultivate adaptability to unlock the full potential of this transformative shift.

12.14 How Management Embraces the Newcomer: The Hybrid Workplace Model

Below are several correlated and overlapping areas related to management, and in particular HR, which are predicted to develop and change significantly in the future, have a decisive impact, and help define the future of the hybrid workplace model with a distributed workforce (the list is not complete or prioritised, but is listed alphabetically). I address the development of the analogue and digital infrastructure in the subsequent chapters and have there not included them in the implications for management of unfolding the hybrid workplace in the organisation.

The overarching theme for all management challenges can be encapsulated in the concept and implementation of agility. This shift in perception moves agile organisations and workplaces from being considered a "nice to have" to a "need to have", forming the foundation for ensuring competitiveness through the unfolding of the hybrid office model as a Trojan horse.

CALIBRATING WORK TASKS AND JOB FUNCTIONS Adapting and adjusting work tasks and job functions in a hybrid work environment to ensure that employees can work efficiently and effectively, regardless of their location. For example, organisations may need to implement faster onboarding processes to ensure that employees are productive from the start, as they may be changing jobs more frequently in a hybrid work environment. This approach can be summarised as "from the best man for the job to the fastest fit for the job". The trend of recalibrating job functions is in line with the growing emphasis on specialised work functions, simpler work and decision processes, initiatives to retain employees, and faster adaptation to changing work environments.

COLLABORATIVE AND TEAM-ORIENTED CULTURE The hybrid model necessitates deliberate efforts to build and maintain team cohesion and culture across virtual and physical spaces. Leaders must promote collaboration through tools, platforms, and practices that encourage regular interaction. Establishing shared goals and creating opportunities for teamwork help foster a collective sense of purpose, bridging the gap between remote and in-office employees. Management should therefore champion inclusivity, ensuring all voices are heard and valued, regardless of an individual's work location.

COMMUNICATION AND INFORMATION Strengthening communication between employees both horizontally and vertically and strengthening leadership communication. Organisations working in a hybrid environment must establish communication channels and collaboration tools to facilitate communication and collaboration among employees regardless of time, place, and space. This could include video conferencing tools, instant messaging platforms, and project management software.

CORE CULTURE Strengthening the company's culture is essential to create the optimal sustainable hybrid workplace ecosystem. A workplace culture that supports all employees, regardless of their location, is necessary to ensure a cohesive and productive work environment. The organisation needs to place more emphasis on the value and culture provided to employees in the workplace.

The cultural differences between workplaces were already significant pre-pandemic, but with the introduction of the hybrid workplace, they will become further differentiated and polarised across regions and countries (e.g. Zarte et al. 2024). There will be a need and demand for more culture-building initiatives since with remote work, employees can feel disconnected from the organisation and their colleagues, which can have a negative impact on the organisation's culture. Maintaining a sense of belonging and shared purpose requires a deliberate effort from the organisation's leaders. Culture can ultimately be assessed based on two key components: alignment and connectedness (Kotter and Heskett 1992). Alignment refers to employees understanding and acknowledging what the culture of the organisation is and genuinely believing that it is appropriate for the company. Connectedness, on the other hand, pertains to employees' identification with and emotional investment in the culture of the organisation, demonstrating that they genuinely care about it.

This brings us back to the ongoing challenge of balancing short-term individual preferences with a cohesive organisational culture, and how leadership and management will address this tension. One possible approach is tribal leadership, which harnesses the power of belonging and shared purpose, fostering a workplace where employees feel part of something greater. This sense of connection can enhance engagement and drive organisational success (Logan et al. 2008). However, all tribes inherently exclude, underscoring the need to balance this workplace equation carefully. Leaders must find a way to foster a sense of belonging without creating divisions, ensuring inclusivity alongside a strong shared identity.

DIGITAL AND ANALOGUE DEXTERITY Securing the infrastructure and, more importantly, promoting and enhancing digital and analogue dexterity throughout the organisation are crucial in a hybrid workplace where employees work both remotely and in the office. Digital and analogue dexterity are essential skills for success. Digital dexterity refers to the ability to effectively use digital tools and platforms, while analogue dexterity involves adapting to different communication styles and environments and collaborating with colleagues both remotely and in-person. To develop these skills, employees can attend training and development programmes, seek feedback and coaching from supervisors and colleagues, and practise working in different environments (Fayard et al. 2021). Employers can also provide support and resources to help employees develop these skills, such as access to digital tools and technology, training programmes, and mentoring opportunities.

DIVERSITY, EQUALITY AND INCLUSION Management can ensure DEI by focusing on the hybrid workplace model. A hybrid workplace that implicitly creates new opportunities for employees who may have been excluded from traditional office-based roles due to geographic location or other barriers. The hybrid workplace is a much-demanded model for families with children, especially mothers, as it makes the daily work life more synchronised with the routines and rhythm of childcare, school, and after school activities (Mcnall et al. 2010). It can also help promote work-life balance and accommodate the needs of employees from diverse backgrounds, including those with caregiving responsibilities or disabilities. The hybrid workplace strives to "include all exclude none".

EMPLOYEE DATA AND GDPR Collection, processing, and storage of personally sensitive data for analogue and digital touchpoints in the workplace are crucial for the development of the hybrid workplace. As employees' activities and behaviour can be captured in both the digital and analogue workplace, a range of legal, ethical, and perceptual challenges arise. With the digitisation of the analogue workplace, there is an increasing opportunity to monitor the behaviour and activities of individual employees, and the recording naturally increases in the digital realm through monitoring of activities on mobile or computer devices.

ENCOURAGING SOCIAL INTERACTION In a hybrid workplace, it is essential to create opportunities for employees to socialise and build relationships with each other. This could include virtual team-building activities, social events, and informal chat channels. There is an even more significant issue concerning social connections and how they can be endangered or completely lost when working remotely. We understand that professional networks and mentoring relationships are crucial for career advancement, and it is already a challenge for women and minorities to build and maintain these connections. Research also shows that personal relationships are socially nourishing and vital for our psychological well-being (Haas 2022). With hybrid working arrangements, there is a risk of creating a "dominant class" consisting of those who feel central to the organisation and strongly committed to it. On the other hand, an "underclass" may emerge, comprised of individuals who feel peripheral and disconnected not only from the work itself but also from the social interactions that create meaning and foster stronger bonds among employees and the organisation. The consequences of this divide can include less satisfied and less dedicated employees who are more likely to seek opportunities elsewhere.

Taking a closer look at the physical office, there is a growing movement to further develop the office as a meeting place—not only to strengthen strong ties, but also to foster weak ties within the organisation. The office is evolving from simply placing a coffee machine in each department to recognising that social interaction must be intentionally created. This is done by establishing shared gathering points where employees are either encouraged or subtly nudged to move across distances to access unique or common services and experiences. This approach breaks away from the traditional idea that services should be placed as close as possible to the employee's workspace. Examples might include barista-style coffee, specialised meeting facilities, food, fruit, or outdoor spaces. By doing so, the organisation strengthens weak ties across the organisation, fostering a stronger culture and sense of cohesion.

ENVIRONMENTAL SUSTAINABILITY The hybrid workplace aligns well with the promotion of environmental sustainability, and management has the potential to reap its benefits. A hybrid workplace can reduce the organisation's carbon footprint in several ways. With fewer employees commuting to the office, there is a significant reduction in transportation emissions and traffic congestion. Additionally, the hybrid workplace reduces energy consumption by decreasing the need for heating, cooling, and lighting in the office. It also leads to reduced water consumption, and less waste generation from paper, food, and disposable products due to fewer employees in the office. The increased use of digital tools can also reduce the need for paper-based communication and document management, further contributing to sustainability efforts.

ENVIRONMENT OF RECOGNITION Recognition plays a pivotal role in maintaining morale and motivation in the hybrid workplace. Management must ensure achievements are acknowledged promptly and meaningfully, whether through formal rewards or informal praise. A balanced approach to recognition ensures that both individual contributions and team efforts are celebrated, creating a culture where employees feel valued. In hybrid settings, management should use digital platforms and in-person opportunities to make recognition visible across the organisation, reinforcing a sense of community and belonging.

FRAMEWORKS AND OBJECTIVES Leaders must design comprehensive frameworks that offer structure and consistency, even in a decentralised working model. These frameworks should define processes, workflows, and performance metrics that guide employees in their roles. Objectives should align with the organisation's strategic goals while being SMART (Specific, Measurable, Achievable, Relevant, and Time-bound). Clear objectives help employees understand their contribution to the bigger picture. Robust frameworks also create a shared sense of purpose, enabling teams to work cohesively despite physical separation.

FREEDOM TO EXECUTE TASKS Autonomy is a fundamental element of the hybrid workplace. By empowering employees to make decisions and manage their responsibilities within established boundaries, leaders foster a sense of ownership and accountability. This freedom not only boosts creativity and innovation but also enhances job satisfaction, as employees feel trusted and valued for their expertise. Effective leadership and management in this context require balancing autonomy with regular check-ins to ensure alignment with organisational goals and to provide support when needed.

INNOVATION In a hybrid work environment where employees work both remotely and in the office, there are specific challenges to creating an environment that fosters innovation, such as communication barriers and difficulty collaborating on ideas. Nevertheless, it's vital for organisations to make innovation a priority to remain competitive and fulfil the evolving requirements of their customers. This may entail establishing a culture that esteems creativity and risk-taking, offering resources and assistance for innovative projects, and utilising technology to enable collaboration and idea-sharing among employees working remotely and in the office. Hybrid work poses a threat to two types of creativity (Haas 2022). The first one is collective creativity, which is the ability to generate ideas through collaborative efforts. While people can brainstorm via Zoom, structured schedules and formats for idea generation may not be as effective as the spontaneous conversations, informal discussions, and unexpected interactions that occur when bouncing ideas off others or working together to solve a problem. Individual creativity is also at risk. We know that spending quiet time alone can help individuals come up with new ideas and insights. However, it is uncertain whether working alone for extended periods of days or weeks will be conducive for employees who need to constantly be creative or innovative. On the contrary, there is reason to believe that some level of social interactions and spontaneous conversations with colleagues, observing random objects in each other's workspaces, and even the change in environment from home to the workplace can play a significant role in fostering creativity.

However, the challenge of fostering innovation through the relationship between in-person collaboration and disruption is unlikely to remain constant over time. Indeed, the costs of coordination and communication over distance have significantly decreased in recent decades, following remarkable advancements in information and communication technologies (Baldwin 2019). The evolving relationship between geographical dispersion and disruption provides evidence that the premium for onsite collaboration has diminished over the decades, suggesting that the benefits of physical co-location have lessened, particularly after the ICT revolution (Presidente and Frey 2022). This is unsurprising. While some tools, such as Skype and Dropbox, gained traction in the 2000s, it was only after 2010 that many of the key remote work technologies emerged, including Trello/Office 365 (2011), Zoom/Google Drive (2012), Slack (2013), Overleaf (2014), and Microsoft Teams (2017). Consistent with the notion that advances in remote work technology are reducing the premium for face-to-face collaboration, we find that co-location becomes less crucial for disruptive discoveries when teams are distributed across countries with robust digital infrastructure.

HYBRID WORKPLACE STRUCTURE, RHYTHM AND ROUTINES The process of creating a framework or system that outlines what flexibility means within the organisation and how it will be implemented. This may involve defining specific policies and procedures related to flexible work arrangements, such as telecommuting or flexible scheduling, and establishing guidelines for how these arrangements will be approved and managed. It may also involve developing training programmes for managers and employees to help them understand the benefits and challenges of flexible work and how to effectively manage a flexible workforce. By setting up a clear and well-defined model for flexibility, organisations can ensure that they are able to reap the benefits of a flexible work environment while minimising potential challenges and risks.

LEARNING ORGANISATION The implementation of the hybrid workplace model requires more emphasis on a learning organisation. An organisation that is committed to continuously improving its processes and practices through ongoing learning and development (Senge 2006). The most successful organisation working hybrid is this type of organisation that values knowledge sharing, innovation, and collaboration among its members, and encourages a culture of continuous learning and feedback. The learning organisation creates innovation faster and with significantly fewer resource requirements. In the learning organisation, it is considered valuable to fail quickly, and in times of great change, a learning organisation culture is on the rise.

MENTORING AND ONBOARDING In a hybrid workplace, there is limited in-person interaction between mentors/colleagues and mentees/new employees. This lack of physical presence can make it challenging to build strong relationships, establish rapport, and effectively convey non-verbal cues. On the other hand, the hybrid workplace can provide opportunities for the development of structured hybrid processes with potentially better options for mentoring and onboarding than the previous model, which relied heavily on in-person interactions in an often more unstructured manner (just being physically present). Addressing the mentoring and onboarding hybrid workplace challenges requires proactive initiatives such as structured in-person attendance, leveraging technology for effective communication, providing comprehensive resources and support through digital platforms, fostering digital collaboration and engagement, and promoting a culture of open communication and feedback. At Microsoft, studies have found that employees benefit from the best of both worlds: flexible work and in-person connections (Microsoft 2024). Their research reveals that while some in-person time is important, additional time spent onsite beyond that does not necessarily offer further advantages. Instead, the key to maximising value, particularly for onboarding, is to be intentional—create structure, and offer opportunities for in-person interactions, while also providing new hires with the flexibility to choose what works best for their success.

NETWORK AND COLLABORATIVE In a hybrid workplace where some employees work from home and others work from the office, it is important to establish a strong network and collaborative culture to maintain a sense of team cohesion and ensure that everyone is working towards shared goals. This includes coordinating, sharing knowledge, and developing as close to each employee's perceived reality as possible. Increasing collaboration, networking, and building trust. The more hybrid the more emphasis on equality and psychological safety, which make ample room for vulnerability.

PERFORMANCE MATRIX Nothing changed—but the devil is in the detail when working hybrid. Insight and assessment of employee work performance where there is growing focus on output (value) and less on input (hours). Movement from hard to smarter—monitoring employees' performance smartly. Increased pressure on the matrix for how work is measured for both individuals and teams, with an increasingly autonomous and decentralised work life and workplace. Building a hybrid performance matrix involves developing a system for evaluating employee performance that considers both in-office and remote work. A hybrid performance matrix should measure both productivity and job satisfaction, and it should be tailored to the specific needs and goals of the organisation.

PURPOSE Purpose and shared value can be challenged with a distributed workforce and employees working from home, as it can be difficult to maintain a shared purpose of the organisation. The hybrid workplace must take measures to enforce and build a shared sense of purpose. It is not enough to rely on previous measures that relied on repeated in-person touchpoints, but rather it needs to be amplified for the hybrid workplace. Organisations can ensure that employees understand their roles and responsibilities, and how they contribute to the organisation's overall mission and goals.

REMOTE LEADERSHIP Remote leadership is a type of leadership where the leader is not physically present with their team or followers. Instead, communication and collaboration take place through technology such as virtual meetings, email, Slack, instant messaging, and other online tools. Distance leadership as a discipline has naturally become growingly popular in recent years due to the rise of remote work and the globalisation of businesses (Barnes et al. 2024). They embraced softer leadership skills and developed more humanistic leadership behaviours and developed an introspection practice to maintain their mental and psychological balance and they mastered time management in an always-on world. This requires strong communication skills, trust-building, and the ability to adapt to different cultural and technological environments. Some common challenges faced by distance leaders include maintaining team cohesion and morale, ensuring clear communication, providing regular feedback and support, and managing time zone differences. With the hybrid workplace model, situational leadership with distance management is on the rise. The model was developed by Paul Hersey and Ken Blanchard. In a major study conducted by the Technical University of Denmark, it was found that leaders who build their leadership on relationships are more challenged by the distance from their employees, as it is difficult to maintain relationships remotely. While it is possible, it places high demands on the leader's social, empathetic, and communicative skills. There is currently a discussion about whether we will eventually see completely new types of leaders emerging as a result of more people working from home (Ipsen et al. 2021).

SHARED AND ADAPTIVE LEADERSHIP In distributed management, employees and formal managers share management tasks (Zhu et al. 2018). This can be done by the manager assigning management tasks to employees or by employees taking on management tasks themselves without being asked. It is important to recognise informal and empathetic leadership and create a culture of high trust, where disagreements about which direction to take are minimal (Joy 2021). Distributed leadership brings greater flexibility and adaptability, enabling organisations to respond swiftly to shifting circumstances. Decentralised management empowers lower-level managers and employees to address changes directly in their areas of work, reducing delays often associated with top-down decision-making. When additional complexity is introduced, the need for adaptive leadership becomes essential. Such leadership fosters a collaborative, problem-solving approach that integrates diverse perspectives, effectively navigating complexities in a dynamic work environment (Nelson and Squires 2017).

SUPPORT AND FEEDBACK MECHANISMS In a dispersed workforce, accessible support systems are critical. Management must ensure employees have the resources they need, including technological tools, professional development opportunities, and mentorship. Constructive feedback mechanisms, such as regular one-on-one meetings and performance reviews, help employees refine their skills and align their efforts with organisational goals. Open feedback loops also allow employees to voice their concerns and share ideas, fostering a culture of continuous improvement and engagement.

TRUST AND PSYCOLOGICAL SAFETY Trust is the cornerstone of successful hybrid workplace leadership. Leaders must demonstrate confidence in their employees' abilities, empowering them to take ownership of their tasks without micromanagement. Psychological safety, where employees feel secure to express ideas, raise concerns, and take calculated risks, is essential for fostering innovation and engagement. Management can cultivate this environment by practising active listening, addressing concerns with empathy, and modelling behaviours that promote inclusivity and respect.

WELL-BEING The happiness, contentment, and fulfilment that employees experience in their work environment are crucial for the success of the hybrid workplace model. Employee well-being can be affected by various factors such as job satisfaction, work-life balance, work environment, leadership style, and employee benefits. Employers who prioritise employee well-being tend to have more engaged and productive employees, lower rates of turnover and absenteeism, and a better workplace culture overall. However, some challenges may arise from the hybrid workplace model, including isolation and loneliness, blurred boundaries between work and private life leading to burnout and fatigue, inequities in resource access, lack of social support and interaction, and technology-related stress, such as difficulty using digital tools and platforms (Montañez 2024).

WORK AND DECISION PROCESSES Leaner, less complex, and faster. With greater hybrid and flexible work arrangements, there is a greater incentive and opportunity to redesign organisational structures, decision, and work processes. This is especially important as employees are staying in each job for shorter periods of time. As a result, the time it takes for employees to become productive after being hired needs to be reduced, even though this task has become more challenging with the introduction of hybrid work. To facilitate remote work, employers can identify tasks that can be done remotely, such as administrative tasks, research, and analysis. This will allow employees to work from home when appropriate and reduce the need for them to be in the office. Employers should also ensure that communication tools, such as video conferencing software and collaboration tools, are in place to allow employees to communicate and collaborate effectively, regardless of their location. Additionally, employers can reduce the need for in-person meetings by using video conferencing software for meetings, allowing employees to attend meetings from wherever they are.

12.15 Challenge: The Manager–Employee Relationship Trumps All Workplace Initiatives

Want a successful hybrid office workplace? Shift focus and resources from interior design, perks, and experiences to the manager–employee relationship. The employee relationship with the proximate leader is more crucial for productivity, retention, and attraction than a fancy office workplace. Creating an impressive office environment is often simpler than establishing a strong manager–employee relationship. Yet, the real challenge lies in managers adapting their approach and expanding their leadership toolkit to foster meaningful connections and effective support within the team. This transformation requires more than aesthetic changes; it calls for a shift in mindset and the development of new skills that prioritise trust, open communication, and empathy (Tigar 2020). Therefore, most organisations post-pandemic are creating attractive offices in line with the best first-order thinking, whereas the focus should perhaps be more on supporting engaged employee–manager relationships. To put it plainly, studies unequivocally show that employees do not leave because of poor office design, but rather due to poor manager–employee relationships.

The managers' engagement and manager–employee relationship stand as one of the most defining factors in the formation of the successful workplace (Farndale et al. 2013). When managers are engaged at work, non-managers are also more likely to be engaged. While economic prosperity and labour protections strongly correlate with reduced misery at work, engagement is more closely tied to interpersonal relationships with one's manager. An effective manager motivates team members, moving them from indifferent to inspired. Managers drive engagement through goal setting, regular, meaningful feedback, and accountability. Great managers help employees find meaning and reward in their work. As a result, employees take an interest in what they do, leading to higher productivity and enjoyment. The office is just one of many contact points between managers and employees. However, given the importance of the relationship between leader and employee, and recognising that the manager's engagement is crucial for the employee's productivity and well-being, the office should focus on supporting and developing the perceived relationship between leader and employee and strengthening the manager's engagement. There are indications that traditional employee engagement metrics and industry approaches to monitoring workplace design and management do not fully reflect the recent shift to hybrid work patterns (Surma et al. 2021).

The contemporary workplace model for knowledge workers must though ensure that employees view managers as exceptional and engaged leaders. This is not achieved by prioritising an office-first approach, but through a strategy that emphasises engagement and close relationships between individuals, regardless of their hierarchical role as an employee, middle manager, or senior manager, and irrespective of the time, place, or environment in which the work is carried out or the relationship is developed. In terms of time and the current focus on enhancing leadership, efforts may be best directed towards nurturing manager–employee relationships and refining processes as they evolve. Emphasising these relationships allows leadership to adapt dynamically, meeting the changing needs of the workplace and fostering an environment that supports growth and engagement over the long term (Shamir 2011).

In other words, it is not primarily about fancy premises, activity-based workplace design, flexibility, or croissants and barista coffee. It is mainly about ensuring that employees view their immediate supervisor very positively and engaged. The physical office can make a significant difference, just as the relationship and contact outside the physical office working can. The challenge lies in striking the right balance between the factors that, on their own, foster engaged managers and those that enhance employees' perceptions of their relationship with their manager. An example of this office manager–employee dilemma could be that a manager prefers to work full-time physically in the office and is therefore most engaged when this is possible, while their employees have a different approach to the hybrid and more flexible workplace. Or a manager is placed isolated from his employees in the office in his own cubicle to work more efficiently and confidentially, while their employees have a desire to have easy and immediate access to their manager.

References

(Atlassian 2022) Trends worth tracking https://www.atlassian.com/blog/state-of-teams-2022#trends-worth-tracking

(Baldwin 2019) Globotics and development https://www.wider.unu.edu/sites/default/files/Publications/Working-paper/PDF/wp-2019-94.pdf

(Ballisager 2023) Kandidatanalysen 2023 https://ballisager.com/kandidatanalysen/

(Barnes et al., 2024) Barnes, Kristian; Vione, Katia; Kotera, Yasuhiro Effective leadership practice among senior leaders working from home and in the hybrid workplace across COVID-19. SN Business & Economics (2024). doi: https://doi.org/10.1007/s43546-024-00651-4 https://ideas.repec.org/a/spr/snbeco/v4y2024i5d10.1007_s43546-024-00651-4.html

(Bartsch et al., 2020) Bartsch, Silke & Weber, Ellen & Büttgen, Marion & Huber, Ariana. (2020). Leadership matters in crisis-induced digital transformation: how to lead service employees effectively during the COVID-19 pandemic. Journal of Service Management. ahead-of-print. https://doi.org/10.1108/JOSM-05-2020-0160. https://www.emerald.com/insight/content/doi/10.1108/JOSM-05-2020-0160/full/html

(Bolino and Phelps 2024) HBR April 2024 3 Challenges to Hybrid Work - and How to Overcome Them https://hbr.org/2024/05/3-challenges-to-hybrid-work-and-how-to-overcome-them

(Christensen 1997) Harvard Business Review Press *"The Innovator's Dilemma: When New Technologies Cause Great Firms to Fail"*

(Dijcke, Gunsilius, and Wright, 2024) Return to Office and the Tenure Distribution https://ideas.repec.org/p/arx/papers/2405.04352.html
(Ding and Ma, 2023) Return-to-Office Mandates https://papers.ssrn.com/sol3/papers.cfm?abstract_id=4675401
(Farndale et al., 2013) Implementing Performance Appraisal: Exploring the Employee Experience https://onlinelibrary.wiley.com/doi/abs/10.1002/hrm.21575
(Fayard, Weeks and Khan 2021) HBR March-April 2021 Designing the Hybrid Office https://hbr.org/2021/03/designing-the-hybrid-office
(Flassak et al. 2022) Flassak, Konstantin & Haag, Julia & Hofmann, Christian & Lechner, Christopher & Schwaiger, Nina & Zacherl, Rafael. (2022). Working from home and management controls. Journal of Business Economics. 93. 1-36. https://doi.org/10.1007/s11573-022-01123-7. https://www.researchgate.net/publication/366247139_Working_from_home_and_management_controls
(Fortune 2023) Employees are fighting hard to keep working remotely - but it can come with a high emotional cost. 4 experts break down how to stay sane https://fortune-com.cdn.ampproject.org/c/s/fortune.com/2023/01/04/remote-work-tips-mental-health/amp/
(Garelli 2016) Why you will probably live longer than most big companies https://www.imd.org/research-knowledge/disruption/articles/why-you-will-probably-live-longer-than-most-big-companies/
(Haas 2022) HBR 5 Challenges of Hybrid Work - and How to Overcome Them https://hbr.org/2022/02/https://hbr.org/2022/02/5-challenges-of-hybrid-work-and-how-to-overcome-them
(Hastings et al., 2020) Hastings, Reed and Erin Meyer. No Rules Rules: Netflix and the Culture of Reinvention. New York: Penguin 2020. https://www.amazon.com/No-Rules/dp/0753553635
(Ipsen et al., 2021) Christine Ipsen, Associated Professor DTU Management 20121 januar Hvordan ændrer hjemmearbejdet lederens opgaver? https://www.dtu.dk/nyheder/alle-nyheder/nyhed?id=%7B22F69C96-D819-4EB2-BF32-8A8ADCD10176%7D
(Ipsen, Kirchner, Andersone and Karanika-Murray 2022) Becoming a Distance Manager: Managerial Experiences, Perceived Organizational Support, and Job Satisfaction During the COVID-19 Pandemic https://www.frontiersin.org/journals/psychology/articles/10.3389/fpsyg.2022.916234/full
(Joy 2021) The future of leadership: skills to look for in business leaders post-COVID-19. Chieflearingofficer. https://www.chieflearningofficer.com/2021/03/11/the-future-of-leadership-skills-to-look-for-in-business-leaders-post-covid-19/
(Kirschner 2023) Crafting the Future of Work: Phil Kirschner, McKinsey & Co. https://at.cafe/blog/phil-kirschner-crafting-the-future-of-work-at-mckinsey-co
(Klinghoffer, Kocher and Luna 2024) HBR June 2024 Onboarding New Employees in a Hybrid Workplace https://hbr.org/2024/06/onboarding-new-employees-in-a-hybrid-workplace
(Kotter and Heskett 1992) Corporate Culture and Performance https://www.hbs.edu/faculty/Pages/item.aspx?num=139
(Lagowska, Sobrao, Furtado and Grobman, 2020) Leadership under crises: a research agenda for the Post-COVID-19 era. Brazil Admin Rev. https://doi.org/https://doi.org/10.1590/1807-7692 bar2020200062
(Lederstof 2022) Ledelsesløse organisationer er en komplet illusion https://www.lederstof.dk/professor-ledelsesloese-organisationer-er-en-komplet-illusion
(Liang 1997) Liang, Andrew. New Patterns of Work: The design of the Office. UK, York, Architectural Press 1997
(Logan, King and Fisher-Wright 2008) Harper Business, Dave Logan, John King, Halee Fischer-Wright, Tribal Leadership: Leveraging Natural Groups to Build a Thriving Organization https://www.amazon.com/Tribal-Leadership-Leveraging-Thriving-Organization/dp/0061251321
(McChrystal, 2015) McChrystal Stanley. Team of Tems: New Rules of Engagement for a Complex World. New York: Portfolio/Penguin 2015. https://www.amazon.com/Team-Teams-Rules-Engagement-Complex/dp/1591847486

(McKinsey & Company 2023) Is your workplace ready for flexible work? A survey offers clues https://www.mckinsey.com/industries/real-estate/our-insights/is-your-workplace-ready-for-flexible-work-a-survey-offers-clues#/

(Mcnall et al., 2010) McNall, L. A., Masuda, A. D., & Nicklin, J. M. (2009). Flexible Work Arrangements, Job Satisfaction, and Turnover Intentions: The Mediating Role of Work-to-Family Enrichment. *The Journal of Psychology*, *144*(1), 61–81. https://doi.org/10.1080/00223980903356073

(Meyer 2010) Forbes The four keys to success with virtual teams https://www.forbes.com/2010/08/19/virtual-teams-meetings-leadership-managing-cooperation.html#53ed19e130cc

(Microsoft 2024) In the Changing Role of the Office, It's All about Moments That Matter https://www.microsoft.com/en-us/worklab/in-the-office-it-is-all-about-moments-that-matter

(Montañez 2024) HBR March 2024 Fighting Loneliness on Remote Teams https://hbr.org/2024/03/fighting-loneliness-on-remote-teams

(Morieux 2011) Yves Morieux, Harvard Business Review September 2011 "Smart Rules: Six Ways to Get People to Solve Problems Without You" https://hbr.org/2011/09/smart-rules-six-ways-to-get-people-to-solve-problems-without-you

(Nelson and Squires, 2017) Addressing complex challenges through adaptive leadership: a promising approach to collaborative problem solving. J Leadership Educ 16(4):111–123 https://www.semanticscholar.org/paper/Addressing-Complex-Challenges-through-Adaptive-A-to-Nelson-Squires/f3af03527bd823cd0c6e57e39244befd78d8192c

(Oygür, Karahan and Göçer 2022) Hybrid Workplace: Activity–based office Design in a Post–pandemic Era. Journal of Interior Design, 47(3), 3-10. https://journals.sagepub.com/doi/abs/10.1111/joid.12218

(Ozcelik and Barsade 2018) No Employee an Island: Workplace Loneliness and Job Performance https://journals.aom.org/doi/abs/10.5465/amj.2015.1066

(Presidente and Frey 2022) Disrupting science: How remote collaboration impacts innovation https://cepr.org/voxeu/columns/disrupting-science-how-remote-collaboration-impacts-innovation

(Senge, 2006) Senge, Peter. The Fifth Discipline: The Art and Practice of the Learning Organization. Rv. Edt. New York: Crown Business 2006 https://www.amazon.com/Fifth-Discipline-Practice-Learning-Organization/dp/0385517254

(Sevcenko, Ayoubi, Choudhury and Jang 2024) Office at Offsite: How Temporary Colocation Shapes Communication in an All-Remote Organization

(Shamir 2011) Leadership takes time: some implications of (not) taking time seriously in leadership research. Leadersh Q 22(2):307–315 https://www.sciencedirect.com/science/article/abs/pii/S1048984311000191

(Surma, Nunes, Rook and Loder 2021) Assessing Employee Engagement in a Post-COVID-19 Workplace Ecosystem https://www.mdpi.com/2071-1050/13/20/11443

(Tigar 2020) The 7 soft skills that will matter the most in 2021. Ladders. https://www.theladders.com/career-advice/the-7-soft-skills-that-will-matter-the-most-in-2021

(Wholers 2015) Choosing where to work at work – towards a theoretical model of benefits and risks of activity-based flexible offices https://www.tandfonline.com/doi/abs/10.1080/00140139.2016.1188220

(Zarte et al. 2024) Zarate. Dolls, Davis, Bloom, Barrero and Aksoy WHY DOES WORKING FROM HOME VARY ACROSS COUNTRIES AND PEOPLE? https://wfhresearch.com/wp-content/uploads/2024/04/w32374.pdf

(Zhu et al., 2018) Zhu J, Liao Z, Yam KC, Johnson RE (2018) Shared leadership: a state-of-the-art review and future research agenda. J Organ Behav 39(7):834–852 https://en.rmbs.ruc.edu.cn/docs/2022-07/69d49b7c51c644eb96a7844696999466.pdf

The Future Digital and Analogue Workplace Infrastructure

13

Abstract

The hybrid workplace integrates both analogue and digital workspaces, creating a balanced symbiosis to meet organisational needs. The physical workspace, increasingly a semi-luxury and optional choice, will focus on complex and value-creating interactions, while the digital workspace becomes the primary environment for work and collaboration. As remote work rises, workplaces will adapt by reducing physical office spaces and enhancing digital capabilities. The future hybrid model balances individual autonomy with collective needs, aiming for an optimal work environment that fosters productivity, engagement, and organisational success.

13.1 The Analogue and Digital Workplace Infrastructure

With the spread of the hybrid workplace, the office workspace is essentially divided into two infrastructure formats that work together in a balanced symbiosis to meet the organisation's present and future needs. On the one hand, we have the analogue infrastructure that must be rethought, redesigned, and transformed for a hybrid work reality. On the other hand, there is the digital workspace and infrastructure, which increasingly form the backbone of knowledge workers' work lives and the hybrid workplace. The contrast between the two is, by nature, stark. The digital workplace is inherently flexible, existing quite literally in the cloud, and stands in direct opposition to the analogue workplace, which remains grounded and inflexible despite efforts to introduce flexibility.

The workspace, regardless of format, is being digitised and becoming hybrid. Hybrid is much more than just digitisation and is a fusion of physical and digital with differentiated use and exploitation of channels and formats freed from time and space. The hybrid workplace is defined digitally and built on the digital reality that

C. Sneppen, *The Future (R)Evolution of the Office Workspace*, Future of Business and Finance, https://doi.org/10.1007/978-3-031-85229-9_13

the workspace creates value in networks and collaboration. Therefore, the hybrid workplace is much more than the activity- or experience-based workspace based on an analogue approach. The future successful hybrid workplace is born digitally and must be thought of digitally—and strengthened through the physical workspace to ensure productivity and efficiency, regardless of where employees are physically located. With the development, as previously stated, the workplace has become a consumption channel in an omnichannel approach to consumption of worktime in exchange for productivity and personal fulfilment.

Central to the development of the physical and digital workspace is analogue and digital dexterity at both the organisational and employee levels. The design and use of the digital and analogue workplace will be essential in the future and still require competent and differentiated approaches. This is expressed in "The Paradox of the Digital Office". We digitise and evolve work life at an unprecedented speed and simultaneously hold on to the office as the true centre of work life for knowledge workers. But the office as the work epicentre for knowledge workers collides with ongoing technology advancements. The more digitalised the office becomes, the less it is used. It is, therefore, merely a question of time and management skills before, not if, knowledge workers are further freed from the constraints of time, location, and physical space in performing their work. The preservation of an analogue approach to the office will only take place if or when analogue work proves to be more competitive than the digital workplace—in other words, if digitalisation levels off.

This is illustrated in Fig. 13.1. Pre-pandemic, organisations were not up to date and did not sufficiently exploit the available technology and digital opportunities. The analogue workplace was overly dominant, leading to a lack of flexibility. During the pandemic and the great office workspace experiment, the opposite was true. Post-pandemic, the general balance has shifted towards a predisposition for the analogue office, with a set analogue workplace complemented by flexibility,

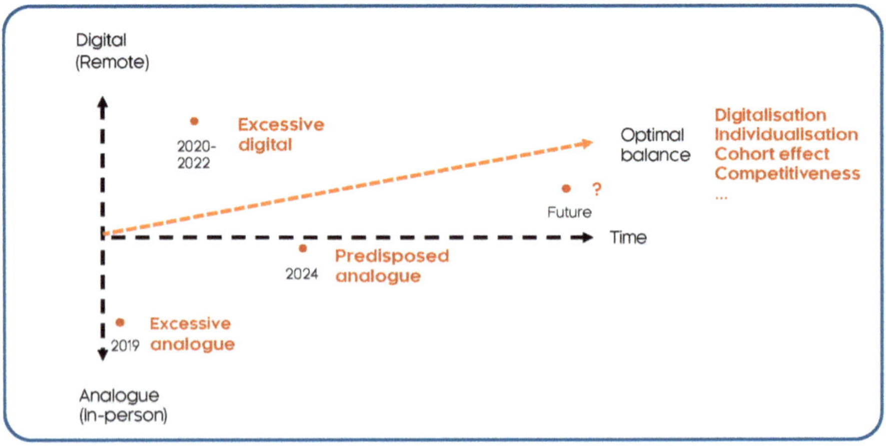

Fig. 13.1 What is the future optimal hybrid workplace model flexibility balance?

typically around two working days per week. Looking further ahead, we expect that the evolution, driven by the defined megatrends, will push the balance towards even greater digitalisation and there for a further distributed workforce no less.

13.2 The Analogue Office Workplace

I anticipate that, in the future, the physical office workplace will evolve into a semi-luxury item and, to varying degrees, an optional yet deliberate choice. The physical workplace will truly be physical and differentiated from digital distance work. The physical office workplace that is a poor copy or replica of the home or digital workplace will be absolute and perish.

The physical workplace itself will become digitised and designed from a network perspective, supplemented by what is uniquely analogue. This means a primarily network-based workplace design of layout and organisation, focusing on value-creating interactions, collaboration, and a radical break with the function-based workplace. In short, the physical workplace will focus on what is important, complex, uncertain, and unpredictable and creates the most value analogously. All other activities will take place within the digital workplace, in a meeting booth, or remotely.

Ultimately, in the distant future, access to the physical workplace will become more limited and selective, with individuals granted access based on time and need. Not everyone will have constant access to the physical workplace at all times. There will be a reduction in administrative, routine jobs through automation, AI, and those that do not create more value by being in a physical office. The bookkeeper is for example anticipated to be increasingly pushed away from expensive square metres in centrally located offices.

The physical workplace will in most organisations remain prioritised as a crucial identity, culture, and brand marker, realising and confirming what the organisation truly is and what it purports to be. Individualisation of workplace design and services in relation to the employee will continue, and an increase in solutions to ensure employee well-being, engagement, attraction, and retention is anticipated. Nevertheless, the physical office workspace will be significantly reduced in size and operating costs while becoming more scalable and flexible. Successful office workplaces will increasingly seek synergies with other workplaces or partners, and will differentiate themselves within an ecosystem of spaces in and beyond the office (Gensler 2024). Workplaces will move closer together to achieve synergies (Fig. 13.2). At the same time, workplaces will decentralise by locating smaller workplaces closer to employees' homes, where they can work quietly or hold meetings. Physical meeting places, such as smaller workplace satellites, will emerge near residential areas primarily in and around major cities. The reduced daily commute will also free up the workplace from being located near main traffic arteries and entry roads on the outskirts of larger cities and make it possible to move workplaces closer to attractive areas and achieve synergies with surrounding city life (which does not exist in isolated office locations in monochrome office cities and

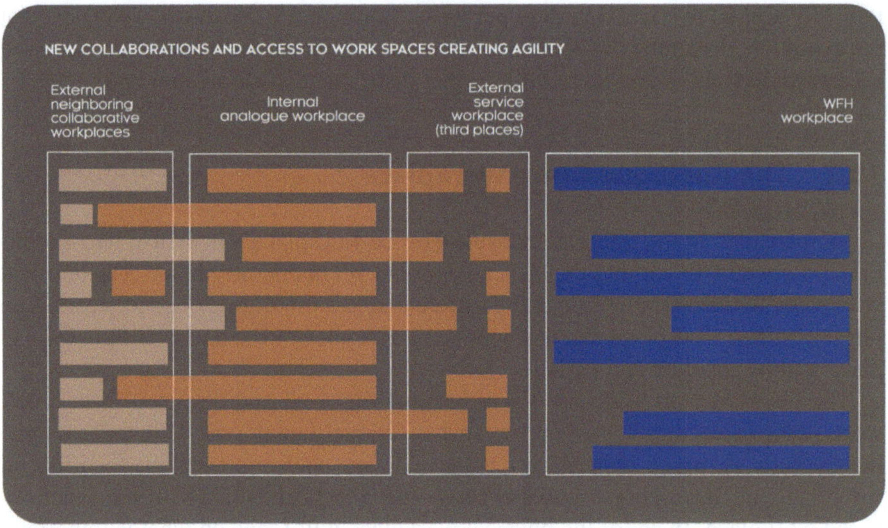

Fig. 13.2 External shared spaces for the hybrid office workplace model

districts). This will make the workplace more attractive and a welcome break from the isolation of home.

13.3 The Digital Workplace

The digital workplace will be defining for the hybrid workplace and will fundamentally offer to fulfil all workplace needs regardless of time, place, and space. It will simultaneously ensure individual work while providing a network-based collaborative approach to work.

Knowledge workers—and eventually other employee groups—will increasingly be able to work from home or other locations, regardless of their tasks, instead of relying on the physical workplace. Widespread remote work will become increasingly standard for knowledge workers, surpassing the current situation, where it is now essential to introduce frameworks and solutions that clarify physical, digital, or hybrid presence during workdays or meetings.

The digital development enables an increasingly larger replacement and conversion from the physical workplace through the development of new digital products that allow for relationship-building, co-creation, and innovation reducing transaction costs and enhancing workplace design through digital tools (Spitzhirn et al. 2022). The ultimate development point will be when—and if—it becomes predominately better and faster to collaborate in the digital universe than when participants meet physically at the workplace.

The digital universe and workplace will growingly become an identity and culture creator. This will be necessary as more and more employees alone will have—or choose to have—limited and sporadic contact with the physical workplace.

13.4 Defining Office Workplace Scenario Dimensions

The crucial scenarios for the future hybrid workplace are built around two dimensions: individual-collective and analogue-digital. The scenarios are not either-or, but a starting point for understanding and proactively considering the primary approach to creating the future hybrid office workplace. Virtually all hybrid workplace models will contain elements of these different scenarios.

The presented scenarios and subsequent descriptions are merely proposals for what the development may imply for the future hybrid workplace. The descriptions are not final or comprehensive; they are intended solely to inspire and potentially stimulate discussion. The detailed scenarios description and lists have been produced through workshops with organisations and have only been partially edited.

ANALOGUE OR DIGITAL (UNPLUGGED OR PLUGGED) (Fig. 13.3): Whether the workplace of the future will be predominantly analogue or digital is seen as a premise for future businesses that each individual company must conform to (although each organisation has the option to go against the trend, this concerns the direction of the market). Can work be done digitally or must it be solved analogously? Analogue is necessary and digital is possible. Technological development will increasingly make it possible and more value-creating to perform work digitally. At the same time, the execution of work is necessary to be carried out analogously—both objectively and based on employee behaviour.

WE OR ME (HETERONOMOUS OR AUTONOMOUS) (Fig. 13.4): Whether the individual company is built around a "me-autonomous" or "we-heteronomous" approach, should it be an individual-oriented approach or a "we-heteronomous" approach—e.g. an orientation around the community? This scenario dimension will inevitably be influenced by whether society as a whole is further oriented towards individualisation or not, but it is primarily an organisational choice, and therefore an active choice that needs to be clarified before the strategy for the future hybrid workplace is established. The "me" and "we" approach is continuously challenged in the interfaces and relationships between organisation, leadership, and

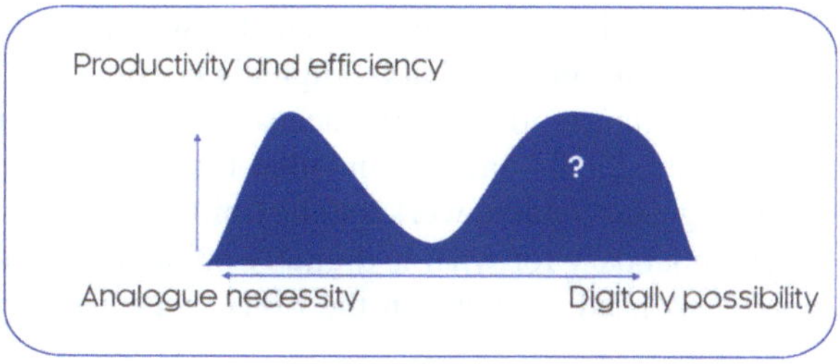

Fig. 13.3 What is most important for productivity and efficiency? The computer or the physical workplace?

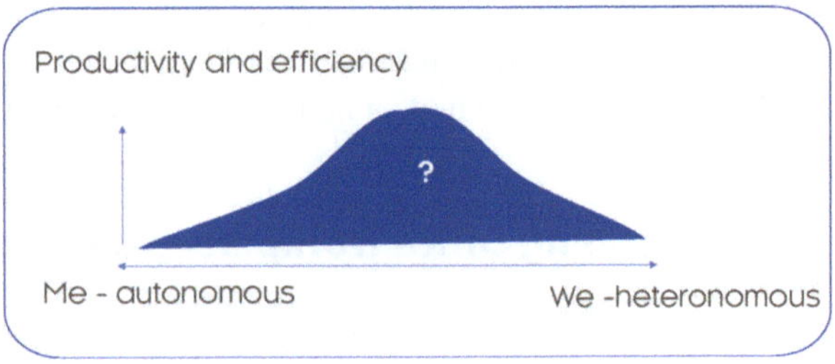

Fig. 13.4 What is most important for productivity and efficiency? The "me" or "we"?

individuals. What is the optimal social capital present at any given moment in an organisation to support the hybrid workplace model?

"Ask not what the workplace can do for you, but what you can do for your colleagues," an adapted version of John F. Kennedy's iconic (1961) inauguration speech, challenges the ego's focus on individualism in favour of the collective and the greater good of the organisation. The same can be said for the hybrid workplace, where knowledge workers are becoming increasingly ego-centred around their own needs and preferences. This development creates a big dilemma for knowledge workers in the hybrid workplace: individual work-life organisation versus the needs of the organisation and colleagues! It may be that I am more productive on my direct tasks by working from home today, but on the other hand, it may be that my colleagues are more productive if I come to the office. How can these two considerations and approaches be balanced in a way that creates the optimal balance for colleagues, the organisation, management, customers, and last but not least, the individual worker? Should employers maintain the dominant approach so far, where workers organise their work life with limited freedom and a high degree of physical presence? Or should the worker have a high degree of freedom to solve tasks liberated by time, place, and space?

13.5 Envisioning Future Scenarios for the Office Workplace

The current interpretation of the hybrid workplace model is merely a first and initial step towards the future design of the hybrid workplace. As we have previously established, development is dynamic and will mainly be defined in interaction with digital advancements and employee behaviour. Using the two scenarios, dimensions and dilemmas emerge, shaping the following possibilities for the development and evolution of the future hybrid workplace (Fig. 13.5). The dilemma of "me" versus "we" carries significant implications for workplace design in an increasingly digitised reality, balancing what is "digitally possible" with what is "analogously necessary". The future office workplace scenarios offer a more enlightened and clearer picture, revealing—once again—that the development is not static but is moving towards greater remote work and flexibility.

The boundary for what is digitally possible coincides with how much less time employees need to spend in the office, with varying degrees of time shifts. The

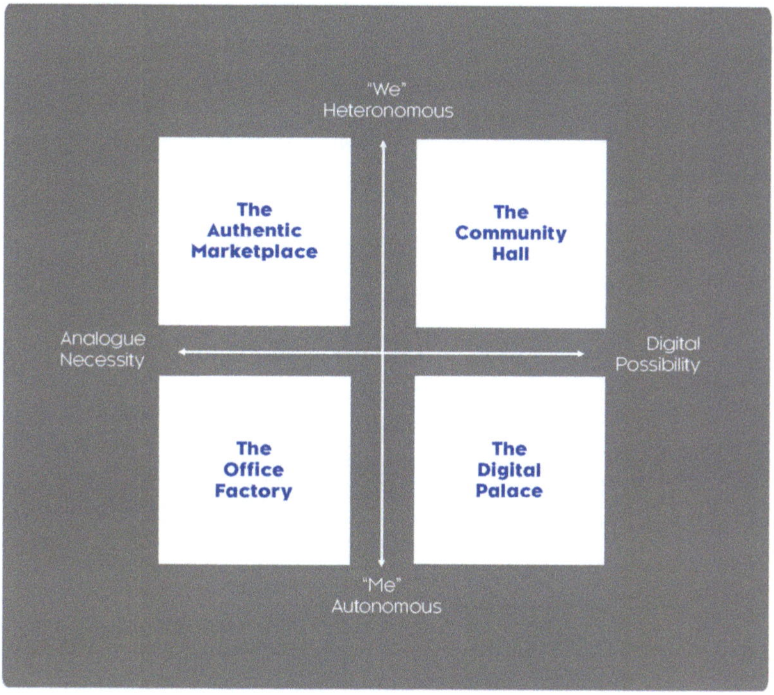

Fig. 13.5 Four scenarios: the hybrid office workplace

dividing line between what is digitally possible and analogously necessary can be determined objectively based on the nature of the work, or subjectively based on the individual employee's or leader's preference. The major question is how this distribution will look in the future: in other words, to what extent organisations and employees have been able to translate these possibilities into behaviour and increased competitiveness.

The pace of evolution between the different scenarios is not uniform. While some organisations have already entered the digital realm, others continue to thrive and maintain competitiveness in the post-industrial age. However, as outlined previously, we anticipate that work will increasingly become more asynchronous and symmetric, regardless of its format, as the boundaries blur and dissolve with the advent of new, advanced technologies such as AI and the Metaverse, and with the adoption of a more non-linear approach. We aim to eliminate asymmetric interactions, given their significant limitations. Our trajectory is towards a more aligned and balanced future, one that leverages the best of both worlds while adeptly navigating the conditions at hand (Fig. 13.6).

2020: The Office Factory

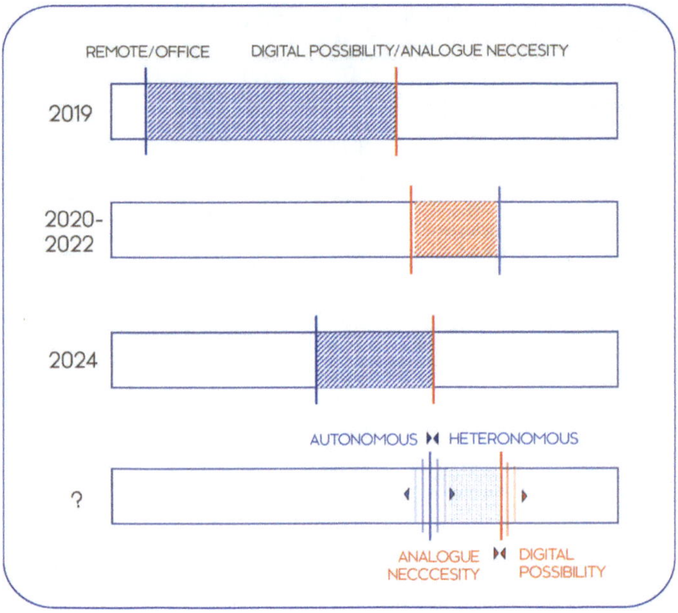

Fig. 13.6 Anticipated digital/analogue development of the future hybrid office workplace

Pre-pandemic workplaces were predominantly characterised by in-person presence at the office. While it was digitally possible to work more remotely, workplaces primarily maintained a 9-to-5 linear and synchronous approach. The workplace, as the office factory, is history as we look towards the future.

2020–2022: The Grand Workplace Experiment

With the pandemic, the workplace for knowledge workers shifted to their homes to such an extent that even analogue necessities for most productive interactions and collaborations were moved remotely. This extreme experiment shifted awareness and highlighted the digital possibilities and analogue necessities. In the workplace scenario model, the great workplace experiment can be viewed as a precursor to the digital palace, where neither technological development nor, in particular, behaviour was ready for this shift.

2024 (Present): The Authentic Marketplace

The post-pandemic workplace has moved the distribution between remote and in-person work for knowledge workers closer to the boundary between digital possibilities and analogue necessities. The boundary for what is digitally possible has also shifted earlier, as technological advancements and adjusted user behaviour have enabled increased digital work. The office workplace is designed to be activity-based, supplemented with various "booths" and experiences to stimulate senses and collaboration.

Proximate Future: The Community Hall

In the future, the proportion of what is digitally possible is expected to increase, while the analogue necessities are predicted to decrease correspondingly. It is also expected that the proportion of remote work will increase and move closer to the boundary between analogue necessities and digital possibilities. The analogue workplace is expected to be reduced accordingly and increasingly function as a community hall where the organisation and employees can gather by appointment and for agreed-upon events.

Distant Future: The Digital Palace

Looking further into the distant future, a possible "what-if-scenario" outcome of the development is that the in-person workplace is reduced to a palace where employees come by appointment, becoming a place for the few and selected. A variation and extension of the digital palace could involve holding meetings at locations selected by management, including private homes and co-working spaces (e.g. Ghandini 2015).

The future dividing line for employee flexibility, and thus the fundamental structure on which the hybrid workplace model is unfolded, will be determined by a pressure and balancing act between autonomy (me) and heteronomy (we)—ideally in a balance where the employee is capable of autonomously balancing it with a Pareto efficiency and a holistic perspective (e.g. the 80/20 Rule that states that roughly 80% of the results come from 20% of the causes). On the one hand, employees, with an individualist approach, will make narrow, self-interested choices for their work execution but constantly evaluate them against what is best for the organisation and colleagues. When management solely determines the boundaries, there is an increased risk of disengagement among certain employees or groups, leading to decreased retention. Managing the hybrid workplace requires simultaneously setting clear boundaries, ensuring alignment and support, and continuously monitoring and adjusting efforts, as needed, to maintain the balance between the collective "we" and the individual "me" when it begins to shift.

On the other hand, there is a balancing point between what is digitally possible and analogously necessary, where the extent of pressure and counterpressure in the future will be determined. It also depends on how employees and organisations translate digital possibilities into behaviour. Regardless of the areas of tension, there will undoubtedly be a narrowing of the borderland between the small heteronomous "we" and big autonomous "me", as well as between the plugged digital and unplugged analogue, as this will unleash increased competitive strength for the organisation.

13.6 External Winners and Losers in the Office Workplace Evolution

The scenario descriptions uncover implicit future changes and developments that will have significant impacts and consequences for external workplace actors. The changes are presently and looking forward causing a chain reaction in the value chain associated with the workplace. A dramatic change in work-life behaviour of office workers has unpredictable consequences for the value chain. For example, office buildings, workplace suppliers, physical retail, neighbourhoods, and even cities and regions are experiencing drastic structural changes due to the liberation of office work in terms of time, location, and space.

For instance, office-dominated neighbourhoods or cities that solely focused on office workplaces, filled between the hours of 9-to-5, have experienced significant impacts on the ecosystem due to increased distance work. This shift from pre-pandemic levels has resulted in approx. US$12 billion annual decline in commercial consumption in New York alone (Forbes 2023). As always, the list is not exhaustive or necessarily accurate. It is up to each individual actor to address the changes as either a threat or an opportunity (Investopedia 2023). Looking at the US office markets collectively, there has been a value loss of $556.8 billion (Gupta et al. 2024). Higher-quality buildings have been somewhat shielded by a "flight to quality", while lower-quality office spaces face the risk of becoming stranded assets. These shifts in valuations have important implications for both financial stability and local public finances, as they reflect broader economic and market trends impacting the commercial real estate sector.

Types of external businesses and organisations, all other things being equal, are set to benefit from the hybrid workplace revolution:

- Organisational and "new ways of working" consultants.
- Office architects and designers.
- Office hubs (third places to work) (Yang et al. 2019; Moriset 2013).
- Technology companies especially workplace infrastructure stakeholders.
- Owners of "worthwhile the commute" offices and buildings (Krause 2024).

- Home improvement companies and contractors (upgrading as employees spend more time at home).
- Real estate agents (employees relocating further away) (Akan et al. 2024).
- Office furniture suppliers (B2B and B2C).
- Suburbs and municipalities (named the "The Donut Effect") (Akatsukaet et al. 2023; Ramani & Bloom 2021).
- Residential and house owners (upgrades and price increase) (Ghent et al. 2024).
- ...

Various types of external businesses and stakeholders may be adversely affected by the lasting shift to hybrid work arrangements:

- Office cleaning and maintenance services (less maintenance).
- Office suppliers (print, etc.).
- Owners of marginalised or redundant offices.
- Financial institutions with loans in unattractive office buildings (Anenberg et al. 2024).
- Corporate food services (less attendance at the office—partly upset by food upgrades).
- Commute-dependent businesses for consumption on the go or convenience (less traffic).
- Public transport linked to commuting (less commuting) (Zheng et al. 2024).
- Business travel (less business travel).
- Monochrome business areas and districts (unattractive).
- Conservative business attire businesses (casual attire is gaining grounds).
- Cities and municipalities dependent on monochrome business districts (unattractive).
- Car maintenance... (less commuting). (Potentially creating a perfect storm, as some regions and countries are simultaneously transitioning to electric vehicles while also reducing overall daily car usage).
- Smaller household incomes are being pushed out of the market due to rising property prices in and around cities (Ghent et al. 2024).
- ...

References

(Akan et al., 2024) 5 March 2024 WFH Research, Mert Akan, Jose Maria Barrero, Nicholas Bloom, Tom Bowen, Shelby Buckman, Steven J. Davis, Luke Pardue and Liz Wilkie Americans Now Live Farther from Their Employers https://wfhresearch.com/wp-content/uploads/2024/03/DistanceToWork.pdf

(Akatsukaet et al., 2023) Akatsuka, H., Toyoda, M. Analysis of the relationship between urban dynamics and prevalence of remote work based on population data generated from cellular networks. *Sci Rep* **13**, 20139 (2023). https://doi.org/10.1038/s41598-023-47513-x

(Anenberg et al., 2024) Work-From-Home and Commercial Real Estate: Effects on Bank Balance Sheets, Credit Availability, and the Real Economy https://drive.google.com/file/d/15daN6aAPPrIUPSqr6uPUgNkIbGHqBr__/view

(Forbes 2023) New York City Is Losing Out On $12 Billion Annually Because Of Remote Work https://www.forbes.com/sites/jackkelly/2023/02/14/new-york-city-is-losing-out-on-12-billion-annually-because-of-remote-work/

(Gensler 2024) GLOBAL WORKPLACE SURVEY 2024 Moving beyond employee presence to workplace performance https://www.gensler.com/doc/research-global-workplace-survey-2024.pdf

(Ghandini 2015) The rise of coworking spaces : a literature review https://air.unimi.it/handle/2434/618721

(Ghent et al., 2024) Winners and Losers from the Work-from-Home Technology Boon https://papers.ssrn.com/sol3/papers.cfm?abstract_id=4768634

(Gupta, Mittal, and Nieuwerburgh, 2024) Work From Home and the Office Real Estate Apocalypse https://papers.ssrn.com/sol3/papers.cfm?abstract_id=4124698

(Investopedia 2023) The Economic Impact of a Hybrid Office https://www.investopedia.com/the-economic-impact-of-a-hybrid-office-5200417

(Krause 2024) Empty Offices and Urban Transitions: The Impact of Working from Home on Commercial Real Estate https://drive.google.com/file/d/1ViqMceSzNs7kzFzJwO0cTQKKut6YJjWw/view

(Moriset 2013) Building new places of the creative economy. The rise of coworking spaces https://shs.hal.science/halshs-01369753/

(Ramani and Bloom 2021) Ramani and Bloom The donut effect of Covid-19 on cities https://www.nber.org/system/files/working_papers/w28876/w28876.pdf

(Spitzhirn et al., 2022) Spitzhirn, M., Benter, M., Heindl, C. *et al.* Hybrid work systems - platform-based work planning - designing productive and human-centered work processes. *Z. Arb. Wiss.* **76**, 489–509 (2022). https://doi.org/10.1007/s41449-022-00342-6

(Yang, Bisson and Sanborn 2019) Coworking space as a third-fourth place: changing models of a hybrid space in corporate real estate https://www.emerald.com/insight/content/doi/10.1108/JCRE-12-2018-0051/full/html

(Zheng et al., 2024) Zheng, Y., Wang, S., Liu, L. *et al.* Impacts of remote work on vehicle miles traveled and transit ridership in the USA. *Nat Cities* **1**, 346–358 (2024). https://doi.org/10.1038/s44284-024-00057-1 https://www.nature.com/articles/s44284-024-00057-1

The Future Digital Office Workplace 14

Abstract

The future digital workplace will revolutionise work by enabling seamless collaboration, independent work, and leadership unrestricted by time, place, or space. As organisations transition to a blend of digital and analogue workspaces, digital infrastructure will increasingly dominate, enhancing efficiency and productivity. The digital workplace will likely include AI, automation, cloud-based technology, IoT, and advanced collaboration tools. As workplaces evolve, balancing digital and analogue elements will be crucial for maintaining competitiveness. Organisations that embrace digital advancements will lead the way, while those that delay risk falling behind in the rapidly changing work environment.

14.1 The Digital Workplace: Where Innovation Meets Magic

The future digital workplace aims to fulfil all workplace requirements (Fig. 14.1). The digital workplace and infrastructure will undergo revolutionary development in the future, leading to unpredictable consequences for our current understanding of the workplace and work life for knowledge workers. Digital advancements will empower independent work and leadership, free from the constraints of time, location, and space, while greatly enhancing efficiency and productivity—reflecting the ideas expressed by Marc Andreessen in his article "Why Software Is Eating the World" (Andreessen, Andreessen Horowitz 2011).

Office workplaces are currently, and will continue, transitioning into a blend of digital and analogue working, with in-person interactions being utilised selectively. This leaves organisations in a transitional phase presently, where they must balance the evolution of the workplace with daily value creation. The ambitious pioneers at the forefront of developing the hybrid and highly digitalised workplace strive for an

C. Sneppen, *The Future (R)Evolution of the Office Workspace*, Future of Business and Finance, https://doi.org/10.1007/978-3-031-85229-9_14

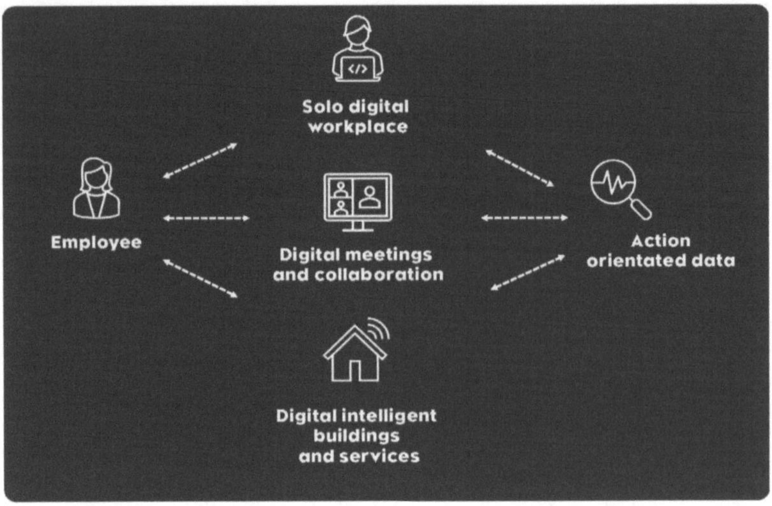

Fig. 14.1 The future digital workplace

almost fully digital workplace. While achieving digital nirvana may not be guaranteed, the digital workplace pioneers avoid being burdened with obsolete and backward-looking real estate and management obligations. On the other hand, those who wait may benefit from the experiences and knowledge of the early adopters, but they risk losing competitiveness in the short to medium term. Many digital tools are already available to organisations and employees. They simply need to incorporate these tools into their everyday work processes further. However, one of the challenges is shifting from hyper-responsiveness and real-time communication towards more asynchronous communication and collaboration using digital solutions (Glaveski 2021).

The digital infrastructure contains the tools that truly grant individuals the freedom to decide when and where to work. Shared documents empower people to work on the same document asynchronously, eliminating the need for version control. Instant messaging plugins can replace email and enhance communication. Ultimately, the effectiveness of digital tools depends on how effectively they are utilised, and alignment between managers and employees is crucial for successful digital transformation. As we move forward, the digital office workplace relentlessly aims to enable all office work for knowledge workers to be done digitally. Objectively speaking, the digital workplace will be capable of addressing work tasks just as well as the analogue workplace, if not better in some cases. However, for certain tasks, the traditional analogue in-person workplace is still anticipated to be more suitable when we look a few decades ahead. Looking even further ahead …who knows? From a market economy perspective, the share of total time spent in offices by knowledge workers is evidently declining, signalling a shift away from the traditional analogue workplace.

With the hybrid workplace model, the focus has shifted from a primarily physical office to a digital infrastructure, complemented by analogue office spaces. While this was already the case for many employees before the pandemic, the continued expansion and development of the hybrid workplace will lead to a future where the digital workplace takes precedence. What is digitally possible will set the standard for the hybrid workplace. The digital platforms will undoubtedly offer increasingly better solutions for collaborative platforms for hybrid work life—platforms that ensure digital and hybrid collaborative spaces and tools, platforms for retention and development of an organisation's culture, management-supporting digital infrastructures, digital user interfaces in the interface between analogue and digital infrastructure, etc.

The big question is what digitisation will offer for products compared to the extent to which organisations and employees translate it into real daily behaviour and value creation. In particular, the behavioural effects surrounding the hybrid workplace will have a crucial influence on the development of digital infrastructure. To what extent are opportunities translated into real digital dexterity? There is a long way from a product being available to employees using it in everyday life. An example of this delay effect is Skype. Skype first introduced the capability for video meetings in 2006, and was subsequently acquired by Microsoft in 2011, later evolving into what was reintroduced as Microsoft Teams in 2017. At the time, the feature was called "Skype video". This was a significant development for the platform, as it allowed users to communicate face-to-face in real time, regardless of their location. The breakthrough for digital meetings only came 15 years later in 2020 with the pandemic and the impossibility of holding traditional in-person meetings. But it is evident that the gap between when a digital product or service becomes available and when it actually becomes widely used is becoming shorter. The digital products are increasingly becoming more user-friendly and intuitive, while users are becoming increasingly digitally competent. The latest example is evident in AI and the possibilities of using algorithms to solve work tasks. To what extent can, should, and will organisations, management, and employees translate digital opportunities into concrete behaviour in future work life and the hybrid workplace? How are organisations going to balance the analogue and digital workplace in the hybrid model?

The digital workplace of the future is very likely to be significantly different from the traditional and existing office workplace in several ways. The digital workplace is likely to be highly advanced, characterised by cutting-edge technology, seamless collaboration, and a strong focus on employee experience. It will be characterised by flexibility and require organisations to be more agile and adaptable to change. Organisations will in the future place a strong emphasis on employee overall experience, recognising that a positive workplace culture is essential for attracting and retaining top talent through engagement. This will involve investing in tools and technologies that enhance employee well-being, such as health and wellness programmes, flexible work arrangements, and digital tools that promote work-life balance.

Some of the elements of the future digital workplace include (the list is not complete, overlapping, and not prioritised):

LOCATION-AGNOSTIC: The digital workplace will be less tied to a physical location. Remote work and flexible work arrangements will be more common, allowing employees to work from anywhere in the world. This will require robust digital infrastructure to enable seamless collaboration and communication between team members regardless of their location.

ARTIFICIAL INTELLIGENCE (AI): AI will play an expanding important role in the digital workplace, automating routine tasks, providing personalised assistance to employees, and helping to identify opportunities for process improvements and efficiencies.

AUTOMATION: The digital workplace will rely more heavily on automation, with machines and algorithms taking over repetitive and time-consuming tasks. This will allow employees to focus on higher-value work that requires creativity, problem-solving, and critical thinking.

CLOUD-BASED TECHNOLOGY: Cloud-based technology will continue to be a major trend in the digital workplace, allowing employees to access information and collaborate from anywhere with an Internet connection. This will require robust cybersecurity measures to ensure the safety and security of company data.

INTERNET OF THINGS (IOT): The IoT will enable greater automation and connectivity within the digital workplace, allowing employees to control and interact with their environment in new and innovative ways. For example, sensors could be used to monitor office temperature and lighting, adjusting settings automatically based on employee preferences.

VIRTUAL AND AUGMENTED REALITY: Virtual and augmented reality technologies will become more prevalent in the digital workplace, allowing remote workers to feel more connected to their colleagues and the company culture. For example, virtual reality could be used for team meetings, training sessions, or even social events.

COLLABORATION TOOLS: Collaboration tools will be more advanced and integrated, allowing employees to seamlessly work together on projects and share information. These tools will include things like video conferencing, instant messaging, project management software, and cloud-based document sharing.

DATA-DRIVEN DECISION-MAKING: The digital workplace will rely heavily on data to make decisions. Analytics tools will be used to track employee productivity, customer behaviour, and business performance, helping companies to make data-driven decisions that improve efficiency and effectiveness.

CYBERSECURITY: As companies become more digital, cybersecurity will become an even more critical concern. Companies will need to invest in robust security measures to protect their data and intellectual property from cyber threats.

VIRTUAL WORKSPACES: Virtual workspaces, such as virtual reality or augmented reality environments, will provide employees with a way to collaborate and interact with each other in a more immersive and engaging way, even when they are not physically together.

References

(Andreessen, Andreessen Horowitz 2011) https://a16z.com/why-software-is-eating-the-world/

(Glaveski 2021) HBR Remote Work Should Be (Mostly) Asynchronous https://hbr.org/2021/12/remote-work-should-be-mostly-asynchronous

15 The Future of the Analogue Office Workplace

Abstract

The traditional office is facing significant challenges as remote work and hybrid workplace models reduce the demand for physical office space. Pre-pandemic occupancy rates of 40–50% have dropped to around 25%, with further declines expected (if office space volume is not reduced). This shift has led organisations to reconsider their office needs, often opting to downsize or repurpose surplus space. As a result, commercial real estate faces a decline in value, particularly in city centres, while suburban and small-town areas experience increased activity. The future of workspaces is leaning towards more flexible, decentralised hubs and co-working spaces near employees' homes, offering reduced commute times and lower carbon footprints.

15.1 The Declining and Changing Analogue Office

Once the initial flexibility of work—concerning time, location, and space—has been addressed from a broader digital and hybrid perspective, the necessary adjustments must then be implemented within the office environment and considered through a more focused, analogue lens. The implications are that the office, both as a physical building and as a concept, is facing challenges in the market as the dominant workplace for knowledge workers. This trend is expected to intensify further (Balemi et al. 2021).

Prior to the pandemic, office working hours occupancy rates were typically around 40–50% (on an average day and at a given time). However, with the rise of remote work and the hybrid workplace, the demand for physical office space has significantly decreased. It is essentially about cost reduction, enhancing collaboration, and improving the office experience. In this context, there is once again a widespread focus on the desk-sharing ratio of workstations to employees, as well as

C. Sneppen, *The Future (R)Evolution of the Office Workspace*, Future of Business and Finance, https://doi.org/10.1007/978-3-031-85229-9_15

on flexibility ratios. However, this focus on ratios risks perpetuating a misleading discourse, as the overarching goal should be to address the organisation's critical objectives and challenges, rather than fixating on ratios.

The traditional office was designed to accommodate all employees simultaneously, but with increased flexibility and the hybrid workplace model, the daily occupancy rate has dropped dramatically. Occupancy rates have decreased from 40–50% to approximately 25% in the same office space (Time 2023; Børsen 2021). As a result, very few workplaces are interested in expanding their area, and the vast majority are considering alternative utilisation of surplus office space or reducing their office area. This is evident by observing the empty office areas and workstations that remain vacant on a daily basis in workplaces with a high number of knowledge workers.

There are several indicators, apart from office occupancy rates, which illustrate the significant changes in the daily use of office space (Fig. 15.1). These include among others decreased rush hour traffic on selected days and times, reduced use of public transportation for daily commuting, negative impacts on businesses relying on daily office movements, and an increasing number of vacant office leases.

The basic math is quite simple. If employees spend less time in the office space and more time at home or third places, there will be a decline in the office space and an increase in the use of home offices and third places such as hubs, co-working spaces, and cafes. The reduction or alternative utilisation of physical office space faces challenges due to long-term lease agreements that are often non-terminable. Looking onwards, we anticipate that there will be a further drop in daily user footfall as remote working will increase.

Office space has traditionally signalled not only current space utilisation but also anticipated future growth. However, over time, the footprint per employee has steadily declined due to densification strategies and the repurposing of surplus space after the Great Recession. While there was initial speculation that social-distancing

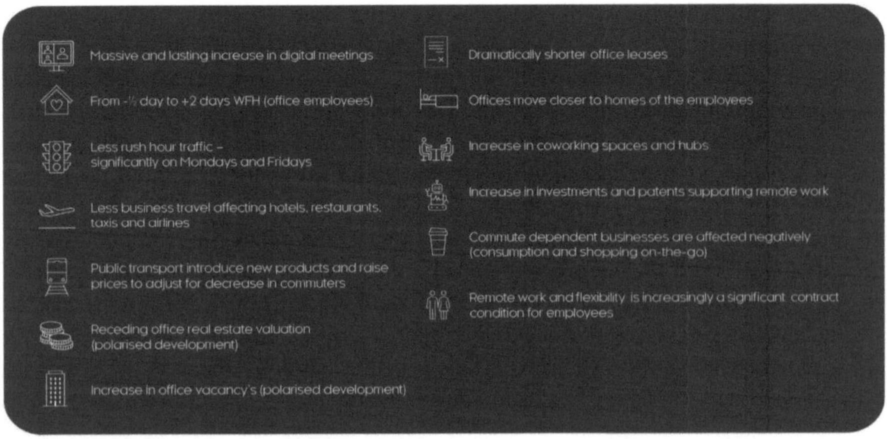

Fig. 15.1 Structural work-life changes—Data indications

measures introduced by the pandemic might increase space allocations per employee, this trend has yet to materialise. Instead, the shift towards hybrid work has driven space per employee even lower than pre-pandemic levels. While leaner office footprints can offer substantial cost savings and a reduced carbon footprint, they may also constrain future growth potential. This shift may reflect economic uncertainty or a belief that additional space can be acquired at favourable rental rates as needed. For the commercial real estate sector, this trend poses challenges, as many organisations are terminating leases, vacating properties, or reducing their square footage.

Some cities and areas are particularly threatened, as entire cities or neighbourhoods have seen their ecosystems disrupted due to the significant reduction in daily footfall from employees who now work remotely (Fig. 15.2). The changing ecosystems of office work have a significant impact on office buildings, as a substantial number of them will need to be remodelled, converted for alternative uses, or simply demolished. San Francisco, for example, has been offering tax breaks and revival plans for its struggling financial district, while New York City is seeking eased rules for converting commercial buildings into housing (Bloomberg 2024; Commercial Observer 2024). The data demonstrates that now, in a post-pandemic world, corporate decision-makers are considering a wider range of business factors when formulating their future corporate real estate strategies.

While city centres have experienced a decline, many towns and suburbs have seen an increase in footfall on their high streets, especially those with a "15-minute city" design, where shops, offices, and housing are all within walking distance (:15

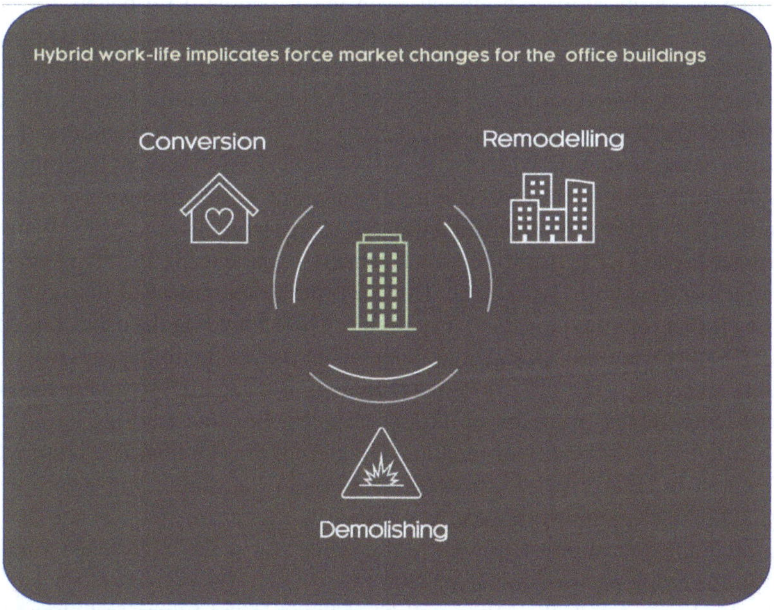

Fig. 15.2 Office owners and investors: structural changes now and ahead

City 2024). The decisions made by chief executives regarding office spaces will have far-reaching effects. Researchers estimate that office real estate values will drop by 39% from pre-pandemic levels in the coming years (Gupta et al. 2022). Economists predict a "doom loop" for urban commercial areas, where fewer people commuting to downtown neighbourhoods leads to the decline of retail and services, resulting in even fewer people commuting and a subsequent drop in tax revenue that could further impact downtown services like public transportation. Additionally, economists foresee a potential economic crisis as a significant number of commercial real estate loans come up for renewal in the coming years, with rising interest rates, inflation, and a declining market for office space.

Alongside the development, it is from a macro perspective observed that total working hours are still decreasing in society which, in isolation, would result in fewer people working in person at the office (Gaittino and Artiz-Opsina 2020). The number of knowledge workers has been steadily increasing over the decades but is also challenged by the development. For example, what will AI mean for the development of the workforce within each organisation, including to what extent it will amplify the need for in-person collaboration or make individual employees more autonomous? In isolation, projecting the growth of knowledge workers in an individual organisation in the short to medium term would not be able to compensate for reduced in-person activity at the office. The argument is often made that surplus office space is necessary to ensure flexibility in extreme situations with high occupancy. An analogy is made to buying a van for the few times it is needed in a normal household. Surplus and unused square footage is threatening to the workplace and potentially a death spiral for the physical office. When the office is empty, it functions like an empty store and attracts even fewer people. Life begets life. At the same time, cost reductions especially during economic hardship will add pressure on reduction of office space. A further trend contributing to the reduction of space is the rise of the shared economy, which adds pressure on unused areas. The shared economy impacts both internally, with employees sharing desks, and externally, as we utilise shared external workspaces.

In the short term, there has been a movement to justify the existence and relevance of the existing physical office through more, larger, and enhanced employee experiences. The idea is that exceptional sensory experiences can solve many of the challenges of the hybrid workplace. However, the development of the future office goes beyond the employee sensory experience while attending the office and focuses on establishing frameworks and guidelines for employee flexibility in terms of time, location, and space. The office as a hotel analogy is often used to justify the continued existence of the office based on experiences. But this analogy doesn't completely align with the reality of the liberated employee. The liberated employee has the freedom to choose where to sleep, in a hotel or at home, and where to work today, at home or in the workplace. Is it primarily the sensory experience that motivates the employee to physically go to the office? Or is the experience a marginal factor in the employee preference equation?

All else being equal, the office will be reduced in the future and aligned more closely with daily usage and occupancy rates. There is a need for occupied offices, not deserted ones, as life creates more life. At the same time, there is a need to scale the office for peak loads in specific situations. This can be achieved through collaboration with neighbouring workplaces to share and coordinate workspace utilisation in shared facilities or gaining access to additional office space at variable costs. The cost of the office, both financially and in terms of perception, will put pressure on further reducing its size.

15.2 Surge in Third Workplaces: The Rise of Office Hubs and Co-working Spaces

As the centralised office diminishes, it is anticipated that there will be a surge of new decentralised office space through the establishment of third working spaces such as hubs and co-working in the vicinity of employee's homes or existing offices. Co-working represents a complex social phenomenon, integrating work solutions, learning opportunities, and social relationships (Marchegiani and Arcese 2018).

The functionality and prevalence of the hybrid work model has given rise to a flexible workplace portfolio and a need to reinvest in locations to provide a more engaging workplace experience for employees. Hubs strive to deliver the best of the centralised office but closer to the home and therefore reduce the commute time of the employees.

One benefit of working from third places is a massive reduction in carbon footprint. A recent report analysed various work scenarios, including commuting to a downtown office 5 days a week, splitting time between home and a central office, and working from a nearby co-working space or satellite office within a short bike ride from home (15–20 min) (Fast Company 2023). The study compared not only transportation emissions (assuming short commutes still involved driving in many cities) but also energy consumption in each building. The findings showed that working from close-to-home offices resulted in a carbon footprint up to 90% smaller than working in a central headquarters every day. The report was a collaboration between Arup, a global design and engineering company, and IWG, a company that develops co-working and shared office spaces worldwide (with a vested interest in this research). Six cities were examined as examples, and it was discovered that the environmental benefits of hybrid work varied depending on the city. In car-dependent Los Angeles, traditional commuting had three times the impact compared to London, where a greater number of people use public transportation for their commute. The lowest-emission scenario in L.A., with people working near their homes, had a similar impact as the worst-case traditional commute in London. In Los Angeles, transitioning from standard commuting to working at a local office could reduce emissions by 87%. Shifting from a typical American commute to a combination of remote work, a local office, and a central headquarters could result in a 79% emissions reduction. In Atlanta, working at a local office had the potential to cut emissions by 90%. The satellite hub or co-working space primarily serves as a low-investment option for employees, breaking the isolation of working alone from home. One example of an early mover organisation embracing an extreme hub model is Standard Chartered, which is making every effort to stay ahead of the changes the pandemic might bring to people's work-life balance (Business Standard 2020). The emerging markets bank plans to "push the boundaries" for half of its 85,000 staff, who work in 9 out of the 55 countries where it operates. Starting early 2021, it will offer these employees the option to work from a "near home" location, which it will rent from an office-sharing company. Employees will also have the permanent choice of working from home more frequently.

Workspace Case: Woods Office
Woods Office was established and is operated by Nrep, a leading Nordic real estate developer, investor, and integrated property operator. Nrep is part of Urban Partners. Our mission is to develop properties that are rooted in the needs of the end user. As tenant requirements evolve, our focus is on creating flexible, high-quality office workplaces that offer a meaningful and effective work environment. We strive to design offices that are not only worth the commute but are also created in a sustainable manner.

Adapting to a Post-Pandemic Landscape:
In the aftermath of the pandemic, we've evolved towards offering a much more diverse range of workstyles and spaces, combining service efficiency with optimised use of space. By conducting various generational studies, we have crafted a workplace that invigorates our tenants, ensuring an exceptional experience with welcoming hosts, flexible layouts, common areas suitable for both social interaction and work, and meeting centres equipped with modern technology. Our services complement these features, such as easy booking via our dedicated app and healthy lunches provided in our on-site restaurant.

Woods co-working space. Image credits: Woods Office

Our Vision:
We aim to create an authentic, vibrant office environment that promotes creativity, communication, and a sense of appreciation among employees, transforming offices into engaging and energising spaces where individuals can thrive and grow.

Future Outlook:
We foresee a rising demand for human-centric, personalised workplaces with improved indoor climates and well-being-focused environments. Coupled with locations that offer urban livability, we are embracing the hybrid way of working, whether through smaller hubs or larger office properties. This approach aligns with our goal of providing convenience and diversity in a modern and increasingly blurred work-life balance.

Objectives:
Our primary objective is to engage knowledge workers and stimulate creativity and collaboration. We aim to support tenant growth by providing low-carbon environments and implementing experience-based designs to drive transformative changes.

Challenges:
In the short term, the main challenge in future-proofing workplaces lies in managing operational complexities and balancing efficiency with flexibility. Over the long term, the challenge is to remain relevant by adapting to functional and digital offerings while maintaining a sustainable approach.

Recommendations:

- *We stress the importance of understanding the expectations and needs of emerging generations, ensuring that the workspace is technologically advanced, flexible, diverse, and convenient, while also supporting collaboration through enhanced connectivity and opportunities for focused work.*
- *Avoid "one-size-fits-all" solutions, as they are outdated and impractical. Tailoring spaces to meet diverse needs is crucial for driving future progress in office workplaces.*

Woods co-working space. Image credits: Woods Office

An increasing number of offices and organisations are considering and establishing hubs in their own vacant office spaces as they downsize their offices. This horizontal displacement of vacant office space will have an impact on the overall need for office space. Individual organisations must carefully consider whether there is a market for their specific co-working space and to what extent it will provide value beyond monetary value to the organisation. It is anticipated that many organisations will not succeed and will opt for the simpler solution of reducing office space by moving out and finding alternative uses for the surplus office space.

There are in most cases alternative, more value-creating approaches that organisations can adopt to proactively utilise surplus office space. Approaches that not only create more rooms, experiences, and opportunities for employees who come to work but also involve collaborations with external organisations that can access office space at a reduced or no cost, where their presence in the office adds value to the organisation and employees. This can be compared to the development seen in shopping malls and commercial areas in Denmark, where marginalised square metres are allocated for free or at a reduced rent to businesses and organisations that generate footfall and thus revenue for the shops, for example, doctors, dentists, chiropractors, public offices, art galleries, package distribution, and charitable organisations. In a retail context, these areas are mainly allocated to units that attract high daily footfall: in other words, attract people.

References

(:15 City 2024) https://www.15minutecity.com

(Balemi, Füss and Weigand 2021) Balemi, N., Füss, R. & Weigand, A. COVID-19's impact on real estate markets: review and outlook. *Financ Mark Portf Manag* **35**, 495–513 (2021). https://doi.org/https://doi.org/10.1007/s11408-021-00384-6

(Bloomberg 2024) San Francisco Is Making It Easier to Turn Empty Offices https://www.bloomberg.com/news/articles/2024-03-12/san-francisco-offers-tax-break-to-convert-empty-offices-to-homes

(Børsen 2021) Nedskæring af kontorplads er et hedt emne i mange firmaer. Udlejer oplever virksomheder, der vil skære op til 30 pct. https://borsen.dk/nyheder/virksomheder/hjemmearbejdsbolge-fjerner-kontorpladser

(Business Standard 2020) How Standard Chartered wants to go way beyond WFH for 85,000 staff in nine countries https://www.business-standard.com/article/companies/how-stanchart-wants-to-go-way-beyond-wfh-for-85-000-staff-in-nine-countries-120110901207_1.html

(Commercial Observer 2024) A New York City Office-to-Residential Conversion Wave Builds https://commercialobserver.com/2024/08/new-york-city-office-residential-conversion-incentives/

(Fast Company 2023) Working from a local workspace instead of the office could cut emissions by 90 percent https://www.fastcompany.com/90884379/working-froma-local-workspace-instead-of-the-office-could-cut-emissionsby-90

(Gaittino and Artiz-Opsina 2020) Are we working more than ever? https://ourworldindata.org/working-more-than-ever

(Gupta, Mittal and Nieuwerburgh 2022) Work from Home and the Office Real Estate Apocalypse https://www.nber.org/system/files/working_papers/w30526/w30526.pdf

(Marchegiani and Arcese 2018) Collaborative spaces and coworking as hybrid workspaces: friends or foes of learning and innovation?. Learning and Innovation in Hybrid Organizations: Strategic and Organizational Insights, 51-71. https://www.researchgate.net/publication/320235839_Collaborative_Spaces_and_Coworking_as_Hybrid_Workspaces_Friends_or_Foes_of_Learning_and_Innovation

(Time 2023) Return-to-Office Full Time Is Losing. Hybrid Work Is On the Rise https://time.com/6281252/return-to-office-hybrid-work/

The Future Analogue Office Space

16

Abstract

The physical office remains a vital component of the hybrid workplace model, even as remote work becomes more widespread. In a hybrid setup, the office serves essential functions, providing space for collaboration, fostering company culture, and offering resources that may not be accessible at home. However, the traditional role of the office as the central hub for work is diminishing, with the employee now becoming the epicentre of the workplace model. The future office must be adaptable, supporting flexibility and catering to the varied needs of employees. This includes providing conducive environments for specific tasks, facilitating social interactions, and accommodating individual preferences.

The concept of "Purposeful Presence" is crucial, as employees plan their office visits around specific activities. The physical office should not just replicate the digital workspace, but it should offer unique value through in-person interactions. As the workplace evolves, the physical office will need to become more dynamic, flexible, and tailored to the needs of a digital and hybrid workforce, ensuring it remains a relevant and valuable part of the work environment.

16.1 The Collaborative and Individualistic Analogue Office

Overall, the physical office is anticipated to remain an important and essential component of the hybrid workplace model for most organisations, even as remote and distributed work becomes increasingly more prevalent.

In a hybrid workplace model, the physical office serves crucial functions. It provides a space for employees to meet and collaborate, which is particularly beneficial for tasks requiring in-person interaction, such as brainstorming sessions, team activities, training, onboarding, and meetings with clients or partners. It also fosters a sense of company culture and community as employees work and socialise together.

C. Sneppen, *The Future (R)Evolution of the Office Workspace*, Future of Business and Finance, https://doi.org/10.1007/978-3-031-85229-9_16

The office additionally serves as a hub for technology and equipment that employees may not have access to at home, such as printers, scanners, and specialised software. It ensures that employees have the necessary resources to perform their job functions effectively.

But one thing is abundantly clear: the office will increasingly cease to be the epicentre of the work life for knowledge workers. Going forward, it is not the building and the office that are the organisations' manifestation and branding platform, but the workplace model with the employee as the new epicentre. In the book *Knudsen: A Biography*, William S. Knudsen is quoted as saying, "If you wanted to build a factory, the thing to do was to make a layout of your machinery and the flow of material, and then build a building around it" (Beasley 1947). (William Signius Knudsen was a leading Danish-American automotive industry executive and an American general during World War II.) The same principle applies to the hybrid workplace, but now the analogue office is no longer the sole defining factor for employees. However, the core remains unchanged. During the industrial era, it was the machines that defined the structure; in today's knowledge society, it is the employees and the digital infrastructure. Thus, the manifestation of a successful hybrid workplace hinges on how an organisation has designed and implemented its unique method of creating value in this new hybrid environment. Can an organisation truly be considered innovative if it clings to a more traditional approach to the workplace? In the short term, is a traditional office model—albeit with modern design, layout, and flexibility—truly innovative? More crucially, in the long term, can organisations continue to attract and retain highly sought-after innovative employees with a workplace model that places the office as its central hub?

Thus, the future analogue office solution must, in its simplest form, address and resolve the complex challenges outlined below, which encompass the diverse approaches and preferences of multiple generations. All of this must be built upon a foundation that continuously evolves in alignment with the key forces shaping the workplace—including megatrends, multigenerational dynamics, workplace tenure, and life-phase considerations (Fig. 16.1).

In summary, the future role of the office is to support the flexibility that hybrid work provides to employees (FM Update 2022). If there is a need for meeting spaces, the office should have suitable meeting rooms. If there is a need for focused work, the office should provide a conducive environment. The office's purpose may change from day to day, hour to hour, and it is essential to have a comprehensive understanding of who intends to use the office and how they plan to use it. Hence, the office should be able to adapt and evolve with minimal friction and effort over time.

The concept of "Purposeful Presence" becomes significant in building future hybrid office workplace models. Visits to the office have become intentional and planned around specific activities, as opposed to my earlier discussion of the office being the default setting. Employees who willingly return to the office do so for specific reasons. They seek a space that supports certain activities better than their

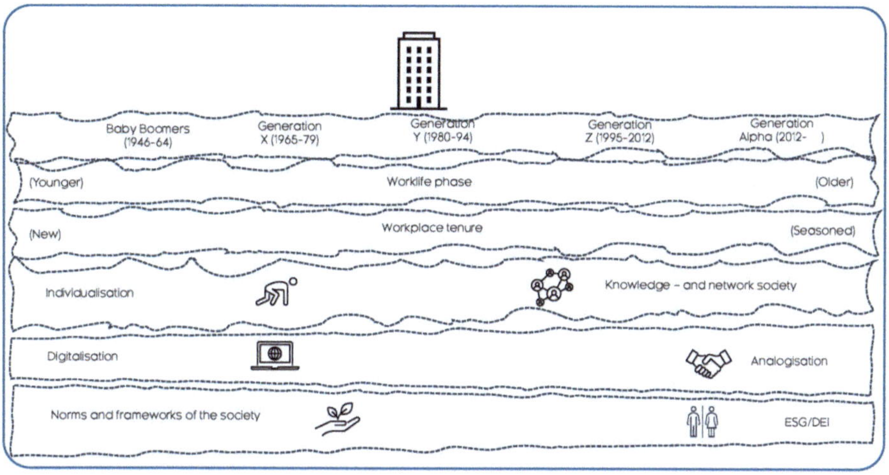

Fig. 16.1 The office model constructed on moving foundation

homes and allows for social connection. They want the office experience to be worthwhile and supportive of tasks that cannot be performed as effectively at home. Employees will spend more time planning their visits, ensuring the necessary facilities and colleagues are available. Data plays a crucial role in proactively supporting employees' intentional use of office space, helping organisations understand where employees can do their best work and where investments will have the maximum impact.

On the other hand, the future office space also serves management and organisational objectives by supporting the new ways in which today's organisations operate—teamwork, flattened hierarchies, telecommuting, and cross-functional collaboration (Becker et al. 1995). In this sense, the office workplace can play a strategic role in advancing business objectives, energising employees, and fostering a more competitive organisation. A clear example of this is evident in the current trend towards Activity-Based Working office design.

The future office emphasises a balanced and aligned approach where the needs of both the employee and the organisation are met in a physical workplace distinct from the more individualistic digital workspace. The differentiated analogue office fulfils the needs of both employees and organisations in areas where the digital and remote workplace may have deficiencies. This can include collaboration, relationships, culture, sensory tasks, and physical tasks. Despite the increased individualisation, the sharing economy has also found its way into the workplace. Contemporary office designs have shifted from "my desk" to shared desks and from "my workplace" to "our shared workspace." The sharing economy serves as a counterbalance to the increasing focus on individual preferences and aligns with initiatives to reduce the carbon footprint (Botsman and Rogers 2010).

Woods co-working space. Image credits: Woods Office

The digitally mature physical office is not simply a replication of the digital workplace in a slightly different format. It is a unique meeting place that focuses on physical meetings and interactions, supporting the growing importance of digital work for knowledge workers. The future of the analogue office lies in making it more physical and leveraging the value of in-person employee meetings as a differentiating factor. The physical workplace should be truly physical, not just a subpar copy of the digital workspace. Additionally, the office must accommodate individual preferences and behaviours of employees and teams.

Workspace Case: Arla Foods

At Arla Foods' headquarters in Viby, Aarhus, there are approximately 1500 employees. The office is designed according to the activity-based working model, which means that employees work in the zone that suits their current task. As a result, we see many employees moving around the office during the workday. However, we also see how most employees prefer the same workstation as yesterday when they are in the work zone. The allocation of workstations per employee is 0.7: 10 employees share 7 desks as a starting point. This matches the trend we see: Many employees work from home on average 2 days a week, which is why many workstations would be unused if we had a 1:1 ratio. With that being said, we always want the office to be the preferred place to work.

The past 5 years confirm that the trend of working remotely for one or more days a week is likely here to stay. It is valued and used by most employees. Work is no longer a place, but a state of mind. Therefore, we have introduced a "remote zone" as part of the zones in the activity-based working model; guidelines are needed for this zone as well as all other zones. The activity-based layout has been the guiding principle for office design in the past 5 years, and all new employees are offered an onboarding session for activity-based working.

Arla office. Image credits: Arla Foods

An ongoing challenge related to activity-based working is the conflict between the need for more traditional workstations due to an increase in the number of employees and the desire to incorporate the other zones in the office landscape (team, break, meet, etc.*). The size of our buildings poses a natural limitation. In other words, it is a challenge to create an attractive office environment that can accommodate an increasing number of employees without adding square metres. This confirms that our current work to create a cohesive Arla Campus, which includes adding square metres to the buildings, is highly relevant.*

We are currently working on a comprehensive rethinking of our office buildings at Arla's headquarters in Viby. The goal is to create a more cohesive and attractive Arla Campus that meets both current and future needs. A massive data collection process for this work is underway. Overall, the headquarters should physically connect better and be upgraded with facilities that go beyond the fundamental work facilities. For example, a restaurant-like cafeteria, an exclusive employee shop, inspiring green outdoor areas, and facilities for services such as hairdresser, physiotherapist, and massages are being considered. The headquarters should be so attractive and inspiring that it encourages attendance at the office, retains talents, and attracts new ones.

We want to strengthen Arla's headquarters as a workplace that is so attractive that employees want to come to the office to work. A workplace that promotes collaboration across teams and departments, supports a variety of tasks, and offers employees more than just work facilities. The workplace should contribute to better integration of each employee's daily life, for example, by offering a range of everyday services on-site. At the same time, the workplace should provide employees with a setting that is worth coming in for. Arla's headquarters already has a strong focus on this today, but the ambition is to further enhance this strategy.

We continue to design the workplace according to the activity-based working model because it offers flexibility that can adapt to changing times. This makes Arla a workplace that continuously offers conditions that match the type of work employees are engaged in. For example, extensive data collection among Arla employees in Viby shows that meeting with colleagues and collaboration within and across teams and departments are the primary reasons for coming to the office. By designing the workplace based on this trend, we create an attractive workplace that meets employees' needs for optimal performance. Furthermore, our focus on creating a comprehensive and attractive work experience through exclusive benefits and inspiring design contributes to making Arla a strong workplace compared to other large companies.

It is undoubtedly a challenge to future-proof the office workplace model for an unknown future. We live in a time where changes in the job market can happen quickly due to new digital possibilities and a world with significant unknown factors that can directly influence daily life as we know it today. We invest a lot of money in creating an attractive workplace that is worth coming to for each employee, but if the trend towards and desire for remote work for various reasons were to be further reinforced, it would be a costly investment. However, we hope that with the activity-based working model, we are equipped to keep up with the times and support the trends we will see in the future due to the flexibility of this working model.

Recommendations:

If employees are not informed about and comfortable working with activity-based working as a new and flexible work model, it will quickly lead to wasted resources in terms of time and finances. Without actively adopting new habits, the old ones will always prevail. Therefore, we strongly recommend incorporating change management as a central aspect of implementing and re-implementing the work model. Psychological safety in the workplace is directly linked to job performance, making it essential to ensure that all employees feel secure in utilising the office effectively.

Overall, our recommendation is to choose an office work model that is flexible and multidimensional and therefore robust during changing times. Relying solely on good workstations, a good cafeteria, or good collaboration facilities is too fragile. The focus should be broad. The workplace is more than just a desk, screen, and office chair. It is also present in most homes. The workplace should consider the whole person and offer benefits and experiences that cannot be obtained from home. We call it "the espresso experience – less but stronger": When our employees come to the office on fewer days than previously, those days must be filled with better experiences than they can get at home.

When future-proofing the office workplace, one should avoid basing the strategy on assumptions. It should be based on solid qualitative and quantitative data collection. Even this can fail because the future remains unknown, but a data-driven approach, including the involvement of future employees, is a solid starting point.

Arla office. Image credits: Arla Foods

As frequently highlighted, the office serves primarily as a meeting place where tasks are completed, well-being is fostered, engagement is reinforced, and social connections are nurtured. Does your analogue workplace primarily support meetings and interactions in an expanding digitised reality? Or is it merely an office filled with desks, supplemented with a green sofa and a coffee machine, and limited meeting rooms?

The design of the office has evolved because of changing contexts and interactions among employees, rather than being the primary defining framework for work life and the hybrid workplace. In a hybrid workplace, the office must facilitate genuine human interactions while allowing for solitude.

16.2 Challenge: The Office as an Identity Creator Is Increasingly Obsolete

As a hybrid workplace futurist and advisor, it is outside my comfort zone to predict, but not to anticipate. So, I limit myself to anticipating that the era of the office workplace as an identity creator for employees is receding. This is mainly because office employees are spending less time in the office as the hybrid workplace unfolds and evolves. Much like physical shops are losing ground as identity creators to the digital realm.

The ultimate aspiration for any office workplace architect is most likely to be commissioned to design a headquarters like Apple's in Cupertino (an organisation iconic with abundant resources and cutting-edge technology, aspiring to maintain its reputation as a global frontrunner). Apple has encountered significant challenges in bringing employees back to the campus, despite management's preference for in-person work (The Human Capital Hub 2024). One might ask whether we have reached the pinnacle of this approach to designing office palaces that truly embody an organisation's identity. In the post-industrial mindset, the 9–5 office had a central role as an identity marker for employees. It was the pivotal epicentre of employees' work life and, to a certain extent, their personal lives. However, as more and more knowledge work can be done regardless of time, place, and space in an increasingly digitalised reality, the role of the office is undergoing changes and becoming less important.

Going one step further into the receding role of the office as an identity creator, the development is reinforced by the following overlapping and correlated trends:

- **Seniority is diminishing** as employees tend to change workplaces more frequently.
- **Employees increasingly take responsibility for their own professional and personal development**, and less responsibility is placed on the employer. This does not mean we do not wish to work; we simply work less for the workplace and more for ourselves. We are becoming more individualistic because the developments support and amplify individualism.
- **The Gig economy is rising** with fixed or freelance engagements where professional responsibility and goals are clearly defined. The focus is increasingly on the task rather than the employer.
- **Increasing focus on life-work balance** rather than work-life balance.
- **Distributed hybrid work life**—the office is no longer the fixed epicentre; it is increasingly where the employee is, digitally or physically.
- **Branding has shifted from labelling to relationships and trust (content)**. Significant content is increasingly important. Here, the office loses significance and ground to more meaningful markers with real content and purpose for both the individual and society.
- **Rising "bullshit" detectors and aversion to spin** and "buzz word bingo" among employees.
- **Growing demand for closeness, not distance, in relationships**, and highly branded and staged offices tend to have an element of impressiveness and distance.

In other words, the office and organisation must increasingly limit their ambition to attract and retain employees through branding at the office and instead deliver value on selected, recipient-specific parameters regardless of where employees perform work. This means a segmented and differentiated approach to internal marketing and communication at the hybrid workplace, reflecting that employees' behaviour and preferences have shifted towards more personal flexibility.

For the office, this means that grandiose branding with an imposing central office is increasingly giving way to the individualised and close-knit. An office that strives to be a decisive identity creator and ensure that employees spend large parts of their lives in-person at the office is increasingly shrinking and becoming a relic of a bygone era. The identity-creating office workplace has become obsolete and is a marker of past approaches to the office.

Can a successful organisation, in the current evolution of the hybrid workplace, thrive without an imposing, branded office? Quite simply, in an era where organisations can flourish without a fixed physical space, individual employees might well question whether the organisation is truly dynamic, or merely clinging to the conventional notion of an office as a creator of identity. Unless the organisation is one of the few genuinely driven by a greater societal purpose (and not one invented by the communications department in an era where everyone must have a purpose), and where the office genuinely embodies this purpose.

What does this mean for identity creation in the physical office? It should not solely strive for grand branding and impressive effects, but it should adopt a more balanced approach, focusing on creating value for employees in their immediate and daily lives, regardless of whether they are working from home, a café, the office, or the beach.

16.3 The Office Is a Place Where Employees Shop In-Person Working Time

The survival and success of the physical office workplace lies in its role as a meeting and interaction place for live human beings. The physical office workplace is undergoing changes, as the concept of a "dead office" with significantly fewer employees in the physical office became a reality with the pandemic.

The digitisation of work for knowledge workers has exploded. What is the future successful physical office workplace in an expanding digitised reality? The office will transform into more of a consumer product (The New York Times 2023). Similar to any other consumer product, the office will have to constantly compete for customers and fulfil their requirements. Offices will need designated spaces for various tasks such as focused work, team brainstorming, client presentations, and employee training. They will also need to prioritise the needs of individuals, even if those individuals work for large organisations. As a product, offices and hybrid workplace models must reinvent themselves at an accelerated pace. Embracing the concept of "failing fast" is a much better alternative than remaining stagnant and ending up in a precarious situation.

If the workplace model is treated as a monopolistic product, with management imposing an unwanted product on the employees, the consequences are grim. The market for workplaces is rarely monopolistic, and the days are long gone when talented employees would line up to find work. Now, employees shop for workplaces and increasingly choose those that offer flexibility. Regardless of the model and approach chosen, there are implicit and explicit choices of employee target groups. If management chooses an approach where the workplace should accommodate everyone—akin to a shopping mall—there will be employees who are not attracted to and will not be satisfied with that workplace model in the future.

Simply because there will be other workplace models in other organisations that better fit the individual employee's preferences and behaviour. The market for workplace models and the degree of flexibility, as previously described, has become market-driven and targeted to segments, thus differentiated.

The implementation of models can be described sharply in a retail analogy outlined below. Changes in retail are also driven by digitisation and an increasing focus on and higher demands for customer/employee experience:

SHOPPING MALL—ONE-STOP OFFICE WORKPLACE SHOPPING The analogue workplace that can do everything and provides all possibilities to solve all work tasks in the organisation. The shopping mall workplace is challenged in the hybrid workplace model as an almost empty shopping mall is not attractive, and with low occupancy, the workplace may be at risk of a downward self-reinforcing negative development. At the same time, a shopping mall workplace is not attractive to all target groups of employees. Has the workplace and organisation consciously considered whom they attract and exclude with the implicit and explicit choices of the workplace model?

STREET MARKET—SOCIAL OFFICE WORKPLACE SHOPPING The analogue workplace as a vibrant and lively market with a primary focus on sensory experiences and social interaction while work tasks are being performed. The market approach may be challenged by too much focus on interaction and collaboration and too little predictability and established routines in the workspace. The bustling and buzzing marketplace is attractive to some employees while others prefer the shopping mall.

SPECIALTY SHOP—TARGETED OFFICE WORKPLACE SHOPPING The analogue workplace targeting a segmented and specialised group of employees who are attracted to a common passion. The challenge with the specialty shop is that it caters to a segmented target group, which is narrower and smaller. Nevertheless, this approach will challenge and push the boundaries of the mass market for workplace models because the "special" approach will attract and retain sought-after employees. Employees that the marketplace and shopping mall approaches also want as colleagues.

ONLINE SHOP—EFFECTIVE OFFICE WORKPLACE SHOPPING The analogue workplace is replaced here by the digital one and largely rendered obsolete. It represents a fully remote workplace model where, as previously described, there is a small and highly segmented labour market for this workplace model. In the extreme no-office work place scenario, this is represented as the Digital Palace.

The trend is pointing in only one direction, and that is towards more digitisation of working time consumption. Virtually all traditional analogue workplaces have made extra efforts to digitise parts of their workflows during the pandemic, and that development continued and intensified after the pandemic released its grip (2023). A growing number of employees experience that the digital workplace creates more value than its analogue counterpart. Employees are undergoing a transformation, and they are developing new habits and experiences. Work preferences have been formed to handle specific tasks and challenges in two very different work marketplaces—the digital and the analogue.

The marketplace originated with the establishment of cities around 2000 years before our current era, and from the marketplaces emerged the permanent stall "the shop." The marketplace is the place where people meet, socialise, network, share knowledge, gossip, and trade. The industrial society's approach with large, efficient physical workplaces as a central monopolistic marketplace for work execution has been surpassed by a more efficient and easier way of trading working time for productivity—namely, the digital marketplace.

The physical office is steadily being outcompeted—or at the very least, losing its monopolistic hold—to the more efficient and convenient digital realm of "worktime commerce." In the digital workplace, employees are treated as datasets but are always recognised and have quick and easy access to most of what they need to solve individual tasks. The physical workplace offers a unique advantage: it enables co-creation, development, inspiration, networking, and rapid knowledge sharing—all with greater enjoyment, once employees are present.

The trend was already present before the pandemic with increasingly specialised, segmented, and differentiated workplace models, and it will gain even more momentum. As previously described, the boundary for what we need to physically meet for is shrinking. It is important to once again distinguish between what we believe and prefer (bias) and what will increase the competitiveness of the organisation.

With digitisation, the "market" and "space" for the consumption of working time have become more fragmented and polarised. The development leaves the physical workplace with a smaller market but plenty of "space." The need to meet, collaborate in person, and network physically is still very pronounced despite digitisation.

As a counterbalance to an expanding digitised reality and preferences for working time, it is anticipated that there still be a demand for "old-fashioned" interpersonal collaborative interaction for selected tasks and challenges. A demand that possibly could be growing as technology makes human in-person interactions increasingly important.

The good news is that the office has a unique opportunity to become the future social meeting place full of work passion. The physical office is a threatened species on the savannah, but there is still a great demand for social and collaborative meeting spaces. A hybrid workplace may be omnichannel in the future, but with a clear differentiation in what creates the most value for both digital and analogue consumers of working time.

In an international survey (with Danish participation), it was established that human activity is limited to 25 fixed physical locations throughout life (Alessandretti et al. 2018). Humans periodically replace meeting places with new ones, but constantly have places that are part of the movement patterns at any given time. This raises two important questions you should ask yourself: Firstly, is your analogue office one of the 25 meeting places for your employees? And secondly, whether the office should even be a meeting place, or if it is more valuable for you and your target audience to design a different value chain? One thing is certain: There will be a competition among workplaces to become a meeting place for employees, and many will fail in the race by being labelled as unattractive workplaces.

16.4 Challenge: Your Office Workplace Model Inherently Excludes Valuable Employees

Which qualified knowledge workers is your organisation, consciously or unconsciously, opting out because of your specific office workplace model? The exclusion of valuable and sought-after employees is not immediately natural or desired but is implicitly a consequence of the organisation's specific workplace model design. Retaining or attracting valuable employees poses an ultimately difficult dilemma for organisations in the context of the implementation of the office workplace model.

Nevertheless, it is a necessary question for all organisations to explore the answer, as the workplace model is crucial for the type of employees the organisation can attract and retain in the shift from a standardised 9–5 office workplace model to increasingly differentiated and unique office workplace models in terms of time, place, and space for work execution. Therefore, the attraction, or conversely, the repulsion, of valuable employees will occur whether it is unconscious or conscious through the specific design of the office workplace model by each organisation.

The dilemmas are numerous and varied: "Are employees who want to come to the office every day attracted and retained?" "Are employees who want to meet on specific and selected days attracted?" "Are those attracted who want immediate and easy access to mentoring?" "Are employees who want freedom attracted?" "Are employees who only live close to the workplace attracted or those who live far from the office attracted?" etc.

The post-pandemic hybrid and flexible office workplace functions as a marketplace—both internally and externally. The employee is at the centre—attracted by internal and external offers. From an employee perspective, it is about perceived individual value in relation to time spent and where freedom to have maximum decision-making power is increasingly crucial. This means that organisations must understand and design the workplace based on employee preferences to the same extent as they approach the marketplace based on a deep understanding of customer behaviour and preferences. The workplace model cannot be designed to attract and retain all employee preferences equally. Therefore, the conscious exclusion of valuable employees is a natural consequence of the organisation's priorities for attracting and retaining valuable employees. I've termed it the Hybrid Employee Paradox in the hybrid workplace: While attracting and retaining valuable employees, you simultaneously exclude other valuable employees. Moreover, heightened flexibility and the option to work remotely also increase the risk of losing valuable employees. You're damned if you do and damned if you don't.

To further complicate the challenge, one must also consider the continued trend towards increasing digitisation, sustainability focus (ESG), and growing individualisation in employee behaviour, all contributing to the employee dilemmas of the hybrid workplace. Time does not stand still, and the systemic and structural change of the office workplace is ongoing and significant for the organisation's future ability to attract and retain employees.

In the design of each organisation's hybrid workplace model, some employees are prioritised while others are, consciously or unconsciously, excluded. Which potentially qualified employees does the organisation exclude or repel? Can the organisation afford these priorities in a labour market where there is increasing competition for qualified knowledge workers, both in the short and long term?

16.5 Earn the Commute

The "traditional" office workplace value chain is being challenged, transformed, and replaced by new value chains for work life—chains that generate greater value for both the organisation and the employee. The perceived value for the employee is crucial and decisive for the success of the hybrid workplace value chain. And thus, defining the future development of the analogue workplace. In a time when the whole world is literally within reach of employees—with the faithful companion of the mobile phone with 4G, 5G, and soon 6G coverage—employees are increasingly aware of how they spend their working time.

Time is precious, and employees are growingly breaking habitual value chains and habits to replace them with optimised use of irreplaceable working time. In isolation, commuting is considered a waste of time, and the development has shown that employees, across the board, are willing to do a lot to avoid it (even take a pay cut of up to 8 per cent) (Bloom et al. 2021). The transaction cost of working from a shared analogue office is basically considered high for the employee. This is the case despite commuting often being after rationalised and described as a space for personal time, to unwind, have phone calls, listen to audiobooks or music. All of this is an expression of employees trying to make the best use of their time when there is no alternative. But now there is a real alternative, namely working from a distance and eliminating the wasted commute time. With the possibility of remote work, the approach to commuting has changed with a significant impact on the surrounding value chain. If employees don't have to commute daily but only a few times a week, the radius of how far they are willing to commute expands. In other words, employees can either move further away from the workplace, often driven by the optimisation of living conditions, or potentially switch to a new workplace that is located further away. Employees have become more free and less bound, resulting in more choices for both place of residence and workplace.

Data reveals that employees with the longest commutes are, unsurprisingly, the least likely to spend the majority of their week at the workplace, while those with the shortest commutes are the most likely to do so. Evidence suggests that, in workplace models requiring in-person attendance, an ideal commuting distance is less than 15 min. In other words, employees have a preference to work from the office if the distance is short. When factoring in primary mode of travel alongside commute duration, a more nuanced pattern emerges: employees who drove to work were generally less likely to feel that their commute positively impacted their overall quality of life compared to those who walked, cycled, or ran. This difference is especially pronounced for longer commutes. The data points to a growing trend of minimising the distance between home and workplace, supporting a broader movement towards "15-minute cities," such as the model Paris is actively developing. This urban planning concept envisions cities where essential services and workspaces are accessible within a 15-minute walk or bike ride, aligning with employees' preferences for proximity and improved quality of life.

How would employers design the workplace model if they were to pay a salary for commute time? At first glance, this may appear to be a highly hypothetical and unrealistic "what if" question. Nevertheless, please entertain the idea and consider the implications for organisations and employers if they were to create a hybrid and flexible workplace model where commuting incurred a salary cost for the organisation. How flexible would the workplace be in this imaginary scenario? Would employers establish more hubs closer to employees' homes? Would the office be downsized and restructured? With the hypothesis that employers should compensate for commuting time, an office-first approach leaves organisations with two main choices: either to recruit locally, drawing from a smaller talent pool and consequently requiring more time spent in the office, or to expand the search radius and access a broader talent pool, accepting that this will result in less time spent in the office. Alternatively, they can abandon the office-first approach altogether and embrace greater flexibility. The truth is that, in the post-pandemic office environment, employers are indeed covering the costs of their employees' commuting time (Ma and Ye 2019). The new cost dynamics of the hybrid workplace are unfolding, despite some employees attempting to resist this new reality. In some cases, they are striving to return to the post-industrial 9–5 office model where employees bore the

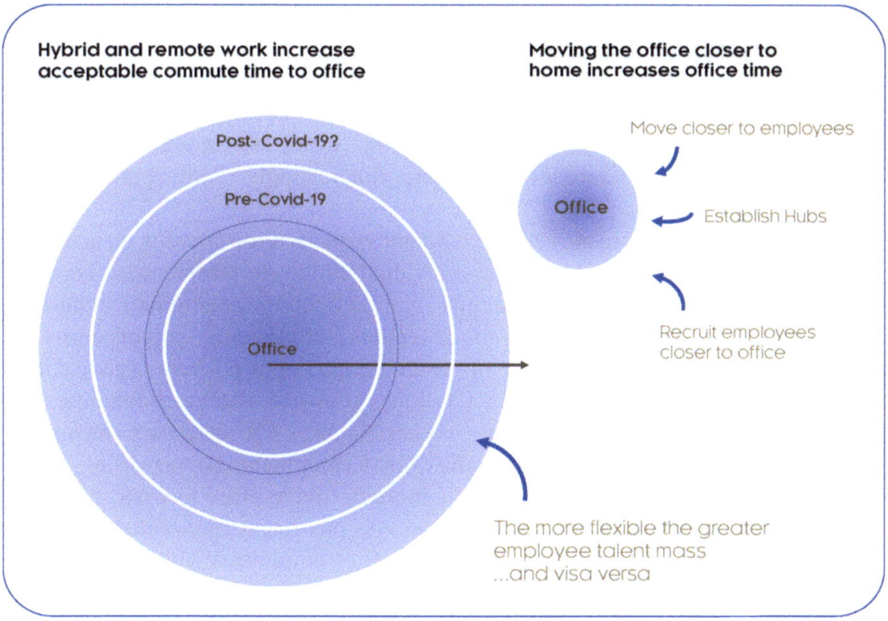

Fig. 16.2 Hybrid workplace model and commuting: two perspectives

expense of commuting. In the hybrid workplace, commuting is no longer a freebie for the employer.

The cost to the employer can be examined from two closely intertwined perspectives. The direct cost of requiring employees to commute is that employees spend approximately half of the time saved on commuting working for the employer (Aksoy et al. 2021). In other words, an employee who saves 2 h on commuting spends an extra hour working on any given day. The indirect cost refers to the potential boost in associated with a more flexible office model—one that is digitalised, more ESG-compliant, cost-effective, and superior at attracting and retaining talent. Such a model not only enhances employee engagement but also holds the potential to increase productivity, provided that the hybrid workplace is designed and implemented intelligently (see Chap. 18).

From an employer's perspective, freeing up the employee from daily commuting places the organisation in a position to consider how to ensure that the physical workplace is successful and thus supports the value creation (Fig. 16.2). In relation to commuting, employers can reduce commuting by moving the workplace closer to employees, including creating hubs, and in the future, recruit employees closer to the office. Naturally, this development also enables organisations to attract and retain employees from a larger area, and though raising the quantity and quality of potential employees. The development is not straightforward, and once again, the hybrid workplace has created new dilemmas.

16.6 Approaches to Make the Analogue Office Work in a Hybrid Set-up

Hypothetically, there are two contrasting approaches to modernising the office: one that makes the office more attractive than remote work, and another that does the opposite, making the office less appealing. Interestingly, both approaches are applied in practice today.

To make the office more attractive, companies can focus on creating an appealing physical environment catering for the individual employee preferences. This may involve investing in stunning surroundings, natural lighting, and modern technology that facilitates collaboration and communication. Additionally, organisations can foster a sense of community in the office by cultivating a positive organisational culture and organising team-building activities. They can also offer amenities and benefits that are not available to remote workers, such as free snacks and beverages, on-site fitness facilities, and opportunities for development. By providing advantages, organisations can make the office a more desirable place to work, hoping to increase employee engagement and retention. (As previously mentioned, this is not the case when comparing fully remote and in-office employees with those in structured hybrid workplace models.) Making the office more attractive is very much about making the employee have a sense of psychological security once at the office. If organisations focus on the physical layout of the office and the possibility for each individual employee to feel like themselves, there is a direct correlation between stress and the lack of opportunity to be oneself (as opposed to pretending and adopting behaviour that is not in line with how the employee perceives themselves). The feeling of psychological safety is ensured in the relationship with colleagues and can be influenced through the design of the office. While some employees feel secure in an open office environment, others feel the opposite in a more isolated location in the office. Employees are not identical and moving forward, they will need to be accommodated individually. Alternatively, the organisation should target the workplace model to a defined and segmented target group of potential employees who specifically demand the model that the organisation has established. Do your colleagues feel like themselves and secure at work and at the office?

On the other hand, organisations can make remote work less attractive by implementing policies that discourage employees from working remotely (the monopolistic approach). Such strategies may include limiting the number of remote workdays per week, requiring in-office attendance for key meetings or events, linking advancement opportunities to physical presence, or offering incentives to encourage employees to come into the office. Additionally, companies might restrict access to certain resources or equipment exclusive to the office, thereby making remote work more challenging. However, deliberately making remote work less appealing could, over time, undermine the organisation's ability to attract and retain valuable knowledge workers, potentially impacting overall talent retention and competitiveness.

It's once again important to note that not all employees may prefer working in-person at the office, and some may have personal circumstances that require them to work remotely. Conversely, others may prefer working exclusively in the office. For this reason, organisations once again face the dilemma of finding a balance between remote work and office work. By striking this balance, organisations can create an office environment that is appealing to employees while supporting the overall success and growth of the organisation.

16.7 Upgrading and Redesigning Offices

The introduction of remote and hybrid work has necessitated the upgrade and redesign of traditional office environments. With more employees working from home or remote locations, companies have had to rethink the design and functionality of their physical office spaces to accommodate a more flexible workforce.

A basic upgrade that companies have made to their office spaces is the integration of technology that supports remote and hybrid work. This basic upgrade includes implementing video-conferencing software and hardware, increased cloud-based storage and collaboration tools, and remote access to company networks and resources. By investing in technology that supports remote and hybrid work, companies can ensure that employees have access to the tools they need to be productive, regardless of their location.

Another fundamental upgrade to the office environment is the reconfiguration of physical space to accommodate a more flexible and collaborative workforce. This can involve creating dedicated collaboration spaces, such as more open meeting areas or breakout rooms, as well as redesigning individual workspaces to allow for more mobility and flexibility. Additionally, organisations are investing in new furniture and equipment that support employee health and well-being, activity-based workplaces, adjustable heating, and adjustable lighting. The upgrade of the office environment aims to create a space that supports employee productivity, collaboration, and well-being, regardless of their location or work style. The most common office upgrades are interpretations or implementations of the activity-based working design concept.

Workspace Case: Danske Bank

Danske Bank DK comprises a range of different business areas, including large corporates & institutions, personal customers, business customers, technology & services, as well as the subsidiaries Danica and Realkredit Danmark, along with various support functions such as HR. In the Copenhagen area, we employ around 6000 staff across these areas, all of whom have now been relocated to our new headquarters, Copenhagen Central. In an era defined by globalisation, rapid technological change, and an increased emphasis on sustainability and Corporate Social Responsibility (CSR), it is relevant to explore new ways of working that respond to emerging opportunities—particularly with the hybrid workforce requirements that emerged post-COVID. By consolidating all employees from the

Copenhagen area into one location and introducing an activity-based work model, Danske Bank aims to foster a stronger sense of community, enhance corporate culture, and, overall, create a positive employee experience.

HQ Danske Bank. Image credits: Danske Bank

Key Facts:
During the pandemic, Danske Bank was quick to adopt the hybrid way of working. Employee feedback about this arrangement, and the flexibility it offered, was overwhelmingly positive and appreciated for the balance it provided between personal and professional life. Variants of Activity-Based Working (ABW) had been tested across various locations and offices for some time, but they were never fully implemented as a Group-wide concept and standard way of working. With the move to the new Copenhagen headquarters, ABW has now become the standard approach across all departments and job roles. For some employees, this transition was relatively minor, as they were already accustomed to a similar set-up, while for others, it represented a significant change in their daily work environment. Our goal is to create a modern, sustainable, and dynamic workplace that offers robust and relevant development opportunities for all our colleagues, supported by responsive leaders who cultivate an inclusive culture.

ABW Is Here to Stay

However, it is unlikely to be a "one-size-fits-all" model. Four months into the transition, we have observed that in certain areas, the ABW model fully supports daily work, while in others, working from a traditional workstation for a full day is still necessary. Generally, we find that more "flexible" job roles thrive within the ABW framework, while more "fixed" job roles face greater challenges. Nevertheless, employees across all roles are enjoying the benefits of being in a single location and the proximity to colleagues, which enhances cross-collaboration. However, the effective execution of daily tasks requires a diverse ABW setup.

Despite some resistance and challenges with activity-based work, we are embracing it and finding that it promotes collaboration, reduces silo mentalities within the organisation, and strengthens our employer brand as an attractive and modern workplace.

Objectives

Our primary goal is to ensure internal collaboration across different business areas—for example, encouraging pension customers at Danica to also become bank customers or converting business customers into personal banking customers. Additionally, we aim to retain our current employees and attract new talent from outside the organisation.

Our Biggest Challenge

Our greatest challenge at present is moving away from the traditional work culture of fixed desks and workstations for everyone and instead realising that different tasks can be completed in different locations, depending on the nature of the work. We are still working to break old habits and establish new ones in this regard.

Recommendations

1. *Start by assessing the ways of working and the needs across the organisation to ensure that the set-up you introduce genuinely supports daily work.*
2. *Continuously evaluate and adjust the office set-up—it will likely require ongoing development and adjustments, so make sure you have dedicated resources within the organisation to support this evolution.*
3. *Start communicating to the entire organisation as early as possible, involve as many people as you can, repeat key messages, and stick to the plan and strategy as much as possible.*
4. *Avoid doing the opposite of the above.*

16.8 At Home at Work

The trend of "At Home at Work" in the office refers to the idea of creating a work environment that emulates the comfort and familiarity of a home environment. This trend has emerged as a response to the rise of remote and hybrid work, which has blurred the boundaries between home and work life. Work has invaded the home, and now the home invades the workplace.

Woods co-working space. Image credits: Woods Office

The "At Home at Work" trend involves creating an office environment that feels more welcoming and comfortable, with the goal of enhancing employee well-being and productivity. This may include incorporating more natural elements, such as plants or natural light, into the office design, as well as creating spaces that resemble a home environment, such as lounge areas or communal kitchens. One aspect of the "At Home at Work" trend is the use of residential-style furniture and decor in the office space. This may involve incorporating soft seating, area rugs, and warm lighting to create a more inviting and comfortable atmosphere.

Additionally, companies may incorporate personal touches, such as artwork or family photos, into the office design to make employees feel more at home. Another aspect of the "At Home at Work" trend is the inclusion of amenities and services typically associated with home life, such as on-site childcare or pet-friendly policies. This can help employees balance their work and personal lives while creating a more inclusive and welcoming work environment. The conventional office attire and business are anticipating very different market conditions for suiting up the workforce of knowledge workers.

16.9 The In-Person Office as the Opposite of Home

To ensure the office remains attractive, there will also be a continued reinforcement of the physical elements that home doesn't provide. The physical office should, therefore, explicitly provide those elements that individual employees prioritise for a fulfilling work-life, elements that are not available in their home environment. This could include areas of total tranquillity and optimal conditions for concentration. It could involve direct access to nature, bustling city life, or inspiring views. In other words, the workplace should simultaneously feel like home and a special place to work. In the future, employees will increasingly strive for the best of both worlds.

Future office development should once again prioritise the individual, addressing employees' experiences and needs. This approach will mark a definitive departure from the traditional office features that were once designed to project efficiency, productivity, and success to the external world. Positioning, and therefore distance, created through the choice of particularly expensive or imposing buildings and furniture will take a backseat in the future, as contemporary value creation increasingly happens through presence and eye-level interaction. Building trust in organisations occurs through relationships, and the physical office of the future will serve as a relationship builder among equals. The future physical office is anticipated to signal that it is a workplace where we achieve success through collaborations and where all employees thrive.

16.10 Challenge: An Office Designed Like a 5-Star Hotel Risk Failing

An office designed like a 5-star hotel risk failing to foster organisational cohesion effectively—it may possibly achieve the opposite. Enhanced sensory employee experiences when present in-person at the office may well be counterproductive to the overarching goal of developing a sustainable approach to fostering cohesion, culture, and interpersonal social capital within the organisation. It is a double-edged sword that simultaneously increases in office presence and could jeopardise and limit the more pressing challenge of nurturing a shared and unique culture, as well as interpersonal social capital and trust.

The office upgrade trend, often referred to as the "hotellification" and/or "homefication" of the analogue workplace of knowledge workers, aims to make the office as attractive as possible (and consequently partly justifying the commute and in-person attendance) and to accommodate individual employee's immediate demands and preferences to the greatest extent possible. This is exemplified by current widespread initiatives such as better barista coffee, exquisite food, the possibility for massages, hairdressing services, and evening meal take away, all of which make office life more pleasant and convenient for individual employees. Some organisations have taken this concept to the extreme by providing employees with the option to sleep overnight at the office, allowing them to live their lives for extended periods at or near the workplace (The Verge 2023).

From an overall organisational perspective, post-pandemic there has been a heightened focus on fostering a shared and unique culture, as well as on building interpersonal social capital and trust—challenges that most organisations identified as key during remote working in the pandemic. These factors are closely linked to an organisation's sustainable innovation, employee attraction and retention, all of which ultimately contribute to overall productivity and competitiveness of the organisation.

The current extensive upgrade of offices, services, and employee experiences is partly based on the assumption that when employees are present in the office synchronously and working linearly, culture, community, and social capital are created by default, best and most effectively. But is this truly the case? In fact, studies contradict this view, as hybrid workers tend to demonstrate higher levels of engagement and attachment to their organisation compared to fully in-office employees. Hybrid work arrangements can enhance employees' sense of connection to the organisation (Microsoft 2022). Employees with the flexibility to choose where they work often feel more trusted and valued, which strengthens their attachment to the organisation. In contrast, fully in-office employees may feel constrained, leading to a diminished sense of belonging.

The contemporary and dominant hybrid workplace model for knowledge workers operates with distributed work in time, place, and space. Consequently, work is increasingly non-linear, asynchronous, and asymmetrical, in stark contrast to the pre-pandemic post-industrial era, which was predominantly the opposite. There is no doubt that physical synchronous presence develops communities and cohesion—but digital presence can do so as well, along with in-person interactions anywhere.

The key question moving forward is where and how formation of organisational cohesion happens intentional best and most effectively. Therefore, the solution for the present hybrid workplace might not lie in the past habitual default solution of in-person office attendance, given all the limitations and challenges that arise from applying post-industrial solutions to a hybrid and flexible work-life reality. Essentially, a singular focus on the individual office experience risks jeopardising the overall objectives and may require a different allocation of resources and a more balanced targeted approach.

When the office aims to be more attractive and caters to the individual demands of employees with enhanced services, it will naturally be able to increase in-person attendance. But does "hotellification" effectively enhance organisational cohesion? In my assessment, the response is at best a maybe, but most likely that a predominant focus on the office and the allocation of attention and resources to it will prove counterproductive. An office offering beautiful surroundings and high levels of service is not the same as effectively creating high social capital or a shared organisational culture—it's more about trying to maintain the office as the epicentre for knowledge workers by making it more appealing.

Workplace experiences should primarily serve to create relationships and network with fellow co-workers—and not focus on pleasing the individual employee only. The experiences function as community-building activities and facilitate the formation of the cultural fabric of the organisation. Therefore, these experiences are the essential ingredients that foster trust and relations among colleagues. Simultaneously, they increase the sense of belonging, well-being, and ultimately enhance efficiency and productivity through better collaboration. In the forward-looking design of the workplace, it becomes increasingly important to identify the significance of experience touchpoints and subsequently design, prioritise, and monitor the dosage of employees' experiences to achieve the desired effect in relation to the overall objectives and challenges. This requires the collection and ownership of user experience data, as well as the subsequent ability to take real action and responsibility regarding the significant experience touchpoints creating cohesion.

Using the hotel analogy, good hotels do not create communities but rather provide excellent individual and attractive customer sensory experiences, aligning with the megatrend towards increasing individualisation. The best community building, in the hotel analogy, actually takes place at no star hostels with less focus on individualistic demands. Equating a high level of individual service and positive experiences with organisational communities and cohesion is simply premature. Individually oriented experience design often risks being counterproductive to the development of organisational communities and cohesion. Communities are best created through experience designs that focus on fostering collective experiences rather than individual ones.

The individual experience focus can be seen, among other things, in the recent increase in the quantity of internal workplace employee experience roles within the internal facilities management or people organisation, which is a direct result of the increased focus on attracting employees to the office. It is much rarer to see internal roles focused on community and cohesion, even though the fundamental overall key objective is closely linked to these aspects. A focus on hybrid workplace community design would be a departure from an almost one-sided focus on individual employee experience.

At a more operational level, this could be exemplified by a shift in focus from individual to cohesion, such as the increasing introduction of shared breakfast or lunch gatherings, communal seating at long tables during mealtimes. Both solutions sacrifice the individualistic service experience approach to foster interrelation social capital and connections. An example of community-building on a broader scale would be reinforcing offsite internal communal events, which have been proven to be highly effective in fostering communities and building social capital—and often much better than similar initiatives in the office.

In conclusion, and simplifying, a 5-star office filled with excellent individual employee experiences and high service levels increases the risk of overall failure in addressing the objective of cohesion due to "hotelification" for two reasons:

1. Prioritising individual sensory employee experience implicitly neglects the creation of community and cohesion.
2. A dominant focus on sensory office employee experience allocates resources and attention to the office, thus deprioritising the broader development of the hybrid workplace and all the competitive advantages it offers.

Increasing office services and sensory experiences is essentially yet another defensive move to maintain an office-first approach considering the current ongoing trend of employees demanding greater flexibility.

16.11 Home—Where Employees Spend Most Time in the Same Place and Space

The office has moved into the home of knowledge workers just as the home is moving into the office (At-Work-at-Home). The lines between the office and home are to a certain extent blurring. Simply put, employees are investing time and money into creating bespoke homeworking environments and are sacrificing space in their homes to do so. Suffice to say, the magnetic force around the homeworking environment is getting stronger for a greater proportion of employees adding to the expanding development of digital possibilities for remote working. The home-work environment has a substantial impact on productivity, suggesting that employers should take a keen interest in supporting employees' remote set-ups (Arkesteijn et al. 2021).

For many, the homeworking environment better supports the majority of working activities as the average home supports the average employee better than the average office. But there are still activities that the office does better. And employees will more willingly succumb to the desire for some organisations to see more people back working together, if the office can show how much better it can be at supporting these activities than their employees' homes. There is also another force at play: the proportion of respondents with "A dedicated work room or office" in their homes has been steadily increasing since 2020 (not surprisingly as employees spend more time working remotely), which suggests, will very likely increase the proportion of employees having a positive home-working experience.

In a Danish survey, the perceived disadvantages of remote working during the pandemic was, respectively, home office constraints, work uncertainties, and inadequate tools—and the advantages improved work–life balance, work efficiency, and greater work control (Ipsen et al. 2021). As a note, national regulative variations have implications for the home office. In Denmark, there are regulations on how the home workplace should be designed and equipped when employees spend more than 2 days a week working from home. These regulations aim to ensure the best possible working conditions and thereby reduce long and short-term work-related injuries, and they were changed from 1 day to 2 days in the spring of 2022. Further studies confirm that challenges associated with full-time remote work include professional isolation (loneliness), a less-than-ideal telework environment, increased workload, and heightened stress levels (Saba et al. 2020). These findings highlight the importance of addressing social connection, workspace adequacy, and work-life balance to support remote workers effectively.

16.12 The Office of the Future Has Plasticity

As flexibility and agility become more prevalent, the office itself will increasingly become adaptable, all in support of the liberation from the constraints of time, location, and physical space in a digitised world.

As a result, walls and buildings have a lesser defining impact on work life. The future physical workplace is created around flexible square metres with embedded plasticity where the office continuously becomes smarter in a digitised reality. In other words, it becomes a mouldable and flexible workspace. Square metres plasticity are intelligent square metres in an ever-changing daily routine. The central workplace that stands as a castle and manifestation of organisational success is growingly giving way to office plasticity. A workplace plasticity functions in symbiosis and constant adaptation with its users and surroundings.

The plasticity of the workplace encompasses various mechanisms and processes by which the office can change. There are two primary forms of plasticity. Structural plasticity refers to changes in the physical structure and connectivity of the office. Functional plasticity refers to the office's ability to reorganise its functions in response to changes in the environment. An analogy to describe the future office is that it should not be perceived as a brick, a fixed and unshakable source of security. Instead, the office is to be like a sponge that is instant scalable, intimate, collaborative, attractive, and absorbent for the employees, just like water to a sponge. But how do you design an office with fixed walls to be like a sponge? How do you create the organisational space and processes to achieve that?

The future-oriented office will transition towards becoming an instantly scalable space that adjusts its availability based on foot traffic. This is done not only to lower costs but also to bring vitality to areas accessible to employees on a given workday. The office will be designed in a way that allows floors to be dynamically activated or deactivated. During busy periods, all floors will be open, while on days with lower attendance, surplus floors can be closed. In essence, the office will expand and contract, consistently maintaining the ideal size for the number of people present on any given day.

This development will contribute to making the workplace much more flexible in terms of dividing and allocating fixed areas and offices to employee groups and managers. Flexibility will encompass all employees in the future office simply because the entire office becomes flexible. Therefore, the office is faced with the need for remodelling and redesigning to accommodate an increasingly liberated, flexible, and digitised workforce. This trend will be further reinforced with the establishment of dispersed offices through the creation of decentralised hubs as stand-alone or co-working spaces. In essence, the development means that overconsumption of physical square metres is a thing of the past, and intelligent square metres based on the sharing economy are the future. What does the concrete reality of the future plastic and physical office workspace entail? As we move forward, it means fewer physical square metres in one location, more flexible square metres, collaborations with external organisations regarding square metres, and involvement of external users, surroundings, and services. This also means that we will see a rising number of co-working spaces and hubs where employees have the optimal conditions to work closer to home. And it will see a dramatic rise in an ever-improving home office.

In the future, hybrid workplace leadership must take control of significant touchpoints for employees' workplace experiences, with a keen focus on the impact hierarchy and the overall value creation. This control includes minimising the time from data to efficient and targeted responses to adjust and optimise efforts. This supports the development of a facility management approach where data and opportunities for real-time responses are connected to a VUCA (Volatile, Uncertain, Complex, Ambiguous) reality. Compared to the past, the future analogue workplace will be radically more changeable and adaptive, reflecting the ever-changing digital workplace. What does this mean for the office and office building? Many will need to be redesigned, while others will need to be converted for other uses such as residential or storage purposes. There will also be offices that become obsolete, unusable, and eventually demolished.

16.13 The Future Analogue Office Creates "More"

The future will see the analogue office offering more. "MORE" serving multiple objectives but, in sum, making the office more valuable for the employees and organisation (the list is not complete or prioritised) (Fig. 16.3). The list could, of course, have been revised to state the opposite, and though applying to the pre-pandemic analogue workplace not evolving, with "less" put in front of each sentence.

- More individualisation: Creating office workspaces and services that are tailored to individual employees' needs and preferences.
- More collaborative and interactive: Creating workspaces that encourage and curate face-to-face interaction and teamwork.
- More external options, conveniences, and offers: Creating ways to provide benefits and offers that extend beyond the internal office environment. Access to conveniences and shops in close proximity to or integrated into the office.
- More digitisation and automation of the office: Creating operational "clever buildings" enabling flexibility through the collection and use of data.

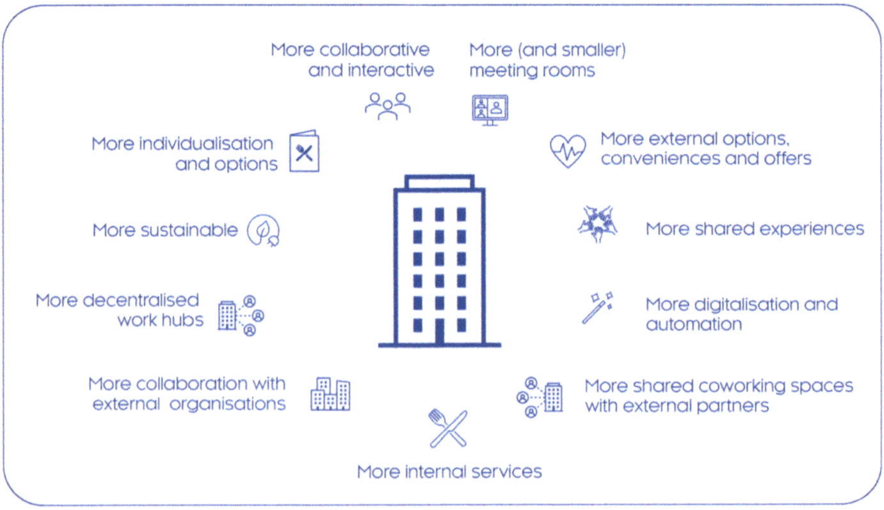

Fig. 16.3 The future office creates more. More or the employees and Organisation

- More shared co-working spaces with external partners: Creating scalability of the diminished office in co-operation with external partners.
- More internal services: Creating more services to make the office more attractive for the employees.
- More shared experiences: Creating experiences that facilitate the relations between employees and the organisation.
- More collaboration with external organisations: Creating more collaborations with external organisations supporting the ambition of creating a marketplace worth spending valuable time at.
- More decentralised work hubs: Creating workplace office hubs that create an attractive workspace closer to home and, at the same time, facilitate collaboration, communication, and community-building.
- More and smaller meeting rooms: Creating and accommodating for more and smaller meetings, either digital or analogue.
- More sustainable: Creating a more sustainable and inclusive office.
- More accessibility: Creating an office with greater accessibility to managers, mentoring, and management.
- More equality: Creating a shared office reality and culture regardless of position and hierarchical placement.
- More trust: Creating and building trust among employees and managers.
- More psychological security, ultimately enabling employees to be safely vulnerable.
- More quiet and secluded workspaces for in-depth work.
- ....

Maersk HQ. *Image credits:* Tomas Bertelsen PLH Architects

From an isolated analogue office perspective, it is anticipated that in the short to mid-term, significant efforts and upgrades will be made to ensure the office remains attractive, potentially making remote work less appealing. However, the question remains: what will the long-term implications be for the analogue office? Will it continue to evolve in response to changing work habits, or will it face a decline as digital and hybrid models dominate?

References

(Aksoy, Maria, Bloom, Davis, Dolls and Zarate 2021) https://www.nber.org/system/files/working_papers/w28731/w28731.pdf

(Alessandretti, Sapiezynski, Sekara, Lehmann and Baronchelli 2018) Evidence for a conserved quantity in human mobility https://www.nature.com/articles/s41562-018-0364-x

(Arkesteijn et al., 2021) Arkesteijn MH, Jansen SJT, Kieft B, Appel-Meulenbroek R, Hoekstra B, Jongens-Van der Schaaf P (2021) The influence of the physical home work environment on perceived productivity during the COVID-19 pandemic https://www.cfpb.nl/media/uploads/publicaties/upload/2021_influens_of_physicalhome_on_perceived_productivity_Arkersteijn_Hoekstar_et_al.pdf

(Beasley, 1947) "Knudsen: A Biography" written by Norman Beasley. Published in 2017 by Papamoa Press. Originally published in 1947. Page 54.

(Becker et al., 1995) Becker, F.D, and F. Steel. Workplace by Design: Mapping the High-Performance Workscape. San Francisco: Jossey-Bass 1995

(Bloom, Barrero, Davis 2021) Why Working from Home will Stick https://www.nber.org/system/files/working_papers/w28731/w28731.pdf

(Botsman and Rogers 2010) "What's Mine Is Yours: The Rise of Collaborative Consumption."

(FM Update 2022) Hvad er kontorets rolle på fremtidens arbejdsplads? https://amp.issuu.com/dfm-net/docs/fm-update_nr3_2022_ny/s/17310779

(Ipsen, Veldhoven, Kirchner, Hansen 2021) Six Key Advantages and Disadvantages of Working from Home in Europe during COVID-19. https://www.mdpi.com/1660-4601/18/4/1826

(Ma and Ye 2019) Does daily commuting behavior matter to employee productivity? https://www.sciencedirect.com/science/article/abs/pii/S0966692318307269

(Microsoft 2022) *Work Trend Index*

(Saba et al., 2020) Carillo, Kevin & Cachat-Rosset, Gaelle & Marsan, Josianne & Saba, Tania & Klarsfeld, Alain. (2020). Adjusting to epidemic-induced telework: empirical insights from teleworkers in France. European Journal of Information Systems. 30. 10.1080/0960085X.2020.1829512. https://www.researchgate.net/publication/345943371_Adjusting_to_epidemic-induced_telework_empirical_insights_from_teleworkers_in_France

(The Human Capital Hub 2024) Work from Home with Apple https://www.thehumancapitalhub.com/articles/work-from-home-for-apple-what-you-need-to-know#Insights%20into%20Work%20from%20Home%20for%20Apple%20from%20the%20Employee%20Perspective

(The New York Times 2023) Dror Poleg: The Future of Offices When Workers Have a Choice https://www.nytimes.com/2021/01/04/upshot/work-office-from-home.html.2021

(The Verge 2023) Google's $99 a night company hotel advertises 'no commute' as a perk https://www.theverge.com/2023/8/4/23820061/google-hotel-bay-view-campus-return-to-office

Part IV

Recommendations for Ensuring the Continued Success of the Hybrid Office Workplace

Dominant Hybrid Workplace Objectives (Potential Competitive Advantages) 17

Abstract

The dominant objectives of adopting a hybrid workplace model vary, but they largely aim to align the workplace with societal and market developments. Management is not the sole driver; external pressures and future expectations play a significant role. The hybrid model offers flexibility, balancing individual and organisational needs, and is increasingly recognised as essential for maintaining a competitive advantage.

Key motivations include digitalisation, which boosts productivity, employee attraction, retention, and well-being by providing greater flexibility. The hybrid model also supports sustainability, inclusion, diversity, and cost reduction, particularly in office expenses. Moreover, it can, if applied cleverly, foster innovation and enhanced productivity through flexible working options.

Although challenges remain, particularly around full remote working, the hybrid model's ability to reduce costs and improve efficiency ensures its relevance. Organisations must strategically develop their hybrid workplace models, as the future of work increasingly demands a balance between digital and physical spaces, flexibility, and innovation.

17.1 Five Dominant Hybrid Workplace Objectives

What are the dominant and present goals and motivations of office workplaces that embrace the future hybrid model? The goals and motivations for introducing this hybrid and flexible workplace model vary widely. In summary, it can be stated that this is being done to align the workplace and work life with the developments and opportunities in society and the market. In other words, the main driving force for the spread and adoption of the hybrid workplace is not management. It is primarily the external environment and expectations for future developments that "pressure"

C. Sneppen, *The Future (R)Evolution of the Office Workspace*, Future of Business and Finance, https://doi.org/10.1007/978-3-031-85229-9_17

organisations to gradually introduce the hybrid workplace, either due to urgent needs (burning platforms) or through slow incremental adaptations towards greater competitive advantages.

There are nearly as many different motivations and solutions as there are organisations venturing into the "unknown" with the implementation of the hybrid workplace. There is no universal or "one-size-fits-all" solution for the hybrid workplace. The transformation is taking place while there is very limited historical data to support the establishment of the hybrid workplace model. It is inherently the responsibility of management to determine how the hybrid workplace evolves and fits into their specific market and organisation. As repeatedly emphasised throughout the book, this development is primarily driven by digitisation, evolving employee behaviour and societal expectations, and the transition from an industrial society to a knowledge-based, networked society. Over time, this shift will place traditional workplace models and organisations at a competitive disadvantage, as the benefits of moving towards a dynamic hybrid workplace model will continue to accelerate.

I have identified five present main goals and motivations that, across organisations, crystallise why management is grappling with the establishment of the hybrid workplace (Fig. 17.1).

They have been generated by the Copenhagen Institute for Futures Studies' countless workplace foresight studies and projects with both researchers and practitioners from the business community and public organisations.

1. Hybrid workplace is positively correlated to work digitalisation: The hybrid workplace model results in a more digitally grounded work life (e.g. McKinsey & Company 2021; Microsoft 2022). Organisations that were digitally mature and had the digital infrastructure and a corresponding management system in place before the introduction of the more flexible model have documented a significant increase in productivity with the hybrid model. Conversely, organisations that introduce a hybrid workplace model experience that the workplace and work life become more digitised. Popularly formulated, the need for paper and physical control decreases when employees work digitally from a distance.

2. Hybrid workplace is positively correlated to employee attraction, retention, engagement, and well-being: The hybrid workplace model offers employees greater flexibility and autonomy over their work schedules while still allowing

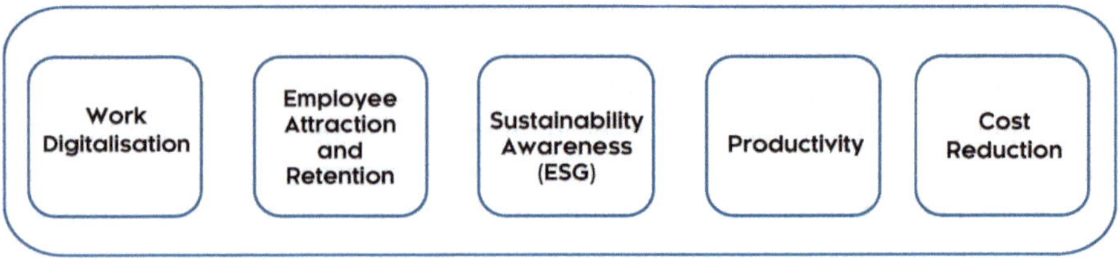

Fig. 17.1 Five present main objectives for the hybrid office workplace model

for in-person collaboration with colleagues (Fig. 17.2). There is a strong correlation between the hybrid workplace model and employee attraction, retention, and well-being (e.g. Bloom, Han and Liang 2024). The work flexibility and autonomy imbedded in the hybrid model is a significant and often decisive motivation for employees e.g. (Cushman & Wakefield 2020). Firstly, the hybrid workplace model can be an attractive feature for potential employees. Many employees now prioritise flexibility and work-life balance when choosing a job, and the hybrid model offers this. Organisations that offer a hybrid workplace model may be more likely to attract top talent who value flexibility and autonomy in their work. Secondly, the hybrid workplace model can increase employee retention. Giving employees the freedom to work remotely part of the time can help to reduce burnout and increase job satisfaction. This, in turn, can lead to increased loyalty and retention rates. Lastly, the hybrid workplace model can have a positive impact on employee well-being. Allowing employees to work from home part of the time can help to reduce stress and increase job satisfaction. Additionally, employees who have a better work-life balance are often healthier, happier, and more productive. A study revealed that when people have flexibility, only 14% report burnout symptoms, compared to 36% who have no flexibility (Atlassian 2022).

When we look at the proportion of organisations that are established from the outset as hybrid workplaces, all workplaces will eventually become hybrid. The establishment of a hybrid workplace is a point of no return for the less flexible office workplace. Unless management is prepared to lose a large number of employees, flexibility is valued and highly prioritised by employees. Overall, the hybrid workplace model can be a powerful tool for organisations to attract and retain top talent while also improving employee well-being. Organisations that are able to successfully implement this model may be better positioned to compete for talent and create a positive work environment for their employees.

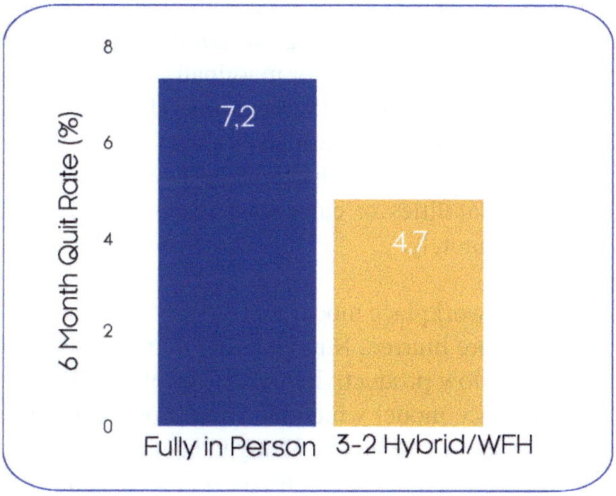

Fig. 17.2 Hybrid WFH lowered employee quit rate by 35%. Source: Barero, Jose Maria, Nicholas Bloom, and Steven J. Davis, 2021. "Why working from home will stick", www.wfhresearch.com

3. Sustainability awareness (ESG) pushes the hybrid workplace model: The hybrid workplace makes the organisation more sustainable and therefore more future-ready. At the same time, hybrid workplaces experience that the more flexible work life increases inclusion, diversity, and equality in the organisation (DEI).

   Addressing employee well-being, studies have shown that time allocated to leisure has increased, while time spent on work has decreased among more remote roles. In other words, remote jobs afford employees more leisure time. Notably, the same study found that these reductions in labour supply were not linked to declines in productivity; in fact, sectors with a higher intensity of remote work experienced greater productivity growth (Makridis 2024).

   Increased equality, diversity, and inclusion are correlated to hybrid work life (part of the sustainability agenda). The hybrid workplace model addresses the need to alleviate time constraints on families with children. These families are constantly struggling with a lack of time, and the fast-paced and structured nature of society only adds to the pressure. Family logistics are tightly scheduled, and since most families rely on dual incomes, mothers in particular appreciate the added flexibility of hybrid work (see Fig. 11.3). The previous rigid model allowed very little room for adjusting daily schedules, resulting in families "suffering". At the same time, it is worth noting that when both parents have flexible work arrangements, mothers tend to undertake a disproportionate share of household chores (Pabilonia et al. 2023; Biehl et al. 2024). Once again, mothers, who traditionally assume the role of a primary caregiver, were greatly affected. They had to compromise their career ambitions and prioritise their families. They often arrived at work at the last minute, left early to pick up their children from school, and took sick days to care for their kids. With the hybrid workplace, employees with children can achieve greater equality, especially mothers.

   In fact, the hybrid and flexible work model may be the key initiative that promotes gender equality in the workplace, particularly in the next decade. By providing individuals with more flexibility in terms of time, location, and space for work, as well as reducing commuting, working hybrid promotes equality and enhances the well-being of families, particularly mothers (e.g. Tito 2024). Families with children or marginalised employees are more likely to be attracted and retained to hybrid workplaces. The hybrid workplace model can help create a more inclusive culture, as it allows for greater flexibility and accommodation for employees with different needs and preferences. For example, employees with disabilities or caregiving responsibilities may benefit from being able to work remotely.

4. Hybrid workplace model is positively correlated to productivity: Now it becomes a bit more blurred. Randomised control trials, natural experiments, and surveys suggest low productivity on the correlation between productivity and the hybrid workplace model which indicates a productivity increase of between 3 and 5% for office workers (e.g. Mutiganda et al. 2022; Barrero, Bloom and Davis 2021: Prithwiraj et al. 2021). Of course, this depends on how the specific organisation

defines and implements the hybrid workplace. A significant part of the productivity increase comes from more working hours saved by employees' daily commuting time, as well as increased employee well-being. For example, an employee who works from home twice a week can have 1–2 extra hours of work per week (see Fig. 11.8). In terms of employee well-being, it is simple: happy and engaged employees are more productive. The introduction of the hybrid and flexible workplace creates significant challenges and dilemmas. The "old" predominantly analogue workplace model did too.

The hybrid workplace model can—contrary to common belief—enhance innovation and, consequently, boost productivity for certain types of tasks. An increasing part of the value creation of knowledge work is innovation, and a study revealed when employees have flexibility in working options, 71% report their team is innovative, compared with 57% without flexibility (Atlassian 2022).

Nonetheless, it is imperative to acknowledge that organisations that have adopted the hybrid workplace model exhibit a higher degree of digitalisation. Given the impending acceleration of digitalisation in the realm of work, the most substantial yet unrealised potential for enhancing productivity may well be linked to the correlation between digitalisation and the hybrid workplace model.

When we consider the extreme model of a fully remote workplace (without any physical office), the best evidence suggests that it may reduce overall productivity associated with 10%–20% lower productivity than fully in-person work (Barrero et al. 2023). This is most likely because it is, among other things, more difficult to train and mentor employees remotely, innovation can be hindered, and communication and building a strong company culture can be challenging. The reason for a fully remote model is primarily cost, as fully remote roles do not require office space and at the same time employees can be hired from different locations, which helps keep wage costs down. The expanded talent pool can make up for the productivity losses, as it allows for the attraction of highly specialised employees. In other words, there is a tipping point in the balance between the design of workplace model and productivity.

An even further transitioning from fully remote work to a work-from-anywhere arrangement has an impact on productivity. Work from anywhere is a growing form of remote work that grants employees geographic flexibility, allowing them to choose where they live. In a study conducted at the US Patent and Trademark Office (USPTO), researchers examined the productivity effects of employees shifting from a work-from-home (WFH) to a work-from-anywhere (WFA) set-up (Fenizia and Kirchmaier 2024). The findings revealed that the transition from WFH to WFA led to a 4.4% increase in employee output, with no increase in rework. Another study, focusing on the public sector and published in 2024, found that working from home (WFH) increased productivity by 12%. The productivity gains in the study were primarily driven by reduced distractions and were not attributed to differences in quality, shift length, or task allocation. Interestingly, the productivity gains more than doubled when tasks were assigned by a supervisor.

5. Hybrid workplace model is positively correlated to cost reduction (Effectiveness): The hybrid workplace provides the opportunity to reduce fixed and variable office expenses, but on the contrary, it will lead to increased investments in other initiatives to support a successful hybrid workplace.

   The hybrid workplace offers the possibility of reducing the fixed and variable office costs, but will, on the contrary, divert increased investments in other initiatives to support a successful hybrid workplace.

   The hybrid workplace model has major advantages in terms of reducing hiring and potential turnover costs. (Conversely, organisations can reduce redundancy costs by enforcing a full return to office policy, thereby encouraging employees to leave voluntarily.) Both of these clearly matter in a recession as they do in a boom.

   Fully remote workplace models obviously result in significant savings on office space and salaries, so it's clear they are here to stay. The force now promoting hybrid working for organisations is that it lowers costs and raises productivity, and this is if anything more important in a potential economic recession.

Another perspective is to examine the broader market assessment of an organisation's value in relation to workplace flexibility. A recent study demonstrates a positive correlation by analysing the link between corporate reliance on alternative work arrangements and long-term stock performance (Lattanzio 2024). The research shows that an equal-weighted portfolio of the "100 Best Companies for Remote Working Jobs" (annually published by Forbes) achieved an annualised four-factor alpha (a metric used in finance to evaluate a portfolio's performance by adjusting for four key risk factors) of 7.44% from 2014 to 2019, outperforming an industry benchmark by 6.17%. Firms included in the ranking also showed significantly stronger positive earnings surprises and announcement returns. These findings have three key implications. First, work-from-home arrangements enhance firm value by boosting employee satisfaction and productivity, aligning with human capital-based theories of the organisation. Second, the stock market fails to fully value alternative work arrangements, even when data are readily accessible across numerous publicly traded companies. Third, a greater reliance on flexible work arrangements strengthens organisations' resilience to long-tail risk (withstand unexpected, rare, and disruptive events such as a pandemic).

To summarise, the above outlines five key advantages pursued—albeit to varying degrees and with different priorities—by hybrid organisations. Provocatively, and perhaps pushing the question too far, one might ask: what leadership, without considering specific goals and challenges, would not wish to become more digitalised, attract and retain top talent, and be more ESG-compliant while simultaneously potentially boosting productivity and efficiency?

References

(Atlassian 2022) Trends worth tracking https://www.atlassian.com/blog/state-of-teams-2022#trends-worth-tracking

(Barrero, Bloom and Davis 2021) Barrero, Bloom and Davis Why Working from Home Will Stick https://www.nber.org/papers/w28731

(Barrero, Bloom and Davis 2023) WFH's staunchest proponents just dropped a bomb: Fully remote workers are officially less productive https://drive.google.com/file/d/1kqbngD8pemqxAkZmWCOQ32Yk6PXK9eVA/view

(Biehl et al., 2024) Biehl, A.M., Hayter, J. & Hill, B. Remote work and the effects on secondary childcare. *Int Rev Econ* **71**, 813–830 (2024). https://doi.org/10.1007/s12232-024-00466-7

(Bloom, Han and Liang 2024) HBR October 29, 2024 One Company A/B Tested Hybrid Work. Here's What They Found https://hbr.org/2024/10/one-company-a-b-tested-hybrid-work-heres-what-they-found

(Cushman & Wakefield 2020-) WORKPLACE ECOSYSTEMS OF THE FUTURE https://www.cushmanwakefield.com/en/insights/the-future-of-workplace

(Fenizia and Kirchmaier 2024) Not incentivized yet efficient: Working from home in the public sector https://cep.lse.ac.uk/pubs/download/dp2036.pdf

(Lattanzio 2024) Does the Stock Market Fully Value Alternative Work Arrangements? Work From Home and Equity Prices https://www.efmaefm.org/0efmameetings/efma%20annual%20meetings/2021-leeds/papers/efma%202021_stage-2049_question-full%20paper_id-182.pdf

(Makridis 2024). https://papers.ssrn.com/sol3/papers.cfm?abstract_id=4517661

(McKinsey & Company 2021) The Future of Work After COVID-19 https://www.mckinsey.com/featured-insights/future-of-work/the-future-of-work-after-covid-19

(Microsoft 2022) *Work Trend Index 2022*

(Mutiganda, Wiitavaara, Heiden, Svensson, Fagerström, Bergström and Aboagye 2022) A systematic review of the research on telework and organizational economic performance indicators https://www.frontiersin.org/articles/10.3389/fpsyg.2022.1035310/full

(Pabilonia et al., 2023) Pabilonia, Sabrina Wulff; Vernon, Victoria Review of Economics of the Household (2023) Who is doing the chores and childcare in dual-earner couples during the COVID-19 era of working from home? https://www.iza.org/publications/dp/15118/who-is-doing-the-chores-and-childcare-in-dual-earner-couples-during-the-covid-19-era-of-working-from-home

(Prithwiraj, Choudhury, Foroughi and Larson 2021) Work-from-anywhere: The productivity effects of geographic flexibility https://www.hbs.edu/ris/Publication%20Files/Work%20from%20Anywhere_forthcoming%20SMJ_ee8cc7c5-c90e-4ad9-a1f4-47309d693a5c.pdf

(Tito 2024) Does the Ability to Work Remotely Alter Labor Force Attachment? An Analysis of Labor Market Flows Across https://drive.google.com/file/d/1Tc33G0rb9ydX0FYOEzyjjOZhH65XdQ_A/view

Dominant Hybrid Office Workplace Challenges

18

Abstract

The hybrid workplace, often referred to as the "new kid in town", faces numerous challenges, particularly when compared to the traditional office-first model. While all workplace models have their drawbacks, the hybrid model has introduced its own set of challenges. Some of these challenges existed even before the pandemic but have now been magnified by the shift to hybrid work. The development of the hybrid workplace will be shaped by the balance between its advantages and challenges, influenced by various stakeholders.

One significant challenge is the shift from a centralised to a decentralised workplace culture. Centralised cultures rely on top-down decision-making, while decentralised cultures distribute power and decision-making across the organisation. This transition, driven by advances in communication technology and changing societal conditions, offers benefits like greater flexibility and innovation but also introduces challenges such as the need for clear communication and coordination.

Ultimately, the success of the hybrid workplace will depend on whether the opportunities it presents outweigh the challenges. As organisations adapt, they will need to address these challenges while leveraging the benefits of a more flexible, distributed work environment.

18.1 Abundant Hybrid Workplace Challenges

The challenges of the "new kid in town", the hybrid workplace, are numerous, particularly when viewed against the backdrop of the traditional office-first model (Fig. 18.1). All workplace models come with their own set of downsides as well as upsides.

C. Sneppen, *The Future (R)Evolution of the Office Workspace*, Future of Business and Finance, https://doi.org/10.1007/978-3-031-85229-9_18

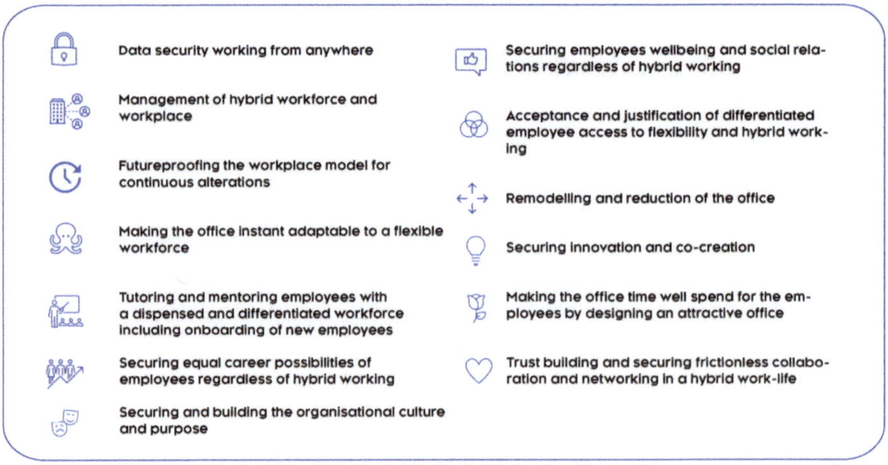

Fig. 18.1 The future hybrid workplace: selected significant challenges

The "old" model had its own, and new ones have surfaced with the introduction of the hybrid workplace—challenges that in most cases already existed in the pre-pandemic workplace but have been crystallised and brought to our attention with the changes. The future hybrid workplace model will be developed in the tension between advantages and challenges and, as always, will be determined by the actors involved.

The legal regulation, rhythm, and structure of society are challenged on a macro level by the increased flexibility of the workforce on one side, and on the other side, they are decisive for the interpretation of the hybrid workplace model within a specific organisation. Ultimately, the framework of any society determines what is possible and impossible, as well as the consequences that the definition of a hybrid workplace will have for both employees and the organisation. The complexity naturally increases when organisations operate across borders.

The transformation towards the hybrid workplace and work life is in a broad organisational perspective a movement from a centralised to a decentralised workplace and culture. The centralised culture refers to a cultural system in which power and decision-making are concentrated in a single authority or entity. In such a culture, decisions are made at the top and disseminated down the hierarchy, with little input or involvement from lower-level individuals or groups. This type of culture is often characterised by stricter rules, clear hierarchies, and a focus on maintaining stability and order. On the other hand, a distributed culture is a cultural system in which power and decision-making are more widely dispersed throughout the organisation or community. In such a culture, individuals or groups are empowered to make decisions and act on their own, without strict guidance or oversight from a central authority. This type of culture is often characterised by a more fluid hierarchy, a focus on innovation and creativity, and a willingness to experiment and take risks.

The shift from a centralised culture to a distributed culture can be seen in many different areas of society, including business, government, and social movements. One key driver of this shift is the expanding availability of information and communication technologies, which allow individuals and groups to connect and collaborate more easily than ever before. Additionally, changing social and economic conditions, such as globalisation and the rise of the knowledge economy, have created new opportunities for distributed forms of organisation and decision-making. The benefits of a distributed culture can include greater flexibility, adaptability, and innovation, as well as a greater sense of ownership and empowerment among individuals and groups. However, it can also pose challenges, such as the need for clear communication and coordination, and the potential for conflicts or power struggles to emerge within the distributed structure. The shift towards a more distributed culture reflects broader trends towards decentralisation and democratisation in many areas of society.

The challenges are often emphasised by workplace actors for the purpose of maintaining the present workplace model. It ultimately boils down to whether the opportunities presented by the future hybrid workplace model outweigh the challenges. We anticipate that the opportunities will prevail as we move forwards and that the challenges will be addressed in the formation of the hybrid workplace model.

18.2 Tangible Infrastructure Challenges

In the organisational perspective, the challenges of the hybrid workplace model can be broadly divided into two overlapping and interrelated groups of tangible infrastructure and intangible human challenges. The list is not prioritised, categorised, or complete list and briefly addresses the challenges and implicit possible measures to address them.

Tangible infrastructure challenges: Tangible infrastructure challenges such as data security, dimensioning of the office, making the office instantly adaptable, remodelling and reduction of the office, making the office time well spent for the employees by designing an attractive office, etc.

- Data security working from anywhere: The paradigm shift towards remote working began even before the COVID-19 pandemic broke out. Since then, local and national directives have confined large portions of the population to their homes. As a result, many businesses have continued operating using a distributed workforce and some have made remote working permanent. These new circumstances demand a different security stance than working from centralised offices, especially when it comes to maintaining the data security that the GDPR requires. If you're suddenly managing remote teams, it can be daunting to think about data security with everything else that's going on. The GDPR requires that companies keep personal data private and secure (Koch GDPR EU 2024).

- Making the office instantly adaptable to a flexible workforce: Making the office instantly adaptable to a flexible workforce means creating a workspace that can quickly and easily accommodate employees who work remotely, on flexible schedules, or who move frequently between different office locations. The challenges are obvious as we move from a predictable workplace model where the analogue office was the epicentre of work life to a dispensed workforce where the occupancy of the office fluctuates by the hour. This may involve implementing technology that enables remote collaboration, designing spaces that can be easily reconfigured to accommodate different work styles, and creating policies that support a more flexible work environment. The goal is to create a workspace that can support the needs of a diverse and geographically dispersed workforce while also maintaining a sense of cohesion and collaboration across the organisation (Hass 2022).

- Remodelling and reduction of the office: Remodelling and reduction of the office with the introduction of a hybrid work model involves rethinking the traditional office space to better suit the needs of a more flexible and remote workforce. This may include reducing the amount of physical office space required, reconfiguring workstations to be more adaptable and flexible, and introducing technology that enables remote collaboration and communication. By reducing the physical office space, companies can save on real estate costs and create a more efficient use of space. Reconfiguring workstations to be more adaptable and flexible can create a more collaborative and dynamic workspace that can accommodate a variety of work styles and preferences.

- Introducing technology that enables remote collaboration, and communication can help create a more seamless and integrated work environment that supports a distributed workforce. Overall, the goal is to create an office environment that is more aligned with the needs and expectations of a modern workforce while also improving efficiency, collaboration, and productivity.

- Making the office time well spent for the employees by designing an attractive office: Making the office time well spent for employees by designing an attractive office involves creating a workspace that employees enjoy spending time in and feel comfortable and productive in. This can include designing the office with features such as closeness to significant collaborating colleagues, natural space for meetings, interacting and collaboration, etc. On a more basic level it involved natural light, comfortable seating, ergonomic workstations, and attractive decor. The challenge of an attractive office is not limited to interior design and services, but includes exterior factors such as employee commuting time and attractiveness of exterior amenities. Is the physical location of the workplace optimal for a hybrid workplace model?

18.3 Intangible Human Challenges

Intangible human challenges include such as management of dispensed workforce, future-proofing the workplace model for continuous alterations, mentoring employees, securing a shared culture and purpose, securing equal career possibilities of employees regardless of hybrid working, mental well-being and social relations, acceptance and justification of differentiated employee access to flexibility and hybrid working, securing innovation, and co-creation. Highlights of specific intangible human challenges are as follows:

- Management of dispensed workforce: All collaborative work involves coordination, but working in hybrid teams presents significantly more coordination challenges than working face-to-face. The risk is that "faultlines", as referred to by researchers, can easily emerge between those who work together in person and those who work remotely. Because of the extra effort required to coordinate with remote teammates, they get left out of small exchanges and minor decisions made by those who are working together in the office. Over time, as people get accustomed to who's looped in and who's not, they can get left out of bigger conversations and more important decisions.

- Future-proofing the workplace model for continuous alterations: Future-proofing the hybrid workplace model for continuous alterations involves designing a flexible and adaptable workspace that can respond to changing needs and requirements.

- Implementing technology that supports remote collaboration and communication: This can include video conferencing, instant messaging, and cloud-based document sharing, which can help ensure that employees can work together seamlessly regardless of their location.

- Creating a modular and flexible workspace: Designing a workspace that can be easily reconfigured or adapted to suit changing needs can help ensure that the workspace remains relevant and useful over time.

- Developing policies and procedures that support a flexible work environment: This can include creating policies around remote work, flexible schedules, and other arrangements that support a more dynamic and flexible workforce (e.g. Eurofound 2022).

- Maintaining open lines of communication with employees: Regularly soliciting feedback from employees can help ensure that the workspace continues to meet their needs and expectations and can help identify areas for improvement.

- Securing equal career possibilities of employees regardless of hybrid working: The "power of proximity" where employees who spend more time at the office and thereby are more visible are more likely to be promoted. The FOMO (fear of missing out) can have negative consequences for the unfolding of the hybrid workplace. When office workers are prioritised, remote workers can't help but feel left out of experiences and opportunities

- Mentoring employees: Mentoring employees within a hybrid workplace can pose distinctive challenges when compared to a conventional, in-person work environment (Fig. 18.2). We know that feedback and mentoring are directly linked to fostering positive engagement (e.g. Pew 2023). The mentoring process for employees, particularly concerning the onboarding of new personnel and guiding younger staff members, becomes notably more pronounced.

- Communication barriers: In a hybrid workplace, employees may not always be physically present in the same location as their mentors, which can make it difficult to communicate effectively. Virtual communication tools such as video conferencing and instant messaging can help overcome this barrier, but they may not always be as effective as in-person communication (Gibbs et al. 2023). It becomes even more evident in actual learning processes.

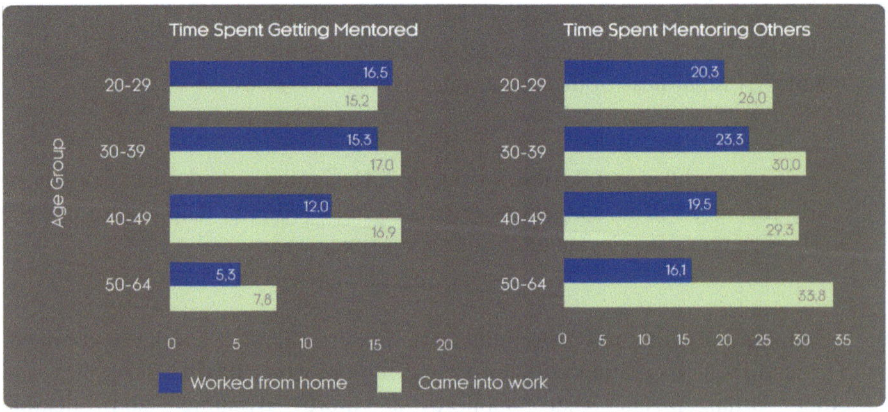

Fig. 18.2 Mentoring time when working from home versus coming into work, age group, percentages. Source: Barrero, Jose Maria, Nicholas Bloom, and Steven J. Davis, 2021. "Why working from home will stick", National Bureau of Economic Research Working Paper 28731. www.wfhresearch.com

- Building relationships: Developing strong mentor-mentee and colleague relationships can be more challenging in a hybrid workplace, where interactions may be limited or sporadic. Building rapport and trust becomes more difficult when regular face-to-face contact is absent.

- Overcoming distractions: In a hybrid workplace, employees may be more prone to distractions or interruptions, which can make it challenging to focus on mentoring activities. Mentors may need to be more intentional about scheduling and structuring mentoring sessions to minimise distractions working can be challenging.

- Time zone differences: In a hybrid workplace, mentors and mentees may be in different time zones, which can make scheduling meetings or check-ins more difficult. Mentoring in a hybrid workplace requires more intentional communication and relationship-building efforts, as well as flexibility and creativity in overcoming barriers such as communication challenges and distractions. It may also require more planning and coordination to ensure that mentoring activities are effective and productive for both mentors and mentees.

- Securing a shared culture and purpose: Like creativity, this is a challenge that management became concerned about as the pandemic dragged on and the prospects of bringing everyone back to the office look increasingly dim. In the initial days and months of working remotely, companies were relieved at how productive and engaged their workers seemed to still be. But this probably owed a lot to the fact that these employees had all worked together closely before the pandemic and knew plenty about how to do so effectively, in addition to their understanding of the company's norms, values, and expectations. In the hybrid workplace model and as existing employees leave and new ones join, an increasingly pressing challenge is how to socialise newcomers and integrate them into the company's culture, whether they're interns, entry-level hires, or seasoned executives. In addition, corporate culture can be critical for signalling the organisation's distinctiveness to potential new recruits, especially in industries where firms compete heavily for talent. If employees never or rarely come to the office or spend time together, how can a company's distinctive "feel" be maintained—and then, how can companies differentiate themselves from each other in the war for talent? (Hass 2022). If employees spend most of the time working from home the overarching organisational purpose ("the why") is naturally fading and becoming more distant as every day goes by (detachment and disengagement). While recognising the importance of culture for newcomers, organisations shouldn't overlook the reality that sustaining a positive culture and strong organisational commitment is at least as important for the many employees who are not new to the company.

- This underscores the need to make the physical office space unique and more closely aligned with the organisation's values. Far too many offices suffer from cognitive dissonance between the values an organisation has formally set out, communicates, or aspires to, and the reality experienced within the office itself. For example, when values such as innovation or sustainability are embedded in the organisation's ethos, there is an expectation that these will be reflected in the office environment. After all, actions speak louder than words.

- Mental well-being and social relations: An issue arises concerning social connections and the potential jeopardy they face, or their complete dissolution, when working remotely. We know that professional networks and mentoring relationships are important for advancing in the workplace and that building and sustaining these is particularly challenging already for women and minorities. Research clearly shows that personal connections are socially sustaining and important for our psychological well-being. Hybrid working risks creating a "dominant class" of those who feel like they're central to the organisation and strongly committed to it and an "underclass" of those who feel peripheral and disconnected not only from the work but also from the social life that creates meaning and bonds employees more closely to the organisation. The consequences can be less happy and less committed employees who are more likely to search for opportunities elsewhere. Two specific challenges that have emerged with more remote working and well-being include human contact, social relations, work and private life merging together, working too much, self-management, and decreasing sense of belonging. Additionally, leaders are more challenged by remote work than employees and are therefore more prone to experiencing dissatisfaction. Research has demonstrated that remote working can create pressure on employees to be constantly available or to work during their personal time. Some remote workers have reported feelings of isolation and conflicts between work and personal life due to the blurred boundaries between the two. However, overall, telework (remote working) improves work-life balance by assisting workers in managing childcare responsibilities, significantly reducing commuting time, and allowing for increased autonomy and better utilisation of working hours. The prevalence of telework is not necessarily influenced by gender. Nevertheless, gender differences exist concerning work-life balance. Women generally faced greater challenges than men in balancing telework with their personal lives during the pandemic. This was due to pre-existing inequalities and gender roles, as women were more likely to shoulder additional unpaid work such as caregiving, housework, and home schooling.

- Securing innovation and co-creation: Two types of creativity are endangered by a hybrid workplace model. Perhaps the most obvious one is collective creativity: people can brainstorm via zoom or Teams, but programmed times and formats for generating ideas may well not prove as fruitful as the more fluid in-person conversation—unexpected things that can happen when people meet in person and bounce ideas around with others or work intensively on solving a problem together. But individual creativity can be endangered, too. We know that quiet time alone can help generate novel ideas and insights. Yet it isn't clear that working alone over many days or weeks will prove generative for employees who must be constantly creative or innovative. On the contrary, there is reason to think that at least some social interactions and spontaneous conversations with colleagues, seeing random artefacts in each other's cubicles, and even the changes of scenery involved in going from home to work may be important to innovation, co-creation, and collaboration.

- Trust and network building: The remote-trust paradox presents a significant challenge in ensuring the success of the hybrid workplace model. When teams lack a culture of trust, the hybrid workplace can become problematic. Unfortunately, many managers don't understand the importance of trust until it's too late. They focus on adapting processes rather than building trust, which can result in fragmented teams. Building trust with remote employees is challenging, especially when there are team members who have never met in person. Although hybrid happy hours can help, they can't fully replace the value of in-person moments. Nevertheless, trust is crucial for success in remote work, as it acts like glue for distant teams' trust (e.g. Costa 2003; Tan 2024). All things being equal, the hybrid workplace will likely enhance small teams and collaborations. Small workplaces have a built-in trust creation factor that larger organisations must strive to match.

- Retention: A new employee retention hierarchy has emerged regarding hybrid workers: those who are predominantly remote, followed by those fully in office, tend to be the least loyal, exhibiting a strong inclination to switch jobs or even relocate. In contrast, employees in hybrid work arrangements are the most engaged and, therefore, the least likely to leave (e.g. Microsoft 2022). The changing attitudes of workers towards their employers are significantly influenced by the adoption of new working patterns. To align with the evolving expectations of the workforce, many employers are now offering greater flexibility, empowering employees to reassess their priorities and values in life. In some instances, this shift has led individuals to distance themselves from their work and explore alternative lifestyles that promise an enhanced quality of life. A significant proportion of employees indicate they would consider resigning if their employers did not provide flexibility regarding remote work. A study published in 2024 found that hybrid working improved job satisfaction and reduced quit rates by one-third, with particularly notable reductions among non-managers, female employees, and those with long commutes.

References

(Costa 2003) Work Team Trust and Effectiveness https://www.researchgate.net/publication/235260441_Work_Team_Trust_and_Effectiveness

(Eurofound 2022) The rise of telework: Impact on working conditions and regulations https://www.eurofound.europa.eu/system/files/2023-01/ef22005en.pdf

(Gibbs, Mengel and Siemroth 2023) Gibbs, M., Mengel, F. & Siemroth, C. Work from home and productivity: Evidence from personnel and analytics data on information technology professionals. *J. Political Econ. Microecon. 1*(1), 7–41 (2023). https://www.journals.uchicago.edu/doi/10.1086/721803

(Hass 2022) HBR 5 Challenges of Hybrid Work – and How to Overcome Them https://hbr.org/2022/02/5-challenges-of-hybrid-work-and-how-to-overcome-them

(Koch GDPR EU 2024) https://gdpr.eu/working-remotely-data-security

(Microsoft 2022) *Work Trend Index*

(Pew, 2023) Pew Research Center, How Americans View Their Jobs, How Americans View Their Jobs https://www.pewresearch.org/socialtrends/2023/03/30/how-americans-view-their-jobs/

(Tan 2024) Why trust is important on a hybrid team (and how managers can build it) https://hypercontext.com/blog/communication/trust-at-work-core-to-high-performance

Strategies for the Future Hybrid Office Workplace: A Strategic Blueprint for Success

19

Abstract

The hybrid workplace, which balances individual and organisational needs, reflects the broader societal and market developments rather than being solely driven by management. In this evolving landscape, leadership must play a proactive role in shaping the future workplace, rather than merely managing change.

Organisations face the challenge of creating a hybrid workplace model that meets diverse needs, with no single solution fitting all. The development of such a model requires foresight, inclusive leadership, and a deep understanding of both employee preferences and organisational goals.

Three strategic approaches—bottom-up (employee-driven), top-down (leadership-driven), and infrastructure transformation—are key to building a successful hybrid workplace. Each approach has its strengths and challenges, but a coordinated and balanced effort across all three is crucial. The future of work demands a departure from traditional office models, embracing both digital and physical spaces that are adaptable and aligned with modern work practices. Ultimately, the hybrid workplace model must be tailored to the unique characteristics of each organisation, ensuring it remains competitive and future-proof in a rapidly changing work-life environment.

19.1 Challenge: Can Organisations Afford Not to Go All in with a Hybrid Workplace?

An increasing number of organisations are adapting the workplace towards a more flexible and up-to-date hybrid model—a hybrid and flexible workplace where employees can work in the office or remotely in a balanced relationship between the individual's and the organisation's preferences and needs.

C. Sneppen, *The Future (R)Evolution of the Office Workspace*, Future of Business and Finance, https://doi.org/10.1007/978-3-031-85229-9_19

The goals and motivations for introducing the hybrid and flexible workplace model are very different. In summary, it can be formulated that it is about adapting the workplace and working life to the development and opportunities in society and the market. In other words, it is not management that so far has been the main engine for the spread and introduction of the hybrid workplace. Management has overall not led the change but predominately attempted to manage it.

If the workplace model is increasingly being treated as a product, it is tempting to quote Steve Jobs (a popular quote he is credited with) (Inc 2021): "Some people say give the customers what they want, but that's not my approach. Our job is to figure out what they're going to want before they do. In line with this, Henry Ford is often quoted as saying, "If I'd ask customers what they wanted, they would've told me 'a faster horse.' People don't know what they want until you show it to them. That's why I never rely on market research. Our task is to read things that are not yet on the page." Are leadership and management reading the employees and developing tomorrow's workplace winners? Has management taken the leadership in the development of the hybrid workplace, or are they primarily focused on managing the changes?

As the workplace undergoes unprecedented changes, it is challenging to ask workplace participants for a definitive answer regarding the ideal workplace product they truly desire. Most internal participants have an immediate and unconscious response to this question. Management would likely prioritise control, employees desire more flexibility, middle management seeks more support, facility management seeks predictability and less uncertainty, IT aims for increased behavioural adoption of new technology, human resources want support for the digital transformation of the organisation, and finance aims for reduced costs, among other considerations. In this context, it is important to note that research consistently emphasises that the best and most successful workplace models are built upon a high level of employee and team inclusion and influence in the ongoing development process of the hybrid and flexible workplace. Therefore, the above quote from Steve Jobs deviates from the analogy of the workplace as a product. Reimagining work and workplaces as a product not only tackles the widespread disengagement and dissatisfaction within the workforce but also aligns employees' needs with organisational objectives (Anicich and Lindsley 2014). The quote also emphasises that the development of a successful hybrid workplace model largely depends on future insights and anticipation. Do you systematically work with foresight and anticipatory leadership in the implementation of your hybrid workplace model?

There are almost as many different solutions as the number of organisations venturing into the "unknown" with the establishment of the hybrid workplace. There is no "one-size-fits-all" solution to the hybrid workplace. The transformation takes place while there is very limited historical data support for the establishment of the hybrid workplace model. The management's assignment is to determine how the hybrid workplace unfolds and is resolved in their specific market and organisation. For example, Google has decided that employees who consistently stay away from the office may have it considered during their performance reviews (Fortune 2023). Google has thus assessed that they are most competitive moving forward with greater office attendance. This assessment is contrasted with the current knowledge that suggests organisations are generally more productive, efficient, digitised, sustainable, diverse, equitable, and inclusive—as well as better able to attract and retain employees (see Chap. 18). If their assessment and decision are correct, it clearly illustrates that the hybrid workplace model is not a "one size fits all", and should though optimally reflect the unique culture and value creation process of each organisation.

19.2 The Five Key Dilemmas of the Hybrid Office Workplace

There are five significant dilemmas that organisations and management must address in their specific workplace in the context of the future hybrid and flexible workplace. These dilemmas also existed in the "old" predominantly analogue workplace model. However, organisations that embrace an updated and flexible hybrid office workplace will be more digitised, productive, efficient, and sustainable and ultimately face fewer challenges in attracting and retaining valuable employees compared to organisations that stick to a predominantly analogue approach. This refers to a model where the office remains the central point of employees' daily work lives. Can organisations afford to ignore the hybrid workplace model? The straightforward answer is no.

Based on my work with *The (R)Evolution of the Hybrid Office*, I have identified five major and crucial dilemmas that organisations and management must address within their own workplaces (Fig. 19.1). These dilemmas arise because a single workplace cannot provide all the answers to these dilemmas. Therefore, it is necessary to find a balance that will create the greatest competitive advantage in a rapidly changing market and environment, both now and in the future (the dilemmas are not prioritised; they overlap and are interrelated):

1. *ME vs. WE* (individualisation and community/autonomous and heteronomous).
2. *EXPLORE vs. EXPLOIT* (ongoing development of the hybrid workplace and present value creation represented in the ambidextrous office workplace).
3. *CLOSENESS vs. DISTANCE* (management, employees, and teams, and also related to symmetric).
4. *PLUGGED vs. UNPLUGGED* (place and space in a digital reality).
5. *SYNCHRONOUS vs. ASYNCHRONOUS* (time).

ME VS. WE (INDIVIDUALISATION) How to accommodate the individual and collective in one shared hybrid workspace? The workplace dilemma and balance between "me autonomous" and "we heteronomous" in all aspects of the individual and organisational work life. In more mature hybrid working organisations, employees are more mindful of when, where, and how to create value for their colleagues and the organisation, often prioritising this over their own short-term tasks (related to analogue and digital dexterity). From an organisational standpoint, performance

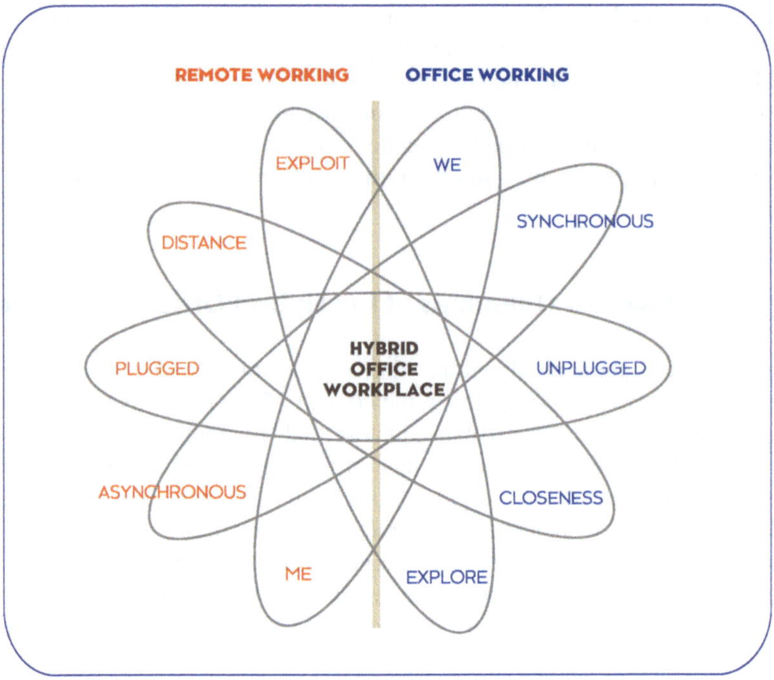

Fig. 19.1 The five key dilemmas of the hybrid office workplace

metrics should be designed to reflect and respond to this dynamic, ensuring that contributions to collective value are recognised alongside individual achievements.

EXPLORE VS. EXPLOIT (DEVELOPMENT) The dilemma of the ambidextrous hybrid office workplace: how to ambidextrously explore and simultaneously exploit the workplace? In metaphorical terms, it can be described as "building the road while driving fast at the same time"—a workplace in continued development and at the same time producing value effectively. The organisation must embrace constant explorations and test and at the same time exploit the very same workplace model to produce value. Learning organisations will all other things being equal have a head start unfolding and reaping the benefits of the ambidextrous hybrid workplace. The organisation, responsibilities, and processes defining the workplace should reflect and respond to the dilemma of continued development.

CLOSENESS VS. DISTANCE (MANAGEMENT AND COLLABORATION) How to navigate proximity and distance from a management perspective? The dilemma of distance management and when, where, and how to be close to the employees and colleagues. The dilemma is not confined to digitally versus in-person, but focuses on the mental distance. At the old workplace working 9-to-5 in the office the closeness was taken for granted (even it often was not the case). In the hybrid workplace, employees risk having long periods with a lack of perceived closeness to the organisation, colleagues, or management. The culture, competences, and all components of communication should among others respond to this behavioural dilemma.

PLUGGED VS. UNPLUGGED (PLACE AND SPACE) When and how to be digital and analogue? The digital versus analogue in-person dilemma at the hybrid workplace, with hybrid adding further complexity to the balancing of the dilemma. The dilemma encompasses analogue and digital dexterity both horizontally and vertically in the organisation. The dilemma is not primarily related to the physical infrastructure but rather to the intangible components such as the culture and competences of the organisation.

SYNCHRONOUS VS. ASYNCHRONOUS (TIME) When to be present and absent in the work life and workplace? The dilemma of when employees work at the same time or work time shifted independently of synchro interactions and collaboration. The dilemma adds yet another dimension to the complexity of the hybrid workplace model. The dilemmas of the hybrid workplace can be approximately divided into the approach to remote working when working digitally and office work when primarily working analogue. The division is purely illustrative but underscores the anticipated need for possessing an understanding of digital and analogue dexterity when implementing the hybrid office workplace model.

19.3 Unfolding the Hybrid Office Workplace Model

There are numerous paths to achieve a successful hybrid workplace, but all organisations contemplate, define, and develop their unique hybrid workplace. Customised workplace models are becoming the new standard. Initially, existing organisations and workplaces have different starting points, with varying digital and analogue infrastructures, employee compositions and behaviours, preferences, management styles, and organisational processes. It is evident that leadership plays a crucial role, and their perspectives on how a hybrid workplace should be defined and implemented vary greatly.

This spectrum ranges from leaders, who mandates that employees be physically present in the office for at least 40 h a week, to leadership teams that have eliminated all office leases, now operating fully remotely (Inc 2022).

Are organisations choosing the easy, difficult, hard, or optimal strategic path to a future-ready workplace model? How can organisations create the optimal, timely, and future-proof workplace? The development of an adapted or new hybrid workplace model can be essentially addressed using three strategic approaches, but the optimal solution arises when all approaches are activated in a coordinated and balanced interplay.

The approaches to the development of the hybrid workplace model encompass key components: management, employees, and the analogue and digital infrastructure. (In the figure, the three main strategic approaches for developing a hybrid workplace for knowledge workers are briefly presented.) If the development of the future workplace model is not considered significant and therefore not prioritised, initiatives will naturally take a tactical and more operational approach to management efforts. On the other hand, a prioritised approach will require a strategic perspective on how resources are prioritised and deployed to achieve the desired benefits. In essence, it can be boiled down to the question of how important a future-proof workplace model is deemed to be by the management.

If the ongoing transformation from the less dynamic and outdated workplace model to the more future-ready hybrid model is not undertaken, there is a significant likelihood that different organisational functions and departments will prioritise the development of the hybrid workplace in different ways. Some functions may solely adopt a limited operational and tactical approach (hence a management approach), while others may take a strategic approach (hence a leadership approach). The lack of alignment can potentially pose significant limitations and challenges to the development of a successful future hybrid workplace model, apart from the obvious misuse of resources. Over time, it may lead to an imbalance in the development of the workplace model, as some functions initiate significant initiatives that subsequently need to align retrospectively with other functions, responsibilities, and departments sharing overlapping responsibility for the workplace. Once again, it falls upon top leadership to ensure alignment and a balanced approach to development, whether it is strategic, tactical, or operational.

Based on our (CIFS) anecdotal observations, we have noticed that FM and real estate departments often prioritise developing the workplace model by adapting the analogue workspace, driven by a sense of urgency as office footfall fluctuates and decreases. In contrast, the IT department focuses on pushing the boundaries of digital workplace development, leveraging emerging opportunities to enhance digitisation. Meanwhile, HR is in a transitional phase, juggling numerous tasks and challenges that require prioritisation. We therefore often observe that HR are reluctant to take the strategic lead in the transformation towards a more future-proof hybrid office workplace model. Top management, keen to maintain productivity, may lean towards simplifying the future hybrid workplace model, favouring short-term, straightforward solutions to reduce complexity and uncertainty. However, it's crucial to recognise that not aligning these efforts and delaying decisions can lead to internal friction, loss of momentum, and potential competitive disadvantages. Therefore, careful coordination among all departments is essential to create a successful and future-proof hybrid office workplace model.

19.4 Three Approaches: Bottom-Up, Top-Down, and the Digital and Analogue Infrastructure

There are essentially three approaches to developing and implementing the hybrid workplace model (Fig. 19.2). The "bottom-up" approach to developing the hybrid workplace model can begin with employees and requires a long and sustained effort. It is a challenging effort as focus and prioritisation need to be maintained over time. However, this approach ensures that the model is anchored and has a solid foundation for continuous development. In the "bottom-up" approach, employees are involved right from the start in considering workplace changes, and their engagement is sustained over time. In an ideal scenario, employees become culture carriers and co-developers of the new way of working and organising the workplace. They become co-owners of the workplace, actively contributing to its evolution and success.

The "top-down" approach to developing the hybrid workplace model involves leadership taking charge and prioritising the development of a unified approach to the changed workplace. This process can be challenging as there are likely to be varying and strong opinions, priorities, and goals within the leadership regarding the workplace model. These perspectives filter down through the organisation and impact middle management, who must interpret and implement them. Positions within the leadership can range from believing the current workplace model is optimal to advocating for evolutionary changes with increased flexibility, such as remote work, to a revolutionary approach where the entire workplace model is reimagined and redesigned.

The primary objective should always be to ensure greater and more efficient value creation for the organisation, which may sometimes be challenged by individual preferences and positions. However, a shared approach by the management and leadership is essential for success. Success is built on a comprehensive overall concept and a plan for the implementation of the hybrid workplace model.

By transforming the analogue or digital infrastructure, it is possible to create new employee behaviours and cultivate a changed work culture. Efforts such as

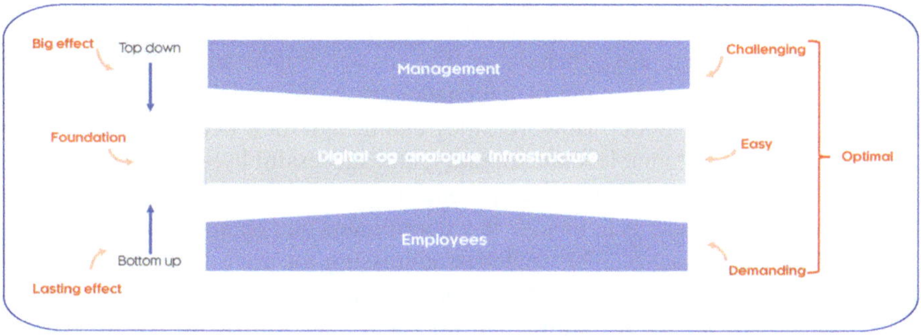

Fig. 19.2 Opting for the easy, demanding, challenging, or optimal solution for the development of the future-proof hybrid office workplace model

implementing new furniture, redesigning layouts, constructing new office buildings, upgrading screens, and implementing new software can all support and develop a transformed workplace model. This approach seems relatively straightforward as it can be achieved through investments. Therefore, the creation of new digital and analogue infrastructure is often seen as a solution to bring about changes in the workplace. Despite describing the digital and hybrid infrastructure as relatively easy to adapt to a hybrid work reality, many organisations are trapped in existing structures and often have a long way to go to be even up-to-date in a fast-evolving market. However, this solution often falls short because changes in the analogue or digital infrastructure are either not embraced or do not significantly impact employees' work lives. How often have you, for example, been provided with access to new digital tools but not incorporated them into your daily routine? How often have new designs or meeting rooms remained unused despite their impressive and costly nature?

Nevertheless, new analogue and digital infrastructure presents an opportunity and the very foundation to create lasting changes. This was evident during the forced remote work period, which accelerated the digitisation of the workplace. As previously mentioned, this sudden shift to remote work highlighted the disparity between behaviour and the potential of digitalisation (Amara's law). When observing the condition of analogue workplaces, a smaller number is up to date compared to the recent significant shifts that have occurred in development. Even fewer are intended and designed for the future development of the hybrid model, reflecting the physical workplace's alignment with the digital workplace in terms of being contemporary. Even relatively newly constructed and designed workplaces pre-pandemic will, for the most part, need to be thought and designed differently today, post-pandemic. In 1943, Sir Winston Churchill famously said, "We shape our buildings; thereafter they shape us." This statement suggests that people adapt their behaviour to the physical spaces they inhabit. From a general perspective, this is a belief held by a significant portion of organisations, as the majority of workplace resources are currently allocated to the analogue workplace. But the big question is whether this will still be the case in the future with changing work practices, behaviours, and increasing digitalisation. What happens to workplace behaviour when employees work remotely? Analogue workplace actors such as interior designers and architects presently argue that the analogue office becomes even more important as a catalyst for employee behaviour. The answer: organisations cannot build or experience-design their way out of the challenges in the transition towards a successful hybrid office model. However, they can design their decision-making processes to create a sustainable, contemporary, and successful hybrid office model.

The objectively optimal strategic approach to creating a timely and future-proof hybrid workplace model is to engage in a coordinated and balanced interplay of all the mentioned approaches. This includes addressing the easy, difficult, and challenging aspects of the office workplace transformation. It requires having a leadership team with a shared vision, concept, and plan, involving employees as co-developers and co-owners, and making contemporary investments in both digital and analogue infrastructure. It is important to note that the evolution of the hybrid

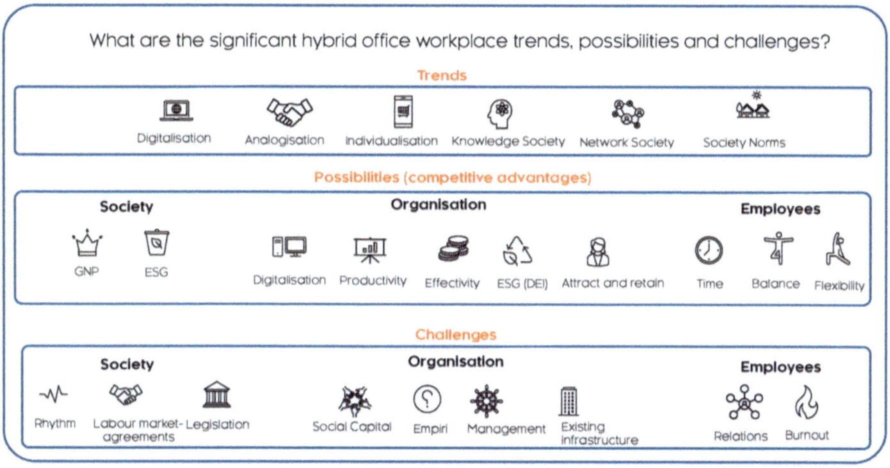

Fig. 19.3 Hybrid office trends, possibilities, and challenges

workplace model is highly dynamic, and the development will continue at a pace not previously experienced. Therefore, the strategic approaches to development and implementation must adapt to this fundamental condition.

19.5 Summarising the Trends, Possibilities, and Challenges of the Future Hybrid Workplace

A brief overview of the expected overarching development over time, as described by the defining megatrends, potential objectives, and challenges, is illustrated in Fig. 19.3. At its core, this represents the tension field that office workplaces must embrace and evolve from.

References

(Anicich and Lindsley 2014) HBR Nov-data Dec 2024 Reimagining Work as a Product https://hbr.org/2024/11/reimagining-work-as-a-product?ab=HP-topics-text-6

(Fortune 2023) Google ramps up return-to-office push by using in-person attendance as part of employee performance reviews https://fortune.com/2023/06/08/google-remote-work-office-attendance-performance-review/

(Inc 2021) This was Steve Jobs most controversial legacy it was also his most brilliant https://www.inc.com/jason-aten/this-was-steve-jobs-most-controversial-legacy-it-was-also-his-most-brilliant.html

(Inc 2022) Elon Musk's Leaked Message Tells Employees to Return to the Office, or Else. https://www.inc.com/nick-hobson/elon-musks-leaked-message-tells-employees-to-return-to-office-or-else-harvard-research-would-urge-caution.html

Specific Recommendations for Futureproofing the Hybrid Office Workplace

20

Abstract

To futureproof your workplace and effectively design a hybrid model, it's essential to adopt a proactive approach that anticipates the evolving nature of work. Through extensive consultations with workplace stakeholders, we have identified ten key principles for the successful design and implementation of a hybrid workplace model. These principles emphasise the need for management to take leadership, ensure top-level buy-in, and develop a cross-functional approach to managing the hybrid environment. The hybrid workplace is dynamic, not static, and requires continuous exploration, measurement, and adjustment to optimise value creation.

Key recommendations include fostering a unique culture aligned with organisational values, practising change management from the outset, and integrating advanced technological solutions. Additionally, HR, IT, and FM functions must focus on their roles in managing a distributed workforce, enhancing digital infrastructure, and creating adaptable, sustainable workplaces. By following these guidelines, organisations can build a resilient and future-ready hybrid workplace that meets the needs of both the organisation and its employees.

20.1 The Grand Office Experiment: Reactive or Proactive?

You are either voluntarily or involuntarily participating in the grand office experiment, regardless of your strategic approach. You can choose to do so proactively, seeking future advantages, or reactively, by maintaining your current perceived competitive edge.

Everything decays and re-emerges in new forms—including the office workplace. The only question is the speed at which these changes occur, and in recent years, the winds of development and change have been blowing strong. The crux of the matter is how quickly your organisation assesses and anticipates the future pace

C. Sneppen, *The Future (R)Evolution of the Office Workspace*, Future of Business and Finance, https://doi.org/10.1007/978-3-031-85229-9_20

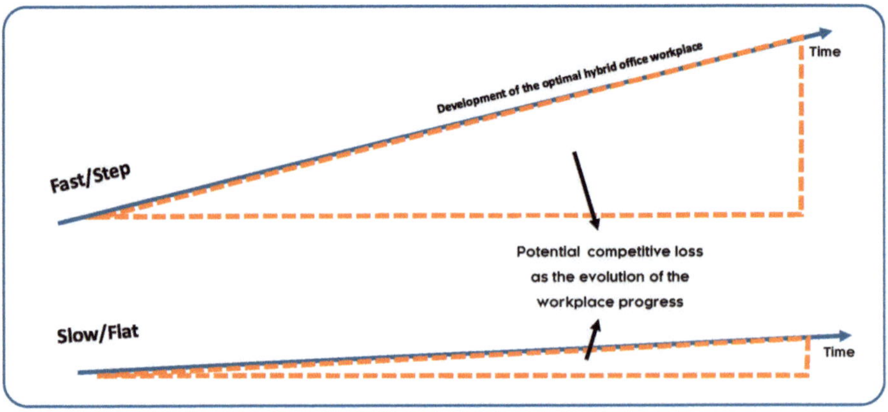

Fig. 20.1 The future pace of development of the office workplace model?

of development of the office workplace model. It's not about what you believe, wish for, or hope, but rather about your objective evaluation.

If the development is expected to be slow, a reactive approach is optimal, and the workplace model only needs to be operationally flexible enough to adapt gradually (Fig. 20.1). However, if greater development is expected, the workplace model should be proactive and agile, constantly striving to unlock critical competitive advantages (this is in line with the thoughts presented in Chap. 2, which covers foresight, and the methods applied to future thinking).

A significant proportion of organisations are reactive, which suggests that they believe the evolution of the office workplace model will be slow-moving, and thus, they adopt an incremental and reactive approach to model adaptation. In other words, they do not anticipate significant or accelerating changes to impact the office workplace through increased digitalisation, regulatory frameworks, or revolutionary shifts in employee and management preferences and behaviours.

The key question is whether slow development will prove to be accurate, or whether organisations with a reactive office workplace model will experience a loss of competitiveness. My assessment of the office workplace model is that it will evolve at a slower pace than I expect but much faster than most would hope for.

***Workspace Case:* Copenhagen Properties, the Finance Administration, City of Copenhagen**

From Cost-Effective to Sustainable Workplaces

The City of Copenhagen is Denmark's largest employer. Therefore, Copenhagen Properties, which manages the municipality's physical workplaces, has developed a department dedicated to strategically designing new workplaces.

Development Over the Past Five Years:

Our department started out with a simpler model in developing and implementing new office layouts. The main goal was to reduce rental and other utility costs in a more effective use of the square footage of the municipality's administrative workplaces. While additionally creating more optimised workplaces focusing on each department's specific needs through the key principles of Activity-Based Workplaces (ABW).

Office environment. Image credits: **Copenhagen Properties, The Finance Administration, City of Copenhagen**

After the COVID-19 remote work arrangements, the need for a more hybrid and flexible work life grew. This meant that more top managers were open towards introducing shared workspaces, and attention was drawn to the physical workplace's role in fostering cohesion.

We have also had an eye on the sustainable effects of our projects. By reducing the square footage of the workplaces, we also reduced the use of electricity and heating, which equalled less emission of CO_2*. We saw a growing opportunity in reusing existing furniture and interior in our projects. This led to a project, where our department established a warehouse and web-shop with used furniture for not only supplying the projects in our department with furniture but also the entire municipality.*

Office inventory warehouse. Image credits: **Copenhagen Properties, The Finance Administration, City of Copenhagen**

Expected Future Development:

An increased focus in our projects has been on satisfying the employees' needs and well-being when designing new workspaces. Currently we are also experiencing a growing need for employees to have a stronger connection to the workplace. We foresee that the future development in office workplaces will increasingly focus on both the employees and the organisation's goals. This means that we will have a job in ensuring that all organisational leaders understand and actively use office design as a management tool, for instance, what different generations in the workforce thrive with in a physical workspace.

Vision:

If The City of Copenhagen should both be and be perceived as a sustainable workplace, then we as a department should strive towards creating more financially, environmentally, *and employee sustainable workplaces.*

Goals:

Our goal is, that the entire organisation recognises, that office design and behaviour in the office spaces are strategic management tools to attract and retain qualified workforce.

We will also continue to save costs in optimising the workspaces for the municipality in both financial and environmental matters. Making new office spaces both cost-effective and environmental and employee sustainable.

Challenge:

As a public organisation, it can be a balancing act to use necessary resources to create attractive workplaces spending taxpayers' *money on what may be perceived as unnecessary by the citizens. At the same time, well-designed workplaces are a key component in attracting and retaining the right employee profiles.*

Avoid:

- *Avoid designing new office workplaces solely as a cost-saving exercise.*
- *Avoid that mid-level managers can make additional furniture purchases during or after the projects are implemented, as this obstructs the function and effectiveness of the design and the behaviour of the employees.*
- Avoid expecting that the design of the new workplace will fit all future changes and organisational needs. Instead, see it as a continuous development process.

Recommendations:

- *Ensure that the organisation's top management take an active part in the change and leads by example,* e.g., *by articulating the goals and benefits of the newly designed workplace.*
- *Ensure that the entire leadership team is involved early and throughout the process so that the purpose, new culture, and strategic opportunities are implemented.*
- *Ensure a good process with both a solid data foundation and active involvement of employees to ensure good, future office workplaces.*

20.2 The Ideal Post-Pandemic Office Is Never Ever Perfect

Do you honestly believe, or simply wish to believe, that the office and workplace of knowledge workers have settled into a new, semi-static balance and modus operandi post-pandemic? My brief response as a futurist is that we are, in a historical perspective, only at the very beginning of the revolution in the way knowledge work and collaboration are conducted as digitalisation progresses rapidly.

Assuming that I am partly right, why are so many organisations acting as if the development of the post-pandemic office workplace model is at most semi-static? An answer would be that habitual knowledge and behaviour dominate most organisation's response to the profound changes currently taking place in the office workplace. In other words, first-order thinking applied to an unknown and never experienced situation. If there is one thing we should have learned about the workplace from the pandemic, it is that we failed to adapt the office to the digital possibilities in the pre-pandemic era, thereby missing out on securing competitive advantages.

The organisation, its environment, management, employees, and particularly digitalisation are in constant flux—and always have been. But knowledge work now increasingly transcends time, place, and space due to technological and digital advancements, necessitating a radical rethinking and redesigning of the physical office as employee behaviour also evolve correspondingly. The office workspace has shifted from static to more dynamic and hybrid. This means that the office as a physical installation is now, and in the future, more flexible and continuously evolving. The office is thus only temporarily optimal and perfect, as ongoing development necessitates continual changes and adaptations of the office workspace. In the past, the post-industrial office workspace and workplace model were predominately static and somewhat resistant to external developments. This became evident during the pandemic and the subsequent return to the office, revealing that the pre-pandemic office had been too immune to development. Over time a significant competitive gap had emerged between the optimal and the actual office workplace model. Retrospectively, the pandemic helped reduce this competitive gap. (Competitive gap arising from the loss of advantages in productivity, efficiency, ESG (including DEI), digitalisation, and the attraction and retention of talent as the optimal hybrid workplace model evolves.)

A vast majority of organisations still regard the evolution of the workplace model as a linear and relatively flat process, attributing current changes solely to the quantum shift induced by the pandemic and believing that stability has either returned or is on the verge of returning in the post-pandemic era (Fig. 20.2). The management

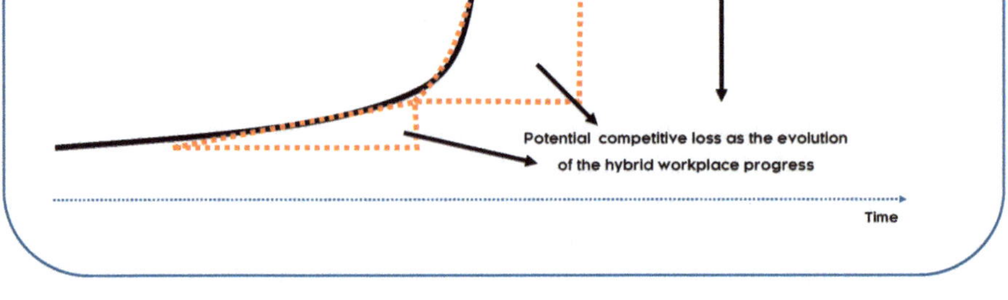

Fig. 20.2 Potential competitive loss as the office workplace evolve—pandemic perspective

approach is somewhat simplistic: "Let's stabilise the turmoil around the office and workplace model and focus on the real work"; "Look at what a great office we post-pandemic have redesigned – now we only have to ensure great employee experiences to stay ahead in the work life game"; or "Let's get the employees back to the office and return to the successful pre-pandemic approach to the office workplace."

An examination of the underlying factors and trends from a futurist's perspective reveals that the anticipated future development of the office workspace model contradicts this static or semi-static approach. It highlights that the future evolution will be dynamic and progressively accelerating, rather than flat or static. In other words, the optimal office workplace model will continue to change at a significantly faster pace than historically experienced (though not as radically/accelerated as during the pandemic 2020–2022). Consequently, the real office work for knowledge workers will be substantially defined by and based on the dynamic hybrid office workplace (Fig. 20.3). Organisations consequently face the challenge of embracing the ongoing development of the office workplace model. Should they opt for continuous adjustments or periodic, more significant changes? My recommendation is continuous adjustments, reflecting that the underlying factors forming the foundation for knowledge work are in constant rapid development, thus the optimal office workspace should reflect this. The productivity and competitiveness loss from delayed periodic major adjustments is simply too great, as the competitive gap between the optimal and realised workplace model becomes too large.

This means that what is most optimal now is increasingly only almost perfect, as continuous micro-adjustments should be made to support the workplace's development. Static, more permanent optimal solutions must give way to forward-looking flexibility. If the ultimate optimal in the moment comes at the expense of flexibility, organisations must increasingly and primarily ensure flexibility and future development.

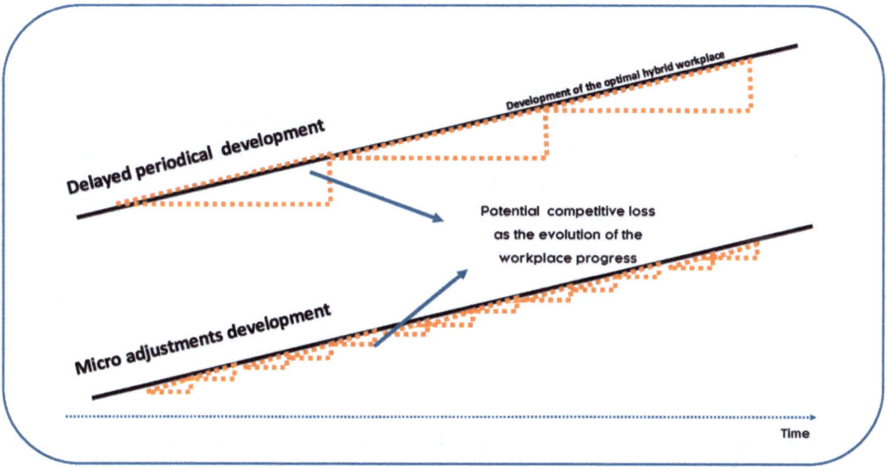

Fig. 20.3 Potential competitive loss as the workplace evolve—post-pandemic

The office is now functioning like a piece of software in continuous development, always in a beta version. It's an office where solutions are implemented but subject to correction and improvement in increasingly shorter intervals. This poses, as previously stated, a challenge for organisations to be ambidextrous, capable of developing and leveraging the office workplace simultaneously. It requires constant optimisation while allowing room for experimentation. The sustainable successful future hybrid workplace raises practical questions for management, such as: How can we establish a process that ensures continuous development? How should we allocate responsibility and resources to achieve this?

The future flexible and evolving office and workspace need room in all dimensions to create change. Practically, this can be achieved by either developing and experimenting within existing office areas or by over-dimensioning the office with rotation to new areas, functioning as experimental and development zones. If an organisation prioritises space optimisation to reduce costs too stringently, it will impact future development, as experimental development requires surplus manoeuvring room both physically and mentally. Flexibility must be prioritised higher than the immediate optimal and most efficient at any given time.

The fact that the workplace, at best, will only ever be temporarily perfect means that all workplace initiatives and efforts are increasingly likely to fail faster over time. This could be because they did not have the desired effect when implemented, or because they will at an increasing speed be overtaken by internal and/or external developments. In other words, it is crucial to fail quickly and continuously adapt the workplace to ensure the organisation's competitiveness. The one thing we all learned about the office workplace during the pandemic was that the competitiveness gap between the optimal and realised office workplace model must never be significant.

20.3 How to Do Hybrid Right

Lynda Gratton (Professor, London Business School) in her article recommends focusing on individual human concerns, not just institutional ones (Gratton 2021). As we emerge from the pandemic, many companies have firmly set their sights on flexible working arrangements that can significantly boost productivity and employee satisfaction. Making that happen will require that managers consider the challenge from four distinct perspectives: (1) jobs and tasks, (2) employee preferences, (3) projects and workflows, and (4) inclusion and fairness. As Rasmus Brandt Lassen, Director of the Danish Building and Property Agency, stated during an interview for this book: "Good leadership has not changed with the advent of hybrid work; it has merely exposed poor leadership in a digital reality with a more distributed workforce."

1. JOBS AND TASKS: When thinking about jobs and tasks, start by understanding the critical drivers of productivity—energy, focus, coordination, and coopera-

tion—for each. Next, consider how those drivers will be affected by changes in working arrangements along the axes of time and place.
2. EMPLOYEE PREFERENCES: Our capacity to operate at peak productivity and performance varies dramatically according to our personal preferences. So in designing hybrid work, consider the preferences of your employees—and enable others to understand and accommodate those preferences.
3. PROJECTS AND WORKFLOWS: To make hybrid a success, you have to consider how work gets done. A manager must not only consider their needs and preferences but also coordinate the work they do with that of the others on their team—and with other functions and consumers of their work. That kind of coordination was relatively straightforward when team members all worked in the same place at the same time. But in the era of hybrid work, it has grown significantly more complex. I've observed executives tackling this in two ways. One is to significantly boost the use of technology to coordinate activities as employees move to more-flexible work arrangements. Other companies are using this moment as an opportunity to reimagine workflows. New hybrid arrangements should never replicate existing bad practices.
4. INCLUSION AND FAIRNESS: As you develop new hybrid practices and processes, pay particular attention to questions of inclusion and fairness. This is vitally important. Research tells us that feelings of unfairness in the workplace can hurt productivity, increase burnout, reduce collaboration, and decrease retention. In the past, when companies began experimenting with flexible approaches to work, they typically allowed individual managers to drive the process on an ad hoc basis. As a result, different departments and teams were afforded varying degrees of flexibility and freedom, which inevitably gave rise to accusations of unfairness. And many employees, of course, had time- and place-dependent jobs that made hybrid arrangements either impossible or far from optimal. They often felt treated unfairly.

Workspace Case: Grundfos

Grundfos is the largest pump manufacturer in the world, based in Denmark, with more than 19,000 employees globally. At Grundfos, we have adopted a hybrid office workplace model—a flexible work arrangement that combines the advantages of working both on-site and remotely. This model offers office employees the opportunity to choose where and how they work most productively, adapting the choice of work location as a tool. As a result, teams, employees, and leaders must select the most appropriate approach based on the tasks they need to complete.

We believe in bringing people together and nurturing a sense of community by utilising both physical and digital spaces. Collaboration in the office is crucial for problem-solving, brainstorming, fostering innovation, and building team camaraderie. We encourage team members to gather whenever possible for activities, meetings, and social interactions. Additionally, we acknowledge the importance of choosing workspaces that align with the nature of each task, whether it's customer meetings, focused work, virtual collaboration, or in-person workshops.

Grundfos office environment. Image credits: HOLMRIS B8

Implementation Journey:

We are currently on a journey to implement activity-based working (ABW) as our standard across all office spaces, with a strong emphasis on creating modern, flexible, and inspiring work environments that support our ambition to make Grundfos a world-class place to work, learn, and grow. Our journey began in 2018 with the first steps towards our hybrid workplace model by launching the initial concept of the "Grundfos Future Office." This was our first step in implementing activity-based working within Grundfos. At that time, all employees were physically present in the office 5 days a week, with all office spaces following a traditional interior design setup—fixed seating, private offices for managers, and bookable meeting rooms. The "Grundfos Future Office" was initially implemented only as a pilot in selected locations in Bjerringbro (hometown of the company placed in rural Denmark).

In 2020, during the COVID-19 pandemic, Grundfos employees experienced remote working for the first time. The pandemic proved to be a game-changer in our hybrid work journey, opening up possibilities beyond the traditional office setup. By the end of 2022, Grundfos' group management launched a global hybrid work policy for the first time, and in this context, the group facility received the mandate to implement activity-based working across all Grundfos offices, whether establishing new offices or remodelling existing ones. In 2023, we developed the first version of our three global standards, outlining how to work with Grundfos workspaces, interior design, and building design to ensure a unified company approach in line with Grundfos' brand and values.

Future Outlook:

We anticipate a rapid pace of development in workplace models and office space design. We believe that the hybrid workplace model will continue to be "the standard" in many companies, offering flexibility while providing clearer structures for when physical presence in the office is expected. This expectation is related not only to specific tasks but also to supporting social interaction, learning, development, and mental well-being.

We expect that employees will continue to have high expectations for physical office spaces, and these offices will need to cater to a wider range of needs, including considerations for different disabilities, as we anticipate an increasing number of employees with diverse needs. To remain an attractive workplace, it will not only be the physical surroundings that matter but also the benefits provided, such as healthy food, quality coffee, and a vibrant, social atmosphere.

Convenience will continue to be key. It should be easy to commute to the office, ideally by bike or public transport. We anticipate that our workplace model and physical workspaces at Grundfos will remain in constant development. Although we expect to maintain a hybrid workplace model, with new generations entering the workforce and changing demands, we must be agile and adapt our workspaces accordingly. Our offices must always be equipped with up-to-date digital solutions and be capable of accommodating more diverse needs and disabilities than they do today. Our aim is to continuously develop our workspaces to support collaboration, knowledge sharing, and social interaction, as these are some of the most significant reasons for being physically present in the office.

The concept of "value for time" will continue to be an important factor, making it crucial for us to continuously develop our physical workspaces to make them attractive and worth commuting to, especially considering that some of our offices, including our headquarters, are located outside major cities. Our focus will remain on establishing modern, flexible, sustainable, and inspiring workspaces to attract and retain talent at Grundfos.

Flexibility and Adaptability:

We are on a journey where we plan to lease office locations on short-term contracts rather than owning many of our offices. This approach allows us to respond proactively to changing needs and ensures that our spaces always fit our current situation. It also makes it more convenient for employees to come to the office to collaborate with colleagues, as these offices will be located closer to larger cities and public transport links. We will increasingly utilise serviced offices in locations where it makes sense to quickly establish an office for short-term collaboration.

Our hybrid workplace model aims to continue attracting and retaining talented employees at Grundfos, ensuring that distance from the office is not a barrier to working with the company. This approach offers a positive advantage in talent acquisition, both for the company and potential employees. We see our hybrid workplace model as a positive contributor to supporting the work-life balance for our employees, offering a high degree of flexibility in planning work activities, as some tasks can be completed remotely.

By working in an activity-based manner within our physical workspaces, we also support our sustainability ambitions by further reducing our organisational CO_2e footprint at Grundfos, designing workspaces that make smarter and more efficient use of available square metres.

Grundfos office environment. Image credits: HOLMRIS B8

Challenges:

One of the challenges in securing our future workplace model and maintaining an attractive workplace is the need to be as agile and responsive as required when facing new trends and demands, given that we are a large organisation with many different locations. As an old family-owned company with core values and a strong DNA, a challenge lies in ensuring employee loyalty and attachment to Grundfos, even with many employees working remotely, and maintaining the values and DNA at the forefront.

In general, collaboration, skill-building, and well-being can be challenged if we do not manage to create optimal, attractive, and inspiring offices that cater to our employees' diverse needs and expectations. We are also focusing on the change management process and skill development as we transition from a traditional office setup to an activity-based office, recognising the difficulty employees may face in adjusting to this new way of working.

Recommendations:

1. *When adopting a hybrid workplace model, it's important to consider how to safeguard the mental well-being of employees. Create an inclusive hybrid workplace where everyone feels a sense of belonging and avoids feeling emotionally distant from colleagues.*

2. *Focus on leadership and change management by providing training sessions that support leaders in managing remote teams and role-modelling the activity-based way of working.*
3. *Establish a clear structure or agreement within the company or departmental teams that aligns with specific needs, outlining the days when physical presence in the office is expected, which tasks and meetings can be done remotely, and which require in-person attendance.*
4. *Involve employees in the development of these agreements to foster engagement, motivation, and ownership, making the hybrid work model a success. The key is to understand the organisation and its various functions rather than assuming a "one-size-fits-all" approach.*
5. *Continuously collect data and monitor if adjustments are needed concerning space or employee needs.*
6. *Avoid viewing the vision of the workplace model as static. Treat it as a dynamic approach, with room for improvement and adjustment. This flexibility will support the ambition to remain an attractive company and ensure the well-being of employees.*

20.4 Transition from Workplace Operations to a Development Organisation

In continuation of the above, one of the significant shifts in the management of the office workplace model, from a pre-pandemic to a future-oriented approach, is the transition from a project and operational focus to one centred on continuous development. As the four central components of the office workplace continue to evolve and, importantly, shift the balance of power, workplace organisation must reflect and adapt to this dynamic landscape. The structure and design of the workplace should be responsive, aligning with these ongoing changes to support a balanced and effective work environment. Are organisations still predominantly structured in the traditional way, with internal silos between IT, HR, Real Estate, and Facilities Management? Does your organisation have a well-balanced, intentional, and aligned strategic approach to developing and implementing the hybrid workplace model?

The hybrid office workplace is becoming increasingly adaptable and flexible, freed from the constraints of time, location, and physical space in a digitised reality. The internal organisation of the workplace should mirror this shift, recognising that the way of operating is no longer defined by static projects and operations, but by ongoing development to support overarching objectives in an ever-changing environment.

The physical workplace of the future will be designed around flexible spaces with inherent adaptability, where the office continuously evolves to become smarter in a digitised world. In other words, it becomes a mouldable and flexible workspace. The concept of "square meter plasticity" refers to intelligent spaces that adapt seamlessly to the dynamic routines of daily work. The traditional office, standing as a symbol of organisational success, is gradually giving way to office plasticity—a workspace that functions in symbiosis with its users and surroundings, constantly adapting to meet changing needs.

Workplace plasticity encompasses various mechanisms by which the office can transform. There are two primary forms: structural plasticity, which refers to changes in the physical layout and connectivity of the office, and functional plasticity, which describes the office's ability to reorganise its functions in response to environmental shifts. The hybrid office of the future must continuously balance two critical needs: moments of efficient utilisation—exploitation—to ensure productivity and effectiveness, and, on the other hand, an ongoing process of exploration to seek new ways of developing the workplace to complement management, employees, and advancements in digital technology.

Consequently, and in my opinion, a key component in the current evolution of the hybrid workplace is an internally reorganised and prioritised dynamic workplace organisation, decision-making processes, and responsibilities (Fig. 20.4). These elements are fundamental to successfully transforming into a long-term successful dynamic hybrid workplace. To achieve a new outcome, you must change the way you've always done things. This begins, among other things, with the internal organisation and responsibilities, as the workplace model shifts from an operational focus to a tactical and strategic role in fulfilling the overall organisational objectives.

Why is reorganising the internal workplace structure, decision-making processes, and responsibilities crucial to a successful hybrid workplace model? The most obvious answer is that, with the transformation and liberation of work time, place, and space, workplace models and solutions have become potentially important, active, and dynamic tools for organisations. The big question is whether leadership has recognised this and seized the opportunity to gain competitive advantages by not attempting to extend the previous model, but by being open and able to view this shift as a fundamental change in how knowledge work is structured and systematised. The parallel to the history of the IT function within organisations is

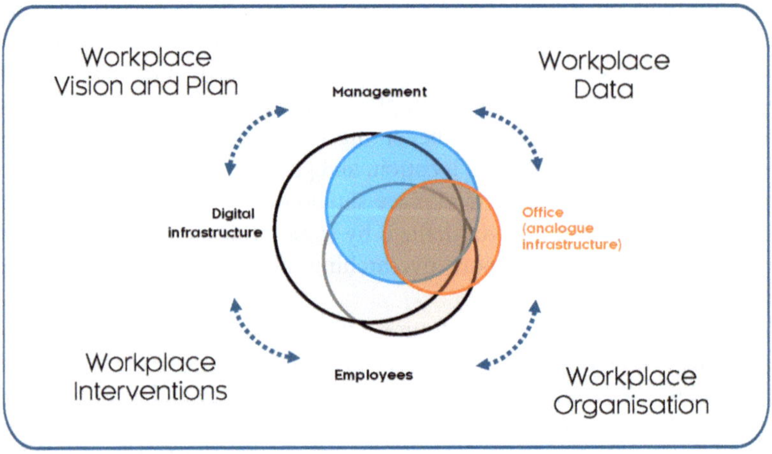

Fig. 20.4 From operation of an office workplace to a business development organisation

straightforward: initially, IT was very operational and focused on avoiding mistakes and minimising downtime. Over time, it has transformed into a vital strategic function crucial to the organisation's success or failure. In my opinion, the workplace model deserves an equally prominent position within the organisation as society progresses towards a digitised, networked, and knowledge-based foundation.

20.5 Office Workplace Function-Related Recommendations for HR, IT, and FM

Is your workplace time equivalent? Do you want to futureproof it? Are you seeking key recommendations for the development and design of a hybrid and more futureproof workplace model?

Based on numerous workshops and dialogues with workplace stakeholders, I am taking the risk of formulating nine key guiding principles and recommendations for the successful design and implementation of a hybrid workplace model. The recommendations may seem fundamental and "boring obvious," but management is recommended to prioritise and take the fundamental changes in the workplace model seriously and prioritise accordingly. We are currently only considering the initial changes initiated by the pandemic, and the changes that will occur in the coming decade are anticipated to radically transform the workplace for knowledge workers. Management can unlock the potential by taking the leadership and designing the optimal mix of infrastructure, employee behaviour, and how the hybrid workforce is led (e.g. Coffey and Wolf 2018).

Common to all workplace function-related actors is the understanding that the development of the hybrid workplace model requires the following:

1. **Anticipate and prepare for a future workplace distinct from the present; avoid first-order thinking. Be time, place, and space agnostic.** Embrace a forward-thinking mindset that assumes the future workplace will look different from today's, focusing on flexibility regarding time, location, and space, rather than on fixed assumptions.
2. **Secure top management buy-in and commitment to the hybrid workplace vision and model. Lead the development with a strategic vision, rather than limiting it to operational management.** Engage top management in supporting and driving the hybrid workplace model with a clear vision, positioning it as a strategic initiative rather than a purely operational one.
3. **Recognise and act on the understanding that the hybrid workplace is dynamic, not static, and will continue to evolve and change.** Approach the hybrid workplace as an evolving entity, remaining adaptable and ready to refine practices as needs and technologies shift. It is important to communicate and adopt a position that the development and evolution of the hybrid office model will be experimental. This is partly due to the inevitable mistakes that will occur along the way, but primarily because of the broader developments within society. Ongoing adjustments and modifications will be essential.

4. **Be proactive not reactive. A waiting approach is unadvisable, as the organisation will invariably fall behind in the ongoing development of the office workplace model. Better to act now than to wait for a "golden" solution.** Take immediate steps towards development rather than delaying for a perfect solution, ensuring that the organisation remains relevant and competitive.
5. **Be authentic and consistent with the organisation's culture values and vision at all tangible and intangible workplace touchpoints.** Align every aspect of the hybrid workplace with the organisation's unique identity, reinforcing its culture and values across all employee interactions and spaces.
6. **Establish a permanent, cross-functional team for hybrid workplace management with a defined mandate and resources.** Create a dedicated team from different functions to oversee hybrid workplace responsibilities, equipped with the authority and resources to make impactful decisions.
7. **Develop objectives, policies, and a plan for the continuous evolution of the hybrid workplace, bridging the present with the anticipated future model.** Formulate clear goals and a roadmap to guide the hybrid workplace's ongoing transformation, balancing current needs with future aspirations.
8. **Implement change management from the initial stages and maintain it continuously throughout the development and implementation of the hybrid workplace, focusing on middle management in particular.** Integrate change management practices from the outset, ensuring sustained support, particularly from middle management, to facilitate smooth transitions.
9. **Collect and analyse forward-looking, actionable data centred on current employee behaviours and preferences.** Prioritise the collection of actionable data reflecting employee habits and preferences to shape an informed, future-ready hybrid workplace (e.g. Rockart 1979).
10. **Continuously evaluate, measure, and adjust the hybrid workplace model to maximise value creation, generating employee engagement and fostering communication as a result.** Regularly and continuously assess and refine the hybrid model to enhance its effectiveness, which in turn supports employee engagement and strengthens organisational communication (in line with the thoughts presented e.g. Brown 2009).

Examining the fundamental organisational functions that define the office workplace, I can summarise the following recommendations for HR, IT, and FM to support the development and establishment of a future-ready and resilient workplace model. These recommendations, while neither categorised, prioritised, nor exhaustive, are intended to provoke thoughtful reflection on the potential implications of the evolving office workplace for the key organisational functions shaping the hybrid model. Each recommendation will, to varying degrees, have a critical impact on the organisation's future operations and overall success. However, they must be carefully balanced against existing responsibilities and tasks, requiring evaluation in relation to the scope and depth of the organisation's implementation of the hybrid workplace model.

HR (Human Resource or PO—People and Organisation)

1. **Assume full responsibility and ownership of the hybrid office workplace model, or at the very least, take a leading role, as it is the human elements—employees and management—that form the core of the modern hybrid workplace model, rather than the digital or analogue infrastructure.** Prioritise people as the central element of the hybrid workplace model, taking full responsibility for its development and ensuring it caters to human, not just infrastructural, needs.
2. **Develop management and organisational capabilities to effectively lead a distributed workforce across time, place, and space.** Enhance leadership and organisational skills to manage teams effectively in a hybrid setting, addressing the unique challenges of coordinating employees who work in different locations and time zones. Offer targeted training to improve digital proficiency and remote work skills among employees and managers, building competence in both digital and traditional working methods. Shift to performance metrics based on deliverables and results, rather than tracking physical presence or time, to support a productivity-focused culture.
3. **Establish flexible policies and procedures that accommodate diverse work arrangements.** Introduce adaptable policies that support various work styles, ensuring inclusivity and accessibility for both remote and in-office employees.
4. **Strengthen awareness of the organisation's purpose and mission.** Reinforce the organisation's core purpose and mission, ensuring that employees remain aligned and motivated, even in a hybrid environment.
5. **Cultivate a strong culture of trust, psychological safety, collaboration, and inclusion to support both remote and in-office employees.** Build an organisational culture that fosters trust and inclusivity, encouraging collaboration and psychological safety for all employees, regardless of their work location. Particularly, implement intentional initiatives by allocating time and resources to accelerate the formation of trust both onsite and, especially, offsite.
6. **Prioritise social connections—both strong and weak—and take responsibility for employee experience and well-being through an "ethnographic" management approach.** Emphasise the importance of both casual and close connections among employees, using a management approach that seeks to understand and intentionally support the workplace culture and employee experiences fully.
7. **Digitise HR by automating routine processes and using employee data to make more informed, workplace-related decisions.** Implement digital HR tools to streamline administrative tasks and analyse employee data, allowing for strategic, data-driven decisions that enhance workplace effectiveness.

8. **Create a comprehensive change management strategy to facilitate the transition to the hybrid workplace model.** Design a robust change management plan to guide employees and management through the shift to hybrid working, ensuring smooth adaptation at all levels.

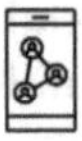

IT

IT

1. **As the unrecognised yet acknowledged leader in workplace infrastructure, it is essential to coordinate all digital workplace initiatives with the holistic development of the hybrid model to prevent siloed thinking.** Align digital workplace projects with the broader hybrid model to maintain cohesion and avoid isolated approaches.
2. **The hybrid workplace must be envisioned primarily from a digital behavioural perspective rather than a traditional, analogue one ("the big digital push").** Design the hybrid model with a digital-first behavioural approach, focusing on processes that enable work and collaboration to be conducted remotely wherever possible.
3. **Invest in robust and secure digital infrastructure to support seamless remote and in-office collaboration.** Ensure the organisation's digital infrastructure is reliable and secure, enabling smooth collaboration regardless of location (Spitzhirn et al. 2022, Anakpo et al. 2023, Marion et al. 2021).
4. **Implement advanced communication and collaboration tools that support interaction, virtual meetings, and teamwork.** Introduce sophisticated tools to facilitate virtual meetings and team collaboration, helping employees stay connected wherever they are.
5. **Develop a digital cultural universe to ensure employee well-being and engagement, whether work is conducted digitally or in person.** Create a cohesive digital culture that supports employee well-being and engagement across all work settings.
6. **Strengthen technical support and training for employees in using digital tools effectively, ensuring that both the organisation and its workforce achieve digital dexterity.** Offer comprehensive technical support and training to build proficiency in digital tools, fostering digital competence across the organisation.
7. **Establish actionable and well-curated data collection points throughout the hybrid workplace—both analogue and digital.** Gather meaningful data at every interaction point within the hybrid workplace, providing insights into its performance and impact.

8. **Continuously monitor, assess, and test the technology landscape relevant to knowledge workers to stay informed on emerging collaborative trends and solutions.** Regularly review and test technological advancements to keep pace with innovative tools that enhance knowledge work and collaboration.

FM (Facilities Management)

FM (Facilities Management)

1. **Transition FM from traditional "janitoring" and space management within a limited operational scope to a business development role. Internalise the business process and development of the hybrid workplace, gaining management control through data ownership.** Bring the development of the hybrid workplace in-house to strengthen data-driven management and strategic control over its evolution. Outsource routine maintenance tasks; Facilities Management (FM) can redirect focus towards higher-value activities, enabling FM professionals to contribute meaningfully to strategic business development. This shift positions FM to support core organisational goals more effectively, bringing it closer to top management and integrating it into strategic decision-making processes. To achieve this, it is essential to foster strong, coherent external workplace partnerships and alliances that work with and for organisationally critical objectives.
2. **Facilities Management (FM) must establish a close and collaborative partnership—ideally through an integrated organisational framework and shared work processes—with other key functions related to the hybrid workplace, particularly Human Resources (HR).** This close cooperation is essential for aligning objectives and ensuring that both FM and HR work seamlessly together to support the needs of a dynamic hybrid work environment. By fostering such collaboration, FM and HR can more effectively address employee requirements, streamline processes, and enhance the overall workplace experience, creating a cohesive approach that benefits the organisation as a whole.
3. **Allocate Facilities Management (FM) competencies to reflect the shift from a focus on costs, maintenance, and physical upkeep to an output-oriented approach that emphasises investing in people.** Position FM to support outcomes related to productivity and employee value by investing in behavioural rather than primarily focusing on operational aspects.
4. **Create a unique, scalable, flexible, and attractive physical workspace that reflects organisational values, including downsizing, remodelling, and co-working hubs.** Assume ownership of the physical workspace as a place for collaboration, focusing on key touchpoints that enhance both organisational and employee engagement. Design communal spaces to support psychological safety

and equality, laying the foundation for analogue collaboration, connection, and community. Design the workplace to be adaptable and reflective of company values, incorporating co-working spaces, remodelled layouts, or even smaller office footprints as needed.

5. **Implement smart building technologies to optimise energy and resource consumption, resource use, and user experience through data collection.** Leverage smart technology to track resource use, reduce waste, and improve the workplace experience, benefiting both sustainability and user satisfaction.

20.6 Challenge: The Future of the Office: Redefined Without the Present Custodians at Its Core

Facilities Management (FM) and Corporate Real Estate (CRE) stakeholders have long been custodians of the physical workplace. However, as the office is reimagined, these roles are increasingly excluded from the strategic core of hybrid work planning. Instead, Facilities Management (FM) and Corporate Real Estate (CRE) are confined to the tactical and operational responsibilities of managing analogue office environments—focused on maintaining spaces rather than shaping their purpose or impact. One might boldly question whether these functions ever truly embraced this challenge. The key stakeholders responsible for the physical office—FM and CRE—have largely missed the opportunity to play a defining and strategic role in the evolution of hybrid work. This absence has far-reaching implications, both for the development of the workplace model and for the broader alignment of organisational strategy with workforce needs.

Why has this happened? Several contributing factors can be identified:

1. Passiveness: A lack of proactive engagement in the strategic discourse surrounding hybrid work.
2. Competency Gaps: Limited expertise in digital transformation and an underdeveloped understanding of the hybrid work ecosystem.
3. Weakened Influence: A diminished voice in organisational decision-making compared to more dominant internal stakeholders, such as IT and HR.

This poses a pressing question for workplace stakeholders: what role, if any, have Facilities Management (FM) and Corporate Real Estate (CRE) played in shaping the office workplace model within your organisation? More crucially, how can they reclaim their influence in defining the future of knowledge work on a broader scale? The marginalisation of the office is not an end but an opportunity—a chance to redefine its role in a way that complements the hybrid work model. For FM and CRE stakeholders, this is a pivotal moment to shift from operational caretakers to strategic architects of the future workplace. What part has FM and CRE played in defining the office workplace model in your organisation? And what steps can be taken to ensure they play a central role in shaping the hybrid work revolution? The answers to these questions will define not only the future of office work but also the organisations that thrive within it.

20.7 Final Recommendation: Steering the (R)Evolution of the Hybrid Office Workplace

In the introduction to this book, I modestly observed that its primary aim was to encourage workplace stakeholders to make small adjustments in their approach to future-proofing the office workplace model, on the assumption that even minor changes could make a meaningful difference for all involved. However, it has become clear that it is not small tweaks or incremental steps that are needed to meet the goals and realise the potential. The pace and scale of change are simply considered objectively too significant.

Therefore, my final and closing recommendation is succinct and addresses the core of the anticipated future development of the hybrid office workplace: be fully aware that the hybrid office environment is both dynamic and significant for the organisation. Organisations must optimally adopt an agile approach in every aspect to keep pace with this evolution. Failure to do so will only increase the risk of falling behind in the ongoing (r)evolution of the office workplace. On a more positive note, those organisations that embrace and proactively leverage their hybrid office models to enhance agility will be well-positioned to secure considerable advantages.

The proactive approach requires organisations to be constantly seeking out and initiating significant workplace interventions that align with and support their objectives. Metaphorically, it is not enough to merely adapt to workplace changes when they create internal friction; instead, organisations should actively seek out changes before they become sources of friction. This involves initiatives that go beyond incremental measures, encompassing the entire spectrum of actions, including radical innovation. As previously mentioned, a proactive approach inherently involves the continuous monitoring and analysis of carefully curated qualitative and quantitative data related to the workplace model, ensuring alignment with the organisation's objectives. To support this, it is vital that internal decision-making processes, mandates, and corresponding resources are structured to allow for rapid and effective action. Herein, we return to the core dilemma for the future sustainable hybrid office workplace: how does one implement an office model today that balances the driving forces of continuous development and flexibility with the many organisational and societal pressures pulling towards a more static solution? Put simply: how do we design and build an office for the long term, when it is highly likely that in the near future, something significantly different will be required? In this light, it is relatively straightforward to establish a modern, up-to-date hybrid office model today, based on current knowledge and existing experiences. However, the opposite is true when future developments must also be factored into the model.

Thus, it is essential to reaffirm: a successful and sustainable hybrid office model cannot be constructed or conceptualised solely based on current workplace experiences and data. Achieving this requires a thoughtfully crafted, ongoing approach to workplace process design embedded within the organisation, enabling the continuous development of a modern and effective hybrid office environment.

Maersk HQ. *Image credits:* **Tomas Bertelsen PLH Architects**

References

(Anakpo et al.; 2023) Anakpo G, Nqwayibana Z, Mishi S (2023) The impact of work-from-home on employee performance and productivity: a systematic review. Sustainability 15:4529 https://www.researchgate.net/publication/369002273_The_Impact_of_Work-from-Home_on_Employee_Performance_and_Productivity_A_Systematic_Review

(Brown, 2009) Tim Brown, Change by Design: How Design Thinking Transforms Organizations and Inspires Innovation. New York: Harper Business, 2009.

(Coffey and Wolf 2018) The challenge and promise of remote work. A brief study of remote work and best practices (Technical Report). Leadership Computing Facility, Argonne National Laboratory. https://doi.org/10.2172/1487022

(Gratton 2021) How to Do Hybrid Right https://hbr.org/2021/05/how-to-do-hybrid-right

(Marion et al., 2021) Marion, Tucker & Fixson, Sebastian. (2020). The Transformation of the Innovation Process: How Digital Tools are Changing Work, Collaboration, and Organizations in New Product Development. Journal of Product Innovation Management. 38. 10.1111/jpim.12547. https://www.researchgate.net/publication/343378966_The_Transformation_of_the_Innovation_Process_How_Digital_Tools_are_Changing_Work_Collaboration_and_Organizations_in_New_Product_Development

(Rockart 1979) Rockart, John. Chief Executives Define Their Own Data Needs. HBR March 1979 https://hbr.org/1979/03/chief-executives-define-their-own-data-needs

(Spitzhirn et al., 2022) Spitzhirn, Michael; Benter, Martin; Heindl, Christoph; Scheder, Noël; Reisinger, Gerhard; Strohmeier, Felix; Behrendt, Wernher Hybrid work systems - platform-based work planning - designing productive and human-centered work processes. Zeitschrift für Arbeitswissenschaft (2022). doi: 10.1007/s41449-022-00342-6 https://www.researchgate.net/publication/366213263_Hybrid_work_systems-platform-based_work_planning-designing_productive_and_human-centered_work_processes

Index

C. Sneppen, *The Future (R)Evolution of the Office Workspace*, Future of Business and Finance, https://doi.org/10.1007/978-3-031-85229-9